MARCH 23,1993

PHILIP MORRISON'S
LONG LOOK AT THE LITERATURE

Philip Morrison's
Long Look at the Literature

HIS REVIEWS OF A HUNDRED MEMORABLE
SCIENCE BOOKS

W.H. FREEMAN AND COMPANY / NEW YORK

Library of Congress Cataloging-in-Publication Data

Morrison, Philip.
   Philip Morrison's long look at the literature : his reviews of a hundred
memorable science books / Philip Morrison.
      p. cm.
   Includes bibliographical references.
   ISBN 0-7167-2107-4
   ISBN 0-7167-2135-X (pbk.)
   1. Science—Book reviews. 2. Scientific American. I. Scientific
American. II. Title. III. Title: Scientific American book reviews.
Q158.5.M67 1990   89-23784
500—dc20   CIP

Printed in the United States of America

1 2 3 4 5 6 7 8 9 0   VB   9 9 8 7 6 5 4 3 2 1 0

Contents

IX

The Staff of Life
243

X

Health
267

XI

The Human Past
295

Preface

Scientific American first came out in the year Texas was annexed to the United States. It was read mainly by confident Yankee mechanics eager for news of ingenious practical devices, and dreaming of patents of their own. It assumed its present form in 1948, the postwar time of a new and confident self-awareness within the scientific and technological community of the United States, a subculture no longer in the least provincial.

From 1948 I had been an enthusiastic friend and occasional contributor to the magazine. A swift and catholic reader, I had always enjoyed the monthly book department, conducted from the start by James R. Newman, a richly talented, witty and committed man. Most months the magazine published an essay review or two on current books, with each review written by some invited specialist. Every month Newman himself wrote a set of shorter reviews as well, on a variety of topics across the whole spectrum of books on science or technology.

The book department thrived, but with a difference. Nearly all journals assign books in science one by one, each to an appropriately specialized reviewer. But it is natural that a magazine intended for the general scientific reader offer instead a regular flow of simpler reviews consistently written by one reviewer, who comes to act as peer and surrogate for the general reader. That was Newman's way. He chose the books for his reviews; he wrote of them reflectively, though hardly ever as a disciplinary specialist.

In late June of 1966 James Newman suddenly died, leaving "a large vacancy in the ranks of the living," as the magazine put it. Almost at once editor Dennis Flanagan appeared in Boston; he asked me as writer and friend to help the magazine out. Try writing reviews for one year, he said; that will meet our crisis. If we mutually agree, you might continue.

Since that visit twenty-three years ago my life has been changed. We live with a kind of free bookshop in the house. One big room is lined with shelves that bear a thousand or twelve hundred new books at any time, all in transit. In they flood by mail and special parcel service, perhaps two hundred books a month on average, delectable and daunting, on topics from Akkadian to zymotechnology. On many days a whole canvas sack of two dozen books will appear in the front hall. Books are sent by one or another among some four hundred publishers, nearly all in North America and Britain, a few books arriving in French or German. Most books appear unsought, now that we have placed our address firmly on the lists of all those publishers; that took some years, and we remain alert to new sources. We order many books directly from the pile of announcements, catalogues and notices we receive, along with a few letters from wistful authors.

Out the books go, too, about as fast as they flow in. No house can expand to store so many bound blocks of stacked paper. We give them gladly to visiting friends, who can carry away only a few at a time; we send them by boxfuls all over the world by agreement to libraries and to distant colleagues. Even the refractory sludge of widely unwanted books is removed by bookish people nearby who maintain regular public bargain book sales for charitable ends. We sell no books.

The physical weight of information is all too evident. Of course it is the message in the books, a torrent of ideas and evidence, that counts most. Newman's example still controls the way I work. Guest reviews of much-heralded books remain an overall editorial responsibility; they appear at a frequency that waxes and wanes with the years. The chief task of the regular reviewer who has no titles assigned to him is an alert, steady and understanding choice. At most one book in fifty can be noticed in print; no methodical system to generate so small a signal amid the noise of complex opportunity is at hand.

The goal of a book review is only secondarily the sale of books. Above all it must please and instruct the readers — and of necessity the reviewer, first reader of all. That implies a wide variety of topics; even an astronomer ought not to review a book on astronomy every month. I look for freshness of matter or of approach, with a middle ground of specialization; no book should be so technical that a summary cannot engage a general reader, nor too close to the step-by-step style of the textbook, nor so idiosyncratic as to elicit mainly criticism.

The books flow in. They are opened, sorted, examined, and placed among their kindred. Perhaps half are removed from consideration at the reviewer's first glance, by title alone. The others survive repeated closer and closer scrutiny, until the time has come to pick among them by comparison with their likes, the month's list for reading in full, more books than can be reviewed in print. The range of possible delay is large. From time to time a book arrives during the days of writing that, once unwrapped, is excitedly read—just what was wanted! That review can be written the very day the book arrives. Other good books simply wait, unchosen but still tempting, month by month, for a year or even more, always evading decision. Finally, they make it, or slide away.

Books interact. You cannot review a book on pigment color chemistry, say, that appears the month after another such book has been summarized. The world is too varied for so much repetition. Thus like books may repel each other. But they attract as well; a little batch of books, say on the tropical forest canopy, may well combine to make a more interesting review than any one might.

Here in this look at the literature we enter a world at second order, hard choices among hard choices, with one review offered for a dozen good books reviewed, and thus one title among five hundred titles received! To appear here, the book itself must have been worthwhile (only rarely is it worth spending scarce space to describe a book that seems wrongheaded). But the review I wrote must have been unusually appealing as well. I hope that fact will help console disappointed authors and admirers of excellent and important books not mentioned here; consider how likely it is that the fault is mine!

Finally, it is not in the spirit of this collection to remain at a distance from the authentic material. We have prepared a list to help readers to seek out—if at some effort—"the books themselves." Preceding the index you will find our list of all the books by title, their authors and publishers and some guidance for its use.

I thank those who have worked with me, Phylis Morrison, partner, acute critic, and dearest of friends among the books; Yvonne Pappenheim, controller of the flow; the postal services; and the editors and the copy editors on Madison Avenue who have watched so expertly over each notion and phrase.

But above all I thank those men and women, in all lands, within all fields, who have themselves formed the living literature of science and technology, the unending bookstream that has refreshed, instructed, and challenged this delighted reader for more than twenty years.

Philip Morrison
Cambridge, Massachusetts
January 1990

PHILIP MORRISON'S
LONG LOOK AT THE LITERATURE

I

Perception, Language and Mathematics

Perception is at the foundation of it all, for the dual task of science and technology is to understand the experiences we gain and to seek new ones. We all know how pathology illuminates health, and in the same way misperceptions clarify perception. Here are books to explain how we come knowingly to see the world, and some to make plain how we fall or are led into illusion.

But it is by language and mathematics, a universal language, that we express and account for what we perceive. Here are a couple of books on extraordinary languages, and more on mathematics, from puzzles and arithmetic to fractals.

Clever Hans (The Horse of Mr. von Osten)
By Oskar Pfungst
Edited by Robert Rosenthal

Hans was a large trotter, owned and lovingly educated by a white-haired old schoolmaster who exhibited the success of his pupil, without any payment, to all who would come around noon to the courtyard of the large apartment house in Berlin where for four years Hans had lived and been tutored. The gentle, if proud and irascible, teacher stood by Hans's right side to question him, a task interrupted by frequent carrots but never marred by the sight of a stick or a whip. Hans was of course mute; he responded by nods and shakes of the head, but particularly by tapping his right forefoot. He read and spelled rather well in German, coding his responses by number pairs that picked out letters from a blackboard array prepared by Herr von Osten. He knew the coins of the realm, the calendar for the year, how to tell time, and he recognized a good bit of music. (His taste in chords and melodies was somewhat old-fashioned.) He could walk toward people he was asked to single out, and could fetch from a row of colored cloths the piece of the color sought. He could recognize people from their photographs. In arithmetic he was outstanding. He could do all the schoolboy arithmetic for numbers up to about 100; tapping too long tired him, but conceptually he was not so limited. He could compute how many times 100,000 was contained as a whole in 659,321. Even fractions were acceptable; he first tapped the numerator, then the denominator, to give such sums as $2/3 + 3/4$. He made a few errors, which he could often correct at once when asked, "By how many units did you go wrong?" He always had a hard time with the answer "One."

The year 1904 was Hans's year. Droves of people came to see him, and he appeared in songs and light verse, as a toy and on liquor labels. Zoo directors and circus trainers, explorers, psychologists and philosophers declared him a horse genius. Educators were classifying him at the fifth-grade level. Some skeptics suspected trickery, but the weight of evidence about the sincerity of his teacher was too great to entertain the thought. As a last resort a learned commission assembled, only to find that Hans in fact would perform just as well for certain other questioners (finally as many as 40 different people succeeded) without even the presence of Herr von Osten. There was no deliberate trickery.

The mystery became the concern of Professor Stumpf, head of the Psychological Institute of the University of Berlin. His young colleague Oskar Pfungst solved the puzzle in a few months, and this reprint of the 1911 English translation of Pfungst's report relates the story. It is so clearly told, the sense of intellectual drama so tense, the personal engagement of Pfungst so evident, the experimental methods so simple, apt and elegant, the entire work so sensitive, penetrating and thorough that the book rightly became a classic of science and its methods.

One experiment, neat and conclusive, was this: When either of two acceptable questioners whispered an arithmetical sum into Hans's ear, the horse could solve the problem. But when one man whispered one number, and the other, not knowing the first number, whispered a second to be added, Hans muffed. If the two men had earlier agreed on the two numbers, Hans could find the sum. Wearing large blinders Hans failed; in the growing dusk Hans failed. Questioned in French, Hans succeeded. Indeed, without any audible question, he did quite well.

It was finally plain that Hans was no schoolboy but a clever and subtle watcher of his questioners. All the three or four people — they included Pfungst — who became very successful questioners gave unintended cues at the correct final tap, by tiny changes in the attitude of the head, relaxing the tension with which they watched the tapping forefoot. Even when Pfungst knew what cue he was giving, he could not easily suppress it.

Then Pfungst turned from analysis to synthesis: he became a human stand-in for Clever Hans. Clever Oskar asked subjects to think of a number between 1 and 100 but not to tell him what it was. He undertook to tap out the right answer, not with a hoof but more humanly with a forefinger. With 23 of 25 subjects tried, he succeeded brilliantly. He even recorded the cuing motions, using the smoked-drum and lever techniques of the era in a fully three-dimensional way, producing a kind of early polygraph.

The implications remain fascinating. The mind-reading act, the rapport of the wonderful pet, the rod diviner, the table-tipper, insofar as they perform as claimed, are subject to the lesson learned from Clever Hans. The polo pony that seems to know the rules of the game and the cavalry horse that knows the commands are probably tactile followers of Hans's. They are behaviorists. They cleverly learn their master's actions but nothing of the logic he follows. (Many schoolchildren are thought to act more like this than is good for humans.) The sensory interactions between organisms as complex as these animals, not to say from man to man, are too rich to prevent an occasional single bit of information from flowing quite involuntarily from one to another.

Dr. Rosenthal brings the tale up to date. Even the albino rat can learn from the way he has been handled whether the "experimenter" expects him to run the maze or not. Second-order experiments have shown such results, experiments in which the "experimenter" is himself the subject of a second experiment and is preloaded with information he then cannot fully conceal from horse, rat or human interviewee.

Finally one is led to quote Pfungst: "In spite of the huge mass of 'experimental evidence,' which has been collected chiefly in England and in America, it appears to me that telepathy is nothing but an unproven hypothesis based upon experimental errors." If 50 years ago Clever Hans had not been studied, a large class of those errors would be unknown. Whether other errors remain in the work of the parapsychologists will always require the insight and the hard work of a Pfungst to decide for sure. Lacking such studies, the claims of extrasensory transfer remain as suspect as the French of Clever Hans.

(March 1967)

The Intelligent Eye
By Richard L. Gregory

The flood of solar photons nourishes all life. Yet the most remarkable optical side effect, an image-forming eye used as an early-warning and pattern-recognition system, is known to no plant, although it is found in most animals of at least the complexity and modernity of the higher mollusks. It is instructive to consider the eyes of the machine. Almost no machines can yet use images to affect their behavior. The familiar elevator door, like most industrial photoelectric devices, merely has a primitive light spot, such as no self-respecting protozoon lacks. The camera and even the up-to-date television chain are not properly eyes: they are only means of transferring images to human eyes. What the machine lacks is certainly not a lens or a retina or many amplifiers; it lacks the subtle circuitry that makes sense out of an image— the intelligence of the eye.

Our eyes are not mere passive image-formers. The retinal image for them is merely a raw input. Their marvel lies in our profound faculty of data processing. The eye-brain-hand system actively uses the incoming image to guide its powerful but quite unconscious selection of the most probable external cause of the image. "Perception must, it seems, be a matter of seeing the present with stored objects from the past." How far that past is experiential and how far innate is not clear. Such is the theme of this compact, attractive, important and fresh volume.

The main topic is the viewing of pictures. Pictures are human arti-facts, always seized of an "extraordinary double reality . . . an essential paradox." Here they are, those puzzling constructions, in their most problematic forms: stereoscopic pictures for three-dimensional viewing, varied perspectives, impossible objects blandly and sharply photographed, pictures of pictures, drawings by Maurits C. Escher, illusions of scale and figure ground. The analysis goes deep, but with little jargon and no mathematics.

Many photographs and drawings are shown doubled in slightly dis-placed red and green tone or line. These yield strong depth perception when viewed through spectacles (provided) with a red filter for one eye and a green filter for the other. Looking even with three-dimensional glasses at such a photograph of the hollow interior of a mask, however, one sees the normal face, with the nose sticking outward, not improbably inward, even though the latter is correct; the stereoscopic cues are over-ridden by the intelligent eye, which—like Lloyd's of London—makes its bet on experience. (Turning the book upside down may destroy familiarity enough to restore the proper stereoscopic result.) There is a step-by-step outline of what you see looking with one eye or with two at a wire-frame cube and at pictures of it. Pictures demand an acquired interpretation. It may indeed be that some statues in ancient temples were made in these ways to seem alive, their hollow heads with that ambiguous depth appear-ing to follow each devotee as he moved in the "gloom of the sacred place." That astrology may have arisen out of the experience that the moon and stars seem to move with the traveler is less plausible. Now that a consciously analyzed form of instrumental perception gives us the true scale of the universe, says Professor Gregory, "all reason for a close personal association with the Universe (hence astrology) is lost." That is unfair; are we not made of star stuff?

In this book Professor Gregory has expanded and deepened a splen-did series of lectures he did one recent Christmas season, which were televised by the knowing and powerful science team of the British Broad-casting Corporation. It has become a well-illustrated essay that readers concerned either with perception narrowly, or with epistemology broadly, cannot allow themselves to miss. Not everyone will agree with his more general conclusions, but the results he exhibits and the views he expresses must be taken into account by everyone who would understand either the world we see or the "essentially unpredictable future . . . a world we cannot see," the world of instruments and of "pictures, symbols, thought, and language."

(November 1970)

The Occult Sciences in the Renaissance: A Study in Intellectual Patterns

By Wayne Shumaker

Giovanni Baptista della Porta published his Latin runaway best seller, *Twenty Books of Natural Magic*, when Galileo was a young lecturer at Pisa. The book ran through 27 editions and was almost immediately translated into Italian, French, Dutch, Spanish "and apparently Arabic." We know it best for its account of the use of lenses; it was almost the first book to refer to them. Lenses had been widely used in spectacles for nearly 300 years but were entirely ignored by the learned. Della Porta even challenged the scholars; he remarked that no one had explained either the effects of lenses or the reasons for them. It has been argued by Vasco Ronchi, the distinguished Florentine physicist and historian of optics, that it was Della Porta's book that led to the first telescope — not Galileo's, of course, but one made in 1590 by an unknown Italian. That instrument was seen in 1604 by the Dutch spectacle grinders, who then produced the toy telescopes whose potential inspired Galileo to develop better ones and turn them to the Tuscan sky.

It was an extraordinary chain of natural magic! Della Porta's treatise itself, however, is almost without readability or credibility today. It is decent enough, the whitest of magic; "no daemonic powers whatever are solicited." All it tells depends on relations and forces seen as being objectively present in nature; there are no prayers, no invocations, no ceremonies. The Neapolitan author searched the world of "Libraries, Learned Men, and Artificers" to bring back "a survey of the whole course of Nature," so that the magician, "a very perfect Philosopher," might "do strange works, such as the vulgar sort call miracles." The magician should be versed in mathematics and astrology and understand optics, minerals, herbs and medicine. Finally, he "must also be rich." Then the seeming miracles can flow. These are passing strange, although supported from analogy or old and traditional wisdom. The tongue of the chattering goose placed in a woman's bed will make her "utter her night-secrecies." Wild olive is an antidote to a chameleon an elephant has eaten by accident. Dromedary bred with boar yields the two-humped camel. And so on, for 20 brief "books," with here and there the nugget of a real lodestone or a burning glass, or even a plausible herbal remedy.

It is plain that the thought of the Renaissance, the centuries in which the modern mind was brought to term, was permeated with such occult material. It is not intrinsic strangeness alone that causes the recipes to lose their hold on us; the story of the telescope and of its fruit for the mind is surely as implausible as curing a mad dog's bite by "a Wolves skin put upon any one that is bitten." After all, the cure we use now — and it very often works — is to mingle with the bloodstream of "any one that is bitten" the ground spinal cord of a mad rabbit, treated with stinking formaldehyde. The difference is a deeper theoretical structure and above all a nexus of trials and tests, much more intricate than the citations from a few ancient writers or the single forced analogy on which the old authors rested their case.

"How did the remotest ancients come to know so much?" It is not just scripture that forms the basis for esoteric knowledge; it is as likely to be some Latin poet, palpably writing fiction. The senses were not seen as reliable guides; illusions are ever their lot. Yet the past, somehow closer to divine inspiration, is a true guide; even its romances are veiled truth. "The real ground for belief was faith . . . in authorities."

So does Wayne Shumaker, professor of English at Berkeley, critic and literary analyst, open to us the tangled growths of the occult. He treats five such sciences: white magic, witchcraft, astrology, alchemy and the curious intellectual movement around certain Greek and Latin manuscripts that trace back to an Alexandrian school of mysticism but were ascribed to one mysterious master, Hermes Trismegistus. There is, of course, an embarrassment of many books on each of these topics, except perhaps the last. But here one sees the occult systems as a whole, not minutely, for the most part, but as theoretical and practical structures with their own aims and methods, to be sifted for meaning and coherence. Often Shumaker compares the doctrines of contending authors; it is not to be thought that all minds agreed on the doctrines or on their validity. He provides long citations, and he has brought his reader indispensable gifts: his expertise and his patience. He has read the dusty old books, in the tongues of all Europe or in Latin, and he has set down what he finds there with many long citations.

He is no believer. Indeed, he is endearingly candid about his concern that "young people have revolted strongly against reason." Therefore he offers a very clear refutation of astrology, for example, on internal and on empirical grounds (much of his stance is taken from the contemporaries of his astrological sources), along with his clear, explicit and compact account of a horoscope. "A decade ago I would not have written [such refutations], and in another decade I hope they will again become unnecessary. At the moment, I could not in conscience omit them."

The long-festering barbarism of the treatment of witches is particularly painful. It was not the Dark Ages but the High Renaissance that tortured so many poor, uneducated, outcast and half crazy old women. A couple of hundred thousand people, mostly women, were burned between the time of the voyages of Henry the Navigator, when Pope Innocent VIII called officially for the extirpation of witchcraft, and "the dying down of fanaticism" in about 1700, after the frenzy had passed even in distant Massachusetts. The scholars' theories justified it all; "each used his sources exactly as his modern counterpart does, balancing one set against another or supporting his own views by multiple citations."

Still, there are crucial differences. We cite ancient authority more as evidence of ancient belief and less as source of fact. Present experience was also then regarded as being important, but it was seldom treated critically. Any statements were taken as being true; old wives' tales were the main burden of evidence, the more acceptable because they resembled the reports of the distant past. There were skeptical and compassionate writers too, and in the end they prevailed. "Ultimately, except in cultural backwaters, the battle for sanity was won." Yet great Martin Luther and lucid Sir Thomas Browne accepted the existence of witches. Montaigne (from a 1603 translation) said what is in the modern mind: "How much more naturall and more likely doe I finde it, that two men should lie, than one in twelve hours [should] passe with the windes, from East to West? . . . It is an over-valuing of ones conjectures, by them to cause a man to be burned alive."

The study is a library project; the laboratory aspect of alchemy, say, is lightly treated. But the annotated lists of references, the period illustrations, the recognition that serious and able minds once differed greatly from our own and the absence of contaminating traces either of condescension or of credulousness give this absorbing volume a special authority and a place on the shelves of any reader or any library where the history of modern thought is relevant. This is a time when the failures of reason lead many who should know better to seek refuge not in clarity but in unreason; that no comfort lies therein can be learned from this honest history.

(February 1973)

The Magic of Uri Geller
By The Amazing Randi

Superminds
By John Taylor

My Story
By Uri Geller

Uri: A Journal of the Mystery of Uri Geller
By Andrija Puharich

R*affiniert ist der Herr Gott, aber Boshaft ist Er nicht.* Einstein said it: The Creator is subtle, but he is not malicious. That is the faith by which the physicist lives. There is order deep in his world, which sufficiently cunning experiment will disclose. But that is no stance in which he can safely buy a used car, appraise the operative statements of a White House press officer or bet against an artist with the cards. Not Einstein, but Machiavelli and W. C. Fields must be his guides then. For things will not be as they seem, plausible assumptions of logical independence ("How could he know?") will usually fail, and systematic mischief will rule the little world. Human beings — unlike electrons — can understand the intent of an observer. In particular, conjurers know the questions likely to be in the minds of the audience and contrive to capitalize on them for their own purposes. The hand is not often quicker than the eye, but the left hand you are coaxed into not watching can work wonders.

These four books span an international misdirection industry that is now a couple of years old in the U.S. It is chiefly a construct of the media, out of celebrity and talk shows on television in the U.S., over the BBC and half a dozen other national networks, and articles in such publications as the *Psychic News, Der Spiegel* and *Paris-Match.* The furor centers on a quick-thinking, handsome, charming, bold but disarmingly informal former Israeli paratrooper named Uri Geller. There are a dozen claimants to this or that occult power in the public eye today, but Geller earns the attention of a general scientific reader because in large measure he offers not mere video wonders but credentials issued by physicists. He has been studied by the Electronics and Bioengineering Laboratory of the Stanford Research Institute (often confused with the great university it neighbors) in work published at length in *Nature.* A few well-known professors of physics, mainly in London, have similarly published their experiences with Geller, which they view as being at least enigmatic and at most revolutionary.

The main Geller effects form a short list: reproducing concealed drawings; bending spoons, keys and the like; starting stopped watches; deflecting magnetic compasses, and recording high count rates on Geiger counters. It is evident that in themselves these effects are ordinary: anyone can achieve those results sans the occult. The issue turns on how he does them: on control. Geller and his believers say he does these things by extraphysical means. Critics observe that almost all the effects belong to the familiar repertoire of stage magicians. The physicists — with no record at all of previous successes in this domain — assert that their experimental skills rule out the paltry tricks of the prestidigitator.

Enters now the Amazing Randi, an elfin gentleman with a white-fringed chin and a flashing wit, a magician of long experience and patent ingenuity. He pursues Geller and finds simply a fraud, "a clever magician, nothing more — and certainly nothing less. . . . Uri's pattern of deception was unmistakable. Clever, yes. Psychic, no."

That ESP of Geller under rigid experimental control? First of all the think tank's shielded room is rendered suspect by their unwillingness to let Randi examine it. The room, which was built for another experiment, has a passage for cables, a passage stuffed with gauze. Geller's one perfect telepathic hit on a sketch of a bunch of grapes, correct to the very number of grapes in the bunch, was too good. For that particular one, Randi feels, "Shipi made a small drawing of the target — an exact drawing — and pushed it through the hole to Geller." (Shipi is Geller's closest associate, a quiet young man, unobtrusive but almost always around.) The psychologists at SRI — not the physicists — ran a doubleblind test, genuinely controlled. Geller did not attempt a specific guess on any of their 100 sealed envelopes. Charles Rebert of the life-sciences division at SRI suspects even the one hit Geller obtained once conditions were somewhat loosened in response to the pleas of the physicists: "I'm convinced that he [Geller] swapped envelopes on us. . . . He flunked our test."

The watch-starting? It works often on studio watches, and it is widely contagious. In Britain, the U.S., West Germany, Japan — in many places — derelict watches long stopped responded nationwide, and happy viewers telephoned in to report the miracles. But in New Zealand: "We sent out a few students to fix broken watches, and out of 16 watches tried, 14 of them started, and seven have kept going for at least four to five days." Stopped watches are often jammed; winding, shaking and holding them enough to warm the oil will get them temporarily under way. Uri takes the credit, as he did in his famous stopping of the funicular near Munich. A reporter suggested that. They tried it out, Geller in the moving car, concentrating. Sure enough, "the cable car stopped right in midair. . . . The main switch had flipped off for no explainable reason." So Geller writes in his own story. Did someone flip that switch? We cannot say, but it was certainly no bent-metal miracle.

So the chronicle goes. When it seems that controls are working, Geller often fails. When he succeeds, there has been uncertainty in the controls, often total collapse. Sometimes he suddenly carries a key off to a nearby water tap; he has found that running water helps keys to bend. Perhaps, but it is surely true that more torque can be placed on a key when its end is inserted into the opening of the faucet. Try it yourself.

How does Geller himself explain his successes? We have his autobiography. It seems that from an early age, since a preschool epiphany in the garden, he has had these strange powers. Since his hypnosis in 1971 by his first American sponsor, the psychic expert Andrija Puharich, he has received mysterious self-erasing messages on tape cassettes; they foretell his future and explain his past. (Puharich's book, probably the most implausible deadpan chronicle to see print in a long time, confirms Geller fully and has identified his sources. Some live on the spacecraft *Spectra*, "fifty-three thousand sixty-nine light ages away.") Geller writes: "The tapes bring with them a tremendous message to the world, even though they do sound like science fiction." One such pregnant message, self-activated and self-erased, is: "The ultimate powers, whether on the particle level or the cosmic level, are in rotation and drawing off the gravitational power from the center of the system. There are special rays . . . where the skin of the envelope of the cosmic rays is utilized for power." Automatic taping seems no more instructive, although it is less objective, than automatic writing was in the old days.

Then there is John Taylor, a reputable London theoretical physicist with an easy pen and a theatrical bent. His last book was on black holes for the layman. (It impressed this reviewer as being wildly uncritical and shamelessly tendentious, with three final chapters on spiritualism, on Christianity and on dialectical materialism, all as they are affected by black holes. The too stern Hume might have wanted to burn such a work, but one has to admit that these are not demonstrable errors but legitimate moral opinions.) The current book goes much further. It centers on the theory and practice of metal-bending. No references are made to Geller's life or Puharich's witness; instead Taylor, hopelessly misdirected by what he has "seen," undertakes to study metal-bending empirically. Measure the bent rod with care. . . . His main discovery is a group of child metal-benders, who will do the Geller bit willingly and repeatedly for Taylor. To be sure, they are 11-year-old innocents, and so he lets them go out of his sight to bend their samples, even go home over the weekend. Sometimes he comes along, but (as Randi quotes Taylor) "this feature of bending not happening when the object is being watched — 'the shyness effect' — is very common." Common indeed! Lately a group from the University of Bath has published experiments with little volunteer metal-benders, drawn like Taylor's from the great British pool recruited by Geller over television. These small adepts, mainly innocent young girls, went to work bending metal. The observer did not see anyone cheating. But the skeptics from Bath had taken one precaution: the room where the experiment was being conducted was being carefully watched by several other observers through one-way mirrors from outside. Result: Five of the six gifted youngsters cheated visibly. They hastily bent metal by hand, tabletop and chair edge, presumably whenever they thought the overt observer was distracted. (The sixth subject bent no metal at all.)

Taylor dimly grasps the idea of experimental control. He sealed some metal samples in plastic tubes. There one is, before and after wonder-bending *in absentia*, a full-page color spread. Alas, Randi visited Taylor and popped the rubber stopper out of such a tube almost inadvertently, without disturbing the sealing wax (which turns out to hold a screwhead and not the stopper itself); "it was a very poor piece of preparation." Randi's drawing and the photograph in Taylor's book form a compelling sequence demonstrating that professors expert in the theory of a complex variable should leave sealing wax to magicians and private detectives.

It has all happened before; it will all happen again. We can laugh at the comedy and the incongruity; we can weep a little at the pomposity, the credulousness, the air of callous exploitation and the crash of reputations. Randi cites a wonderful parallel or two. The two great psychophysicists Weber, then advanced in age, and Fechner, partly blind, were taken in by Henry Slade, a medium who caused knots to appear in a string, the ends of which had been tied in a loop and sealed with wax, after many days of storage. According to the psychologists' astrophysicist colleague (the theorizing Taylor of that day), one Johann K. F. Zöllner, the medium Slade simply had access to the fourth spatial dimension! The magicians of the time knew better, as they do today. A new loop had been substituted. Randi draws a systematic methodological parallel between the aspects of the Geller case and the events of a century ago. His chapter is a telling guide to recognition of the central phenomena.

Not everything is made clear. Randi not only reads sealed envelopes and bends keys unnoticed but also can drive down the street while he is blindfolded with pizza dough and three layers of tested blindfolds. He will not explain that at all. His work is not unique, but magicians by long tradition will not expose their contrivances; they hold that the appeal of their clever art depends on guile. Indeed, Randi has already gone too far for many of his confreres, who see in Geller a new approach to the public. Not human ingenuity but the hint of mysterious power is what draws audiences today. A magician can do better with a bumbling, nervous performance. ("The mentalist who is too perfect loses credibility. . . . Stress, as does Uri Geller, that what you are attempting to do is little understood and doesn't always work on command. . . . They want you to succeed." The elegantly flawless card trickster is being supplanted by a performer who simulates an earnest but uncertain parapsychological striver. The article cited (from an American magicians' periodical) goes on more cynically: "Find out what their budget will allow them to pay. Ask at least that much! . . . Later, concentrate on the best-paying audiences."

The Geller wave seems now to ebb. The contrast between the galactic claims and the limited, banal performance in the end drains interest. Another will arise, and another, just as waves at the shore. Perhaps we shall learn at least this: The physicist is no person to ferret out the truth once *Boshaft* enters. Credentials ought to be more specific; a plasma physicist does not pronounce on the tracks of the magnetic monopole, at least until he has etched many a film of plastic. Clumsy-fisted theorists who trust the innocence of children ought not to set themselves up as knowing investigators. They will generate only more thick documents of human credulousness. Finally, there is no canon of logic or inference from common sense or use of past experience that can speak more strongly to the mind than the simple will to believe.

(February 1976)

The Renaissance Rediscovery of Linear Perspective
By Samuel Y. Edgerton, Jr.

The Magic Mirror of M. C. Escher
By Bruno Ernst

Copernicus was born in 1473; that 500th anniversary rang throughout the world of science. Here we celebrate, along with an imaginative and experimental art historian (of Boston University), a much less arbitrary moment in the growth of the Renaissance point of view. One day in the year 1425 "a short, middle-aged man arrived at the piazza" between the still unfinished cathedral of Florence, pride of the Republic and of its rich and generous bankers and wool merchants, and the famous multicolored marble baptistry that still faces the portal of the great church. That man was the sculptor, architect and artisan-engineer "Pippo di Ser Brunellescho the Florentine." He had with him a small painted panel about a foot square, with a curious hole in it, and a mirror of the same size. He stood within the portal, we may guess, looking out toward the baptistry, with the painting held in one hand "oddly enough, obversely right up against his face." In the other hand he balanced the mirror, which he dropped in or out of the line of vision from time to time. "Is that a mirror reflection in his eyes, or a glint of satisfaction?" He has cleverly matched his painted image (as seen looking through the hole in the painting at its reflection in the mirror) with what the eye sees. It was the first modern demonstration of linear perspective with lines converging to the vanishing point. Indeed, the author of a treatise of the

1460's ascribed that "subtle and beautiful" discovery to Brunelleschi's "considering what a mirror shows to you." It had to be a plane mirror, of flat glass, which at the time was rare and expensive, and so it was the mirror that determined the scale of the small painting.

Professor Edgerton takes the reader to that same portal and shows us with his own mirror and Nikon and a few persuasive plans, drawings and photographs what was the probable field of view, where the painter stood to take his cue from the mirror and even the little tilt he may have given the mirror to balance the sky and the pavement satisfyingly in his image. Other scholars have suggested that Brunelleschi painted directly on the mirror (impractical and unlikely) or that he made the discovery first intricately on paper, merging the elevations and plans of the church he was no doubt preparing. It was of course Brunelleschi himself who closed the big unfinished edifice with one of the greatest cathedral domes in Europe during those very years.

Edgerton's happy experiment makes a strong case (stronger than he seems to think) for Brunelleschi's being the first to paint in perspective, for his learning it from the images in plane mirrors and for his tellingly demonstrating his discovery to his scholarly and painterly friends with his dramatic image-superposition scheme. At the same time, give or take a year or so, his friends the painter Masaccio and the sculptor Donatello created the first works of art clearly to employ linear perspective. His patrician friend the learned Leon Battista Alberti, who was unique in the breadth of his training in science and in letters and who had taken up painting as a relaxation, wrote the first explicit treatment of linear perspective as a device for painters.

Alberti prepared a version of his work in Italian (for the artists to read), which he dedicated to Brunelleschi among others, 10 years after the play with mirrors in the Piazza del Duomo. The wonderful painted panel has not survived, but Brunelleschi's biographer, writing in the 1480's, stated, "I have had the painting in my hand and have seen it many times," and he describes the panel size, the peephole "small as a lentil on the painting side of the panel" and the care, delicacy and accuracy of the work. For the sky the painter had put burnished silver leaf, to reflect the natural clouds so that they might be "moved by the wind when it blows."

Only a fifth of this fresh and lively small book is given to an account of the analysis and reenactment of Filippo Brunelleschi's invention; most of it is a study in the history of ideas from paintings and relevant texts. Alberti gains the most attention; one of the clearest perceptions is into his language, which serves as a sign for the centrality of human experience in his period. He speaks of concave surfaces as "the inner surfaces of egg shells" and of a plane as consisting of "many lines . . . joined closely together like threads in a cloth," making colorful metaphors of the world of everyday experience to replace "the black and white of Euclid."

Edgerton is anxious not to overpraise his protagonists; by the very title of the book he allots first place to the ancients. He asserts that Euclid himself, and Ptolemy too (particularly in the projections described for mapmaking in the *Geographia*, which was first seen in the Christian West in about 1400 in Florence), had possessed the main ideas of Alberti and his contemporaries.

What is plain is that linear perspective fits the grand metaphysics of the Renaissance. It was their "symbolic form," to use the term Edgerton draws by way of the art historian Erwin Panofsky from the philosopher Ernst Cassirer. It constructs a space in which for one moment and one position the observer becomes objective, a space based on his experiences having been abstracted impartially for all. In the end it was more science than art that came to prosper from this discovery on the part of the artists. The entire quality of linear perspective, its empty space free from boundary or change, suits well the spaces of Newton, the lens of Hooke and the traveler's notebook of Humboldt.

Nowadays science has matured. Our projective spaces do not exclude Newton, but they span much more. Our world is buzzing, various, half-chaotic, half-patterned. One impartial standpoint is no longer enough; time and chance happeneth to it all. The artists too have made peace with this world view, but they have not led it. It has been a long time since the perceptions of science have been pioneered by the painter. Remarkably enough, one modest Dutch printmaker came to express visually in his meticulous and ingenious woodcuts and lithographs a great deal of what our bold new postulates and richer instrumentation have added to the lucidity first grasped in Alberti's city.

Bruno Ernst was a friend and neighbor of M. C. Escher's, and a teacher of physics and mathematics and editor of a mathematics magazine for Dutch students. In this fine book he presents many of Escher's best-known prints in the context of models, sketches, personal confidences, influences and the hopes Escher expressed to him and to others. Vanishing points? Of course Escher used linear perspective with uncommon crispness. But here is the famous "High and Low," where there are two vanishing points, one dragging our gaze up to the tiled ceilings, the other pulling it down to the tiled floor. Relativity has entered; the same small patch is at once the ceiling and the floor, depending on where the observer stands. The finished lithograph is reproduced, and with it four or five sketched versions and Escher's own account of how one vanishing point can and should be made to function for two observers, high and low.

Here too is Escher's remarkable grid in which the scale grows steadily as we encircle a point in the center of a drawing. The print space bulges enormously; the window mullions of the print gallery reveal to us not a ship print but a great ship in the harbor. Scale has become explosive; what Escher had done, the "learned gentlemen . . . once tried in vain to convince me," was to draw on a Riemann surface. He was not trained in mathematics, but he came to its conceptual schemes by his artist's vision and his determination to present that vision consistently. "So far as I was concerned it was merely a question of a cyclic expansion or bulge, without beginning or end." Even specialized modern theory can speak to a reflective percipient.

Escher's themes are marshaled and exemplified: different structures of space interpenetrating; the flat surface made to fill, to contain an approach to infinity within a limited bound, to reflect becoming no less than being; the conflict between the optical devices of perspective and the intricate algorithms of the unconscious by which we judge depth and position in pictures. It is all a rich legacy, to which every admirer of Escher will repair for a sense both of the man and of his methods. The little horsemen ride by, the one melting into the other; the last pages show us Escher's last work, a twining of three elegant, colorful snakes into a double interlacing of rings, suggesting infinity at both the edge and the center.

The book begins with a magic mirror, Escher's mirror, which sets its little beasts free to walk around on a tiled table. Overleaf we see the end point of linear perspective, Andrea Pozzo's great baroque trompe l'oeil ceiling in Rome. The plenitude of the world lies still uncaught by art or by science. The book shows a color snapshot of Ernst with Escher a few weeks before the artist's death, with the touching quotation: "I consider my work the most beautiful and also the ugliest." It is here again remarkable how one can catch in apparently conventional work of student days the prefiguration of an artist's maturity.

(July 1977)

Whistled Languages
By R. G. Busnel and A. Classe

Twenty years have passed since Professor Classe first explained in this magazine the remarkable language Silbo, with which the herders and farmers of La Gomera in the Canary Islands proudly maintain an acoustic citizen's-band surrogate among the steep, dry, canyon-cut landscapes of their island. He and his colleague have since delved deep — they are fluent in Silbo — into this remarkable cultural achievement, known to outsiders since the 17th century but poorly understood. It turns out that Gomera is not unique: in the high-Pyrenees valley of Ossau in France a single village, Aas, developed a similar scheme, which has dwindled and all but vanished as the people left their hard mountain homes. In the highlands of northeastern Turkey close to the Black Sea coast a "whole population of highlanders," some 30,000 men, women and children, depend on whistling as we depend on the telephones of the city. The three schemes are remarkably similar—almost surely by convergence rather than by diffusion, since each is tightly based on its distinct language, French, Spanish or Turkish, and no contact whatever is suggested. (A fourth whistled language, of a rather different kind, is used among the Mazateco people north of Oaxaca in Mexico.)

This book is a thin monograph that compactly summarizes what is known and how it was learned. Sound spectra, landscape photographs, careful linguistic and phonetic analyses, measures of intensity over distance, experimental tests of critical points and hints (none too easy) on how to do it, with photographs of adepts—all are offered in a work that is hard for a general reader to put down even though it is intended for the specialist in linguistics. Why Silbo and its cognates? The answer seems clear: they function adaptively. The landscapes and the work life of the three places are similar. There are no roads and the paths are winding and difficult. Crops are cultivated high in the hills, which are rather barren and, in the Turkish case, terraced. An isolated population has for a long time been given cause to think about a message channel that would carry better, with less effort, than a shout. Once built, the language becomes—as all human social accomplishments become—a source of pride and a mark of community, in these cases with the advantage of concealment from outsiders. (In the Spanish Civil War military signals were on occasion cast in Silbo, but there were Gomerans on both sides and so the measure-countermeasure drama soon ran its course.)

Does it work? Here are the data, both in general and from direct measurement of the propagation of sound in natural conditions. The whistlers are well aware of acoustic shadows, both topographic and thermal in origin. The noise is low; except when the trade wind is blowing La Gomera yields "the impression of profound quiet." (From time to time blackbirds sound false signals, imitating human calls!) A line of sight helps; vegetation strongly damps the signal. In wooded open valleys the useful range is one or two kilometers, but in narrow rocky valleys from eight to 10 kilometers can be reached. The whistlers do not use their lips, but with tongue on teeth or with one or two fingers in their mouth they generate rather pure piercing tones, some 120 decibels at a distance of a meter—as loud as a trumpet.

The information is placed on this carrier by frequency modulation as well as by all the start-stop amplitude rhythms of speech. Consonants and stops are coded into the tone by natural patterns of quick pitch change, quite parallel to the modulation of the ordinary voice during consonants, since the motions of the mouth are the source of both. Anyone can try simply whistling out an articulated phrase, particularly working with an open language such as Spanish. It is then convincing to read the study of the whistle speech in detail. It is an almost complete phonetic recoding of speech; users can recognize and repeat words from a language they do not know if they are whistled properly. Single words can be recognized, according to careful direct tests, with an error rate of some 30 percent, compared with only 4 percent for normal speech; it is the redundancy in longer messages that makes the channel fully workable.

The Mexican case is different. Children and men whistle but not grown women; this is lip whistling, much less loud and not practiced over distances greater than a few hundred meters; it is used at close quarters (say in the marketplace), unlike the other three languages. Among these people group work is more usual and there are no distant herds or flocks. The coding is quite different: their spoken language is tonal, and in the whistle language only the melodic line of speech is presented. The sentence is thus merely outlined, transposed to a high lip whistle modulated in a narrow frequency range, about half an octave around 2,000 hertz. (In Silbo the frequency range is as much as two octaves, although most of the time the carrier stays at about the same mean, which is the region of best signal detection over natural noise.) The Mazateco cannot recognize any words that lack the tonal structure of an existing word in their own language; theirs is not a full phonetic mapping. Indeed, they are reported as substituting the same whistled form for such prosodically similar names as Modesto and Gustavo.

A final chapter touches on animal signals, drum languages and the like. Maybe porpoises could learn Silbo; like canaries, they can mimic whistles. Whistle languages are almost as fast as ordinary speech and much more efficient than the very redundant talk of drums. Here is a folk technology of telecommunication, demonstrably effective and in no way occult, mystical or telepathic.

(May 1977)

Everyone Here Spoke Sign Language: Hereditary Deafness on Martha's Vineyard
By Nora Ellen Groce

This brilliantly argued and lively book first examines a concrete problem that random nature coldly set human beings and then traces out an unexpected solution devised by human

human nurture. Dr. Groce is a medical anthropologist at Harvard; her information consists of the oral history she herself garnered from some 50 witnesses, almost all more than 75 years old, and the documents in print and in manuscript that cross-check and extend their firsthand accounts. Human genetic theory, ethnographic counterparts and a clear-eyed account of social attitudes are the analytic tools that form her brief and telling work.

The famous Vineyard is 100 square miles of moor, woodland, field, pond and beach five salt miles off the Massachusetts mainland. Thomas Mayhew, Sr., of Watertown near Boston bought the rights to the island (and several other islands nearby) for £40 and a beaver hat in the year 1641. No Europeans were yet there at all, and the Indian bands assumed and remain in a reasonably peaceable stance toward their new neighbors. For a generation or two a few families moved to the island each year, first from lands near Boston and later from the nearby Cape Cod shore. By 1710 immigration had stopped: there were open lands elsewhere, whereas the island was settled.

After American independence Martha's Vineyard became a small maritime power, like Nantucket a nursery for the far-flung New England whalemen. But its westernmost township, Chilmark, a quiet up-island settlement with only a small harbor, lived by its subsistence farms, the sheep pastured among long stone walls, and one-man fishing dories, daring daily the pounding surf off South Beach. Few men there signed on as whalers, and even a day's trip to the hustle of the down-island seaports was a major event.

People lived close among their kin, in farm neighborhoods that could be traced back to the first settlers. In 1850 there were some 650 people in Chilmark, four-tenths of whom bore one of five surnames: Mayhew, Tilton, West, Hillman or Allen. The place was a genetic isolate, its lines of descent intricately knotted. New blood hardly entered the inbred up-island community. By the 1850's the percentage of those who could count no ancestor with a Kentish surname such as Tilton, one of the families that had come before 1710, was negligible.

The founders left to their people more than a name. In the mid-19th century the number of deaf individuals in Chilmark was about one in 25; 39 individuals are known to have been born deaf there in the course of two centuries, in a town whose average population was only 350. That rate is crudely 100 times higher than the rate for the entire American population in the 19th century.

Deaf parents did not always have deaf children, and hearing parents sometimes did. The origin of the condition was then a mystery. Not until Mendel's concept of recessive inheritance became known early in this century did the cause become clear. A mutation can alter the normal development of the complex circuitry of hearing, but the single mutant gene does not affect the one who carries it. It is passed at random, still hidden, to one of his or her children. (There is no sign of sex linkage, by the way; men and women were affected alike.) A great many genes induce recessive deafness; it is highly unlikely that a child can inherit deafness unless the parents share a common ancestry and each happens to donate the same hidden mutant gene.

Congenital deafness is gone from the island now. The last person to be born deaf there died in 1952. Chilmark today is no isolate. Young people go off-island to work and often return with a spouse. Many immigrants have married islanders. The American Asylum for the Deaf in Hartford by 1860 was enrolling many of the deaf children from the Vineyard. They were the largest group in the school. Quite a few married a deaf classmate. But there was much less chance of finding a carrier of the island recessive gene among that group than there was among hearing islander relatives.

Where did the mutant gene arise? The Vineyard families among whom deaf members were first documented knew each other well, but they were not related. They had all settled in Scituate south of Boston, the second-oldest town in Plymouth colony. Together they had moved to the Cape shore, and 25 years later on again to the Vineyard for new land. They had begun to intermarry; the birthrate was high and the death rate was low. They multiplied.

Those families were united by the sufferings of civil war, depression and dissent. Most of them had been Puritan clothworkers in the isolated poor, chalky lands of The Weald of Kent — once a wild forest, the largest in Roman England — 40 miles southeast of London. The Reverend John Lothrop, their godly minister, led them to Boston in 1634, all migrating in a loyal party, most in a single ship. During the next years more "men of Kent" from nearby villages of The Weald joined them in Scituate. The Weald was no island, but its secluded villages were also something of a genetic isolate. When the Kentish folk settled at last on the Vineyard, among them were many carriers of that hidden mutant gene. Most of the deaf Vineyarders shared three early colonists as ancestors; probably all three of them had borne the gene.

In the spring of 1714 Judge Samuel Sewell of Boston engaged some island fishermen to guide his party to Edgartown after a long trip across Vineyard Sound. The judge was "ready to be offended that [one of the men] spake not a word to us. But it seems he is deaf and dumb." He was Jonathan Lambert, born in 1657 at Barnstable on Cape Cod of Kentish parents, the first recorded case of deafness on the island. There is no record of widespread deafness in The Weald of Kent. There is a hint, however, in the witness of Samuel Pepys himself. He noted during the

Great Fire of London that a political acquaintance of his used sign language with deaf people engaged in intelligence work. That London official had grown up in a market town in The Weald around 1630.

Incomplete, the case is still compelling. Vineyard deafness was certainly the outcome of an old mutation. The place of that genetic event is almost surely within a dozen miles of the village of Egerton in The Weald of Kent, whence Lothrop and his congregants had come. The time remains uncertain; the single error could have occurred generations before the transatlantic migration.

The islanders' marriages with their neighbors shuffled the replicated gene widely enough so that the gene could often find its partner, and deafness, without other symptoms, could appear. Full expression came in the 1850's, after the gene had replicated for a dozen generations more or less in hiding.

Is molecular biology, to be sure with a good deal of help from society, to be viewed as destiny after all? Some people, plainly, were destined by nature to live without hearing. But chromosomes do not and cannot make a handicap out of that mere disability; it is society that handicaps. It was nurture, not nature, that fixed quite a different destiny for the deaf men, women and children who inhabited this engaging island.

Never were they treated as handicapped; never were they outcast, impoverished or isolated. The islanders instead actively adapted their society to the pattern of frequent hereditary deafness. "'Oh, they didn't think anything about them, they were just like everyone else . . . everyone here spoke sign language.'" For almost three centuries the deaf were part of the whole, free to vote, free to marry anyone, active in church affairs, legally fully responsible. They were farmers, militiamen, dorymen, carpenters. They were on hand at every social affair, all those merry chowder suppers, now winning and again losing at whist and checkers, practical jokers, once in a while celebrated horse traders or even memorable storytellers "in deaf and dumb," always part of the main. "As far as can be ascertained, deaf Islanders did not perceive themselves as a distinct social group."

Deafness just happened to some infants; it might enter any family as a minor problem of no deep importance, and it was best to get on with life. Nathaniel Mann, fisherman and dairy farmer, was born deaf; in 1924 he died the richest man in Chilmark. Tax and bank records indicate that there was in general no financial difference between deaf and hearing people. In today's America the deaf earn on the average about a third less than what hearing people earn.

Hearing and deaf islanders learned sign language in childhood, as naturally as the hearing learned spoken English. In hearing island families the children had no formal teaching in sign, but they picked it up from wide exposure; deaf adults and deaf children were important all around them. One old man reported that his hearing cousin learned to sign with her deaf father before she could talk with her hearing mother. Deaf children today are observed to gain vocabularies in sign as early as and at about the same rate as hearing children learn words; bilingual learning appears to be easy—sign and speech. Language is wider than speech, social communication is wider than language and our children are adept at it all.

Signers who could hear recalled that the syntax and word order of island sign was not the same as that of English; off-island, many hearing signers did follow English word by word rather than use the swifter forms of American Sign Language. Down-islanders who wandered into the Chilmark general store were often disconcerted by the silent general conversation passing around them among the locals, both the hearing and the deaf. The *Boston Sunday Herald* reported charmingly in 1895 on "singular pantomimes": neighborly morning gossip in sign carried out through spyglasses between Chilmark back doors an eighth of a mile apart.

It is now plain that sign languages are not dependent on spoken tongues. Most children born deaf have hearing parents who need to develop a home system of communication. Whenever there are enough deaf people in the course of time to pass along a system, a mature sign language may develop. There are recent studies of the use of signs by groups of deaf individuals in half a dozen villages around the world—in Yucatán, Surinam, Ghana, the Solomons. . . .

The origin of signed languages was long held to be Enlightenment Paris, where the good Abbé de l'Épée invented it at his schools for the deaf, said to have been the first such institutions. The Abbé himself did not claim to have invented signing. He knew there was at least a regional sign language already in use among his pupils. It seems plain that such a sign language has served Vineyarders since Jonathan Lambert's time. It is likely to have come from Kent. Indeed, British sign language is little studied, although there is evidence of its use since the Middle Ages. It is probable that there were many regional dialects.

Once the deaf children from the Vineyard went off to school in Hartford at state expense, the Chilmark sign language began to merge with the official American Sign Language that had come from France. Groce's elderly hearing informants found it hard to understand deaf off-islanders, or the signers they saw on television; the Vineyarders must have signed in an interesting creole.

"I was born in Chilmark," writes John W. M. Whiting, a distinguished Harvard psychologist, in an eloquent foreword, "and am related through my mother to most of the families in that community. . . . I never learned to sign, but I saw sign language used . . . [at] the annual county fair . . . and when I went fishing. . . . Knowing how to use sign language was, like knowing French, something to be envied. With the influx of new residents . . . the incidence of hereditary deafness . . . declined and finally ceased altogether. But this benefit was countered by the destruction of a microcommunity as a strongly supportive network, something that is sadly missing in our modern industrial world."

We need to weave anew; this persuasive and compassionate investigation has uncovered a gleaming old design.

(April 1987)

Mathematical Circus
By Martin Gardner

The Incredible Dr. Matrix
By Martin Gardner

The Annotated Alice: Alice's Adventures in Wonderland and Through the Looking Glass
By Lewis Carroll
With an introduction and notes by Martin Gardner

The Ambidextrous Universe: Mirror Asymmetry and Time-reversed Worlds, Second Edition
By Martin Gardner

Fads and Fallacies in the Name of Science
By Martin Gardner

Science: Good, Bad and Bogus
By Martin Gardner

Confessions of a Psychic
By Uriah Fuller

Further Confessions of a Psychic
By Uriah Fuller

The Flight of Peter Fromm
By Martin Gardner

To praise Martin Gardner by these books: So long ago that the redoubtable Richard Feynman of Cal Tech was still a Princeton graduate student, Feynman and a few others developed the remarkable recursively folding paper structures called flexagons. In 1956 a professional free-lance editor and writer, a man with not one college course to elaborate his high school flair for mathematics but with a lively and trained philosophical mind, undertook to elucidate flexagons, then known only through the journals of recreational mathematics, for the readers of this magazine. The piece ran in December, 1956, to wide interest. The editors of *Scientific American* perceived a public thirst for informal mathematics.

Here the fibers of connection wind tightly; the wonderful four-volume *The World of Mathematics* compiled by the first author of this book-review column, James R. Newman, had in 1956 begun its unexpected rise to the runaway best-sellerdom it so patently deserved. The editors popped the question; Gardner agreed that recreational math could support a monthly column. "I rushed around New York and bought all the major references I could find . . . and started a library." Today Gardner has a couple of rooms full of books and papers, "all the books that come out on recreational math," a file of the issues of some 10 journals and a fruitful worldwide correspondence with knowing readers, many of whom send in new ideas. His column has appeared some 300 times; it has become the focus of a recognizable subculture.

This year Martin Gardner turns 65. Douglas Hofstadter, a young, wide-ranging mathematical mind as familiar with language as it is with computers, is the continuator of Gardner's column, and Gardner has moved from the Hudson River shore to the quieter hills of North Carolina. There he will continue to write in his own rhythm within his best-loved philosophical vein.

Most of those monthly columns have been collected into nine volumes issued over the years by various publishers; all but one are still in print. (The magazine columns are all indexed in the valuable 1979 cumulative-index volume of *Scientific American* from the start through June, 1978; no one has yet prepared an overall index to the collections in books.) Here we review only the latest book of the series; consult *Books in Print* for the rest.

It seems fitting to list a few of the columns that have left a permanent mark on this reviewer, however idiosyncratic the choices may be. (Remember that responses by letter, often more complete in the later book version than in the magazine, offer a rich trove.) To begin with word games, there was a fine response about pangrams, those sentences that seek economically to use all 26 letters. The best pangram (September, 1964) is ascribed to the famous theorist of communications, the mathematician Claude Shannon: Squdgy fez, blank jimp crwth vox. It is formally perfect, meaningful although it requires an explanatory context. The most erudite reader response (November, 1970, and *Mathematical Circus*) is surely that of George L. Hart III, who offered a classical palindrome in Sanskrit, a poem of 32 syllables called *sarvatobhadra*, "perfect in every direction."

Then there was the game of "life" (October, 1970, and February, 1971), a set of recursive rules that generate moving plane patterns whose asymptotic limits are remarkable. It must have consumed in its period of epidemic spread enough computer time to show up in the G.N.P. The studies of tiling, or tessellations of the plane, provide a swift path into serious math for people with no mathematical training and no facility with numbers. (These appeared in April, 1961; July, August and December, 1975, and January, 1977.)

The magnificent April Fools' spoof in 1975 gave an illustrated set of ingenious hoaxes. It drew several thousand responses, mostly from people who had found the mistake within their own specialty but were pleased to read of surprising breakthroughs against those other stodgy truisms. Nearly a thousand physicists wrote to defend special relativity against the well-known paradox displayed in the column. When an Australian paper some years later printed the fact that two Illinois mathematicians had proved the four-color-map theorem, one loyal reader protested that this proof must be wrong because Gardner had published a map that was a counter-example! More skeptical readers had colored the "counterexample" and sent it back to Gardner.

The most telling of the responses were to a hilarious column about Irving Joshua Matrix and his daughter Iva, which appeared in June, 1974. The two were then running a wonderful pyramidal factory producing pyramids with magical properties (here a long, authentic citation of the claims in the marvel literature was given) at Pyramid Lake in Nevada. In spite of everything in the pages, including a pudgy Paiute super named One-Tooth Ree, so many readers drove to Nevada to visit the site that even those who wrote later to complain that no trace of the establishment could be found were numerous. Even sadder was the invitation immediately extended to Gardner by a reputable New York publisher to put out a quick book on pyramid miracles. When that enthusiast learned the whole thing was a hoax, he was not dismayed. His offer stood; write the first book at once and then put out a second in refutation! (The account appears in *The Incredible Dr. Matrix.*)

Gardner's own favorites are the more philosophical columns; memorable ones include those on Newcomb's paradox of decision theory (July, 1973, and March, 1974), and two tours de force on nothing and on everything (February, 1975, and May, 1976). In August, 1977, the column gave an account of the unbreakable public-key cryptography system growing at M.I.T.; this helped to raise a controversy over censorship between the research community and the National Security Agency that has only lately calmed.

The most widely known of Gardner's books is his delightful *Annotated Alice*. A big volume, with the indispensable original drawings by John Tenniel, it presents long marginal notes in witty and learned explication and amplification. Although there is "something preposterous about an annotated *Alice*," as Gardner himself concedes in the first line of his introduction, the book is in fact both useful and endearing. To "Jabberwocky," for example, there are 25 notes, including the texts of the clever translations *Le Jaseroque* and *Der Jammerwoch*. Even more to the point, there is an early Carroll gloss on the difficult words, written years before *Alice* and fuller than the interpretation given by Humpty Dumpty. The success of Gardner's *Alice* induced several similar annotated classics, including a 1967 *Casey at the Bat*, now out of print. Gardner is predictably a devotee and a savant of Oziana and L. Frank Baum; so far he has published only introductions to various editions of Oz works.

Gardner's college training, like his general predilection, was directed toward philosophy, particularly the philosophy of science and of knowledge. Gardner has written four or five books expounding science for general readers. The new version of *The Ambidextrous Universe* is a special pleasure. Its reach includes the look of flipped photographs and paintings, a delightful palindromic (by words) short-short-short story, the Korean flag, the violation of parity and the intimate history of its discovery, the symmetries of magnetism, entropy, Dr. Edward Anti-Teller and a good deal more. Fresh, clear and sensible, it is a small classic of popular science; the current edition includes a few new pieces on difficult questions of time invariance.

Gardner's first general book, a little timeworn but still in print, is *Fads and Fallacies in the Name of Science*. Here a new theme first entered the extraordinary output of this more than mathematician and philosopher. He was a boyhood magician, and he has ripened into a keen critic of magic and a prolific designer of magical effects, with a wide publication in those esoteric circles. He never performs, not even as a public speaker; the closest he ever came to a direct appearance as a conjurer was in Christmas demonstrations of magic at Marshall Field's in Chicago before World War II. A direct union between his philosophical concern with the nature of evidence and his own behind-the-scenes experience with magic turned him quite naturally into an assiduous and effective critic of pseudoscience.

The early book began this theme, and Gardner's very latest (*Science: Good, Bad and Bogus*) is a collection of nearly 40 book reviews and magazine pieces mostly on the passing and disparate parade of unreliable wonders, such as the psychic surgeons, the learned Dr. Velikovsky, those many adepts who manage over the decades to see through blindfolds, and some academic self-deceivers such as John Hasted and John G. Taylor. Professor Hasted studies, among other things, young people who can, if they are not watched, somehow pass distorted paper clips into a sealed glass globe. Well, not quite sealed; you do need to leave a small hole, or curiously the paraphysical effect does not work! It is all in print, incredible at two levels. Here is our Gardner as an acute and responsible if polemical discussant; responses are by no means suppressed.

The two booklets by "Uriah Fuller," relatively expensive (as the publications of the magicians' world are), lead any serious reader close to the methods of the pseudopsychic conjurers. Those fancy Dans are audacious and subtle by turns. The key is not a special technique, although there are plenty of clever ones. The real base of the effects is the adaptive stream of intellectual and physical misdirection and deceptive simulation. The magician-psychic will exploit any small opportunity, will vary method, sequence and intent, will make use of any interruption of attention and any chance hint to attain the imprecise goal, which itself changes. Control over such behavior lies only in mastery of the details, through stratagems as clever and knowing as the tricks they seek to expose. It is no art for mere credulous professors.

One small example: psychologists have learned that a breath can move a light object that is otherwise quite untouched. A control is a glass jar placed over the object that is presumably to be moved by mental forces. Does this also eliminate the use of an unseen thread? No; on a hard tabletop every jar edge is likely to leave at some point enough clearance to freely pass a nylon fiber of microscopic diameter. Somehow an adroit magician can operate an obedient dancing handkerchief "on a well-lit stage before thousands" and it is just an unexplained trick, perhaps done with thread. But "a crude demonstration by Nina, in her dimly lit Russian apartment," supports volumes of pseudo-learned commentary, darkly threatening the repeal of Newton's laws.

Finally, this engaging but tough-minded man has a productive hand at fiction. Gardner will soon publish a book of poetry for children; for eight postwar years he prepared a story and a poem each month for the children's magazine *Humpty Dumpty*, with a frequent trick or stunt that on being performed physically damaged the page it was printed on, an amiable delight of the author. There are plenty of his short stories, mostly humorous ones, in *Esquire* and other magazines of the period.

Gardner's one full-fledged novel, with a complex genesis, is now out in paperback. It is a genuine *Bildungsroman*; the young protagonist — and maybe the older man whose novel it purports to be — shares Gardner's life. Youth gave him a profoundly fundamentalist religious background. It was undergraduate study of philosophy at the University of Chicago that carried him beyond the passionate simplicities of a Tulsa upbringing. Exactly this happens to Peter Fromm, the name echoing Sören Kierkegaard, and the book also supplies a vivid journal of life on a destroyer escort in the Atlantic, Gardner's own wartime experience. The core of this intellectual novel is a comprehensive examination of the most important trends in Protestant theology of the past few decades, particularly the subtle Christology of Karl Barth. Fromm (and surely Gardner) leaves the tub-thumping certainties of his youth to enter a domain of doubts and searchings, from which Gardner will certainly comment in the fruitful years ahead.

(The above remarks owe much to the kindness of two mathematician-admirers of Gardner, Peter Renz of W. H. Freeman and Company and Dana Richards of Indiana University at Indianapolis, who made available to this reviewer both published and private material from their treasury, and to *The Two-Year College Mathematics Journal* at Menlo College. To praise Martin Gardner buy these books!)

(October 1981)

Les Objets Fractals: Forme, Hasard et Dimension
By Benoît Mandelbrot

There is a short list of works that display for the mind's delight the profound role of geometric form in the fabric of the world. D'Arcy Wentworth Thompson's *On Growth and Form*, with its account of living creatures large and small, bridges and backbones, honeycombs, cracked mud and rhinoceros horns, heads the list. The geometry therein is Greek in topic and simplicity. Hermann Weyl's marvelous lectures on symmetry in nature follow closely, extending the mathematics to obey the demands of repetitive rigid displacement. The papers of Cyril Stanley Smith — summarized by him in this magazine some 15 years ago — first made clear how foams and tissues and polycrystalline metals evince the struggle between the Gibbsian play of local energies and the overall rule of topology, Eulerian in epoch. This French paperback is a fresh addition to that notable shelf, bringing to the knowing viewer of natural artificial form the unexpectedly diverse application of the theory of real variables. It is proper 20th-century mathematics nucleated around names such as Minkowski, Besicovitch and Kolmogorov.

The book and in some sense the ideas begin with Jean Perrin, whose study of quantitative Brownian motion visibly displayed the reality of the kinetic theory before World War I. Perrin reminds us that for mathematicians, with their nice analysis, "curves which have no tangent are the rule, and the well-regulated ones, such as the circle, are very interesting but highly special cases." These views *seemed* only an "intellectual exercise, without doubt ingenious, but . . . sterile. . . . Nature presents no such complications and does not even suggest the idea. *But the contrary is true*, and the logic of the mathematicians has kept them closer to reality than the practical representations of the physicists." Even the great analyst Charles Hermite once wrote to Thomas Jean Stieltjes of turning away "in fright and horror from the lamentable affliction of functions which have no derivative."

Most appreciators of mathematics have long understood this point on the molecular level. What Dr. Mandelbrot has shown is a world of visible form that is governed by the properties of Brownian motion, suitably generalized by the work of many hands, including his own original studies.

Take the analyst's "snowflake" curve (named here after its discoverer, H. von Koch), which is made in an elementary way from an equilateral triangle of unit side by replacing the middle third of each side with a "cape," itself the two jutting equal sides of a triangle a third as large as the original, and so on, repeating indefinitely. With each repetition the length increases by the factor 4/3. Such a continuous curve has in the limit no tangents, infinite length and zero area.

The mathematicians have presented a number of measures applicable to such a remarkable curve that can distinguish it overall from a circle, even though it too is merely a one-dimensional manifold. Consider two properties of the snowflake curve. It is self-similar: magnify any section and you see under the magnifier just the same form on a smaller scale. Step off its length with a pair of dividers; with dividers set at one unit distance the length you measure will be three units. Next try a one-third-unit divider setting. The length is now four units. The stepped-off length will increase continually as the divider setting grows smaller, following a simple power law, with the calculated exponent .26.

A straight line shares some properties with the snowflake. It too is self-similar, but its stepped-off length is the same for every divider opening. It has a dimension of unity, in our usual way of thinking. Here arises the book's title: it is now plausible to assign the snowflake curve a generalized dimension (applicable to self-similar curves) that is greater than that of its tame kindred, a straight line. The general formula sensibly assigns a generalized dimension 1 to the straight line and "dimension" log 4/log 3 = 1.26 . . . to the grander snowflake. Hence the book's title. Dr. Mandelbrot offers us a new word, fractal, suited to the tongue in both French and English, to convey this meaning of intermediate dimensionality. ("Fractional" itself would grate if it were applied to a number that is in general not rational.)

Where is the physics? Here lies the novelty and the bulk of the book. Of course we have no physical snowflake curves. Nature gives no infinities, not even within molecular collisions. There is a cutoff at the angstrom level. Still, surprises abound. The land-sea shorelines of the real world approximate the snowflake curve! Two modifications are needed. There is no such formal regularity in the coast of Brittany; it is self-similar in the statistical sense only. A map at a 10-kilometer scale shows some complex bays and peninsulas; so does a map at a .1-kilometer scale. On the average the forms do not differ (apart, of course, from any particular fishing cove we know). Empirically the stepped-off length of a coastline on maps at varying scales obeys a power law like the snowflake curve's, from a scale of hundreds of kilometers down to one of perhaps meters, where geography stops and pebbles begin. Only the exponent differs.

The book shows us simulated coasts, from which we form the impression that the dimension 1.1 is too small for the real map and 1.5 is clearly too large. It seems that mountain relief, islands, lakes, the holes in Appenzeller and Emmenthaler cheeses, the craters of the moon, the distribution of stars close to us in the galaxy and a good deal more can be described by the use of generalized Brownian motions and the idea of the fractal dimension. The cosmos itself may in the end prove to be no uniform domain but a random assembly in space, uniform only statistically, finite in mass and yet infinite in extent. Turbulent eddies, word frequencies, computer components, even the incomes of the population share some of these properties, formed out of the infinities of measure theory and the play of correlated probabilities. There is much more to be done, and it is not reasonable to assume that these results imply one mechanism.

The author has given us a delightful "macédoine" of a book, between monograph and popularization. It makes an irresistible mix, with lots of graphics, few formulas, careful and yet informal exposition, even biographical notes on the often eccentric but fascinating people who have been his predecessors in this new domain. One original philologist, a Harvard lecturer named George Zipf, published a law of word frequencies in 1949, but he "justified the Anschluss by a mathematical formula" in the same book. "One sees with him, in the clearest fashion — even in caricature — the extraordinary difficulties that attend any interdisciplinary approach."

Dr. Mandelbrot has overcome all such barriers; he is a well-known applied mathematician, trained in France but working chiefly in this country, where he is a fellow and scientific adviser to the director of research at IBM. His small volume is a good bet to become a classic of its deep yet elementary genre. Some American publisher ought to get it into English soon.

(November 1975)

From One to Zero: A Universal History of Numbers
By Georges Ifrah
Translated by Lowell Bair

The accountants have provided that most potent of contemporary finalities, the bottom line. Now it appears that they produced the top line too. The first writing, according to Georges Ifrah, seems to have been "invented by accountants who had to deal with economic operations much too complex and varied to be entrusted to a single memory."

The time was 50 centuries back; the places were Sumerian Uruk on the old Euphrates and Elamite Susa east of the Tigris. The first documents are clay tablets, marked while they were soft with a simple pointed tool (not yet the sedge used for cuneiform). The entries show pictographs for date palms and mutton legs. Adjoining them are coded marks for numbers. There is a precursor to this full-fledged account book: a couple of centuries earlier we find clay envelopes that resemble a tennis ball in size and form. They enclose a set of small clay tokens, almost certainly themselves the descendants of pebble counters. (An X-ray photograph of such a specimen at the Louvre is redrawn here.) The tokens are numerical symbols; a little sphere, say, means 10 units. An impression from a cylinder seal on the outside authenticates the secured record.

Within the past decade various French expeditions and scholars have uncovered level by level a scheme that was steadily elaborated in the course of a few centuries. First, the envelope becomes merely a legal record; its numerical content is marked again on the outside so that it can be read without destroying it: the stylus marks match the enclosed tokens. Next the envelope evolves into marked, solid tablets of account, again validated by cylinder-seal impressions. The fourth step at Susa shows minor neatening. In Uruk at that same time new tablets appear, between 3200 and 3100 B.C., bearing engraved marks. These marks sometimes box together the numerical symbols based on the tokens with new signs that code for the commodities being counted. The symbols are as realistic as a sketch of a bird, or as abstract as a crossed circle representing a sheep.

Writing has certainly appeared, although not as yet the richness of a real written language. Accountants tend to be frugal.

A delightful illustration shows the basis for the identification of Sumerian numerals: the scribes followed the helpful practice of putting totals on the reverse of many tablets. The example shown is a formal accounting for 15 bags of barley, 30 bags of wheat and so on. The total is written on the overleaf (overclay?) as 145 bags in all. Given many tablets, the checking method allows unique decipherment.

This interesting volume by a gifted and enthusiastic amateur scholar (a polyglot French teacher of mathematics) offers almost 30 chapters that range over the entire story of number systems, both written and unwritten. Ifrah draws all the many figures in his "archeology of numbers" with his own hand; the unity and clarity gained are a pleasure for the reader. There is a price: the sense of evidence is necessarily diluted by all those figures plainly written in the same style, whether they originated as Chinese, Hebrew, Roman or Zuñi.

Most of the story can be seen as a tension between the early iterative and the later structural. One-to-one correspondence lies at the taproot, but that seems no very new insight for our species. There are good accounts of the mapping of numbers on body parts, not merely the 10 fingers to which all forms of numeration except for machine language still bear homage, but systems such as those used in the Torres Strait, where ankles, knees, hips and more gave a visual representation that ran up to 33. A table of the first 10 number words in a couple of dozen Indo-European tongues, from Sanskrit *dvi* and *tri* to Icelandic *tveir* and *prir*, bears out their kinship. The words have lost all meaning but the digital (that trendy word has kept both meanings); were our number words also once "names of parts of the body"?

The number base is a brilliant recursive early invention. The role of anatomy in its origin is clear. The pedigree of base 60, however, is obscure. We use it for telling time and in circular-arc numeration, a practice we can ascribe to the Babylonians and to the Sumerians before them. A little eased by an auxiliary use of 10, it saved them the labor of inscribing symbols. If 10 was *u* and 60 was *gesh*, it was nice if not fully consistent to call 600 *gesh-u*.

Why 60? In a fine page Ifrah collects the theories, by now antique. Theon, a Hellenic author, was the first to offer one answer, known to generations of the mathematical: 60 is uniquely full of divisors. Perhaps two peoples, one using the base 6 and one the base 10, came together — an unfounded conjecture made in 1904. One subtle argument began with the Babylonian double hour, a twelfth of the full day, spanning an arc 60 times the angular diameter of the sun.

Cantor himself, the founder of set theory, held that the beginning was the rough day count of the year, 360; then the simplicity of the hexagonal division of the circle, the chord equal to the radius, further privileged 60. Cantor gave this up when critics objected that neither astronomy nor geometry could explain a numeration system. Once one learns that Chinese reckoners long ago divided all circles not into 360 degrees but into 365^1/$_4$ degrees, he is led to think Cantor ought to have held firm. Perhaps in the oldest times few people other than astronomers needed to compute with large numbers. The early tablets already use the standard Sumerian system with its mixed reliance on 10 and 60.

To the Babylonian sexigesimal computers we owe both the first place-value system of notation and the first use of zero. Their entries are strictly positional in the base 60, although their cuneiform numerals are formed by symbols for 10 and 1 combined in a simple way (thus 32 is made of three marks for 10 and two for 1). The notation for 610 requires a crescent for 10 in the 60's place and then another crescent for 10 in the units place. But now the scribe was worried: that might look like 20, two crescents side by side. He spaced his marks carefully. After 1,000 years or so, practice had moved ahead. The sign for a separation, used in many prose texts for such purposes as marking the end of one language and the start of another in bilingual documents, was drafted to fill the necessary empty space. In the Babylonian mathematical documents that device appears only when the zero is medial, never at the start or end of a number. The astronomers went further; they used it wherever necessary.

It remains uncertain that the sign could be read as a true abstract null, say the result of 20 minus 20. Instead the authors of some texts resort to a more concrete statement, for example "the grain is exhausted." Such was the dawn of a written zero, an event that probably preceded the first records we have of the zero, which date to the fourth century B.C.

The elements of our 10-digit system are called Arabic numerals, for thence they came to the West; yet they are almost surely southern Indian. They can be seen here in a variety of Indian documents dating from the sixth to the ninth century A.D. The decimal place-value notation, with its zero explicit and free, most of its digital forms swift and abstract, is there in full consistent use; even a few of the signs are familiar, although not all 10 are recognizable. That numeration is the "only real universal language" of our times. The original forms were entirely Indian; the system itself might have owed something to old Babylon. We do not know; it is most likely that the entire scheme was an Indian invention whose antecedents are the place notation and the place holder in a counting board. The treatment here of the many documentary and interpretive issues involved is particularly full. The idea of a mark for nothing touched the imagination of Europe; it seemed almost magical—in a way it is—and the word recalls that sense. The word comes from the Arabic for the void, sifr, after the Sanskrit with the same meaning. In English we hear in the word cipher the general notion of number and a hint of the secret or mysterious as well.

The volume is a full and clear account. It is at its best close to the documentary record; it loses a good deal of authority when it discusses the origins of counting as described in ethnographic and psychological literature, where secondary sources and speculation perforce take a larger role. There is plenty of fine reading here as well as quite a few sign and number puzzles. Although they are unraveled, they should still challenge readers who have a bent for such tasks. We miss an index, and the inviting citations, particularly for the wealth of figures, are unfortunately incomplete, a style not unusual in France

(November 1986)

Capitalism and Arithmetic: The New Math of the 15th Century
By Frank J. Swetz
Including the full text of the Treviso Arithmetic *of 1478*
Translated by David Eugene Smith

Already mature in this first of all printed books of mathematics in the West are the kind of arithmetic problems that still call forth schoolday groans: "Three men, Tomasso, Domenego, and Nicolo, entered into partnership. Tomasso put in 760 ducats on the first day of January, 1472. . . . And on the first day of January, 1475, they found that they had gained 3168 ducats, 13 grossi and 1/2. Required is the share of each, so that no one shall be cheated." The solution is worked out neatly — if wrongly, as one of the many problem conditions is misstated. Partner Nicolo is found to gain 1,173 ducats, 22 grossi and 17 pizoli, all checked. (Business was good; they earned some 40 percent per year on capital invested.)

We are at the flourishing of the Renaissance, printing is lively in the cradle. This is the still expansive Venetian Republic. Even the town of Treviso, 15 miles away, about a day's travel from the capital city, supports half a dozen printers. No other book in mathematics has reached print, not even famous Euclid; the academics would have to wait a few years more for the first printed *Elements*. Perhaps the scholars were not as attractive a market as the many young merchant's sons for whom the affairs of imagined Tomasso and his partners were so meticulously set out. Geometry, moreover, demands all those costly labeled diagrams; even the numerical examples were not easy for early printers. Here they made do with the letter i for the numeral 1 to save time or type. (The inexpensive book at hand is not a facsimile, although the edition is both typographically attractive and evocative of the rare original.)

This sprightly piece of scholarship presents in 300 readable pages the text of the anonymous old practica itself, a documented analysis of its operations and techniques in the context of the applied mathematics of the day. A concise and colorful perspective view of the thriving mercantile society that this arithmetic text so artlessly reflects, ducat by golden ducat, emerges from the book. The text, originally written in the Venetian dialect, was put into clear-running English before World War I by David Smith, a well-known Columbia University historian and teacher of mathematics. Smith never published it in full. It was noticed among his papers a few years back and given this delightful form by Dr. Swetz, a scholar at the Harrisburg campus of the Pennsylvania State University.

Untitled, anonymous, the *Arithmetic* was a working textbook for young students of the new commercial arithmetic. It was the first to see print of a large number of books that expounded the new math in many European vernaculars. They were called algorisms, after the Baghdad savant Muhammad al-Khwarizmi, whose ninth-century arithmetic on the new numbers had been among the earliest to gain Latin translation. Also in use were Latin theoretical arithmetics of medieval provenance, based on Roman numeration.

Other books were at this very time in embittered competition with the algorisms; they were also practical in intent but dealt with the venerable techniques of the counting table, how to use its movable tokens and ruled lines. By 1400 the new numbers written in ink on paper had won their way in the south but not in northern commerce. Even the University of Padua had required as late as 1348 that book prices be written out in Roman numerals, "not by figures but by clear letters." It was thought the strange new digits could be more easily falsified.

It is no mere chance that many words of modernity—such terms as bank, discount, net, credit, opera, science, even ghetto—are Italian in origin. All the action was there. Prosperous and up-to-date German families from the 14th century on had sent their sons to northern Italy to learn the new ways of ciphering and the double-entry bookkeeping already in wide use. The apprentice merchants studied the texts of their masters, who ran the special reckoning schools. Such a master was our unnamed author of the Treviso arithmetic; in all, we know of 30 practica like his printed by century's end, about half of them still in Latin.

Those people who would become literate began study in a basic school where the three R's were taught. On that foundation a good student with support might go on to grammar school, where he would become proficient in Latin and the Roman authors. He might then make his way through the university to become a cleric, a lawyer or a physician. One such career would be that of Nicholaus Copernicus, who came from Baltic shores to study at Bologna and Padua; he was still a child when the

Treviso arithmetic came out. The strongest educational alternative to grammar school for middle-class youths was the reckoning school. Mercantile education beyond that vocational level meant wide travel and the mastery of foreign languages. The 200-year-old model of the Venetian merchant Messer Marco Polo set the pattern.

This arithmetic is broadly familiar. In our time we still place it with the force of law before all our pupils. The 10 digits that served the merchants of Treviso in 1478 are the ones we use today. There are differences. No number word beyond *million* appears; *billion* and the rest entered a few years later. The algorithms for adding and subtracting are still familiar, although curiously no exercises on adding long columns are set. Multiplication tables up to 10 times 10 appear early in the book, although that powerful operation is clearly less than routine. Long and short division are treated with special care and taste. Several clever schemes are described that lay the work out by the column, the cross, the chessboard. As many as eight algorithms were current. Saving on expensive paper seems one criterion for choice. Checks of computation are regularly taught, including the trick of casting out 9's. Although units of money and weight are much discussed, the tables of equivalents and exchange ratios are not as elaborate as those in other works of the time. The Rule of Three for ratios is a big set piece. Fractions are assumed, but they are not much elaborated. The systematic use of decimals lay a century ahead, although percentage and the utility of place notation are already well appreciated.

As one might expect, the otherwise intensely practical book begins with some neo-Aristotelian philosophy of number (perhaps misunderstood) and closes with a few fancy problems on rates: "If 17 men build 2 houses in 9 days, how many days will it take 20 men to build 5 houses?" These are not in fact relevant to commerce; they are, "in a sense, a boast of the power of mathematics." Students, amaze and puzzle your friends! There is not the least hint of astrology for the young businessman; instead there is a final page or two on calendrical computations that fixed the holidays.

The goods most in trade in these problems are crimson cloth, raw silk and French wool, beeswax for candles, and spicy ginger, pepper, saffron and cinnamon. Relative prices are not grossly discordant compared with those of today — not even the price of sugar, then perhaps grown on Venetian-held Cyprus. On the 10th day of December, 1478, the Trevisan *maestro d'abbaco* closed his book with an affectionate farewell to his dear friends, the diligent students. "I promise you the same gratifying usefulness." That mind and attitude remain familiar 500 years and an ocean away from the Rialto, embodied in our Harvard M.B.A.'s.

(June 1988)

II

Tales Old and New

Myth and folklore lie deep within our world view, and the writers of fiction speak volumes. Three books of ancient myth, one old and marvelous reworking of folklore and a modern novel of science and technology, brilliant but icy cold, are offered in example.

Legends of the Earth: Their Geologic Origins
By Dorothy B. Vitaliano

Hot-tempered Pele, goddess of volcanoes, dwells to this day with her many relatives in the fire pit called Halemaumau, deep in the caldera of Kilauea in the Hawaii National Park. Their shifting dwellings are the lava mounds built up when a fountain of fire jets high above the surface of the lava lake. For a century before 1924 Pele's lake of flame rose and fell continually: fiery surf for family sport. Since then the climate has grown less favorable. A congealed gray layer conceals the glow; only during specific eruptions do fountains leap and do flung bombs bear witness to the games and the temper of the gods. Not since 1790 has angry Pele hurled a violent explosion from her abode. Then she acted in defense of the ruler of Hawaii, her protégé Kamehameha, who in the end came to hold sway over all the islands. She reduced the rebellious army of the great chief's cousin Keoua by a third, engulfing it with a rare blast of steam, ash and rock just as it passed her crater. An entire day spent in appeasing her had been inadequate to win her neutrality.

Pele has not always lived in Kilauea. When she first came to the islands, it was to Kauai in the northwest, where she left only an eroded core of a volcanic cone, now long extinct. Next she went to Oahu, where a fire pit she left became filled with salt water to make a lake, and then, island by island, she moved southeastward, at last to dwell in fiery peace near the tip of Hawaii. She still leaves Halemaumau from time to time, but only by "a road under the ground from her house in the crater to the shore." It is an apt enough account of flank eruptions, the latest of which began in 1969 and is still in progress.

The dramatic and coherent legend of Pele is a fine example of geomythology, the subject of this unusually interesting book. Pele's story includes both types of earth legend: the euhemerist, which incorporates actual observed geological events and is a kind of folk field report, and the causal, or etiological, which is rather a folk theory conceived to account for features of the environment, from odd minerals such as tektites to landforms, floods, volcanoes and earthquakes. Many photographs (some taken by the geologist author herself), detailed maps and drawings enrich this book, whose clarity and liveliness are no less visible than the informed scholarship manifested in a multilingual list of references citing 277 books and papers.

The folklore (and some fakelore) presented is catholic indeed, spanning the world. Iceland, Japan and Hawaii are evidently particularly rich veins, and they are well worked here. The lore does not stand alone; it is supported by detailed and skeptical appraisal of the real geological situations, both in the relevant locality and as more general analogy. One chapter makes it clear that the slow motion of most geologic process has not come to the attention of the legend makers. "Man adapts to the slow-but-sure changes so naturally that in most cases he forgets them completely."

In almost every part of the world there are traditions of a great flood, such as the deluge Noah alone escaped. Once even geologists believed that the marine fossils of the high mountains bore mute witness to such a worldwide event. It is now clear that the imprints refer to no single time, and even clearer that worldwide rains of the most remarkable volume and simultaneity could at most flood many large rivers but never the sea.

Immanuel Velikovsky is the most important remaining proponent of the folkloric evidence of a universal flood (which, since it cannot be of normal geological origin, he ascribes to "worlds in collision"). Tsunamis in the wide Pacific littoral, meltwater floods from postglacial lakes and disastrous river floods augmented by typhoon conditions are some more likely events behind the tales. For flood stories are not literally worldwide; they are conspicuously lacking in Africa, where the main rivers are seasonal and floods such as the Nile's are often not evil but benign. "Velikovsky gets around the lack of African flood traditions with an ingenuity that must be admired: he invokes a 'collective amnesia.'" The verdict is plain. It is just as implausible to ascribe the widespread deluge stories to an actual worldwide flood as it is to claim that all the stories derive from one diffused account of a great overflow of the Euphrates. "Flood traditions are nearly universal, partly because of the efforts of [Christian] missionaries, but mainly because floods *in the plural* are the most nearly universal of all geologic catastrophes."

Nearly half of the book is given over to a fascinating argument (owing much to the Greek scholars and scientists Spyridon Marinatos and Angelos Galanopoulos), some of it based on direct work in the field by the author (and her husband). The topic is the Bronze Age eruption of the caldera of Santorini, southernmost of the Cyclades Islands in the Aegean. There stands the sea-flooded broken ring of the volcano, 10 kilometers in diameter. Deep-sea cores show a layer of tephra, the ash of the explosion, over many hundreds of miles of sea floor. (Krakatoa's ash shows up very little in comparable cores, and so we can argue that at least one paroxysm of the event of Santorini must have been more powerful than the 100 or 150 megatons of TNT equivalent estimated for Krakatoa, a well-studied eruption of the same type.)

Santorini erupted around 1500 B.C., the dating coming most surely from the presence of Minoan pottery in "sealed Late Minoan I A" levels in easternmost Crete. (Pottery styles, but not carbon-14 dates, are specific enough to fix the complicated sequence of events.) The event of course destroyed the Minoan colony on Santorini, but not the colonies on Crete or other islands, and yet within a generation the Minoan culture had given way to the mainlanders from Mycenae. Were the mainlanders the beneficiaries perhaps of a "knockout blow from Nature . . . not all at once, but in the form of a one-two or even a triple punch"? The Minoan decline was the aftermath of ashfalls that ruined crops, followed by moderate but repeated tsunamis and finally by a major earthquake that decimated fisheries, towns and royal courts. In the end there was a massive emigration and final surrender to powerful Mycenaean expeditions of conquest.

The author provides this scenario in one interesting chapter of "science fiction." The classical deluge of Deukalion, the Platonic tale of sunken Atlantis, the plagues of Egypt (ashfall and its consequences), the parting of the Red Sea (a tsunami on the Mediterranean coast of Sinai), the flight of Icarus and even more have been ascribed to Santorini. The euhemeristic relationship of all these classical and Exodus events is still to be proved; it remains possible until tested by more reliable absolute dating. "Until then in these cases . . . we are left swimming in a sea of speculation. But is it not a delightful sport?"

Here is excellent, skeptical, and knowing geology, fused with the sensible folklore insights so much at home at the Indiana University. Travelers, the fortunate dwellers in many interesting places, those who teach earth sciences and their more imaginative students all need this book.

(July 1974)

Inanna, Queen of Heaven and Earth: Her Stories and Hymns from Sumer

By Diane Wolkstein and Samuel Noah Kramer
Art compiled by Elizabeth Williams-Forte

At the eastern edge of the alluvial plain of the lower Euphrates in southern Iraq the archaeologists have for two generations been working at the mounds of Uruk, biblical Erech and modern Warka, one city-state of ancient Sumer. The site has disclosed marvels, the oldest written documents and the first great monumental temples, their mud-brick walls, huge columns and high platforms encrusted with a colorful patterned mosaic of cones and beakers of painted terra-cotta. The time of Uruk's flowering was a period of 500 years and more from about 3500 B.C.; Sumer endured, waxing and waning in the flux of human affairs, for another couple of millenniums.

The glory that was old Uruk was not forgotten: its beliefs and forms were recorded with learning and passion on clay. That very technology was Uruk's accomplishment. Here and there in newer cities throughout the land between the two rivers there accrued libraries of the hand-size tablets, marked in swift cuneiform by scribes and scholars who knew the past, even though they were of a different people. In the 19th century tens of thousands of tablets were found and preserved; it has been a triumph of our century to have translated many of them. Among all those temple accounts and tribute lists and school lessons we hold as well a literary treasure, "more than thirty thousand lines of text, mostly in poetic form, [constituting] the oldest written literature of significant quantity and variety so far uncovered." It includes "twenty myths, nine epic tales," 200 hymns, with laments, dirges and diverse texts of antique wisdom. The principal source tablets for the Inanna cycle are dated at about 1800 B.C.; their story is surely much older.

The poets and the people of Uruk listened and sang; the scholars of later Sumer recorded their liturgy in all piety; the dusty tells held the bone-old records safe until the artful diggers came; the scholars unraveled the crowded wedge signs into English, French and German texts. The lapidaries represented the sacred date palm and the Holy Fly of the Underworld, the nude Lilith and the radiant Inanna.

This volume of collaboration takes us one inviting step further. The young senior author is a gifted storyteller, an experienced folklorist, with a sense rare in our literate times of the demands and the rewards of the spoken tale. Searching for a grand story of a woman, she came to realize that the tale cycles of Diana, Demeter, Cybele and Persephone and the others are all scattered and incomplete. It is Inanna, the oldest story of all we know, who alone spans the whole of the mythic life.

A girl, Inanna claimed her womanhood with the aid of her hero-brother Gilgamesh; she brought the sacred *me*, the root of all order, to her city Uruk to enter first on her queenship. She made joyous love with her chosen shepherd-king Dumuzi. Reigning, she journeyed to suffer the tyranny of the Underworld in death; she returned to the Great Above after exacting a partial sacrifice from Dumuzi. Finally she ruled Sumer in all her aspects, celestial and temporal, "mighty, majestic, radiant and ever youthful," patroness alike for sweet fruitful love and the bitter emptiness of death. Like Venus, she is together the Morning Star and the Evening Star, 2,000 or 3,000 years before the astronomers of Hellas.

The distinguished junior author, Samuel Noah Kramer, is the recognized dean of Sumerologists. His own scholarship has for 40 years given us most of the meaning we can now find in the tablets. He prepared the relevant Inanna texts in up-to-date form, some drawn from very recent translations and newly pieced fragments, taking account of all current work. Those texts, the best we have, he turned over to Diane Wolkstein, the storyteller. She has spent three years preparing her cycle of Inanna, more than 100 pages true to the resonant but unrhymed verse line of Sumerian. Not one tired archaism is left, no days of yore. She has shaped order and flow, keeping "as close as possible to the power, wonder and mystery" of the old texts. She has eliminated enough repetition to allow the story to breathe, and yet she has retained enough of it to give the novelty of a ritual authenticity long hidden.

Half of the book is this newly alive story of Inanna, half is a readable, varied and documented commentary from three points of view: that of the epigrapher, that of the writer and storyteller and that of the art historian and archaeologist. The gloss explains the complex written and visual material of this unusual and exciting volume, at a little-visited frontier between meticulous scholarship and vivid theater. Within the text there may well be lightly encoded one important constituent of the astronomical understanding of the time, only hinted at in this book.

"As Inanna ascended from the underworld.
The *galla*, the demons of the underworld, clung to her side.
The *galla* were demons who know no food, who know no drink,
Who eat no offerings, who drink no libations,
Who accept no gifts.
They enjoy no lovemaking.
They have no sweet children to kiss.
They tear the wife from the husband's arms,
They tear the child from the father's knees,
They steal the bride from her marriage home."
The hymns celebrate the bride's return in peace:
"My Lady looks in sweet wonder from heaven.
She looks in sweet wonder on all the lands
And on the people of Sumer as numerous as sheep. . . .
I sing your praises, holy Inanna.
The Lady of the Morning is radiant on the horizon."
(October 1983)

Hamlet's Mill: An Essay on Myth and the Frame of Time
By Giorgio de Santillana and Hertha von Dechend

In our times it is mainly amateurs who recognize particular stars. The experts have it all in books and photographic plates; the ship's captain is more likely to think about the jitter on his loran screen than about the constellations. The current revival of astrology is touching and repellent by turns. Yet from Cape Kennedy the morning papers now and again write of the bright star Canopus, somehow fixed on, and once in a while lost by, the automatic star-seekers of the latest space vehicle. Why Canopus? That star has long been the *gubernaculum*, or steering oar, of the starship Argo, just as it is marked in the first printed star map of 1603. To be sure, the designers of space vehicles may never have heard of this tradition, and it was surely not the basis of their selecting Canopus. Still, they are not entirely independent of it; their rational choice and the old tradition, which we can be sure arises in part from reason, rest on the same fundamental fact. The bright point of Canopus defines a line of sight nearly perpendicular to the plane of the ecliptic, where the lines of sight to the sun and all the planets lie. That makes the star useful for fixing an axis in space. The same fact makes Canopus (also called Ponderosus and in Arabic "the weight") the plumb bob of the sky, a fitting steersman's instrument.

The pole star is motionless to the eye of a man; it is steadfast for his lifetime. It moves nevertheless. It moves in the slow precessional motion detectable by our instruments; it moved for the classical discoverer of the precession of the equinoxes, Hipparchus, who had instruments of stone and bronze and the powerful instrument of Greek geometry. Above all, and this is the central theme of this marvelous and exasperating book, the pole and the entire sky tilt in the sight, not of any one man, but of a culture of men linked over millenniums by oral tradition. Before the invention of writing 5,000 or 6,000 years ago men were not dull or unobservant or barbarous. Genius flowered from time to time. One contemporary anthropological style, stemming from the school of Claude Lévi-Strauss, likes to think of great unlettered minds of the past expanding the logical matrices implicit in kinship schemes to construct traditional arrangements we can barely grasp today. Esoteric world systems are related in small African tribes.

Hamlet's Mill, following not a single tree to its roots but a banyan grove of correspondences, takes up a complex skein of myth. The authors, two learned historians of science, present case after case, allusion after allusion, in support of the general view that before men could write they thought deeply as they watched the order of the heavens. Hamlet is no mere orphan prince; Shakespeare had a source. That source, Saxo Grammaticus, is here, and in his tale the figure grows more heroic and more mythic. Even Saxo had his source, in oral myth. His Amleth the Dane was Icelandic Amlodhi, whose mill was the sea, grinding rock to sand. It is not even the classical tales of the Roman kings, where philologists at the turn of this century grounded the whole story, that begin it. Indeed, the steering oar and the mill and many another curious item can be traced to the Finnish epic the Kalevala, to the Persian hero Kai Khusrau and to Aryan myth. In the human warmth, glory and tragedy of all men's epics there is embedded a technical account of the "frame of time." Kai Khusrau, for example, was not only a great sovereign of Iran but also king of the zodiac, "from Pisces downward to the Bull's head."

A golden age may be a perpetual component of man's wishes, a part of his unconscious, but there was a genuinely luminous period around 6000 B.C., not on earth but in the sky. At that time the area of the sky where the plane of the ecliptic crosses the celestial equator (the equinox) was occupied both by the Milky Way and the bright stars in the belt of Orion. In *Hamlet's Mill* numbers, animal names, a "Star Menagerie" and all manner of other clues are pursued. We voyage from Kepler, Dante and Plato back to the Old Testament, the epic of Gilgamesh and the Milky Way tale of the Arawak. The book presents scores of works of art of the most puzzling kind (mighty churns of the Sea of Milk and Scorpion ladies) and almost 40 learned appendixes.

It is natural that so rich and complex a first unriddling is flawed. It is less necessary, but it is true, that the authors cannot conceal their impatience with translators and clumsy metaphysical assumptions. There are scholars who, purporting to disdain all metaphysics, hold that social evolution is simple and direct, from an unthinking barbarism through Aristotle straight through to modern times. It is hard to deny that translation from the dead tongues is an art that does not often go with a knowledge of positional astronomy. The word *Himmel* is given in the standard dictionary as the translation of no fewer than 38 distinct Egyptian hieroglyphs. That must represent a large loss of what well could be technical astronomical information. For Sumerian the case is no better. The book is polemic, even cocky; it will make a tempest in the inkpots. It nonetheless has the ring of noble metal, although it is only a bent key to the first of many gates.

"This book reflects the gradually deepening conviction that, first of all, respect is due these fathers of ours," says the preface. Plato explained in the *Phaedrus* that trust in writing was bound to discourage the use of memory, so that the invention of writing was a mixed blessing. Readers "will therefore seem to know many things, when they are for the most part ignorant and hard to get along with, since they are not wise, but only appear wise." Here is a book for the wise, however it may appear.

(November 1969)

The Journey to the West, Volumes 1, 2 and 3

Translated and edited by Anthony C. Yu

Fifty years ago Sir Aurel Stein loaded the saddlebags of his camels with drinking ice for a winter trip across the arid Gobi. His adventures on central Asian tracks from India to China became famous, but long before him other men of learning had undertaken the perils of that trip. The annals name a hundred earlier pilgrims: Chinese monks who traveled similar routes both ways, seeking the dharma in the West, in that India from which the lessons of the Compassionate Buddha had reached out to engage Chinese faith. Their travails spanned four centuries, the last pilgrim returning as an old man to China in A.D. 789.

One such scripture pilgrim, neither the first nor the last, was the monk Hsüan-tsang, called Tripitaka. He set out under the second T'ang emperor, to return years later to Ch'ang-an in A.D. 645, bearing nearly 700 items, "three baskets of Mahāyāna scriptures." But his story alone, not without the quality of myth, was fused into a new substance, an intoxicating elixir of fantasy, audacity, satire and overreaching adventure within the crucible of the Chinese mind over almost 1,000 years. These folktales and popular texts were newly worked in about 1580 (probably by Wu Ch'êng-ên, an otherwise obscure scholar of Kiang-su) into a 100-chapter narrative, half epic and half Ming novel, poetry embedded in prose, with the high art of an unchallenged master.

It is those 100 chapters we are now being given for the first time in English. (Several truncated versions have appeared, one of them still available in paperback, a single volume by the gifted Arthur Waley with the title *Monkey, Folk Novel of China*.) But never before have we had a chance to approach the real thing, "one of the four or five lasting monuments of traditional Chinese fiction." This *Journey* is alive today both in China and overseas, wherever inked characters are read. The skillful paper cutouts offered in China for a few coins often show the silhouettes of the four companions of the journey. The Peking Opera plays their story regularly; the action drawn out in modern cartoons fills four thick paperback volumes in comic-book format for sale in China and Hong Kong. An issue of colorful stamps of the People's Republic celebrated the *Journey* in 1979.

How can an ocean of tales be sampled? The arduous trip is turned into a magical epic, a combat not only against mundane thirst and endless rocky paths but also against a diverse multitude of monster spirits and demon kings. No human heart, not even that of the good, if timid,

Tripitaka, could survive alone. He is accompanied by three supernatural bodyguards—disciples and intercessors—with a white horse that is an errant dragon in disguise. Elder Brother among the three reprobate immortals is the half-repentant Monkey King, Sun Wu-k'ung, born of a stone and self-styled as a Great Sage, Equal to Heaven. His all but boundless powers, his ceaselessly fertile invention, his daring irreverence, his cocky self-assurance and his feisty combativeness make him at once the hero rebel, the sly, ugly-faced trickster and the invincible warrior. He, like the others, bears his allegorical burden lightly; he is the Monkey of the Mind, at once the glory and the peril of our cruel and marvelous species.

Would you read of strange instruments? Try the imp-reflecting mirror, the pineal phoenix eye, the Compliant golden-hooped iron rod, which can grow from an embroidery needle concealed in Monkey's ear into a weapon as thick as a rice bowl or even to the height of a mountain. (There is evidence that once it was the axis of the earth.) Would you find a surprising turn of events? The good monk and his second disciple Piggy drink of the cool, clean river. Half an hour later, what a stomachache! "Their bellies began to swell. . . . Inside their abdomens there seemed to be a clot of blood or a lump of flesh . . . kicking and jumping wildly about." It had been the Child-and-Mother River in the Nation of Women, and the men were pregnant, although they were "without any birth canal." "That water your master drank was not the best," says an old woman in some amusement.

Is it mortal combat and all the martial arts you seek? This story is the very fount of kung fu; the play of sword and rod, fire and wind, cloud somersaults and wild stratagems is unending. Magical transformations? A single hair of Monkey is often turned into a fighting little monkey ally, and in need an entire handful can be torn out, at once a loyal army. Cormorants, crabs and flies are familiar guises for Monkey; indeed, such efforts are no newer than the old Sumerian tales. But to become a pangolin? Or what of the occasion when old Monkey changed "into a little temple for the local spirit. His wide-open mouth became the entrance, his teeth the doors, his tongue the Bodhisattva and his eyes the windows. Only his tail he found to be troublesome, so he . . . changed it into a flagpole." There never was such a temple with a flagpole behind it; that architectural eccentricity gave him away.

The scenes of ever fresh quandary and conflict are played out under the engaged gods above. Those rulers include the magical theocracy of Buddhism, the stars in their constellations and the masters of the deep lore of Taoism. There is a well-staffed heavenly bureaucracy in T'ang style, from grooms and gardeners to the examiners, magistrates and ministers of the Celestial Court.

Professor Yu, in a crisp vernacular, lively and lighthearted, never affected or cute, sets it all down for a flood of pleasurable reading.

Hundreds of passages of poetry, mainly scene descriptions or fast-paced chronicles of exalted combat, are here to be enjoyed. The personages we encounter span this world and the next; we meet, among a few dozen other demons and monsters of character, the terrible young demon king Red Boy (the master of true fire), a passel of thunder squires, a false Monkey (really a magical six-eared macaque), Lao Tzu and Kuan-yin, Mars (the Star of Fiery Virtue), the Divine King Water Lord of the Yellow River (ready to drop on any adversary from his chalice the waters of the entire stream), the monster Clean Iguana and the comic little fish spirit Busy Bubble. There are many more, friends or foes of Pilgrim Sun Wu-k'ung.

Plenty of learned footnotes explicate the allusions that tumble past modern readers, particularly those unfamiliar with the culture; without pedantry the notes often cite the sources in Chinese. Alchemy, astrology and medicine are all sketched out as Monkey uses them or deals with their adepts. Great Sage undertakes to treat the Western monarch, King of Scarlet-Purple Kingdom, whose grave illness has defied all local therapies. He invokes the *Classic of Medical Problems* and applies the rare technique of taking the pulse by the feel of three long threads of gold, each tied to a point on the king's pulsing wrist, as the unapproachable patient sits up in his dragon bed. Pilgrim Sun studies the revealing signals with meticulous care, making "his own breathing regular." The diagnosis is full, and Great Sage's pharmacology offers the cure. Sun orders three pounds each of all the 808 flavors of medicine, both raw and cooked, along with all the mortars and pestles he may need. This is a professional ruse, to guard his prescription by misleading the imperial college. Actually only two flavors and soot are used to roll three large pills. The active ingredient is horse urine, to be sure, taken from a loud-talking horse that was "originally a flying dragon." Sourceless water is required for taking the pills, and a dragon rain obliges. In a little while the king is literally purged of his illness: it is a complete cure and a hyperbolic look at ancient medical ritual.

One volume is still to come; it will end the pilgrimage in victory, surely freed from illusion. Dear Great Sage! His diamond pupils see all; his spirit is marked by an irrepressible "heroic gall." We last hear him, at the end of Chapter 75, speaking from within a demon who has swallowed him. Undaunted, the Monkey inside threatens to use his portable frying pan from Canton to grill liver, chitterlings, stomach and lungs, so preparing the authentic southern dish *tsasui*: a chopped-up miscellany. By sea change four centuries later it is our American chop suey!

(June 1981)

Gravity's Rainbow
By *Thomas Pynchon*

A V-2 missile links the two ends of the ballistic parabola that is gravity's rainbow. At one end is London, dogged and ingenious; the other end is by extension Germany itself. This bulky, intimate, particular and detached novel, a work of the first magnitude, is a tale of V-2.

There is a protagonist at each root of the parabola: in London, Slothrop, the young New England intelligence lieutenant, with a hidden childhood under psychological experiment; on the Continent, a mad and perverse S.S. officer, Captain Weissmann, commander of a V-2 battery. Slothrop leaves London to spend the year in fugue across shattered nations, in a search for the unique rocket, serial number 00/000, that Weissmann once requisitioned and launched with the S-Gerät, strangest of all the payloads of the Wehrmacht. The prose is intricate, turbulent, streaming without rest in a spate of idea, event and allusion.

Here we merely note that this is a novel of a new sort. James Joyce grounded his flowing work on the ledges of epic, myth and folklore. *Gravity's Rainbow* instead founds its intricacies and expertise of allusion on science and technology, adjusted to the wartime *ambiance*. There are a number of remarkable set-piece essays, one on organic chemistry and its origins, one on operant conditioning, another on rocket dynamics. Ackeret and Leibniz, the Poisson distribution and double integrals are references as natural to Pynchon as limericks and vintages are to other novelists. To sketch one example, an apt connection is made between the serial wood engravings of late medieval German art, the calculus of Leibniz, the successive frames of an Ufa film and the unfolding time trajectory of the rocket, striking unheard a theater in London. Not all readers will persist up the wordstream past the bizarre and explicit sexual couplings, diverse as molecules, into the analytic heart of the novel; those who do will gain a richness of thought and motive, for which they must pay in spiritual coin. The literary reviewers have treated the novel as seriously as it deserves; it is a brilliant book, but be warned, that glow is icy cold.

(October 1973)

III

Lives and Careers

Individual lives, told us in biography or in letter and journal, can bring into focus a time, a discipline, a career that a less personal account may blur. Most of these reviews recount such examinations, often in the first person, over the last couple of centuries. Half a dozen more tell, not of individuals but of particular vividly described groups.

The Collected Papers of Albert Einstein, Volume 1: The Early Years, 1879-1902

John Stachel, editor, with six associates
English translation of the German texts of Volume 1, Anna Beck,
translator, and Peter Havas, consultant

A thriving scholarly industry centered in the University of Cambridge has for years documented the lives and works of Isaac Newton and Charles Darwin. Although it is under some linguistic handicap, American competitiveness here asserts itself with a first heavy and handsome volume in condign response, the massive written legacy of our fellow citizen, this century's symbol, at once its hero, victim and unintending culprit.

Einstein once explained that because he had never deferred to authority in his youth, Providence punished him in the end by making him quite an authority himself. This first volume uniquely skirts that punishment by showing us the young Einstein intimately before he had become anything of an authority at all, even before the work of the *Wunderjahr* 1905. It meticulously presents and annotates 134 documents, although all his published papers, even the two of 1901 and 1902, are held over for Volume 2. Here are the letters to and about him as well as from his hand, exams, records of his schoolwork, legal forms he filed and character reports made by the authorities — even his birth certificate, accompanied by photographs of the period as well as copies of sketches and drawings. The book has all the expert apparatus we expect: map, footnotes to identify the people who are mentioned, helpful comment on the more technical material, a chronology, thumbnail biographies of friends, family and teachers and an excerpt from a reminiscence his younger sister wrote in 1924. The texts are in German, although all the editorial apparatus is in English. An accompanying paperback gives a literal translation of the texts but does not repeat any of the editorial matter.

The second item is Einstein's mother's note to her sister, written as he finished second grade at the local public school in Munich. "Yesterday Albert got his grades, once again he was ranked first." The myth of the backward child is plainly false, although his sister had heard that he had been slow in learning to speak; it is certainly true that he was not a top student at all levels and times. He listened to drummers near and far. Young Einstein left Munich at 16, before finishing secondary school, to seek more education in Switzerland and probably to avoid conscription. His family had already moved for business reasons to Italy. The rest of the events in this volume take place in the Swiss setting, except for visits and holidays in Milan, Genoa, Pavia and the mountains.

Einstein failed the general part (but probably not the scientific part) of the entrance examination for engineering at the ETH in Zurich (the Federal Polytechnical School). He had attempted the exam even though he was two years younger than the age of regular admission. He was advised to spend an additional year at the cantonal school in Aarau, a secondary school known for its liberal and secular bent, and good in science.

That year is endearing to read about, and Einstein would recall it fondly all his life. The cantonal inspector reported on an examination of the violin students. Bowing technique seemed a little stiff here and there, but "one student, by name of Einstein, even sparkled . . . rendering . . . a Beethoven sonata with deep understanding." Here too Albert fell in love for the first time, with Maria, the young daughter of the family he lived with; his host was a teacher of Greek at the school. "How different it is," he wrote to her while he was away on a visit to his family, "to play a simple, sweet little song with one's sweetheart than to overcome . . . an admittedly difficult sonata with straight as ramrod, decked-out Pavia ladies." He broke off the innocent romance about a year later. It was in Aarau too that Einstein, not yet 17, wondered what would happen to a light wave if one ran after it fast enough to catch the thing — "the first childish thought-experiment that had to do with special relativity," he would recall at 60.

Nearly a third of the text transcribes two Einstein notebooks that record a year of physics lectures by H. F. Weber, his ETH professor. The student Einstein plainly enjoyed experiments and their results, and he was particularly pleased when a theory would unify empirical results that had seemed to be unrelated. The biographical sensation of the volume is a set of 50 documents never before published, letters exchanged between Einstein and another physics student at the ETH, Mileva Marić from Zagreb. Their letters are funny, tender, intimate and practical, with much comment on physics — if more on jobs and apartments. The lines are full of diminutives; he is Johonzel, little Johnny, for reasons unknown; she is usually Doxerl, a form of Dolly.

Mileva bore to Albert a daughter they called Lieserl, born in Serbia a year before the two were married in Bern, a match much against the Einstein family's wishes. "This Miss Marić is causing me the bitterest hours of my life," the angry mother-in-law wrote. The fate of the baby girl is not known; she may have died in Serbia of a childhood infection. Albert and Mileva had two sons in the marriage, which lasted for nearly 20 years until divorce.

The young physicist tried for every kind of post, "honoring all physicists from the North Sea to the southern tip of Italy with my offer," as he put it. He advertised private lessons in mathematics and physics "given most thoroughly" by Albert Einstein, diplomate. The fees were a help; better were the lifelong friendships he formed with a couple of interesting students. Finally, in June of 1902, through the good offices of a classmate at the ETH, he got a position at the Patent Office: provisional appointment as Technical Expert third class at 3,500 francs to start. "Ehrat thinks . . . one cannot live on 4,000 fr. with a wife. But we will prove by deeds how fabulously that can be done!" Salary, young wife and son, degree, leisure to work: it would be done well. A few months earlier he had written to Mileva that he was working "very eagerly on an electrodynamics of moving bodies, which promises to become a capital paper." There was truth in that too.

Some 30 volumes lie ahead. The monument being built is a grand one; here is the entrance, lively with the sights and sounds of youthful life.

(September 1987)

The Wild Boy of Aveyron
By Harlan Lane

The chief acts and ideas of the Enlightenment and its revolutionary aftermath have a local habitation: the Seine's Left Bank in Paris. It is the intellectual legacy of one event there that is chronicled in this lively, informed and arguable book. The author, a psychologist at Northeastern University, begins in the Luxembourg Gardens, where on a summer day in 1800 the wild child they had brought from the forest first met the young physician Jean-Marc-Gaspard Itard, a brilliant student of the psychiatrist Philippe Pinel (he who had just ordered the inmates of the asylums of Paris unchained). "I retraced their steps," Lane writes, in "the boiler-room 'archives' . . . , the dusty attics of the Sorbonne and School of Medicine (with the priceless view of Paris rooftops accorded only to students and cleaning ladies) [and] a dozen other places but especially the cavernous hushed reading rooms of the National Library: these were my joyful haunts." He brings from those quarters much solid material, forgotten accounts by various actors in the drama and a step-by-step unwinding of the origins and implications of Itard's five years of intimate work with the "disgustingly dirty" Victor, "who swayed back and forth ceaselessly like certain animals in a zoo." What we examine as much through debate as in careful narrative is the history of the concept of the perfectibility of humankind.

Itard saw hope for Victor. Pinel had given a darker prognosis, which he delivered before the Société des Observateurs de l'Homme. Lost for many years, the report was published in 1911; it was rediscovered by Lane, and he cites it at length. Pinel believed nothing whatever could be done for the boy he deemed to have been abandoned at the age of nine or 10 by his parents as being incapable of education. Itard, and following him Lane, reject the idea; they blame the boy's symptoms, including his inability to speak, on his enforced isolation. Lane, citing modern cases, rejects the diagnosis of retardation and of autism; the conclusion follows that "prolonged isolation deprived him of the crucial skill . . . of imitation," just as Itard had written that "the foremost faculty of human intelligence, that of imitation, is annihilated." Not every reader will be persuaded that Pinel was wrong; the issue seems to turn on the uncertain condition and age of the boy when he was left in the forest. All the comparisons seem to depend strongly on the developmental stage and the duration of isolation.

The theater of these ideas is much wider than the intimate two-person drama played out over five years. Victor lived in Paris on a state allowance until he died at about 40, still without speech, under the devoted care of his kind but uneducated governess. Itard went on to teach the deaf with striking success. It was the work of Étienne Bonnot de Condillac that gave him theoretical support. Itard saw education as being neither the imposition of an intrinsic logic that arose out of the subject matter of instruction nor a merely empirical set of practices and hints. For him, and for the hopeful philosophy of education that we still pursue, instruction is determined mostly by the person taught, by the careful observation of his maturing and his needs, which are not uninfluenced but are experimentally managed in their antecedents and their consequences. New needs are created, social and above all sensory, often by the invention of instructional devices. Itard used a black-painted board "on which everyday objects were placed and their outlines chalked," together with cutout letters, a red disk, a blue triangle, a black square, a drum, snuff, bells, a vase with nutmeats hot and cold — an arsenal of pedagogy mainly within the spirit of early schooling today. His later success with the deaf depended on his observation that many were not entirely devoid of hearing but could at least make out vowels quite well. He worked at extending their rudimentary discrimination of sounds and often saw great progress.

Itard was the founder of the oral education of the deaf, followed by such figures as Alexander Graham Bell. But Itard himself, who "never learned a sign during forty years among the deaf," became the champion of the opposing procedure, the language of signs. Since the 1760's, when deaf children brought to the home of the Abbé de l'Epée the signs they themselves had improvised to converse with their families, there has been a struggle between oral and sign instruction for the deaf. Today in the U.S. and Canada half a million people use the American Sign Language, which can be shown to have grown from Parisian roots. Thomas Gallaudet brought it to Hartford in 1816 with the deaf young Laurent Clerc, earlier a student and later a teacher at the Paris Institute for Deaf-Mutes; it was Gallaudet's language of sign that spread and grew into today's Ameslan. One great step remained: the sign code had to free itself of the heavy burden of French grammar and inflection that had been added to encumber the "natural language" by the philosophical instructors at the institute. Like Chinese or even English, Ameslan has a structure of context and redundancy, with a swift grammar of position and gesture but no time for inflection or any apparatus that derives from Latinity.

Itard came at last to understand that, given the indispensable little community of the deaf, most of those who cannot hear consonants at all will profit by the sign language. They develop conceptually through that channel and they may later come to use their understanding to gain some control over oral speech. In 1827 Itard made a comparative test of two mute students. He found the student taught by signs to be superior, as has the latest careful study, made in the 1970's, of congenitally deaf children matched for I.Q., age and sex. The signing "twins" did significantly better in reading, writing, psychological adjustment, oral speech, school completion and college entrance. "But the Great Sign Controversy continues to this day."

Itard's student Édouard Séguin went on to teach not only the deaf but also the retarded. Plainly the narrower goals of such instruction made more evident the effectiveness of the method drawn from Condillac. First, Séguin taught, comes motor control, based on an analytical strategy of finding the elements of complex acts. For example, climbing a ladder, with the teacher climbing the other side of the ladder and holding the child's fingers against the rungs, proceeds by easy stages to independence. Sensory training comes in its turn: the sense of hot and cold, warm and cool, light and heavy. The drum and the bells follow, and with them music itself. The child is led to speech and finally to moral education, a domain for which Itard and Condillac had given little guidance.

The regime had its effect, as one American witness touchingly related in 1847. "During the past six months, I have watched . . . nearly one hundred fellow beings who were objects of loathing and disgust . . . these . . . I have seen properly clad, standing erect, . . . eating in an orderly manner at a common table, . . . gaining, by their own labor, the means of existence . . . and singing in unison songs of thanksgiving." Séguin was drawn by inner commitment into the French revolutionary storm of 1848; the Second Empire saw him an emigrant to the U.S., where he worked as a teacher and a consultant until his death in 1880.

The story of Victor is not over yet. Just before the turn of the century the courageous Maria Montessori became the first woman to receive a medical degree in Italy. She was posted to the asylums of Rome, where she found retarded children thrown indiscriminately among the insane. She read Itard and Séguin ("the voice of a forerunner crying in the wilderness"), and within a decade she had opened her first Casa dei Bambini, where she offered to normal preschool children in her own way the hopeful opportunities Itard had set before poor Victor. The drum and the bell, the letter cutouts, the pairing of names and the objects they symbolize—these and much more of Montessori practice were first seen by the wild boy of Aveyron. Montessori's books and her original methods of instruction are now known worldwide. She died in Holland in 1952.

"Itard had set out to train an *enfant sauvage*; by his journey's end he had become the originator of instructional devices, the inventor of behavior modification . . . , creator of oral education of the deaf, and father of special education for . . . the handicapped." The "education of the senses" spread through Séguin to the universal view of education seen by Montessori. The end is not visible; even models as constraining as behavioral modification now appears to be are transient elements of a view of education based, like Itard's, on honest observation of the subtle needs of the learner and a profound respect for human potential. Excesses such as the shock from the Leyden jar and the frightening time Itard held Victor "out of the window, his head facing directly down toward the bottom of the chasm" are matched in our time by shock therapy, the demeaning reward of the tossed chocolate drop and the related pseudo-constancy of the I.Q. score. No, neither Itard nor the behavior modifiers of our own day are always successful or even plausible, yet there is a kernel of hope for a more perceptive pedagogy in the 100-year story of the wild child, if we read it in sympathy and wisdom.

(January 1977)

The Great Barrier Reef
By Isobel Bennett

The Life of Captain James Cook
By J. C. Beaglehole

The Explorations of Captain James Cook in the Pacific as Told by Selections of His Own Journals 1768–1779
Edited by A. Grenfell Price
Illustrated by Geoffrey C. Ingleton

The Coral Seas: Wonders and Mysteries of Underwater Life
By Hans W. Fricke
With an introduction by I. Eibl-Eibesfeldt

The continental shelf outlines a funnel 1,000 miles long on the east coast of tropical Australia. The deep water of the open Tasman Sea is more than 200 miles from the mainland at the southern end and only 10 or 15 miles out at the narrow stem. In May of 1770 H.M. Bark *Endeavour*, her master Mr. Cook, "a good mathematician, and very expert in his Business," sailed into the mouth of the great funnel all unaware. A radiant moon lit the calm sea, and the *Endeavour* "stole along under double-reefed topsails" until "'before the Man at the lead could heave another cast the Ship Struck and stuck fast.'"

The *Endeavour* was the first we know of to go aground (and she got away), but 500 later shipwrecks have been documented on the shelf along the present steamer track, which is now guarded by a hundred lights, marks and radio beacons of the Queensland Coast and Torres Strait Pilot Service. The track is the longest single stretch of pilotage in the world, one pilot alone conning every ship for the entire voyage. Masters can opt instead for the open ocean east of the shelf, to which Cook gratefully escaped through a narrow passage after beaching and repairing the *Endeavour*. Back into the reefs he came a few days later, shoal water and all! He had to flee the heavy ocean swell and the beating surf, which one becalmed day threatened to throw his drifting ship "upon this Reef where the Ship must be dashed to pieces in a Moment. A Reef such as is here spoke of is scarcely known in Europe, it is a wall of Coral Rock rising all most perpendicular out of the unfathomable Ocean."

Isobel Bennett, a marine biologist in Sydney, explains it all in her big, handsome book. There is no single great barrier reef; there are many. The entire 100,000-square-mile wedge of shelf is studded with islands high and low, both the high outcrops of the shelf rocks and the patient low fabric of the coral polyps, 2,500 reefs ranging from a few hundred acres up to 20 square miles, and uncounted smaller ones. The book, at once wide-ranging and intimate, surveys the life and geography of the region as a thoughtful field biologist sees them, at normal scale and mainly from the surface, reveling in the intricacies of that living fabric. In one of the photographs made by the author you can see from the air the surf-streaked *Endeavour* reef as it is today. A steel peg marks the spot where Cook struck and where, five years ago, they recovered six guns of half a ton each, which that prudent and decisive man had thrown overboard along with 50 tons more of stores to lighten his grounded and leaking ship. Overleaf is the richer blue of Cook's Passage. Out through it the *Endeavour* sailed freely, following the lead of the pinnace sent ahead to check the opening Cook had made out from the top of high Lizard Island, to ride at last on a "well growen Sea rowling in." Here his final Providential Channel is only marked on the maps; it would be interesting to see the place of his reentry, "not more than a quarter of a Mile broad," a break in that terrible reef wall where Cook was "happy once more to incounter those shoals which but two days ago our utmost wishes were crowned by getting clear of. . . . The world will hardly admit of an excuse for a man leaving a Coast unexplored. . . . If dangers are his excuse he is than charged with *Timorousness* and want of Perseverance . . . ; if on the other hand he boldly incounters all the dangers . . . and is unfortunate enough not to succeed he is than charged with *Temerity*." The historian comments: "This . . . is . . . hardly even . . . a commander justifying himself to the Lords of the Admiralty; it is a man, not unduly nervous but emerging from one of the dark places of the soul . . . passing judgment on himself."

This Great Barrier Reef Province, as Bennett calls it, is not merely the site of a dozen national parks and tourist resorts, a major route of shipborne trade, a theater of old heroic voyages and the target of mineral and offshore-oil concessionaires. It is all those but it is also home to a web of species: the big violet starfish, the tangled mangroves, the barnacled sea turtles, the palms, the orchids, the crested terns and many others; the faunas of the province have never been completely listed.

Coral is the dominant sea organism. A coral cay is a little like an old tree: just as the strong trunk is the fibrous product of past growth, a growth active only in the outermost layers and in this season's foliage, so is the cay a limestone structure accreted in the past. The luxuriant living coral is found not on the white limy flats or the miles of dead tracts of boulders and old coral heads but only as a thin veneer of life on the seaward edges and in deep pools or at the outer margins of a lagoon. A complex and lengthy sequence of other forms exploits the coralline gift of a limestone foundation. Coral polyps feed only on marine plankton. Their own enzymatic powers do not extend to the digestion of plant tissue, but within the inner layers of many coral animals live specialized single-cell algae, certain dinoflagellates. The photosynthesis of the algae of course requires sunlight. In nature not much coral can grow deeper than the sunlit layers where its internal algae can prosper; in the laboratory, although coral survives in the dark, the internal algae disappear. Until lately it was thought that the algae must have some useful but secondary aid to give their coral hosts, perhaps in waste removal. Now it appears that the corals are really agriculturists: their symbiotic algae supply much of their food energy for life. It was studies at Eniwetok, the bomb-test site, that first suggested the animal plankton were quantitatively inadequate to support the life of the coral; the algae, on the other hand, comprise a greater living mass than the animal tissue does in a typical colony of algae-supporting coral. It has been known for a long time how successful the big clams of the genus *Tridacna* (the largest forms of all occur in the Great Barrier Reef Province) have become at such internal farming. The rich-hued mantles of several such clams are exhibited in the Bennett book, with the lens spots that focus light between the lips of the heavy shell deep into the tissues of the folded mantle where the algae grow, vividly pigmented in violets, greens and blues.

The four books noted here differ greatly. The Bennett book is an engaging introduction to a region of living interest. The biography by J. C. Beaglehole is the fruit of a life's study of Pacific exploration; the noted New Zealand historian spent decades in careful editing of the journals of Cook and of his scientist-shipmate Joseph Banks, prepared a study of the discovery of New Zealand and traveled in the tracks of Cook from Nootka Sound to Dusky Bay, half a world apart. He completed this last, ripened book, but it was left to his son to take up the final task of readying it for the printer. The Price paperback is a high-grade sampling of the four volumes of the *Journals* that takes some advantage of Beaglehole's editorial work; it is a great bargain. Fricke is a daring scuba diver and a behavioral biologist; his book gives a good account of the biology of subsurface life as the scientific diver sees it and celebrates in particular the undersea photographer: his book has 150 color plates supplied by the world's masters of that demanding art. The volume is more cosmopolitan than the rest, but it does not neglect the Great Barrier Reef. Indeed, here one can see a full-face view of the largest cold-blooded fish in those or any seas: the plankton-feeding whale shark, *Rhincodon*, its crevasse of a mouth stretching across the double page, while close above floats the nonchalant diver, arms only partly spanning that great flat head. (The photographer and the diver are themselves intrepid and ingenious members of the fauna of the Great Barrier Reef Province — two filmmakers of Queensland, Ron and Valerie Taylor.)

Cook, science's classic seaman, sailed in the *Endeavour* as part of the flowering of post-Newtonian physics. His first task was not the exploration of the earth but rather concerned the universe. He was posted to observe from far Tahiti the transit of Venus in the year 1769. The injunction had been a legacy. In 1716 Edmund Halley had exhorted the Royal Society to ensure that "many observations . . . might be taken . . . at separate places . . . of a sight . . . on which depends the certain and adequate solution of a problem the most noble, and at other times not to be attained to." The astronomical world had tried hard in 1761, but the first worldwide trial was no success. There would be no chance again until 1874. A supreme effort was needed in 1769, and the Royal Society pressed for many observers, widely spread in both hemispheres, "not merely beyond the Arctic Circle but into the Pacific Ocean." Off went Cook, already known as a careful marine surveyor but in no way famous. A good judge of men in the Admiralty had seen his promise. He became the paragon of explorer-seamen: humane, cool, patient, imaginative and expert. "He had a plain heroic magnitude of mind." Cook sailed amid ironies. He dealt fairly and even nobly with all manner of men, yet weariness and bad judgment in one moment brought him to a violent end, and warrior Hawaiian chieftains who had venerated him fed on his roasted flesh. He proved the new chronometer, measured the parallax of the sun, found the means to end scurvy and left a track on the world's great ocean as fair as any that violent Europe can claim. Beaglehole's own insight and devotion fashioned these eloquent final words to the biography: "There are statues and inscriptions; but Geography and Navigation are his memorials. . . . Geography and Navigation; if we wish for more, an ocean is enough, where the waves fall on innumerable reefs, and a great wind blows from the south-east with the revolving world."

(November 1974)

Science in France in the Revolutionary Era, Described by Thomas Bugge
Edited by Maurice P. Crosland

The Metric System: A Critical Study of Its Principles and Practice
By Maurice Danloux-Dumesnils
Translated by Anne Garrett and J. S. Rowlinson

Metric Change in India
Edited by Lal C. Verman and Jainath Kaul

Prepare Now for a Metric Future
By Frank Donovan

In the summer of 1798, known locally as Year VI of the Republic, in the month of Thermidor, a perceptive, independent Danish astronomer arrived in Paris. Thomas Bugge was privileged: few foreigners came to that revolutionary capital, at once the Peking, New York and London of its day, the source of political and cultural change. His book, which was a quick best seller in several languages, is excerpted and extensively annotated by Professor Crosland, with special attention to the cultural and scientific institutions of France under the Directory. There is plenty of fascinating material, for instance the first school of military balloonists, working with hydrogen-filled taffeta aircraft, the splendid menagerie and the public lectures of R. J. Hauy on minerals and J. A. C. Charles on physics and chemistry. What a stir there was in Paris! Sundays were gone; the day of rest came only every 10th day. (There were, however, plenty of holidays.) Bonaparte and the army were off to Egypt, and in the gardens of the Louvre stood "the large and strong four-wheeled carriages" that had just conveyed to that gallery the rich collections newly liberated from the princes of Italy.

Bugge was no mere tourist. He was an official delegate to the founding International Commission on the Metric System, perhaps the first such congress of scientists ever held. The representatives of the main neutral and satellite nations of Europe were there; they met for some months, but the work of measurement could not meet the schedules of the diplomats. Bugge tells a good deal about the birth of metrology under the demands of the metric system; for example, the density maximum of water at four degrees centigrade was found by L. Lefevre-Gineau "by the most delicate experiments" with the big brass cylindrical vessel whose volume and weight measurements were to give the kilogram as the true weight of one decimeter of pure water. Bugge was admiring but unconvinced. ("States that already have a system of weights and measures have no sufficient reason for adopting the new metric system.") He went home early.

The powers of 10 did not sweep everything before them. The metric time units proposed to set 10 hours to the day, 100 minutes to the hour and 100 seconds to the minute. ("I have seen only two clocks in Paris with dials divided according to the new time.") The clock industry beat this scheme back, for which, as an astronomer depending on old records, Bugge was grateful.

Professor Danloux-Dumesnils, in a personal, reasoned and instructive little volume — good reading for every teacher and student — reviews the present state of units in a tasteful book; indeed, a book refreshingly tart. He seeks a more rational approach to the metric system, in the spirit of Borda, Coulomb, Laplace and the rest. The International System of Units, with its strange concessions to the illuminating engineers, is not without bad faults. Surely the lumen and the candela are illogical as physical standards, and the watt, suitably qualified by visual efficiencies, solid angles and areas, will someday do it all, even for the lampmakers. ("It is outrageous to place the candela on the same footing as the metre, the kilogramme, the second.") Danloux-Dumesnils's logic is matched by the interest of his book, with its clear summaries of history and means of measurement, and admirable logarithmic scales presenting the entire range of phenomena for a dozen important physical quantities.

Danloux-Dumesnils would like to metricate plane and solid angle (already done in part by the founding fathers but never adopted outside France), and he exclaims against "the Chaldaean units," but he will accept the day and the second as admirably international and long-lived. An appendix raises the urgent matter of teaching and using the power-of-10 notation in some compact and publicly welcome form; Danloux-Dumesnils's economical solution — Avogadro's number becomes (23) 602 — will appeal to many readers. This is an urgent notational problem that has existed since Simon Stevin gave us the decimal point.

The history of metrication is rich in implications. It was Talleyrand, acting for the French constitutional monarchy in 1790, who first invited the world to adopt unified units. He insisted that "Franco-British collaboration" was the condition of success. The British Foreign Secretary called the plan "almost impracticable," a "diplomatic expression for the word NO." The U.S. Senate was also negative, simultaneously turning down another decimal plan of Jefferson's on the ground that the metric system was under consideration in Britain and France. Danloux-Dumesnils dryly remarks that the current opposition of these countries can be understood: "When one has refused to collaborate in a scheme, one cannot forgive its subsequent success."

Only the U.S., Canada, Australia and New Zealand remain nonmetric (Britain is en route) among the nations that have appreciable industry. How India converted is the tale of the book edited by Verman and Kaul. It was the political climate of independence from Britain, with the strong support of Jawaharlal Nehru, that set India the double task of going over to decimal coinage and the metric system. The legislation was passed in 1956. After two bank holidays in 1957 and plenty of work on the railroad fare system, in the post office and particularly in the mints, the naya paisa, a hundredth of a rupee, with its multiples, two, five, 10, 25 and 50, has replaced the 16 annas divided into four paise of the British Raj.

A change in currency touches everyone, but this change is simple and the incentives are high. Metric weights and measures are of course far more complex: they extend from maps and milestones to wire sizes, paper dimensions, screw threads, standard lamps, timber, brick and much more. The cheerful and effective civil servants whose essays compose this book tell the detailed story of how the changes were made. Ten years was legally allowed for the task. After seven years the newspapers stopped giving their weather reports in both metric and British units. The paper manufacturers have stopped complaining and instead adjust their machines. The schoolbooks, particularly the more specialized ones, still lag. While both schemes were taught the pupils felt an added burden. The manufacturers of weights first tended to stall; they did not want to make the investment. Then they were pressed and were offered some aid, and so they went ahead. Then they could not sell the weights, just as they had feared.

Finally the legal deadline came. Suddenly all the tradesfolk rushed for new gear. They found the long neglected manufacturers ready to sell what the storekeepers had to have but now at inflated prices!

In retail and wholesale trade the conversion is essentially complete. Land records lag; engineering schools are nearly converted; in engineering, industry, machine tools and the like "a good deal remains to be done." Above all, write the editors, "the common man had proved to be extremely receptive to the new idea and the fact of the change . . . the illiterate . . . more [so] than the more sophisticated and educated classes."

Prepare Now for a Metric Future is a swift, clear, journalistic treatment of the entire problem, its history, controversies (including some chauvinist period doggerel about "A perfect inch, a perfect pint,/The Anglo's honest pound") and the prospects here in the U.S. The Miller-Pell bill of 1968 has set up a serious Federal study of the task. Donovan, a worldly and well-informed writer, reckons that a gradual conversion will soon begin, pushed by Government procurement policy, not by legislative compulsion. Britain too has avoided compulsion. The difference, and it is not slight, is that Britain depends much more heavily on export to the metric world. The push there came from industry.

When the Allies invaded Sicily in 1943, someone asked Enrico Fermi if the advance would be an important step toward final victory. "Maybe it will about make up," he said, "for the fact that the U.S. and Britain do not use the metric system."

(January 1971)

Never at Rest: A Biography of Sir Isaac Newton
By Richard S. Westfall

It is 125 years since the appearance of the "reigning biography" of Isaac Newton, Sir David Brewster's two volumes of Victorian adulation and scholarship. Now we have this hefty but lively modern volume, the fruit of 20 years of work by a distinguished Indiana historian of science. The book is a scientific biography, with Newton's career as a man of learning and research at the core. It is the product of a post-World War II industry of Newton studies, a phenomenon that has brought seven volumes of Newton's letters into print, together with eight volumes of his mathematical manuscripts and a number of fine books on particular Newtonian themes, well documented, perceptive and fresh.

There is still no shortage of raw material: Professor Westfall provides a footnote to establish his own firsthand estimate of the quantity of Newton's manuscripts on alchemy. They alone amount to six or eight substantial books from the writing desk and the laboratory bench; one book-length study has appeared, without new laboratory work. In Jerusalem there is a large collection of Newton's theological and historical papers; in all there are five major collections in his hand. Newton worked steadily over a long lifetime, never at rest. The title of this work is Newton's, taken from a letter he wrote at the age of 51: "A Vulgar Mechanick can practise what he has been taught or seen done, but if he is in an error he knows not how to find it out and correct it . . . ; Whereas he that is able to reason nimbly and judiciously about figure, force, and motion, is never at rest til he gets over every rub."

The newer studies of Newton traverse three main roads. Most of the books have sought to tease out method and influence, assumptions and philosophy. How did he come by this idea or that? The painstaking study of texts lies along this path. We have a two-volume version of the *Principia* comparing the variations among the three editions Newton saw into print. The notorious controversies over priority are encountered along the way. A second path has brilliantly sought out the psychology of the man, so solitary, work-possessed, guarded, fearful, jealous, at times tyrannical. But the route traveled here is taken at a more leisurely pace, with an eye on the landscape; it is a contextual study, setting Newton in his time. What did others say of his claims? Did Cambridge come to a halt while the plague closed down the colleges? So regarded, myths seem a little reduced in strangeness, the inner life a little less hyperbolic, the lonely spirit nearer balance.

Schoolboy Newton was remembered by everyone for his "strange inventions." Sundials he had made filled the house where he lodged. (Even in old age he would "look at the shadows instead of the clock to give the time.") He tied a paper lantern to a kite tail to frighten the neighbors; he built a model windmill powered by a mouse treadmill and a little cart he could run by cranking as he sat in it. "We know now that Newton found many of these contrivances in a book called *The Mysteries of Nature and Art* by John Bate." That antique volume fed his fertile interest as its equivalents in every generation since have nourished the boys and girls who make their adult careers around the laboratory.

Newton was admitted to Trinity College in 1661. The universities had by then become reservoirs of patronage; between them they controlled through their degrees the benefices of the state church. "Cambridge University, like Oxford, drifted toward the status of a degree mill exploited without conscience by those fortunate enough to gain access to it." True, Cambridge had been the center of English Puritanism, and after the Restoration it plainly had to show that it had purged itself of error. Most of the heads of colleges were replaced; their jobs were the juicy morsels of political spoils. The student body, however, grew apace, reaching again the peak size of the days of James I. The life of the mind was all but absent. There is a story that when Newton left home, his educated uncle gave him a book of logic, saying it would be the first book his tutor would read to him, as an earlier tutor had done for the uncle as an undergraduate 30 years before. The prediction was accurate, but there was no vigor left in Cambridge's formal Aristotelianism. It was rote. The disputations had become rituals; even the lectureships were sinecures. No one came to the lectures, and often the lecturers themselves did not appear.

The degree statistics show no signs of decrease during the dispersal of the university for two plague years. Newton never finished his assigned texts; no one cared. Examinations were lax, although for Trinity fellowships they continued. Newton somehow converted his wretched subsizarship (the lowest of grants, requiring its poor student holders to work as valets and waiters for the fellows and wealthier students) into a four-year fellowship in 1664. It seems sure that this preferment came about through the intercession of some powerful advocate.

Isaac Barrow was the one man at Trinity who had the competence to assess Newton's mind and work. Five years later Barrow would write to identify the author of a paper on infinite series: "His name is Mr Newton, a fellow of our College, & very young (being but the second yeest Master of Arts) but of an extraordinary genius & proficiency in these things." Barrow that year resigned the well-endowed Lucasian chair he held in order to obtain it for young Newton. Barrow was eager for, and soon received, other preferment; within three years he became master of the college. It was almost surely Barrow who in 1675 secured a royal dispensation exempting, beginning with incumbent Newton, the Lucasian professors in perpetuity from the need to take holy orders.

That requirement would have been all but impossible for Newton then; he had become in secret totally disaffected from the Trinitarian creed of the Church of England. His refusal not only would have cost him his job but also would have left him vulnerable to the exposure of a kind of heresy that was socially damning in that time of religious strife. Because of a misunderstanding during an oral examination, however, Newton believed that in 1664 Barrow had "but an indifferent opinion of him." Perhaps Newton was misled about Barrow's judgment; perhaps a shadowier senior fellow, a relative of the household where Newton had boarded in his school days, was responsible for that first recognition. We do not know.

Between 1664 and 1667 (with one year off campus) Newton found and mastered Descartes's new analytic geometry, set down questions in his notebooks that presage his entire experimental future in optics and mechanics and made his way self-taught to the "resolution of problems by motion," the idea of the calculus. For Westfall these are three miraculous years, not the traditional single annus mirabilis. They do not leave the 24-year-old Newton in command of "the results that have made his reputation deathless, not in mathematics, not in mechanics, not in optics. What he had done in all three was to lay foundations." What of the falling apple? It seems real, but the record does not support the notion that he carried the full idea of universal gravitation in secret for 20 years. His own notes deny the possibility. That he had some inkling, some half-contradictory hint of magnificent generality, remains credible. Universal gravitation is not, after all, some mere spark of insight; there would be "time to think on it."

The long life unfolds before the reader, always against a full stage. In his London career the now-great worthy is a serious civil servant but no longer a profound original, either in religion or in mechanics. He changed status with the Glorious Revolution of 1688, in which he took some public risk. The *Principia* was then newly set before the world, thanks largely to tireless Halley. One can read of Newton's niece, a young woman of beauty and wit (Swift became her intimate friend, and he once wrote to Stella "I love her better than any one here") who was celebrated in 1703 at the Kit-Kat Klub in baroque verse diamond-scribed on a toasting glass. Such were the pleasures of the great families and their friends who made up the ruling Whig Junto of the times. Worldly Voltaire held that Newton's high post had been gained through the conquest of the minister Halifax by the charmer. "Fluxions and gravitation would have been of no use without a pretty niece."

Conquer Catherine Barton had; evidence is compelling that she became either mistress or wife to Halifax in secret. The brilliant and scandalous minister had, however, already been Newton's close friend for many years; although the talented young man was no student of science, at Cambridge he had joined with Newton and a few others to form the Philosophical Society. As Chancellor of the Exchequer he first named Newton to a post at the Mint, but there is no sign that the "famous witty Mrs. Barton," then a mere girl, had had anything to do with an appointment for which Newton was plainly suited and on which he had some public claim by political service. The affair came years later, with the Newtons already rich and soundly set in London society.

Here is the older Newton as expert parliamentary witness on finding the longitude. He was not very hopeful about good clocks, but he listed all the possibilities we have today, except inertial guidance. (The time signals then proposed were acoustic and of rather too short a range. Still, it is near the coast that most danger lies.)

Newton died at 86. For 15 years he had laundered his most unorthodox views out of the theological works he intended for publication. He died, however, with a gesture; he refused the final sacrament of the Anglican church. A covert man, all his triumphs must have seemed to him incomplete. "He was greatly concerned to leave his image behind him." No one save royalty sat so often for portraits. There are some 20 of them in this book, with about 30 other interesting images, mostly pages and drawings from Newton himself. (We miss any likeness of Mrs. Barton.) This ample volume somehow does not resolve the drama. Not the legacy of Newton's own words by the million, not the careful piecings of the scholars nor their psychoanalytic insights can make clear this unequaled mind, so charged, powerful and lonely.

One impression comes clear. It is only a partial knowledge that was the true fruit of Newton's work. The savants of the time, mechanical philosophers all, lived under the sway of a universal preconception. The occult properties and tendencies of the school philosophers could no longer be tolerated; matter must move only by the mediation of subtle particles in collision. When the gifted Christiaan Huygens was told that the *Principia* was in preparation, he replied: "I don't care that he's not a Cartesian as long as he doesn't serve us up conjectures such as attractions." But attractions we got, and with them profound quantitative and genuine — but incomplete — understanding, widely serviceable unaltered for 250 years. It could be argued that Newton's long hours among the firebrick furnaces he built with his own hands, seeking in the crucible the occult wisdom of the alchemists, showed him that the material world was subtler than the naive models of the Continental thinkers. Until he lost confidence in the soundest metaphysics of his time he could not make real progress.

(June 1982)

Scientists under Hitler: Politics and the Physics Community in the Third Reich

By Alan D. Beyerchen

It was the best of times. From 1925 to the early 1930's a flood of penetrating papers had filled the *Zeitschrift* and the *Annalen*. From Born, Pauli and Heisenberg in Göttingen, from Einstein and Schrödinger in Berlin, from Sommerfeld in Munich and his students ("in 1928 nearly one-third of all full professors of theoretical physics in the German-speaking world were Sommerfeld pupils") had come the most profound of all steps to our knowledge of matter and radiation. Quantum mechanics reached its full powers, still unchallenged after half a century. Of course, the Weimar Republic physicists were not alone: Dirac and Bohr and de Broglie are hardly German names. But the big German universities and institutes, notably the powerful mathematical center in Göttingen around Hilbert, Courant and Weyl, guarded the core of the subject. The reviews and the indispensable texts in their bright yellow covers told it to all, in German.

It was the worst of times. In a year or two the Reichsminister of education, sitting beside Hilbert at a dinner, asked: "And how is mathematics in Göttingen now that it has been freed of the Jewish influence?" Hilbert never temporized. "Mathematics in Göttingen? There is really none any more."

In a cool, meticulous volume, which draws not only on the printed word but also on many oral interviews with participants in the events, Professor Beyerchen, a University of Florida historian, tells how it was done, how the physicists encountered the hooked cross. Nobel prizewinners and bemedaled war veterans, canny university politicos with grant money flowing in and isolated, unworldly specialists—all were swept away under the law (the Law for the Restoration of the Career Civil Service, April 7, 1933, and many supplements), in spite of active public protest, dogged passive protest, quiet protest behind the scenes and the use of legal channels.

In quantitative terms at least a fourth of the physicists were made to go, or took the powerful hints. Qualitatively, many more of the best left. It is to be recalled that atomic physics was not then the discipline it is today, a proverbial source of worldly power by way of thermonuclear weapons, lasers and transistors. It was still abstract, unfamiliar, akin more to academic philosophy or even to science fiction. Bright young scientists whose Jewish background would have barred them from more lucrative and more conspicuous careers in medicine or in chemistry sought this intriguing intellectual refuge, where upright men like Planck and Sommerfeld never hesitated "to promote a Jew when the candidate was highly talented." But the content or quality of the research was never an issue in the years of dismissal. Anti-Semitism came first.

There were lines drawn around matters of substance as well. The tale includes the wretched figures of two able physicists (Johannes Stark and Philipp Lenard), men long alienated by envy and disappointment, who elaborated an Aryan neoclassical physics, the subject freed not only from the infamous Jews and part-Jews but also from the inordinate influence of theory, as from the materialism they could brand as Marxist. Surely it was inconsistent to return physics to Newton as a base: mechanical materialism had always stemmed from Newton's particles, and the new relativity and quantum mechanics are even today widely seen as the negation of strict determinism. But the personal careers of the two leaders and the public ideology of the Third Reich alike demanded this difficult stance. "Aryan physics was a microcosm of National Socialism, a coalition of views just as irrational in form and nihilistic in content. It is a dangerous form of intellectual arrogance to believe that a movement must be rationally consistent in order to achieve political power," writes the historian dryly.

The high point of the Aryan theorizers was the conflict over succession once Sommerfeld reached the age of retirement in 1935. Heisenberg was the obvious man, and he was the choice of the faculty even after the ministry had once rejected his name. In the summer of 1937 the matter, still unsettled, took an alarming turn. The SS journal itself published a piece on the dispute, alluding to "white Jews" and comparing Heisenberg's Nobel prize to the one given the pacifist Carl von Ossietzky during his imprisonment in a concentration camp. The matter was plainly grave.

The first step Heisenberg and his family took to deal with it was extraordinary, a revelation of a lunatic and arbitrary regime. The physicist's mother had known Himmler's parents in old days in Munich. Mrs. Heisenberg went to Mrs. Himmler to seek some redress. "My heavens, if my Heinrich only knew of this. . . . He is such a nice boy—always congratulates me on my birthday. . . . So if I say just a single word to him, he will set the matter back in order." (We owe this remarkable account to Heisenberg himself!) Finally the aerodynamicist Ludwig Prandtl intervened, presuming on a dinner conversation with Himmler. It worked, and Himmler agreed that in spite of the attacks Heisenberg seemed a decent young man, whom the SS might make use of in their world-ice research. Munich circles, however, held enough allies of "Giovanni Fortissimo and Leonardo da Heidelberg," as Sommerfeld called Stark and Lenard, for Heisenberg not to succeed to his old teacher's chair, although Himmler held out hope in writing of an important exonerating appointment at some later time.

Came fission and the war. The professors' demand for academic autonomy and for the exemption of younger men from service at the front was now bolstered by their claim of the new relevance of their work for the war effort. The Aryan ideologues had no way to match the promise of the uranium project. The academics won the fight in that they maintained the old standards of peer judgment, which they themselves consistently pointed out did not at all mean opposition to the Nazis.

The choice had once been to fly or to stay. If one stayed (Jews had of course simple survival to consider), it meant self-alignment with the party, or perhaps "prudential acquiescence." "For many others it was inner emigration away from political involvement. For a very few it was a form of resistance."

This tragicomedy, with its careful letters and agreed statements, its little encounters, influential friends and strong rejoinders, is played very quietly. Offstage a continent burns and shudders. Only once do we see the red glow itself, when on a February night in 1944 the Royal Air Force attacked Berlin and a high-explosive bomb exploded "right in the director's room" of Otto Hahn's Institute for Chemistry.

It was too late for military atoms. Max von Laue wrote: "Absolutely everything conducted in science was 'decisive for the war effort.' . . . Many, many young people owe to this designation the activity which . . . kept them alive. This is the only meaning which the ominous word 'kriegsentscheidend' had in the years 1942–45."

The irony of history has it otherwise. The German physicists, even in the face of published warnings of the truth by such a sharp observer as Carl Ramsauer, president of the German Physical Society after 1940, remained complacent in their evident superiority. Actually the Americans had long since overtaken them. In nuclear and quantum physics particularly the greening of American physics had begun long before the years of forced exile from Germany. There were young Europeans who had sought opportunity in the uneasy years before 1932, for example Samuel Goudsmit. There were bright Americans with postdoctoral years at Göttingen, for example Robert Oppenheimer. There were the energetic experimenters and brilliant planners, with and without European experience, for example Ernest Lawrence and I. I. Rabi. All of them, led and urged on by the illustrious and justly fearful emigrants after 1933, were convinced that "German science was the best in the world, and that if a bomb could be built, the Germans could—and would—build it."

So did our epoch of the bomb arrive. The just cause was pursued to extremity in the fear that our German counterparts—disaffected, complacent, under a regime that had bet everything on the short run, carrying the suppressed guilt of a bloody and unreasoning tyranny, yet so talented—would beat us to it. If you want to examine the fine structure, this book will disclose it to you. It is impossible to close without tribute to the noble few who remained outspoken in their moral opposition to the Reich. Einstein said it well in 1944: "If [the scientists] are different, it is not attributable to intellectual capability but human stature, as in the case of Laue. . . . [He] tore himself loose step by step from the traditions of the herd under the effect of a strong feeling of justice." Not many followed him. To be sure, most were not secure enough, and indeed "their goal of professional autonomy did not demand it."

(May 1978)

Patrick Maynard Stuart Blackett, Baron Blackett of Chelsea: A Biographical Memoir

By Sir Bernard Lovell

Midshipman at the Battle of Jutland, first to photograph a nuclear reaction "by the Wilson method," World War II director of naval operations research, founder of the defense research organization of the new government of India, P.M.S. Blackett played diverse and important roles in the drama of science and society in our century. Sir Bernard Lovell (of Jodrell Bank), who became "one of Blackett's young men" at Manchester in 1936 (Blackett was himself not quite 40), has prepared here no mere impression but a 100-page account of that dramatic life, full, intimate and yet clearly seen. His memoir is published both as a small book by the Royal Society and in the 1975 volume (Volume 21) of the less accessible *Biographical Memoirs of Fellows of the Royal Society*.

Blackett was born in Kensington; his father was an unconventional stockbroker whose "great interests were in literature and nature." Military, missionary and Indian service were all in the family. As a 12-year-old he was put up for appointment to naval college and was interviewed by four admirals, who, playing the usual gambit of testing the candidate's alertness, asked him about the first round-trip flight across the English Channel, which had been completed the day before. Since the boy had been spending his spare time building model aircraft and crystal radio sets, he "bored the Admirals by telling them far more than they wanted to know." He was at the top of his class at Dartmouth when the war began, and he saw action at sea even before Jutland. There he served on the heavily damaged cruiser *Barham*; when he first left his gun turret, he found belowdecks "an extraordinary reek of TNT fumes, which mixed with the smell of disinfectant and blood was awful." The destroyer on which he became fire-control officer was posted to Harwich fresh from the Grand Fleet at Scapa Flow, and within 12 hours it had dashed without permission across their startled new admiral's bows at full speed — to sink a U-boat, the first sunk by the Harwich force, which P.M.S. thought "must have been very galling."

Blackett intended to leave the navy after the war, to seek work with some instrument firm (he already held a secret patent on a gunnery device), but was sent to Cambridge for six months' study as an effort to redress the curtailed education of his wartime class at naval college. He came to Cambridge in uniform. Within a few days he was happily immersed in intellectual conversation and had found his way to the flowering Cavendish Laboratory. He was out of the navy within three weeks, earned his degree a couple of years later and became a research student under Ernest Rutherford late in 1921.

Blackett remains a paragon of the experimental physicist. Like Rutherford, he had a deep grasp of the fundamental concepts behind his experiments; unlike Rutherford, he did not conceal his admiration for theory, and he embraced quantum theory itself. Indeed, when he left

Rutherford to work for a year in Göttingen with James Franck, he was among the first English physicists to reopen contact with Germany. Rutherford found in that one trip two sins: leaving the Cavendish and studying the outside of the atom!

In the early 1930's Blackett wrote an unforgettable paper ("a perfect selfportrait") titled "The Craft of Experimental Physics." One passage reads: "With such varied manual and mental skills . . . does the experimenter go about his work in the laboratory, an amateur in each alone, but unique in commanding them all. It is the intimate relation between these activities of hand and mind, which give to the craft of the experimenter its peculiar charm. It is difficult to find in other professions such a happy mixture of both activities. . . . He must be enough of a theorist to know what experiments are worth doing and enough of a craftsman to be able to do them. He is only pre-eminent in being able to do both." But Blackett's world was no longer Rutherford's string-and-sealing-wax one. He analyzed in depth the practical systems he used: quick-moving pistons, stereographic cameras, good-sized magnets. He improved his apparatus not by improvisation but by systematic expert design and test. His gear was complex by the standards of its time; nowadays, in particle physics at least, that complexity has grown to require big engineering teams for experiments, and Blackett's example for the experimenter is now more a heroic ideal than a reality.

He made major changes in three provinces of physics. The first decade he spent as a pioneer examining nuclear reactions with the cloud chamber. The second decade was one of particle physics as it is revealed in cosmic rays, beginning when he and his colleague G.P.S. Occhialini, who came from Florence for three weeks and "stayed for three years," operated the first counter-controlled cloud chamber. It ended with the first strange particles, found in his Manchester cloud chamber, as modified and operated by G. D. Rochester and C. C. Butler. The third decade was taken up with paleomagnetism and continental drift, a field Blackett entered after his revival of an old theory that regarded magnetism as being generated by the simple rotation of bodies, even electrically neutral ones. He developed the best of magnetometers, with which in a virtuoso experiment he quickly proved his own ideas wrong. In so doing he invigorated the study of the magnetism of rocks over geologic time, and from the data he inferred the concept of continental drift that dominates the earth sciences today. A nuclear physicist in his fifties, he had made a fundamental contribution to another field that "merits his inclusion in the small group of scientists . . . who have done so much to create modern geophysics."

For more than 50 years he spoke his mind on political matters and acted on them. He was throughout "remarkably consistent in his political and social attitudes," although the times often changed around him. He described himself as a Fabian socialist; from his first entry into active naval service he worried about the class distinctions of the navy. The Depression turned him still more clearly toward the problems of wealth and poverty. He was an early participant in the scientific defense of Britain against the Third Reich, a partisan of radar. He applied to air and naval operations his own combination of personal involvement and objective analysis, crudely quantitative and mathematical where possible. Out of this work grew modern operations research. When he left the antiaircraft command in March, 1941, to help with the U-boat threat, the air battle over Britain having been won, his general complained: "They have stolen my magician."

He was no magician, but he joined thought to action. One night at headquarters of the Western approaches his attention was drawn by a wall map of estimated U-boat positions in the Atlantic. He calculated from the hours flown by the antisubmarine aircraft that they ought to be sighting four times as many U-boats as they reported. From informed estimates of how much time the U-boats spent on the surface he concluded that in three cases of the four the U-boats saw the plane and submerged before they were sighted. Not long afterward all the aircraft of the Coastal Command were painted white, to reduce the chance of their being seen against a light sky. (All other bombers were painted black, to reduce the chance of their being picked up by searchlights.) It made a distinct difference.

Lovell lays out the complex story of Blackett's unsuccessful opposition to the bomber campaign to dehouse the German worker. Blackett wrote in *Scientific American* in 1961 of the "fanatical belief in the efficacy of bombing. . . . The only major campaign in modern history in which the traditional military doctrine of waging war against the enemy's armed forces was abandoned for a planned attack on its civilian life was a disastrous flop. I confess to a haunting sense of personal failure."

He was of course not always right. He saw early that the atomic bomb could not be a five-million-pound two-year venture, as was argued by its early proponents. At first, however, he regarded nuclear weapons as bringing no discontinuity in warfare. That cost him much in the Establishment world of the cold war; Prime Minister Attlee once rebuffed a report of Blackett's with the astonishing remark that "the author, a distinguished scientist, speaks on political and military problems on which he is a layman." Although he held the American Medal for Merit for his wartime work, "on one occasion he was arrested when an intended overflight from Mexico to Canada had to make a refuelling stop in the United States."

He was a cosmopolitan, at home in many lands. He answered a question put by Jawaharlal Nehru in 1947, estimating that the newly independent Indian armed forces could be Indianized well enough within two years to fight on their own frontiers. Their British commanders had reckoned on a generation. With that beginning he "came to love the country and its people," and he gave much time to visits and advice impinging on many facets of Indian national life. He spoke and wrote on the economic gap between the rich and the poor, which he hoped science and technology could with goodwill help to narrow. That there is much more than science involved he learned both in ministries of the Labor government in the 1960's and around the world. "Science is no magic wand" to convert a poor country into a rich one; the unities of wartime do not justify the inference that in peacetime people will do what they ought to do for the general good.

There is too much fascination in this man's life to summarize. He and his wife celebrated their 50th wedding anniversary before his death in 1974; Patrick and Pat (as Costanza, Lady Blackett, is often known) walked all that time across the world of physics and government, a striking pair, generous, tasteful, interested without pose, assured without vanity, hopeful without illusion. We remain in debt to him, a debt we can meet in his own style, seeking workable ways to replace war with peace, to narrow the gap between the rich and the poor and to understand this world on scales large and small.

(October 1976)

Black Apollo of Science: The Life of Ernest Everett Just
By Kenneth R. Manning

Like Porgy a generation later, young Ernest Just took ship from the Charleston docks to New York to enter the wider and more hopeful world. The 16-year-old son of a free black couple of middle-class status, himself a new graduate of the state normal school, Ernest made his way to New England as a scholarship student by his brilliance and energy. Acclaimed as classicist, journalist and poet, remarkably handsome and grave of bearing at 23, he stood first in the Dartmouth graduating class of 1907, the only magna cum laude of his year, a biology major with a demonstrated capacity for research. He had won everything save a chance "to enter the white professional world."

He had set his mind on science, although medicine was plainly the easier road to a career. His first job was as an instructor at Howard University, in English and then in zoology. He used his Dartmouth connection to win a chance to work summers as research assistant in the laboratory of Frank Rattray Lillie, professor at the University of Chicago and second director of the Marine Biological Laboratory at Woods Hole, Mass. Their close relationship endured for a lifetime, subtly shifting as just repeatedly sought independence of mind and job.

Just earned his Ph.D. at Chicago in experimental embryology, with a thesis on the mechanics of fertilization, the process with which most of his 80-odd scientific papers were seized. He studied the early development of the eggs of marine invertebrates — sea worms, starfish and sea urchins — at Woods Hole until he left there for good in 1930. For a decade he appeared in research as a gifted young collaborator of Lillie's. By the end of World War I he had built a reputation of his own, particularly for his authoritative and meticulous knowledge of and control over the handling of those eggs and sperm, materials central at Woods Hole. He knew the effects of temperature, he understood the essential nature of careful experimental controls, he pioneered in handling the living cells without damage to them. His expertise was so much in demand that it cost him heavily in time from his own research. Howard University was no place for research; without financial support, he was heavily burdened with teaching duties. He might aspire to a deanship, even the presidency, at Howard, but hardly to science. His haven of investigation, his "Mecca, Woods Hole," would have to nourish him from early spring to fall every year.

This was the Woods Hole of A. H. Sturtevant, T. H. Morgan and Calvin Bridges, great names of chromosome genetics in America. It was the Woods Hole of K. S. Cole and Selig Hecht, the American pioneers of biochemical and biophysical neurology, and of the cytologist E. B. Wilson. It was also the Woods Hole of the quixotic and impulsive Jacques Loeb, a weighty figure in behavior, physiology and public debate. Loeb befriended Just effectively, saw him demonstrate error in some of Loeb's rasher conclusions and then turned against him in a virulent letter of 1923. That letter "squelched" any chance of a research position at the Rockefeller Institute for Medical Research, a position that might have been "symbolic for the whole black race." Loeb had written that he had tried "to help and encourage" Just, but that he had come to conclude "the man is limited in intelligence, ignorant, incompetent, and conceited."

The book is written so quietly, with such unfailing sympathy, yet without sentiment or partisanship, that it reads very much like one of the novels from America between the wars, like some newfound Willa Cather. That tone sounds the clearest when Just first visits Europe, a black American abroad. It was pre-Depression 1928; after years of indecision, the Julius Rosenwald Fund had agreed to support Just's department at Howard, for books, equipment and research, over the next five years. No other black in science had ever had such practical recognition. First of all, Just went off to spend half a year at the famous Zoological Station on the Bay of Naples. Everyone was kind; his research went like clockwork. The

women scientists—one of them recalls his visit with the title phrase
"black Apollo"—were taken by Just's charm and good looks.

Just returned an advocate for life in Europe, and he even tried to raise
American funds for the Zoological Station. In the first half of 1930 he
went again to Europe, this time as guest professor at the Kaiser Wilhelm
Institute for Biology. We know how golden a time it was for him, starved
for scientific community and respect, because there is a witness to the
seminar of June, 1930, when Lillie's 60th birthday was celebrated at
Woods Hole. Five old Lillie students spoke. The last of them was Just, his
most prized student and perhaps his best friend. Just closed his technical
talk, and added: "'I have received more in the way of fraternity and
assistance in my one year at the Kaiser Wilhelm Institute than in all my
other years at Woods Hole put together.' A peculiar silence fell over the
room." He never came to Woods Hole again.

The Depression and the death of Julius Rosenwald ended Just's
Howard grant in 1933. He had fallen in love at first sight with an elegant
young German philosophy student in the summer of 1931. After that he
made seven trips to Europe; his wife and children in Washington faded
from his life. The echoes in America were ominous, and pained friends
and foes. Saddest of all, by 1936 Just wrote a letter from the blue Bay of
Naples: "Il Capo del Governo d'Italia, S. E. Signore Mussolini. . . . As an
American negro who for more than 25 years has contributed to the
progress of biological science without having attained a place . . . which
such service deserves, I desire earnestly the opportunity to continue my
labors in Italy and thereby cooperate [as] your energetic leadership acceler-
ates Italy to a magnificent destiny." The Man of Destiny never replied.

By 1938 Ernest and his Hedwig were living together in France, all but
penniless. Just's big book was about to appear in the U.S., but history put
forward urgent demands. France fell, and foreigners had to leave. There
was nowhere to go in 1940 but America, with Hedwig, now his wife by
virtue of a Riga divorce and soon to be a mother. Ill and unhappy, Just
went back to teaching at Howard. At 58 he died painfully of cancer of the
pancreas before war came to the U.S.

Just belongs to an era of biology when bricks were perforce made
with little straw. Embryonic development is far from our understanding
still, but only the broadest strokes could be made out before the electron
microscope and biochemical cycles and protein sequences and the double
helix. Ernest Just indeed saw the key place of the cell surface in the
economy of the cell; his 1939 book bore the title *The Biology of the Cell
Surface*.

Black Apollo of Science, however, is not a book on the inner logic of
biology. It is a reminder of how much the men and women who construct
the new ideas and artifacts of science are part of a world they never made.
From this story, true and mythical at once, readers can gain a new insight

into the heavy costs still being paid day by bitter day for that most peculiar of the institutions of America's wealth, two centuries of African slavery and its unending reverberations.

(May 1984)

Niels Bohr: A Centenary Volume
Edited by A. P. French and P. J. Kennedy

"Dear Dad," wrote W. L. Bragg, then a physics student at Cambridge, to an older physicist: "I'm so glad you liked the notes on Jeans. . . . I got an awful lot from a Dane who had seen me asking Jeans questions, and . . . came up and talked over the whole thing. He was awfully sound on it, and most interesting." The Dane was Niels Bohr at 26, a postdoc in the Cavendish, soon to make his way to Rutherford at Manchester, just as the nuclear atom was born out of the closely watched scattering of alpha particles. Bohr's own tussle with the ordered spectral pattern of the atom began then and there, in about 1911.

Long before, in 1885, J. J. Balmer had published his remarkable integer formula for the visible spectrum of atomic hydrogen. Bohr was born in that same year; it took physics three decades to explain those small integers in optical spectra. Bohr's atom model was crude and remained seriously incomplete, but it was absolutely on the right track. When he made the first easy extension to the spectrum of helium, interest quickened. In October, 1913, he refined his mechanics a little to take account of the motion of the nucleus itself, since of course the sunlike nucleus did not infinitely outweigh its planet electrons. It moved too. The outcome was a soon-confirmed fit to the measured line positions of helium accurate at the level of a couple of parts in 100,000. George de Hevesy, a close friend, wrote Bohr (in an orthography all his own) of Einstein's reaction to the news: "When he heard this, he was extremely astonished and told me: 'Than the frequency of the light does not depand at all on the frequency of the electron . . . And this is an *enormous achiewement*. The theory of Bohr must be then wright."

Of course it was not right. It resembles the atom no more than a quick pencil sketch resembles a living face, as O. R. Frisch put it. The real Jacob, quantum mechanics, appeared only in the mid-twenties. How much Bohr meant to this second coming, even more as a personal focus of understanding than in published papers, is the next high theme of this volume, glowing with affectionate recollections by half a dozen eminent physicists of the Copenhagen days between the wars. A warmth born of community in the long struggle for understanding is radiated from every reminiscence of Bohr. He was a friend in decisive action no less than in spirit. It is moving to read of his prompt tour of the German universities during the fearful year of 1933 once the Third Reich rose in fire; as he went from city to city and physicist to physicist, he quietly set up "the lines of escape."

The book contains Bohr's published masterpiece, that long review, half history, half reanalysis, of his decades of dialogue with Einstein over whether quantum mechanics can be a complete theory or is only a statistical shadow of a more causal but more hidden reality. He wrote it for Einstein's 70th birthday in 1949. The depth of the issue has kept it alive. Two or three shorter papers summarize and discuss the present-day status of arrangements that allow the experimental choice between two interfering measurables to be delayed until the significant interaction seems long ended. Just as Bohr contended, the new results fulfill the quantum forecasts based on the indivisibility of experiment, but they surely contradict less subtle versions of physical reality.

The third great theme in Bohr's life sounds yet in all our lives. It is fission. That nuclear phenomenon entered the world with the year 1939. It was Bohr who first brought across the Atlantic in person the word of how Frisch and Lise Meitner had explained and confirmed the enigmatic report of the radiochemists that uranium could absorb a neutron and then break into two heavy fragments with an unprecedented release of energy. Bohr and John Wheeler spent six months clarifying the physics of the process, in particular which isotopes would show fission. Their decisive fission paper appeared just as grim war broke out in Europe. It is reproduced here in part, along with a chronicle of the people and the events of that fateful year for physics and the world.

Bohr faced the consequences too. First he escaped from Denmark in the bomb bay of a fast Mosquito, converted so that B.O.A.C. could fly civilians from neutral Sweden to Britain at altitudes above the Luftwaffe's reach. He made his way first to Los Alamos and then soon to the side of Churchill and Roosevelt. The memorandums he prepared for the two leaders are here, again in a mix of anthology and new historical comment. His plea for an open world around nuclear energy release was not heard, during the war or afterward. The P.M. at once took a dislike to that man "with his hair all over his head" and even grumbled that "Bohr ought to be confined" as a "great advocate of publicity."

A section learnedly treats Bohr's philosophy, again by means of old papers and new. It includes accounts of the Copenhagen views both as seen from a base in Sanskrit dialectic and as debated in the U.S.S.R. by the thinkers of Marxism-Leninism. (Hideki Yukawa is cited as observing that in Japan Bohr's complementarity looked quite evident: "You see, we . . . have not been corrupted by Aristotle.")

The book is lighthearted in its admiration, and it does not omit the times when Bohr fell into error: that bad year before the discovery of the Compton effect when he despaired of the conservation laws, or the occasion when he guessed that success in molecular biology would require complementarity at some deep functional level. Light was not the key to life. That turned out, as far as we now see it, to be more closely related to Schrödinger's notion of the aperiodic crystal. But it is striking to read H.B.G. Casimir's remark that it was Bohr who steered him toward the zero-point energy of the photon field as a description of his wonderful derivation of the forces between closely spaced conductors. Bohr seems rather casually to have thought decades ahead, exploring a major puzzle alive in the sophisticated present.

A few pages in context, picture and verse, are reproduced out of the 1932 Copenhagen parody of *Faust*, written essentially by Max Delbrück. The parody's Mephistopheles was clearly meant to be Wolfgang Pauli; the Lord God rather resembled Bohr in a top hat. The entire script was published by George Gamow in his autobiographical *Thirty Years That Shook Physics*.

Plainly an elderly physicist can enjoy the volume, with its cargo of apt figures and citations. About a fifth of the text is given to Bohr's own papers, another fifth to reprints of older studies; the rest has been written for the centenary year. Every student of physics will want some access to these instructive matters, access made so easy here that the volume is a fine buy for every library such students frequent, from high schools on up. The general scientific reader will also find much of interest in this diverse and well-presented collection of 40 papers. (Observe how useful are the notes the editors have provided, as their final admirable contribution to the welfare of the International Commission on Physics Education, which will benefit from the royalties on the book.)

(March 1986)

Robert Oppenheimer: Letters and Recollections
Edited by Alice Kimball Smith and Charles Weiner

Dictionary of Scientific Biography
Editor-in-chief Charles Coulston Gillispie

Myth has twice enfolded Robert Oppenheimer, first in the image of the awesome mushroom of our fears and then in the drama of the state's unpitying humiliation of the mind that had done the state some service. His human qualities now fade from living memory. His hopeful and admiring teachers, except for a couple of remarkable octogenarians, are gone; his fellow students are now the gray elders of physics; his own students and those he led are at the brink of retirement. But his many-sided talents and his luminous thought are still to be made out in this intimate, carefully documented, honest and affectionate book, a collection of 160 of his letters (and some exchanges) over 25 years, augmented by meticulous identification of allusions, by a good deal of later comment from Oppenheimer himself and by interviews with many correspondents and other contemporaries.

The senior author is the chief historian of the postwar political movement among the scientists and was a personal friend of Oppenheimer's since the 1940's; Professor Weiner is a historian of science whose special interest has been the growth of nuclear physics. To the vividness and variety of the letters they have brought a pervasive sense of order in growth. The celebrated events of Oppenheimer's public life, everything after the last war year, are treated in a few understanding pages of epilogue. This is no wartime or cold-war chronicle; it is the evocation of a remarkable life of science in our country between 1922 and 1945.

We meet Oppenheimer, after a useful introduction, in his first week as a Harvard freshman at 18, in the fall of 1922. He left Harvard three years later with a most irregular but steadily brilliant record, graduating in three years with an A.B. summa in chemistry, a deep love for which was fostered, out of his childhood delight in minerals and their variety, by his science teacher in his junior year of high school. Most of the college letters are written to another influential teacher, his high school English instructor and lifelong friend Herbert W. Smith. Wrote the playful sophomore to Mr. Smith: "I might string you out a lengthy miserere . . . how Jane has frozen, because it was rude to understand her dismal notes and unthinkable not to . . . how Jeffries and I miss each other with coy opacity; . . . how I have come lugubriously to the conclusion that the two people at Wellesley . . . that even pretend to pursue me are a sorry and worthless lot; how all that has driven me to whorls of stories and notes on the divgrad of an electrical field and French and merely English verses; and how, in a final catastrophe, I projected said verses toward you."

The years sped past around the Widener Library and weekends at Cape Ann, in gas analysis in the chemistry laboratory and in enriching experiences in class and out with Alfred North Whitehead, G. D. Birkhoff and particularly Percy Bridgman. A skilled sailor and no tyro at the laboratory bench, the young Oppenheimer found he was happier still with the thick books of Cambridge mathematical physics. Although he undertook a study of electrical conduction in rutile for Bridgman, he became convinced that "my genre, whatever it is, is not experimental science." Bridgman concurred; he wrote Ernest Rutherford that Oppenheimer had a brilliant record but that "his type of mind is analytical rather than physical." Somehow Oppenheimer reached the Cavendish, struggled bravely in the laboratory, then found his way through R. H. Fowler's good sense and kindness to theory, moving to Göttingen just as the forge of quantum mechanics glowed hot. By the spring of 1928 he had his Ph.D. and had made his mark. With Max Born as his mentor he could choose among offers. Born wrote to Julius Stratton at the Massachusetts Institute of Technology: "We have here a number of Americans. . . . One man is quite excellent, Mr. Oppenheimer." His vocation was fully in hand; his letters breathe it now in self-assurance, wide acquaintanceships and bubbling plans.

It is sobering to read that Bridgman, a man of perception and limpid integrity, felt compelled to write in 1925 to the Cavendish: "Oppenheimer is a Jew, but entirely without the usual qualifications of his race. He is a tall, well set-up young man, with a rather engaging diffidence of manner." This is about the time of the jacket photograph of this volume, a very youthful poet's gaze at the lens, with an artfully delicate melancholy.

Now times march swiftly. Oppenheimer has chosen to work in Berkeley, with a concurrent appointment in Pasadena. The letters go now mainly to the theorist George Uhlenbeck and to Robert's brother Frank, eight years his junior, himself on the way to a degree in experimental physics via Johns Hopkins and the Cavendish. The world tightens its coupling; the young professor himself becomes the generous focus of a California coterie of students and research associates. He forms close bonds with the experimenters, Ernest Lawrence at Berkeley, William Fowler and C. C. Lauritsen at Pasadena. Here the letters carry the reader into the flowering of modern physics in America. By the early 1930's the theorist's concerns acquire a still familiar tone: electron-positron pair theory, nuclear energy levels, troubles at high energy, cosmic-ray properties (is the meson radioactive?), even neutron stars.

The troubles of the world enter as well; a tithe is pledged to aid the "former colleagues" exiled from Germany, and we hear other echoes of a grievous decade. Literature, although never music, still consoles: "With books it is not so good, new ones. I have reread all Flaubert" and still older works, "the *Meghadhuta* and the *Timaeus*, reading them with a painful pedantry." Spanish and Dutch too were at his command. Only the Sanskrit would have seemed unusual in a well-traveled and cultivated European physicist; in America his fluency was extraordinary. Then the grave final motif sounds far away in January, 1939: "The U business is unbelievable. We first saw it in the papers, wired for more dope." The next week he wrote: "I think it not too improbable that a ten cm cube of uranium deuteride (one should have something to slow the neutrons without capturing them) might very well blow itself to hell."

In time it did, more or less, and took two cities with it. The next period is wartime, "these terrible years." The diffident youth has become the warm, trusted, prescient and tireless leader at 40. He accepts the requirement to form his laboratory under the Army, not under the civilian Office of Scientific Research and Development. "If I believed with you," he wrote to I. I. Rabi in 1943, "that this project was 'the culmination of three centuries of physics,' I should take a different stand. To me it is primarily the development in time of war of a military weapon of consequence, I do [not] think that the Nazis allow us the option of not carrying out that development." (The only text, a carbon copy, omits the needed *not*.)

By April, 1945, the bomb is a few months from completion, as all believe. The Nazis are done for. At the memorial service for Franklin Roosevelt in the theater on the mesa, Oppenheimer spoke in elegy: "When, three days ago, the world had word of the death of President Roosevelt, many wept who are unaccustomed to tears, many men and women, little enough accustomed to prayer, prayed to God. Many of us looked with deep trouble to the future; many of us felt less certain that our works would be to a good end; all of us were reminded of how precious a thing human greatness is."

So is one reminded on reading this book, rich in the texture of feeling and idea, a bright but erratic beam into shifting components of a mind of power and intricacy and on a world in which ever forking paths of choice have brought us to 1980. We still drift downstream from an accurate fix Oppenheimer took for us 18 years ago: "We are in an arms race of quite unparalleled deadliness—I think this is not the place to speak about the amount of devilment that is piled up on both sides . . . ; on the other hand, we have lived sixteen and a half years without nuclear war. In the balance between the very great gravity of the risks we face and the obvious restraints that have seen us through this time, I have no counsel except that of sobriety and some hope." (The passage is not from the book but from a lecture at McMaster University.) The final published scientific paper of Robert Oppenheimer, on a radiation mechanism in algal photosynthesis, appeared in 1950; his travail began in 1953. He died at his home in Princeton on February 18, 1967, after a final year's struggle with a malignant throat tumor, during which he was determined "to maintain as long as possible his connection with physics . . . and communication with his friends."

Dictionary of Scientific Biography, the second work reviewed here, is at once closely analogous and entirely distinct. It is in some way a grand extension of the notion of the biography of a scientist, but on a scale so large as to lose most, although not all, of the quality of the volume directly on and by Oppenheimer. The fruit of a decade's work by a thousand scholars from almost a hundred countries, it presents a summary of the scientific lives of a selection of the men and women who have made world science, in all its branches, from antiquity to the present, albeit excluding all living scientists. The first volumes appeared in 1970 and were reviewed in these columns in March, 1971. The work is now complete: 14 of its volumes offer an alphabetical array of biographical articles, from Pierre Abailard to Johann Zwelfer. Volume 15 for about half of its pages adds a small supplementary alphabet, pieces for some reason delayed past their proper time of issue; its latter half offers a set of expert topical essays on periods in science without easy biographical attribution: mathematics in Egypt, mathematical astronomy in India, our understanding of Maya calendars and computation, and a couple of others. Volume 16 is a useful overall index, in which the 5,000 biographies are set in a much larger context of entries, from the A.A.A.S. and the abacus to zymohexase. The entire work is 10,000 pages long, a heavy three-foot shelf. A general reader will hardly read it all, nor did this reviewer.

The authority and scholarship of the work is beyond doubt. An entire Sanhedrin of boards and consultants assures us, and the signatures on the pieces bear the names of the best historiographers. Since so many subjects belong to this century, many of the accounts are the work of colleagues, even friends of the person described. Most such pieces are the product of reflective working scientists who take up rather gracefully the stylus of Clio. In fact, with striking exceptions, a general reader is likely to gain more comprehension from these somewhat less professional articles than from the others. Partly this represents the sense of historical proximity, but it arises also from the pervasive method of the text, a style much closer to the scholar's lamp than to the scientist's bench. The authors all work, as scholarship demands, directly from the sources, which they list and categorize carefully. But they give the reader little evidence, not even many equations, almost never citing the phrases or reproducing the data, the graphs, the drawings and the photographs that were the work they describe. It is mainly brought to us secondhand; *totus in verba*. Even diagrams are few; it is a real pleasure to see the annotated facsimile of the Dresden Codex or a photograph of the zodiacal ceiling at Dendera with a careful key. Although the quasi-archaeological articles offer evidence freely, the others rarely do.

To read of the thought of Niels Bohr at the hand of his colleague Leon Rosenfeld, or of Desmond Bernal in a moving account by C. P. Snow, is the unforgettable best of the work. Our careless tendency to neglect Europe past the Elbe is wonderfully countered by an entire battery of articulate scholars from the U.S.S.R. and from other lands of eastern

Europe. The brief piece on Aleksandr A. Friedmann, Leningrad master of fluid dynamics, who first set Einstein and the world straight on the expanding relativistic cosmology, is most welcome; we all believe in Friedmann's universe, but we know little of his life. The science of China is left in general to more specialized works, but a few articles on key figures are presented. The essay on the Sung polymath Shen Kua, who left us so much understanding of the compass and printing, chemistry and astronomy, in a few compact pages of apparently casual comments, is a tour de force of appraisal in a very wide cultural context. (It is by Nathan Sivin.)

Five thousand names are a lot, but still a few are missing. One can find Georges Sagnac, who carefully led light rays still in phase around a circle, but one looks in vain for Cipriano Targioni, who consumed the prince's diamond with a burning glass in Florence long ago. Yet the overall choice is wide and wise. The length of the articles is not under much control: Newton gets the full treatment; Darwin's biography, although expert, is rather brief. Pasteur has a few more pages than even Newton draws and Laplace fills twice as many (60 times the average), the careful work of the editor-in-chief, with some help from his friends. The Laplace article—a small book—is about the most elaborate mathematically; Lagrange, in contrast, does not earn a single integral sign. The contributors have plainly taken over. The entire dish is bulky, nutritious, rather dry, doubtless very good for you and your library; here and there you can pull out a delicious plum. Our assessment of 1971 seems to stand: a tenth of the pages opened to direct citations and to visual matter might have doubled the value of a work that will nonetheless stand as a lasting contribution to the world of scholarly books.

(August 1980)

Edward S. Curtis: The Life and Times of a Shadow Catcher
By Barbara A. Davis

Edward Sheriff Curtis was a gifted and energetic young photographer and engraver who lived in Seattle at the turn of the century. Out of that frontier town and busy port the Yukon and the Nome gold rushes gave birth to the brief Harriman Expedition, whose brilliant scientific staff reconnoitered western Alaska for a site that would accommodate a trans-Bering railroad connection by bridge or tunnel. Curtis went along as a photographer; he returned with luminous and dreamlike landscapes of the Arctic world. Soon the life of a city studio no longer fulfilled him.

In a well-documented 100-page biography Davis follows the shadow catcher from youth to his death in Los Angeles in 1952, at 84. From about 1904 to 1930 Curtis carried out against all odds his grandiose scheme to publish 20 volumes of text and image on *The North American Indian*. About 300 copies of the original work with its expensive and enormous photogravures exist, and the text has been reprinted. Most of the biography treats his struggle to complete his work and then to save it from remaindered obscurity. The story is a pageant of the American early 20th century; its characters range from TR and J.P. Morgan to Geronimo, Buffalo Bill, Franz Boas, Robert Flaherty and Cecil B. de Mille. Curtis knew them all, the powerful as erratic patrons, the others as fellow artists, scientists and strivers. He was a cameraman for de Mille on *The Ten Commandments* and an adviser to Flaherty for *Nanook of the North*. He entered the lives of many subjects easily and sincerely; his principles of direction were built around the pronoun *we*, not *I* and *you*.

The volume offers about 150 plates, some of them reproduced from prints made anew from the original copper gravures, some not published before, many of them once celebrated. It is these shadows that establish Curtis as a kind of second John James Audubon, two men seized with a dream that lay between science and art. Audubon worked with brushes, a shotgun and his own unflagging energy; Curtis needed dozens of expert helpers in the field and at home. Audubon pictured the birds of forest and meadow; Curtis, the men and women of 75 cultures over an entire continent during an era of defeat and travail. Both achieved the wide reproduction of outsize images. Audubon painted for the lithographic stone; Curtis, a century later, took his big glass plates for printing by photogravure.

Curtis could not fully succeed. Yet he did not fail. These enhanced shadows are not caught just as they fell. They were seen by an ethnographic eye that sought romance in every image but only rarely allowed the excess called sentimentality. These people and the works of their hands look more beautiful, prouder and more powerful here than in any other sustained evocation.

Of course that is not the whole truth; they were then in real peril and poverty, and there they mostly remain. Yet it is part of the truth all the same. Here is the Canyon de Chelly, riders of the People before the towering pinnacles. Here are the kayaks of Noatak hunters, like seaborne birds in the dusk. Here is a timbered tomb of a chief of the Haida at Yan, a monument looking as ancient and strong as a tumulus on the plains of Europe. The weaknesses of this artist are all too easy to see, as Beaumont Newhall remarks, but his strengths lie deeper.

The collection (it includes a wide variety of Curtis' work beyond the Indian studies) and the text are fine to see and to ponder. It is worth recalling that Curtis completed one motion-picture film, made in the Northwest among the Nootka and the Kwakiutl between 1912 and 1914.

It was shown briefly but soon disappeared from view. One print was rescued and released not many years ago by the University of Washington; the story is told in a 1980 book from that press by Bill Holm and George Quimby. The events of the film are embedded in a staged and costumed drama no subtler than its period, but while masked Eagle and huge Bear dance grandly in the prows of two speeding war canoes the viewer for a moment shares in full the hunter's beliefs. There too we feel the power of this man's art, shadows caught in an unflinching pursuit of a vivid and loving dream.

(May 1986)

Cecilia Payne-Gaposchkin: An Autobiography and Other Recollections
Edited by Katherine Haramundanis

What is the primary substance of the cosmos? In the closing years of the 19th century and the opening decades of the 20th this was plainly a scientific question of the first order. The answer materialized slowly. Orbital motions of double stars demonstrated that their masses were indeed akin to the mass of the sun; the Victorian spectroscopists showed that the glowing stars were composed of chemical elements mostly familiar on the earth. By 1920 the thermal physics of atoms and radiation, although still innocent of quantum mechanics, stood fully ready to reveal the composition of hot gaseous matter. All that was required beyond the laws and concepts discovered by Boltzmann, Planck, Bohr and Einstein was knowledge of the discrete energy levels of the nuclear atoms and of the photons they emitted and absorbed.

In about 1921, from Meghnad Saha in Calcutta came the brilliant "idea that gave birth to modern astrophysics." He applied the equilibrium theory of simple chemical reactions to the ionization of atoms in the hot surface gases of sun and stars. Suddenly it became plain that the stars were roughly uniform in substance; the striking distinctions among their spectra were principally the result of differences not in atomic composition but in pressure and temperature.

One more step was needed to reach the surprising result, which today we accept as commonplace: the cosmos is made of hydrogen, the simplest of the atoms. To be sure, cosmic hydrogen is not quite pure: some eight atoms out of 100 are helium, and two more atoms may represent any of the remaining 94 or so elements. The earth is not at all like that; here hydrogen provides only a modest proportion of all atoms, and helium is rare.

The physicist who first drew that grand conclusion about the substance of the cosmos was a brilliant young graduate student, Cecilia Payne. She came on a fellowship from the University of Cambridge to work at the Harvard College Observatory in the fall of 1923; she was just as young as the century. "Before I left Cambridge, [E. A.] Milne told me that if he had my opportunity, he would go after the observations that would test and verify the Saha theory."

So she did. She was thorough, logical, devoted and hardworking to the point of risking exhaustion and despair; swift to catch and use new ideas, she was also deeply original. Within two years she had published half a dozen related papers in which she analyzed the starry universe. Payne (as she was then) became the first astronomy Ph.D. from Harvard; her thesis, the best one ever written in astronomy, sold out as a book. It was "at the same time an attractive story and a work of reference," as Milne wrote.

Could there really be so much hydrogen and helium? That conclusion was plain from Payne's work, but it was too strange to be believed. This early in the growth of atomic physics there was indeed room for generalized doubt. Princeton's formidable expert Henry Norris Russell ("I respected and feared him") read her manuscript and wrote her about that incredible hydrogen content: "Here I am convinced that there is something wrong with the present theory." She accepted her adviser's doubts as her own, publishing that the inferred hydrogen and helium content of the sun "is improbably high, and is almost certainly not real." Five years later, after the swift sunrise of quantum mechanics and a great deal of enriching new theory and observation, Russell made his own estimates of solar abundance and reported "a gratifying agreement" with Payne's earlier numbers. "Ingrained conservatism" had proved wrong.

Soon the theorists could assay indirectly the unseen cores of stars and the interiors of the giant gaseous planets; mainly they found hydrogen. Not much later the spectra of gaseous nebulas and the physics of nuclear energy sources consistently supported the domination of hydrogen and helium. Investigators in the postwar years observed that the cosmic rays consisted largely of protons; radio telescopes revealed neutral hydrogen clouding the spiral galaxies. Lately both radio and ultraviolet observations offer clear signs that molecular hydrogen gas dominates the composition of those interstellar clouds. Cecilia Payne's first atomic analysis of the heavens has been confirmed in full.

Today the simple atomic makeup of the cosmos is less a result than an unstated premise to every argument about the starry world. (It is important to be precise: the stuff we see in any wave band is hydrogen-rich. Lately, however, we have good reason to believe much more matter than what we can see is out there, matter so dim and scattered that it is invisible. Its presence is disclosed by gravitation alone, and so its nature is well hidden.)

All of this and much more is to be read in the small volume, wherein the reader will encounter Cecilia Helena Payne-Gaposchkin in image and in words, from four or five angles. Her autobiography, written late in life, offers the fullest view; it is self-revealing, even passionate, beyond that of most scientists. Often it is so in ways she must have realized but does not remark on. She does draw the curtain around a few key feelings and events.

There is a warm and knowing appraisal by a younger associate, himself now easily dean of American students of the spectroscopy of stars, Jesse Greenstein. The editor, who is the middle child of Payne's lifelong marriage to a lively Russian astronomer she first befriended in Germany in the 1930's, gives a loving account of this "Renaissance woman": at once scholar, linguist, keen scientist, warm mother, generous neighbor, cultivated traveler, playgoer, musician, something of a political activist, a clever wit and the inspired queen of kitchen and needle. Historian Peggy Kidwell presents a careful study of the early work based on the full record, both published papers and many private letters.

Two unusual pages must be cited. They open: "At the age of five Cecilia saw a meteor, and thereupon decided to be an Astronomer. She remarked that she must begin quickly, in case there should be no research left when she grew up." This delightful character sketch is the work of a dear friend at Newnham College, a young woman whose untimely death was an unsettling tragedy to Payne at Harvard. The whimsical pages gain poignancy because Professor Payne-Gaposchkin, not long before her death at the age of 79, asked that the little text, published nearly 50 years earlier, be used as her obituary. She wrote always with clarity and style; her literary judgment did not falter here, nor does the piece conceal her inmost values.

Sample the autobiography very sparingly. The big names of the time play expressive parts. At Cambridge, Payne was introduced to the Bohr atom by Bohr himself, made "almost incomprehensible by his accent." Rutherford thundered at her, the only woman in his advanced course, seated by university regulation all by herself in the front row.

It was eloquent Arthur Eddington who swept Payne into astronomy. She attended — four tickets had been assigned to Newnham College — the famous lecture in which Eddington presented the results of the eclipse expedition he led to Brazil in 1918. "The Great Hall was crowded. The speaker was a slender, dark young man with a trick of looking away from his audience and a manner of complete detachment. He gave an outline of the Theory of Relativity, as none could do better than he. . . . He led up to the shift of the stellar images near the Sun as predicted by Einstein and described his verification of the prediction. . . . When I returned to my room I found that I could write down the lecture word for word. . . . For three nights, I think, I did not sleep."

A similar epiphany came to Payne a few years later. This time it was young Harlow Shapley in London who spoke intimately of the cosmic picture, with "none of Eddington's classical polish" but with unmatched directness and energy. Again she found she had absorbed the lecture word by word. A much older student, the war-wounded L. J. Comrie, himself bound for a job at Swarthmore, had told her that in America a woman would have a better chance to win a research post in astronomy than she would in Britain. It was he who had taken her to hear Shapley. Comrie promptly introduced her to the new director of the Harvard College Observatory, and she came at once to the point: "I should like to come and work under you."

Edwin Hubble is a looming off-stage presence. Payne recalls the day news came of the blinking Cepheids in the Andromeda galaxy that securely established by Shapley's own methods the scale of the galaxies. "I was in [Shapley's] office when Hubble's letter came, and he held it out to me: 'Here is the letter that destroyed my universe,' he said." His actions then were characteristic: "From that day he planned a gigantic assault on the problem of galaxies . . . Harvard astronomy shifted abruptly . . . to the distant systems."

Payne's research life was rewarding; she valued and loved her science so much that given her full acceptance among peers she could be deeply content. "Everyone who was anybody (and many more besides, who were going to be somebody in the future) came through. . . . We got to know Lundmark, Milne, and Unsöld. . . . How we argued, how we walked about the streets and sat talking in restaurants until the manager turned off the lights. . . . We met as equals; nobody condescended to me. . . . Nobody ever thought of flirting." We do things better here, she concluded, looking back at her 50 years as an American.

There was sadness in this life beyond the death of friends, beyond the lonely years of that young Englishwoman who was so tall, imposing and outwardly reserved. (Yet Payne would often in her new car at dawn burn up the road beside the Charles, the observatory's elderly raffish night assistant "urging me on with 'Step on it, Celia!'"

Harvard College did not by any means do everything better. For years Payne was shamefully mistreated as a professional, "on the material side." She was diverted more than once by fiat from her own research direction. She was chronically underpaid, overworked, denied formal status. She received her first Harvard rank at the age of 38, under the presidency of James Bryant Conant; it was not a faculty position except in its duties. A paragon of a candidate, she had to wait until 1956 to become the first woman professor at Harvard, perhaps 20 years after a man of her achievement and qualities would have earned the post.

President Abbott Lawrence Lowell, autocrat of an older school, had long seen to it that no woman would receive any appointment from the Harvard Corporation. Even the courses Payne taught went uncatalogued until after the war. What dark fears beset an establishment under little challenge?

The book artfully records a life of worth and delight won against obsessive, powerful but not pervasive forces. The record has value beyond its period and its circle. This is a chronicle of affirmation and hope, a near-poetic witness to a burst of profound discovery insufficiently recognized.

(April 1985)

The Path to the Double Helix
By Robert Olby
Foreword by Francis Crick

James Watson a decade ago wrote his narrative of the final push, a tale inward-looking, provocative and brilliant. Like the commando hero he saw in himself, Honest Jim told of anxious pursuit, with Old Alpha Helix cunningly at work across the sea while paper models and smiling popsies filled Cambridge days about equally with tantalizing promises. But battle journals, however honest, are not quite history; they concentrate on the smaller scene, and might misinterpret the hint a dark lady gave when asked for directions at a crossroads. The historians describe it all later—the entire campaign, not just the fight. It is they who first sort the pieces of paper that document the weapons, the battle order and the long struggle for position.

This volume is a "full scholarly account of how the structure of DNA was discovered, set against its proper historical background." So justly writes that other hero of the double helix, who supplied the foreword. Robert Olby is concerned with the entire problem, from the nature of the support of scientific institutions and the rise of schools of research to the logical development of concept and experiment. A professional historian of science at the University of Leeds, he clearly has sound judgment and critical understanding. His sources include not only the published literature (plus theses and notebooks) in the substantive field and the considerable body of memoir and critique that has by now appeared but also a good deal of contemporary private correspondence and many interviews with principals and spear carriers alike. He retains a lively interest in strong personality and incident—and there are plenty along the way—to add color to a coherent narrative of intellectual struggle.

The story is a 20th-century one. True, there is a prehistory of nucleic acid biochemistry, but it left little legacy. We are in the world that emerged after the rediscovery of Mendel, the development of polypeptide synthesis by Emil Fischer and the birth of X-ray crystal analysis before World War I. It would be invidious to try to summarize all the rich texture of this history, but one may outline the chronicle by describing the five stages of the campaign.

The first question (here one sees how the hot issues of one decade become the unexamined "self-evident" axioms of the next) is that of long-chain polymers. James Clerk Maxwell thought the average molecule in living microscopic beings contained about 50 atoms. The term "macromolecule" was introduced about 1925 by Hermann Staudinger. He was ridiculed by his fellow chemists for his ideas, which revived with quantitative support the classical hunches of Kekulé. The work carried him into the "unpleasant and poorly defined" rubber and polystyrene. It was not easy for X-ray crystallographers to rid themselves of the idea that the molecule could not be larger than the unit cell they saw. Nevertheless, by 1939 the X-ray analysts in Berlin and the remarkable laboratory at Leeds under W. T. Astbury, an enthusiast and an original ("I am alpha and omega, the beginning and the end of the whole thing," he said), had demonstrated long fibrous biomolecules and had laid the foundations of a sophisticated method of X-ray analysis via models—although their first results were seductively misleading.

Next one had to part tape from cassette. By 1931 the chemists had found nucleic acids to be rather simple, with only four nucleotides, and had turned their attention to the more complex protein. Here is the story of those infants with air-darkened urine, which led by way of Garrod and Beadle to the genetics of molds and to the clear recognition that genes somehow code for enzyme proteins. Even a direct look at the protein rods of tobacco mosaic virus did not, "after all reveal the chemical identity of self-reproducing units." The denatured virus left a purified RNA residue, but in 1942 they did not check carefully to see if that portion could be infectious by itself. One reason was that the preparation method had damaged the RNA tapes; another was that the investigators were in a "Kuhnian box": no one was prepared for the revolutionary idea of genetic information without protein.

That way was of course found by the medical immunochemists at the Rockefeller. They devoted themselves to the curious transformations of the pneumococcus as a key to immunization against bacterial lobar pneumonia. The bombshell of induced transformation, with its disturbing whiff of Lamarck, was detonated in 1928 by a "quiet and retiring medical officer . . . a civil servant and proud of it," a man who could not be persuaded to leave his bench to attend a meeting or to read a paper. (Once his friends had to bundle him into a taxi to get him to a relevant talk at an international congress in London.) That bacteriologist, Frederick Griffith, was the other side—and fully as English—of Astbury's fine presentation of a puffy John Bull. The answer was found and secured by 1943. Macfarlane Burnet visited Oswald Avery in New York and wrote home of "an extremely exciting discovery which, put rather crudely, is nothing less than the isolation of a pure gene in the form of desoxyribonucleic acid." The final step in preparation for Watson-Crick was the enigma of the base ratios: the one-to-one match of the amounts of adenine and thymine and of guanine and cytosine in DNA over a wide variation in their separate fractions. This had been made clear by the early 1950's by a number of people.

Here the theme changes. The issue is no longer model paradigms, molecule size or protein versus nucleic acid but the rise of complementary schools. One was the informational school of Luria and Delbrück and their friends: physical biologists who worked out the genetics of bacterial viruses, suspicious of biochemists as people who were analyzing the brass in the gears rather than how the watch worked. The second school, no less influenced by the successes and the methods of physics, was that of the British structuralists, dealing in complex X-ray crystallography. By training and tradition the two groups shared an appreciation of the subtlety of the chemical bond and even seemed to hanker for physically new specific forces between biological molecules. There were, it is true, two schools of X-ray structural studies. The British, under the Braggs, with Bernal and Perutz and Wilkins and Huggins, was the best in the world; its members were analysts in all detail, tireless and ingenious. But in Pasadena there was Linus Pauling, whose conviction that the bond lengths and angles of the quantum theorists were reliable guides strengthened the bold strategy—model-building synthesis—with which he outguessed the structures cautiously puzzled out of the spots of the diffraction diagrams. Pauling and his co-workers found and proved the protein helix in 1950 and 1951. By the end of 1951 Perutz was convinced that the Californians were right. The protein helix fit the data neatly and was deeply plausible on general group-theoretical grounds. The helix became fashionable. "You would be eccentric . . . if you didn't think DNA was helical," reports Crick.

Watson met Crick in 1951. Crick was then a confident extrovert, although a theorist without a Ph.D. at 35; Watson, a diffident "loner," was a prodigy, a former quiz kid with a bacteriophage Ph.D. at 22. The structuralists at their most thoughtful had met the informationalists at their most enterprising—and Peter Pauling lived upstairs in Cambridge, a hot line to Pasadena. (Luria and Linus Pauling could not themselves visit England then, because the Age of McCarthy kept those two men without passports. It may be that it was the U.S. Passport Office that fixed the outcome of the hunt for the double helix.)

The last 100 pages cover the final engagement culminating in May, 1953, and extend the tale briefly to 1973. The meticulous study seems to do justice to all the participants in a tangled skein of ideas, personalities and interchanges by design and by chance, but the historian and not the reviewer must be read for that detailed story. The discovery would have been made, "we may be fairly confident," in London or Pasadena a year or two later if Dr. Watson had never come to Mr. Crick.

One important theme is slighted: the computer metaphor supplied by the mathematicians, from Turing's machine to the clever von Neumann theorem on self-reproduction as no paradox. To a physicist the molecular realization of DNA still seems less important than the generalities of its functional structure. The few nucleotide symbols with low interaction, the great length, the helical coiling, complementary replication with the alternation of double helix and single helix—all these seem more general than any particular bases and bonds. It was Crick himself who saw in 1955 that what a single DNA base coil provided was not a set of holes for a long protein template but a spatial pattern of hydrogen bonds. He *predicted* the little adapter molecules that transcribe the code, a byte at a time. It was a glowing fusion of structure and function, and it opened the "tumultuous phase" of molecular biology that is now a richly elaborated scheme, neither mysteriously quantum-mechanical nor naïvely reductionist—nor yet all-powerful in the study of life.

(November 1975)

Adventures of a Mathematician
By S. M. Ulam

In 1949 radioactivity from the first Russian fission-bomb test contaminated the filters of an Air Force reconnaissance plane. Soon the theorists were set hard at work at Los Alamos and at Princeton: Could a fusion bomb be made? At Los Alamos "we started to work each day for four to six hours with slide rule, pencil, and paper." At Princeton the brand-new computer MANIAC was trying to catch up with the Los Alamos mathematician pair, the witty Stan Ulam and his taciturn partner of prewar days, Cornelius Everett. (Everett "used to say, 'I never make mistakes' and this was true. . . . " Once when Edward Teller maintained that Everett had made an error of a factor of 10^4, Everett became annoyed; eventually "Edward had to admit that it was he who was at fault.") Nothing worked; the device on paper would not ignite. Enrico Fermi and Ulam next showed that the paper explosion would not spread, and John von Neumann soon reported MANIAC's concurrence: "Icicles are forming." After a year's elaboration of the basic theory of thermonuclear explosion around a design that could not work Ulam had an extraordinary idea. He proposed a new scheme (which is still classified today), "a repetition of certain arrangements" that became the turning point for H-bomb work, and perhaps for all of us. A similar iterative scheme has presumably since been hit on in secrecy by ingenious people in four other countries.

Three distinguished mathematicians of our time have written well-known autobiographies in English: G. H. Hardy, Norbert Wiener and now Stanislaw Ulam. Ulam, the youngest, knew both of the others. Hardy's donnish disdain for the applications of mathematics and his enthusiasm for both cricket and militant atheism, like Wiener's touching expression of the life of an ex-prodigy who was childishly in need of repeated reassurance of his ability, display almost total eccentricity of style and thought. Ulam is not an eccentric but an urbane original; some of his mathematical inventions have led to profound consequences, one might say to the choice between life and death.

What Ulam tells us of his mind and his times is generally fascinating. He makes little effort to draw us into the mathematical content of his deep and varied work. He is, however, transparently honest, and he is effective in portraying his impatient, ironic and quizzical style, his ambitions, his estimates of others, his interests and his opinions with "a frankness and truthfulness which are sometimes a little strong but never really shocking."

His wordplay and comment draw now on the Latin of his excellent classical studies, now on the logical Jewish jokes of Central European cafés. When it was mentioned that Fermi would soon come to wartime Los Alamos, "immediately I intoned: 'Annuncio vobis gaudium maximum, papam habemus,'" as they say in St. Peter's when the white smoke heralds the election of a pope. Was not Fermi the infallible pope of the physicists? Later, when some mathematicians seeking Government contracts asserted the clear utility of their beloved work for national security, Ulam was reminded of the Jew who wanted to pray on Yom Kippur but tried to sneak in without paying for his seat on that crowded occasion by explaining he wanted only to deliver an urgent message. "But the guard refused, telling him: 'Ganev, Sie wollen beten' ['You thief! You really want to pray']. This, we like to think, was a nice abstract illustration of the point."

A score of such tales enliven Ulam's book, as they embellished the speech of Ulam and von Neumann throughout the years. Stefan Banach, Enrico Fermi, George Gamow and above all von Neumann were friends and colleagues of Ulam's. Banach was the master of his youth as a gifted student in Lwów, one of the centers of the great blossoming of Polish mathematics between the wars. "I recall a session with Mazur and Banach at the Scottish Café which lasted seventeen hours without interruption except for meals." Ideas and proofs flowed from those conversations. Then the decision came to leave war-threatened Europe. (Of more than one of his Lwów group Ulam writes: "Murdered by the Germans.") Ulam was first a Harvard research fellow and then a faculty member at Wisconsin, a rising mathematical worker.

It is von Neumann who came closest to Ulam. They had met first in Warsaw well before the war, and they were parted only by von Neumann's death. The two men were congenial, complementary, intimate. Von Neumann displayed a not uncommon "admiration for people who had power"; indeed, Ulam thinks that in von Neumann there lay "a hidden admiration for people or organizations that could be tough and ruthless." During von Neumann's last days Ulam would read to him, in Greek, Thucydides' gripping tale of the expedition against Melos, "a story he liked especially." Von Neumann was "remarkably universal" and yet avoided "tangents from the main edifice of mathematics." He died too young of cancer, a strict Catholic near death although he had been an agnostic in life, with an enormous reputation and every honor of the mathematical world, yet "not entirely . . . a mathematician's mathematician."

A mathematician such as Ulam works without external aids: no props, no equipment. Without chalk or pencil he may be at work even while walking, eating or talking. He seeks analogies between analogies. Such a person lives by this inner search and by the aid and the appraisal of a small set of peers. No wonder there is a certain detachment, a self-centered world view, an echo of fatalism. A few generous friendships of the kind that are candidly shared here with us are given to the lucky ones, but a certain coolness informs Ulam's estimate of men he found unclear, including Niels Bohr and Robert Oppenheimer. Most touching is the moment when Ulam, grievously ill with a virus inflammation of the brain, slowly recovers consciousness and speech. "One morning the surgeon asked me what 13 plus 8 were. The fact that he asked such a question embarrassed me so much that I just shook my head. Then he asked me what the square root of twenty was, and I replied: about 4.4. He kept silent, then I asked, 'Isn't it?' I remember Dr. Rainey laughing, visibly relieved, and saying 'I don't know.'"

Readers owe Ulam a debt for a book of reminiscent perceptions that have rarely been matched. A plausible conjecture suggests that we owe its coherence of form largely to an acute and sensitive Parisienne, Françoise Ulam.

(June 1977)

Berenice Abbott/Photographs
Foreword by Muriel Rukeyser
Introduction by David Vestal

This is a year of celebration: three American artists have displayed the ripe harvest of a lifetime of mastery. They are Louise Nevelson, the sculptor, Georgia O'Keefe, the painter, and Berenice Abbott. Only Miss Abbott's work is in a form such that readers far from New York can partake of the fruit, through this large paperbound book.

Here are about 125 black-and-white photographs, some given two pages and a few sharing one page with another. They fall into three quite distinct groups that among them clarify our times, apart from the absence of death and of war (although not of tragedy). Miss Abbott's style is one of precision: precision of eye, of mind, of tone value, of composition. She wrote: "If a medium is representational by nature of the realistic image formed by a lens, I see no reason why we should stand on our heads to distort that function. On the contrary, we should take hold of that very quality, make use of it, and explore it to the fullest."

We see first about 40 faces of Paris in the 1920's, portraits of the makers of art between the world wars. Miss Abbott worked initially with Man Ray, and here are the men and women she met at the time. Jean Cocteau, his pistol aimed directly at our eye; James Joyce, somewhat tired and gray but internally assured, and finally Eugène Atget, who sat for Miss Abbott so close to his last day that he never saw the print. There he is, a bridge to memory, "wearing," as it is put in the foreword, "the new overcoat of suffering."

Then we find not the brilliant few of Paris but the entire sweep of New York City, viewed mostly in the 1930's. Steam locomotives puff against a backdrop of skyscrapers; signs of shop and newsstand compose patterns that can still be seen; the gingerbread and clamor of the Barclay Street "el" station arrayed full face, and the steel frames of Rockefeller Center growing from the drilled bedrock, a Manhattan invariant. Cooler, and yet still tense, as beautiful and strange as the world of today's painters, are a last score of photographs from the 1960's. They are science, mainly physics: views of mirrors and of motions, strobe-light shots and close-ups, a foam of square and pentagonal bubble faces, a round colony of *Penicillium*, dotted by rich droplets of its healing liquor. Here is the famous crescent wrench, its center of mass moving superbly in a straight line as the ungainly shape gyrates around it. The poet writes: "Magnets here like faces. Actually, forces like faces."

In the copy at hand the usually reliable printers have allowed an intolerable grayness of tone.

(April 1971)

Working Knowledge: Skill and Community in a Small Shop
By Douglas Harper

Willie's shop, simple although not small, is a length of Quonset hut lying parallel to the paved road it adjoins, out in the hardscrabble farmlands tucked between the St. Lawrence River and the reserve of the Adirondack Park. The empty fields lie snowy and stubble-covered around it. The hut's dooryard is a crowded Saab heaven, where doze a couple of dozen old cars, a cache of parts for that esteemed product of Göteborg, accompanied by a random sample of less esoteric automotive ruin. For 10 years the ethnographer-author and Willie felt out time after time how to talk and work with each other, until 300 pages of transcript were there to be added to Douglas Harper's lengthy field notes and his sequences of photographs.

Now the ingredients have been made into a case study, as warm and lively as it is reflective, that records an important example of "material and folk culture. . . . I want to explain the way Willie has explained to me . . . to show a small world that most people would not look at very closely." Harper is a campus wordsmith, closer to grand ideas and far from the material. To approach the viewpoint there in the small shop he employed a powerful method (ascribed to the anthropologist John Collier). Called "photo elicitation," it seeks to organize the interviews around the photographic sequences. Willie would respond to the photographs. He is an articulate and thoughtful man, sometimes on sure ground, sometimes quite tentative and alert. Therefore he often demystifies "what . . . seems like an intuitive method" of repair, but in fact resembles, apart from calculation, the process of the design engineer.

Harper learned a good deal, just as many others learned who formed part of the shop's circulating group of customers: farmers, the occasional over-the-road trucker and exurbanites such as Harper himself with ailing and indispensable Saabs.

Willie was first taught by his father, a blacksmith who made the transition to auto mechanic as engines replaced horses. His work is not simply craftsmanship; that is not to say it is without craft. It is too improvisatory, imaginative, irregular and full of novelty to fall into the same category as the work of a journeyman who executes with skill the demands of a single trade. The base of Willie's working knowledge — this he shares with the craftsman — is the deep understanding of materials. In a setting where often he must design, invent and modify if he is to succeed, Willie handles a variety of materials: ferrous and nonferrous metals, plastic, wood, refractories.

Fixing is a narrower art than making; Willie is both constrained and proud to do both. Harper relates this style to prestandardized handwork, which was the rule before the artisans' trades were fully formed. It seems also a modern way, found not only on the isolated twig ends of the tree of industry but also wherever a product is made anew, in model shops, mixing rooms and tool cribs; it is an occupation for old hands, crew chiefs and serious young technicians, from Nagoya to Norfolk and Novosibirsk.

The touchstone is a degree of understanding. Those who approach repair as a matter of exchanging some broken part for the right replacement will never be mechanics. They know and see components but not the purposes and problems of design. Among the photograph sequences here several make plain what it is a mechanic can do. One brief page (with a drawing) shows what befell the white metal die-cast door handles that became through some small mistake part of the early Saab 99. The engineers were perhaps misled by matters of cost. The handles were made to be squeezed open, but the plastic ball bearings that bore the hand pressure on the lever would stick, break and fall out after "dirt and stuff" had worked on them. The metal was too weak to hold the pivot shaft for long against the force of a hard pull. The photographs show Willie filing and fitting a new stronger, smaller lever to trip the latch; there is no ball bearing. "The new ones have a different design. . . ."

The book is Veblenian, explicitly so in one sharp passage. It is the instinct of workmanship, said Thorstein Veblen, that is fundamental to human action, to constructive human behavior. Such a view goes beyond analysis to judgment. The last third of the book examines the social context of that shop in the Quonset. First of all comes the stubborn independence of its owner, and the degree to which out there in open country he does his best to avoid relationships (such as those with institutions) that he cannot conduct face-to-face. Next is Veblenian indeed, the impulse to teach: Willie's grown son is a mechanic of high repute, one schoolgirl daughter is already a resource in the shop.

Harper learned much, for "the shop becomes a school, and to get work done you must often become a student." It is no wonder that a community of visitors centers there. Willie has too much work; he allots his own time. He serves the farmers in need right out in their fields during cultivation or harvest. Others may wait interminably. Those who come back share in a certain social reciprocity: they listen, they wait, they lend an occasional hand. Plenty of people in self-interest or carelessness offend the implied rules and drift off; some are slowly brought back in. This is not at all an ideal world, but it is a real one.

Every day alienation grows; every day what they call de-skilling widens. The North Country itself will not change fast, although Willie, who sees this book as a lasting record of his kind of work, expects that such work will be gone soon enough. The dairy farmers begin to trade their equipment in sooner and the automobiles get more complex. Willie's story offers wider hope; technology does not demand, as even Doug Harper thinks, that we human beings remain captives of our own creations. It is not the complexity of machines that presents a hopeless imbalance. We can master any machine, except perhaps our most powerful weapons. What we must learn is how to build social institutions that reflect the spirit of the small shops.

(April 1988)

Akenfield: Portrait of an English Village
By Ronald Blythe

The Shell Book of Country Crafts
By James Arnold

"Village folk have been buried over and over again in the same little bits of churchyard . . . three or four sometimes. I always put all the bones back so that they lie tidy-like just under the new person." So says the gravedigger, come to witness. The 100 houses and 300 people of Akenfield in East Anglia can trace their village back to the Domesday Book. The two square miles of flat fields on the margin of the cold North Sea bear well, their yield of grain, livestock and fruit larger than ever before.

Fifty villagers, change ringer and smith, doctor and farmer, wheelwright and vicar, poet and pig farmer, tell their life story. These tales span the years of man and woman from 17 to 88, and they seek not only to narrate but also to explain and to justify. The stories were drawn out and surrounded by a commentary both beautiful and sharp by a novelist, himself a Suffolk man, whose art it has been to forge an intense and glowing form from these artless, intricate recollections.

The wind is doctrinal over this wide clay plain, "a quite unmysterious wind, dispelling the fuzziness of things. On a clear day . . . you can see as far as you can bear to see, and sometimes farther. It is a suitable climate for a little arable kingdom where flints are the jewels and where existence is sharp-edged." About 85 people work for a living in Akenfield (the name is fiction but the village is real); some 55 work directly on the land, and a number of others in farm-related trades such as flour milling.

The volume is a work of literature; it engages and it fascinates. It is history told by actors playing bit parts, like ourselves. It gains review here as science, as good social anthropology seized with questions wider than the Suffolk plain.

Class interest has ruled this land over the past century. After World War I the slow, silent men of the fields organized an Agricultural Labourers' Union. It was crushed by the farmers, themselves hard, proud, quiet and self-assured men, and "it took a brave man to show his politics in Suffolk all through the 1930s." Wages in the fields are still low but no longer are the young men able to see no future except a half-feudal life in a tied cottage with a claim on gleaning rights. The more imaginative people depart for the less satisfying but better-paying impersonal factory job in the ugly city. "These young men, they changed the farmers. . . . It was a good thing. Their power had got too great." "My father used to say that farm-working was bad pay but a good life."

Now there is factory farming, and the head plowman no longer walks behind the big, slow horses but drives his tractor. "[There is] about 400 acres of cornland and I plough it all." When the plowman's tractor stops, "the village experiences a similar kind of dragging silence to that caused by a clock stopping in a room." The penned hens and pigs are prisoners, and the veterinarian can "hardly bear thinking about" the chickens. The very hogs have changed, now reaching less than half the usual old weight ("With our pigs it is a short life—and a happy one." "It was a world of great pigs. The villagers needed all this fat . . . to keep them warm. . . . The Suffolk women won't buy fat now—perhaps it reminds them of [the] shivering men in the lea of the wind . . . chopping at pure white hunks of the stuff. . . . The miners still like it very much.") Work calories now come from petrol, and body heat is saved by plenty of good warm clothing. "You can hear the paper packs being torn open and in five minutes it's dinner. I don't call that dinner," says the old retired plowman.

The Suffolk mind is opener now, but it remains passive. Most of the people have traveled only in wartime, or to leave the land for good. ("While the others thundered their way through the multiplication tables . . . Michael made rag rugs with incredible speed and ingenuity. . . . He cannot read or write a single letter. . . . It is this which cuts him off. . . . Nobody seemed to realize that a child who could work so hard and who could make such good designs might have been able to learn if learning had been a less rigid thing.")

There is still the book fear that the young learn. They need to read now about pigs and engines, but they reach no further. The magistrate thinks that television doesn't touch the young people, "not yet, anyway." Once there were "scores of Peeping Toms . . . part of the old frustrated cooped-up feeling." Sex "used to be in the hedgerows and now it is in the back of the car." It was never as restricted as people imagined.

The reader will never quite leave Akenfield. The book will greatly reward those who seek in it a village in our day. Let Gran have the last word, as she waters her pot plants. The author writes: "A swing-wing bomber from Bentwaters knifes up the iridescent Akenfield afternoon, its scream momentarily and intolerably trapped in the cottage. 'Blessed Yanks!' says Gran — 'If ever I should swear!' "

Smith, wheelwright and roof thatcher still ply their trades in Akenfield. The master smith there is busy and prosperous, signing his name, as his predecessors never did, to the output of his forge, now almost entirely ornament. *The Shell Book of Country Crafts* is a fulfilling complement to *Akenfield*. In its own right it is a general reader's guide to the cunning crafts of woodland and coppice, anvil and reed roof, and 35 other specific trades of preindustrial Britain. They are each well described, with history, surroundings and a sketch of the craft, its tools and its product. The plaiting of the corn dolly from dampened golden wheat straw to adorn the last load of the harvest grain is Neolithic and continent-wide. The farmers' wives in the Akenfield Women's Institute are reviving the practice ("How dare you think of putting a pagan idol in our church!"), although it was always the men who made them in the old days, and an aging woman near Akenfield had a "kind of goddess wrapped in a plastic bag" that she had watched her grandfather plait. A dolly called "the Suffolk horseshoe" is here in a photograph; it is the old Earth Mother transformed and tame.

(October 1970)

Gypsies: The Hidden Americans
By Anne Sutherland

Gypsy on 18 Wheels: A Trucker's Tale
By Robert Krueger
Edited by Sam Yanes

Real Gypsies are the subject of the Sutherland book, "an ethnographic description of a group of American Rom" as they lived about 1970 in a "depressed town of substandard housing" in northern California, "its most noticeable feature being the maze of railway tracks that form natural boundaries for the various ethnic groups."

The Gypsies call themselves O Rom. They belong to the quasi-nomadic folk, now spread all over the world, who speak a Sanskrit-derived language they call Romanes. It is 1,000 years, more or less, since their ancestors left the north of India and began their wanderings. In all that time, over four continents, through profound economic and political changes in the host lands across which they have nearly always moved as a tiny, outcast minority, they have remained unified, distinct, recognizably as they were described in medieval Europe. The question that motivates this acute and technical field study by a young Oxford-trained American social anthropologist on the faculty of the University of Durham is: How have they done it?

The author is pretty convincing, even though her answer is trendy. The Rom live in a world of social experience cleft into purity (*wuzho*) and pollution (*marime*). All that is non-Rom (*gaje*) is morally wrong. The *gaje* are polluted. They do not even know to keep the upper and the lower body strictly separated, as the Rom do. Let the living room be strewn with discarded food to be swept out into the yard every day. No matter. The house stays pure if the six classes of laundry (male and female, tops and bottoms, food and children) are kept separate, and if food is never handled by *gaje* or by the temporarily unclean. To eat, to sleep or to work among the careless outsiders is manifestly to risk the danger of *marime* and of eventual ejection from the Rom. The Rom always try to cooperate; they work together and not side by side with *gaje*; they must be free to travel widely to fulfill their social duties centered on marriage rites and death rites. The Rom families that are studied here, about 300 people in 33 households, spent almost half of their time away from home, traveling.

The economic life of the Rom, constant through superficial change, remains based on the extraction of support from the *gaje*—shameless people who can command no respect yet are the only possible source of a livelihood based on mobility and separation. Horse trading gives way to coppersmithing; the tinker's art becomes fender-fixing; there is always itinerant farm labor—and now there is welfare, the chief income source for this sample. For 1,000 years the Rom have been persuading *gaje* to give them money on one slender pretext or another: tea-reading or palmistry, doctoring lame horses or fiddling in the street. They have become fully adapted to the way of the hustle. Welfare is only the latest hustle, further proof of the deep gullibility of the *gaje*. Read the I.Q. estimates made of certain Rom who played retarded to avoid having to accept employment. These clever people elicited results such as: "An I.Q. score of 64 . . . a mental age of about ten years. Thinking was markedly concrete . . . motor performance was also poor. . . . Retraining does not seem feasible." But the subject of that report told Sutherland: "The trick is never to protest anything but act like you are doing everything right. . . . I just give some wrong answer . . . there was a picture of this doll, and I was supposed to connect the arms and legs. Well, I put the legs in the armholes and the arms below. She kept trying to help me but I stuck with that like I was sure it must be right." That is the subtle art of pretense, which informs the petty deceits and pilfering long associated with the Gypsies. They are almost never violent and generally engage in a fully temperate parasitism that avoids deep damage to the host. It is a social adaptation.

And the Rom steadily adapt. They remain generally illiterate, although the need to move within a bureaucratized society has begun to persuade them that writing is useful. The most prolonged contact with the Rom the author reports was her time as the principal of a church-supported, Gypsy-controlled "Romany school," which was intended to allow their children to acquire literacy without losing the values of the Rom. Costumes change. The men dress colorfully, with Stetsons, gold badges and flashy colors, but fundamentally in *gaje* modes; children wear normal clothes. Only the women hold to distinctive dress: the 10-yard skirt and a low-cut blouse, echoes of the basis of *wuzho* and *marime*.

The book tells much more, particularly about the complicated kinship system and the elaborate social groupings of the Rom, from the level of "the tent" to the lineage, the community and the tribe. There are documents of Gypsy trials (transcripts of recorded narratives), a glossary of Romanes terms and a critical bibliography. (The reader is warned not to generalize much beyond this one examined community.)

It is not likely that the Rom will be assimilated, although the possibility is constant. Official recognition is the newest hazard they have encountered (they were named an official U.S. minority in 1972), and it may increase their vulnerability. Soon there will be nowhere to go, and territoriality may become their only means of preventing overexploitation of the *gaje*. In Europe a proposal for some Romany Zion has even arisen among them. Once long ago in Romania they were enserfed and settled; that influence is strong still, but it has not integrated the Rom. Their travail of hidden superiority preserves among us a lasting example of human wit and ingenuity, a touching, even romantic memorial to conscious solidarity, to the enduring power of the social recognition of "purity and danger."

The metaphorical gypsy — not the real one — is the theme of the book by Robert Krueger. No work of social science, it is an extraordinary evocation in fine photographs and an edited text: a set of first-person

narratives by truckers themselves of the way of life of the owner-operator
of a five-axle, 18-wheel diesel rig. These lonely blue-collar entrepreneurs,
mostly men but also "a few brave women," roam the concrete ribbons of
the Interstates as the merchantmen from Tyre roamed the wine-dark sea
3,000 years ago. They are profoundly integrated; indeed, theirs may be the
very archetype of American life today. Consider the symbolic intensity of
the highway system itself, the diesel fuel and its tax load, the overarching
mortgage, the Teamsters Union and General Motors, the citizen-band
two-way radio, Radar Alley (where lurks Smokey the Bear), the universal
truckers' café and the waitress's high blue hairdo, the disc jockey and his
country music, Benzedrine, five national trucking publications — and
always one ironic dream: "The problem is that a truck is . . . something
that can be taxed, but it can't vote. . . . The truck driver [is] Don
Quixote all right, but . . . he charges bureaucracies. He could be so free,
like I always dreamed. Workin' hard but havin' fun." There is the dream
made visible in the frontispiece rig pounding up the long smooth hill at
Raton, N.M., nothing else moving under the wide sky.

> I got ten forward gears and a sweet
> Georgia overdrive,
> I'm takin' little white pills and my
> eyes are open wide.
> I just passed a Jimmy and a White,
> I'm passing everything in sight,
> Six days on the road, and I'm going
> to make it home tonight.
>
> *(January 1976)*

The Smugglers: An Investigation into the World of the Contemporary Smuggler
By Timothy Green

Cool and elegant, she sat there across
the corridor of the rocking train, on her slender wrist the massy gold
bracelet, with its finials of lion heads, that could have come only from the
time of Troy! The young British archaeologist bound from Istanbul to
Izmir could no longer contain himself; he sprang the trap. Anna Papastrati
was fascinating; she took James Mellaart to her home and allowed him to

sketch an archaeological treasure. It was the burial hoard of an ancient princess, and about its discovery Anna spoke excitedly but evasively. Mellaart got permission to publish his sketches, but the promised photographs never came. Anna was never seen or heard of again. The Dorak treasure also disappeared; it was never seen by the Turkish authorities. Anna's bracelet (or, as the owners say, a match to it) can be seen in a photograph reproduced in *The New York Times* on December 31, 1969, part of a 10-kilogram gold hoard datable to before 2500 B.C. The treasure has now surfaced as a gift for the Boston Museum of Fine Arts in its centennial year. Why the romance? Presumably an able group of smugglers wanted to establish the authenticity of their valuable finds, and Dr. Mellaart was an incorruptible (if susceptible) appraiser on the spot.

This volume covers art, gold, drugs, guns, people, watches and other commodities in the illicit trade of our times. Its raffish tale is well told, with much detail and documentation in the best style of the London weekly where Mellaart published his sketches, by the paper's former editor on the basis of interviews with both sides of the law around the world, and of loving study of the press and of the police dockets.

The largest single smuggling trade today is the flow of gold bars, all of them the smooth little bonbon size, to the merchants and landowners of the western states of India from the little port of Dubai. That excellent harbor is the capital of a sheikdom of the Trucial States, on the coast where the Arabian peninsula sends out a tooth to narrow the Persian Gulf. Dubai is a quiet, hot, coastal river town, but a dozen dealers there own busy teleprinters rattling with the London gold prices, and the sleepy dhows in the harbor, their deck cargo oil drums and pilgrims returning from Mecca, can waken spectacularly if Indian customs boats draw near. The dhows have modern marine engines below their lateen rigging. In 1968 smugglers brought many millions of dollars worth of gold to the seashore grounds of the Tata Institute and the Atomic Energy Establishment in the beautiful Bombay suburb of Colaba. The guards could be bribed; who would expect contraband to enter such secure government property? The trade is about $150 million a year; a few percent falls into the hands of Indian customs. It is by no means certain that this centralized and measurable trade—perhaps 95 percent of the illicit gold flow to India—is not preferred by the Republic to the universal permeation of the border that existed before the traders of Dubai became active (with much Lebanese capital).

Archaeologists and the engineers thus have a place in smuggling. So have chemists. There are currently two centers of preparative organic chemistry in the smuggling world. One is London, where the task is to prepare LSD from the intermediate ergotoxine. The base drug is supplied from Hamburg, although the manufacturers are in Hungary and Czechoslovakia, working for licit pharmaceutical industries. LSD sells wholesale (the price is falling) for some $1,500 or $2,000 a gram, a threefold markup on the materials cost. Since 1967 the London police have seized nearly 200 grams of the stuff in raids on two separate laboratories: about a million doses, intended mostly for the U.S.

The second chemical center is on the Riviera, where the Corsican operators of the high-priced heroin trade maintain their laboratories. It is the purity of the heroin that determines price: "The French stuff is the champagne of heroin." Here the chemists toil on the kilogram scale, not on the microchemical level of the LSD workers. Heroin is worth only its weight in gold—a dollar or so per gram.

This is a sad, witty, adventurous and convincing book.

(March 1976)

Children's Games in Street and Playground: Chasing, Catching, Seeking, Hunting, Racing, Duelling, Exerting, Daring, Guessing, Acting, Pretending
By Iona and Peter Opie

Voltaire was delighted by Newton, who stayed home with his calculations and yet found the figure of the earth as well as did the Paris astronomers who voyaged to Peru and to Lapland with their costly instruments. Modern ethnographers working deep in the bush, and we who read them, may even more excusably envy and admire the Opies, who extract the details of a marvelous culture from the children in the streets around them. That learned and tireless couple devoted the decade of the 1950's to collecting and recording the lore and the language of schoolchildren, and the 1960's to assembling less verbal parts of that culture. This volume (we are promised another one on games, such as ball games and marbles and hopscotch, that depend on special equipment) is concerned "solely with the games that children, aged about 6–12, play of their own accord when out of doors, and usually out of sight." The string of participles in the subtitle is as good as a review. More than 10,000 children have been their informants, and "there is no town or city known to us where street games do not flourish." Adults, even boys of a ripe 14 years, sometimes maintain that the games are past, because the games are past for them. Even perceptive novelists and professional students of the street have had this illusion, but although the games change, they remain robust and ubiquitous.

Adult interference does weaken a game, and the games given official place in park and playground by well-intentioned people become less popular. There has been a decline of games in which one player is repeatedly buffeted by the others. Novelties arise too, so that the knife game split the kipper has all but driven out mumblety-peg, at least in Britain, after more than 400 years. (The older game is played from New Zealand to Poland, and you can find it in Brueghel's painting.) Conkers, a battle fought with strings of horse chestnuts, is a new version of the game played with hazelnuts until a century or two ago, when the newly introduced horse-chestnut trees provided a better (and inedible) basis for the game.

The Opies provide an account of each game, its rules and its names variorum, its appeal and circumstances of development, and a passage of historical and foreign parallels. The seeking game kick the can (tin-can tommy is its basic name in London) is the game that most commonly disturbs the "repose of the back streets"; the catching game Farmer, farmer, may we cross your golden river? ("fascinating to little girls, partly, it seems, because of the way it draws attention to item after item of their clothing") is the most popular game in British streets today. The U.S. is knowingly treated, although Britain is the main site of the fieldwork.

The authors are indignant that this free culture of children is restricted, both by unneeded efforts to domesticate it to school and other adult-dominated uses and by physical elimination of the complex and obscuring environments in which the games best flourish. These ritual romances and combats thrive alike in the fresh greenwood and in the shabby warrens of the alleys and streets of the city, but they cannot thrive in aseptic, flattened, unobstructed areas of paving called playgrounds or school yards.

Like all human culture, the culture of children is self-perpetuating, but it is not aloof from other cultures. Television has had a marked impact. Games have spread with armies of occupation, with emigration, under a hundred influences. Games arise too from the witness children bear to what we do. In Auschwitz the children "were seen playing a game that proved the most terrible indictment ever made against man, a game called 'Going to the Gas Chamber.'"

There are several interesting maps and some excellent photographs of children at play.

(January 1971)

IV

Physical Sciences and Their Instruments

From telescope and microscope to the theory of light quanta, of the chemical elements, and of the great conservation laws, these admirable books open a few doors into study and lab. Two treat the unexpected technical foundations of sport.

The Invention of the Telescope: Transactions of the American Philosophical Society
By Albert Van Helden

Galileo was not one quick to rush into print. Eighteen years a professor in Padua, he had published only two books, one an instruction manual for a geometrical instrument he had invented and sold out of his own private workshop, the other a witty polemic against a Padovan student who had sought to rip off that very instruction book! But from the time Galileo first heard of the spyglass of "a certain Fleming" until his book *The Starry Messenger* opened the Copernican universe to our extended senses, just 10 months elapsed. He was onto a good thing, and he published it first, in March of 1610.

There were probably three men who had telescopes by early in October of 1608. At the autumn fair in Frankfurt that year a Dutchman was offering one for a high price. And it was not a novel idea to look through such an instrument at the stars. The first printed account from the Hague mentions that the glass showed new stars in the Pleiades, months before any telescope came to Paris, Milan, Venice or Naples. But Galileo worked hard and well, he had the help of a master craftsman in his own shop, he had access to selected lots of the best Venice glass, he ground scores of lenses and chose the best of them, he grasped the importance of a steady mount and he invented an aperture stop to correct the faults of his high-powered lenses. There is no doubt that his was a magnificent and purposeful development, even though it was not an invention; he described the new cosmos, beating out Thomas Harriot, Simon Marius, Christoph Scheiner and the wonderful Paris amateur Nicolas de Peiresc, all of whom were gazing at the sky through telescopes at about the same time.

Professor Van Helden's fascinating and learned little monograph includes Galileo; it focuses, however, not on him but on the "certain Fleming," whoever he was. We see the main evidence in this long detective story: 30-odd key passages from books, letters, journals and official documents, in the original Latin, English, Italian, French and Dutch, all with clear translations. The documents begin with Roger Bacon, who wrote in about 1250 of "Glasses so cast, that . . . starres shine in what place you please." They end with a long passage of 1655 from a book seeking "the true inventor of the telescope" and finding him in an artisan of Middelburg in Zeeland.

One reads the 1609 letter of Giovanbaptista della Porta himself, who says of the new Dutch wonder: "I have seen it, and it is a hoax, and it is taken from the ninth book of my *De refractione*." Nevertheless, the noble Girolamo Sirtori pursued the glass over all Europe, seeking experts who could grind usable lenses. He examined and measured Galileo's own tube and lenses at that famous dinner of the Academy of Lynxes in Rome where the word "telescope" was coined in the spring of 1611, yet he was not able to duplicate the success of the Tuscan artist.

There is a famous journal entry that cites a statement (against self-interest) made by the son of Sacharias Janssen, the strongest candidate for the designation of inventor, suggesting that the father (an unsavory character, a convicted counterfeiter) "made the first telescope in this country in the year 1604, after one belonging to an Italian which bore the date *anno* 190." (Stillman Drake thinks the error was for 1590; since the text clearly intends a date, 1590 is hard to fault.) Another claimant is a Florentine, Raffael Gualterotti, who wrote Galileo in April, 1610, asserting that he, and no Dutchman, was the inventor: "It is now twelve years since I made an instrument . . . for the benefit of a cavalry soldier. . . . A feeble thing."

How can all this be true? How can the telescope have become the cynosure of Europe in a year or two after 1608 and yet have remained unknown for a decade or more before that? Professor Van Helden, a historian at Rice University, offers a persuasive explanation. The erect-image two-lens instrument was indeed not very new. It had been found quite naturally during the 1590's by combining the then common lenses of the spectacle makers. It was of some help to myopics, but its lower power and poor lenses made it a thing of no great virtue. The early optical experimenters, on the other hand, were hoping for wonders like the glass of Roger Bacon's dreams. There was no excitement in "a feeble thing" with magnification well under two diameters. But the concave lenses for the myopic grew better, their focal lengths shorter, the glass clearer; and one of those clever Middelburg artisans, or more than one, saw a new potential. The magnification, close to threefold, was striking.

We can see now, however, that in a way "'telescopes' existed before anyone, *including the men who made them*, were aware of them." The key point was the development of effective higher magnification. That began near Middelburg when the utility came clear. The rich, the curious and the military seized on the device. Galileo speedily developed the concept, pushed the workable power up to near 30 in a few months and put it to work penetratingly. Once the news got around more than one man realized he had already long possessed the same device, but with low magnification and used in a very different way. Quantity is the hero of this story, as it is of much science in the post-Galilean years.

Old Gualterotti put it well: "'Astonishing' will never seem to me what I shall [have to] say about the accomplishments of the Florentines."

(June 1978)

Single Lens: The Story of the Simple Microscope
By Brian J. Ford

The young microscopist had been studying the work of Antony van Leeuwenhoek, trying to decide how the simple microscopes that pioneer had built could have worked as well as they apparently did. Although in 1981 professional historians were halfway through the editing and publication of the large number of Leeuwenhoek's letters long kept in the vaults of the Royal Society of London, Brian Ford wanted to look at the originals for himself. "As I lifted the final leaf of Leeuwenhoek's letter of 1 June 1674, it felt heavy. Pasted to the back of the last blank page was a white paper envelope . . . "

On the book's next page we see a photograph of the contents of that long-unseen envelope, taken after the envelope was opened, the scholar's breath firmly held. They were four small packets of folded paper annotated in the hand of the old Dutch amateur. Each had held a specimen prepared with care by Leeuwenhoek himself for the microscopists of London, and three of the specimens were still in place. A little farther on we see the first specimen found, a section of cork, sliced skillfully with a sharp open razor, the image made at a magnification of 266 diameters through a surviving Leeuwenhoek microscope still held in Utrecht. (A few of Leeuwenhoek's own red blood cells are shown in an electron micrograph. They were found on the surface of another specimen he had cut; no one can avoid leaving some red cells on the blade after a shave. Their unlysed condition implies that their source had shaved with a dry blade, although just possibly it was a cough that sent them there.) Others had seen some of the packets before (nine turned up in the files) but no one had examined them with any care. One set was missed because the translator, working from microfilm copies, mistook the images of the labeled and pasted packets of dissected cottonseed specimens for "drawn rectangles" at the end of the old letter.

This informal, iconoclastic, personal book is both persuasively argued and well supported by modern expertise engaged in firsthand experiences with evidence from the past. The author seeks out and refurbishes the old instruments to see how they work, a powerful method open to historians of science and technology. The author and a Dutch lens expert, J. van Zuylen, measured the magnifying power of all nine of the simple microscopes currently ascribed to Leeuwenhoek. (He may have made as many as 500 of them during his long life.) Five of them magnify clearly by more than 100 times; the most powerful, the lens now in Utrecht, is in fact somewhat nonspherical, which improves its field of view. It was made without any signs of polishing; van Zuylen and J. Nieuwland have since made a similar lens, like a tiny bead, in their own glass-blowing flame. Leeuwenhoek indeed claimed that he had found "a useful way of blowing lenses which were not round."

Some unknown attic in London may hold today 26 of Leeuwenhoek's earlier microscopes, "ground by myself, and mounted in silver . . . almost all of them in silver that I extracted from the ore." Silver is costly, but it is softer and easier to work than brass. His daughter sent those instruments to the Royal Society as her father's legacy, arranged and labeled in a "small Indian cabinet" carefully prepared long before by their fabricator. The microscopist Henry Baker, drawing and describing them 20 years after the legacy had come, remarked in a footnote: "At the Time I am writing this, the Cabinet of Microscopes left by that famous Man . . . is standing upon my Table." No more. That cabinet and its contents are lost. Their last known borrower, in about 1820, was an eminent London physician, a man who published many microscopic illustrations made by able technicians in his employ. An unsuccessful search by the Royal Society in 1855 left a tangled tale. The silver devices remain a tantalizing lost treasure, although less of a marvel than the unmatched specimens Ford came on a few years ago.

The botanist and microscopist Robert Brown, for whom we name the motion of all tiny particles recoiling from the random rain of molecular bombardment, carefully studied that phenomenon in 1828 under his simple microscope. He called the moving bits "active Molecules." Since he noticed them first in flower pollen less than a year old, it seemed natural to him that they might be some microscopic form of life. But after a very careful study of dead and fossil organic specimens, including "a fragment of the Sphinx" within a long list of mineral and rock powders, he found that any substance he could powder finely enough to suspend for a while in water shared the incessant motion. His paper was firm in its conclusion that the motion was neither animate nor the result of currents or evaporation. He never claimed original discovery; others he cited had reported the motion before him.

The author has found Brown's microscope too, dirty, blackened and damaged, and has made it workable. Quite likely it was the very one peered through by young Charles Darwin when he visited the secretive old botanist in London while Darwin waited for the readying of H.M.S. *Beagle*. Darwin later wrote of what he saw, "I . . . believe now that it was the marvellous currents of protoplasm in some vegetable cell," but all the old man would answer to Darwin's questions was, "That is my little secret." Years later Brown published an account of streaming protoplasm in the giant stamen hairs of the spiderwort. Brown ought to be still better known for his recognition and naming of "a single circular areola, . . . or nucleus of the cell as perhaps it might be termed" in each cell. He reported them in many cells of many monocot plants and sometimes in the epidermis of dicots.

Again the discovery is convincingly re-created: through Brown's simple microscope we see cell nuclei quite clearly. In his day the best simple microscopes of the London makers were indeed excellent; they had workable fine adjustments, convenient stands and optics of good quality that could achieve magnification of about 200 powers. This high state of the art brings us to the book's thesis: that the mid-19th-century compound microscope with its optical corrections and conveniences was no precondition for the grand rise of microbiology and the "mushrooming awareness" of microstructure. In fact, it was the simple lens that had made the great earlier breakthroughs, and an instrument as good as van Leeuwenhoek's little Utrecht beauty might easily have served for the discovery of pathogens and for most of the structures resolvable by today's optical microscopes.

Ford's case is strong that the single lens has been underestimated. Its harvest has been rich, and its best performance is demonstrable to a resolution of about one micrometer at an enlargement of close to 300 times, or a bit better. Over the past century the use of well-corrected high-power oil-immersion lenses has brought the resolution down to less than a third of a micrometer. The change is not large, but it may well be important; a clear gain in resolving power by a factor of two or three is not to be brushed aside. Very possibly the arcane art of staining and the refinement of sectioning and fixing techniques were even more important.

The book has much more to say. Ford pretty well clears up the story of the alleged lens from Assyria: not optically usable, it is a striated rock-crystal ornament of the eighth century B.C. He makes a good if rather subtle case for the fact that merchant van Leeuwenhoek began his microscopy on seeing Hooke's best-seller *Micrographia*. The making of simple bead lenses is outlined by Hooke, and van Leeuwenhoek's specimen gifts to the Royal Society recapitulate Hooke's choice of early samples. Not all citations in this book are as complete as they might be, and there are no footnotes.

It is artifacts more than texts that Ford is pleased to read. It would be splendid to see him compare his fine single lenses with the compound microscopes of high Victorian days. Bacteria may be shown well enough by the single-lens view; perhaps it was more the pure-culture techniques of Koch and Pasteur than fine new microscopes that led to classical bacteriology. The dance of the chromosomes is certainly one major performance to which the lenses of the past, single and compound, should be brought in Ford's adept and critical spirit. Clio needs to be made fully at home at the laboratory bench, and this microscopist and writer has already welcomed her there.

(July 1985)

Album of Science: From Leonardo to Lavoisier
By I. Bernard Cohen

Historians of science are tireless con-
struers of the word. This fine collection is exceptional; its Harvard com-
piler, a teacher and scholar well known for his authoritative and detailed
studies of the work and times of Newton and of Franklin and for his lively
book for the general reader on the rise of dynamics, has taken us to the
stacks of rare books. But there we enjoy not texts but images, symbolic
materials closer to perceived reality. Ever since books were first printed,
multiple copies of illustrations have celebrated, enriched and (in fields
such as botany) authenticated knowledge and its accurate transmission. In
a thoughtful blend of the indispensable and the fresh ("I believe that there
are no readers who will be familiar with all of the illustrations in this
book") Cohen reproduces a wealth of engravings, etchings, woodcuts and
drawings.

Most of the 368 illustrations are indeed from printed books; some
excellent ones enter from manuscript or gallery wall, and there are a few
photographs of artifacts. This grand library tour is systematically organized, and each picture is flanked by a paragraph to set it reflectively in the
context of the time of the rise of modern science. The library without
shelves is arranged in a couple of dozen sections. They owe much to
Harvard's own treasury of holdings but are indebted as well to Cambridge,
Florence, Bologna, Leningrad, Leiden, London and many other places
where the archives of the scientific revolution are stored. Each section is
headed by a page or two of comment by Professor Cohen, and the book
ends with a useful annotated bibliography for the reader who would go
further.

If Cohen has finally chosen 368 out of "more than a thousand
absolutely first-rate illustrations," here we can describe only half a dozen.
In 1612 Ludovico Cardi da Cigoli painted within the dome of the papal
chapel in Santa Maria Maggiore in Rome a panel of the Assumption of the
Virgin. The crescent moon is often depicted at the Virgin's feet; Cigoli is
true to that tradition, but his moon is cratered; it is the telescope's moon
first seen just three years earlier by Galileo, the artist's friend. We can
admire the observatory at Danzig (now Gdańsk), until Greenwich and
Paris the finest in Europe. It was private, and we see its keen owner-ob-
servers, Johannes and Catherina Elisabetha Koopman Hevelius, jointly at
work on the big sextant.

A remarkable manuscript drawing, found in a letter sent to Kepler in
1624, unknown until it turned up in Leningrad after World War II, shows
the first mechanical digital computer, a scheme with setting dials and

mechanized Napierian multiplying rods. The principle was extended to a line of successful calculators before World War I, but the original machine was destroyed by fire before Kepler could use it. Kepler's inventive friend at Tübingen was Wilhelm Schickard. Then there is a photograph of the elaborate silver microscope made in 1761 by George Adams for King George III. One can hardly reach the tube for the sculptured figures; usefulness is sacrificed to ornament.

A drawing made for eventual engraving shows Galvani's frog-leg preparation, which twitched each time a spark was drawn from the electrostatic machine nearby. A page of 64 small drawings is the pictorial specification of the proper portable chemical laboratory of 1689. The Frankfurt chemist Johann Becher had an inventory of apparatus quite like a position at any beginning chemistry bench of a few decades ago, without a Bunsen burner but including a glass-cased analytical balance.

The volume ends with the Enlightenment and with science institutionalized. Diderot's *Encyclopédie* acclaims faith in reason, and the hope for a social order as rational as that observed in the natural and technological world. We no longer see progress as a short-term certainty. Yet here too is the crowded collector's cabinet of the Copenhagen physician Ole Worm in 1655. The room contains a bizarre assortment, but there is a fine collection of worked stone implements, then considered to be only a kind of thunderbolt, not human artifacts at all. The history of mankind is slower and longer than they thought, even in the day of Condorcet and Franklin. Maybe there will still be time.

The reproductions are excellent; a few suffer from the necessary reduction in size. The volume is dedicated to Charles and Ray Eames, masters of the images of science, who joined meaning and form in our fast-flashing day.

(January 1981)

Perpetual Motion: The History of an Obsession
By Arthur W. J. G. Ord-Hume

By the time of the cathedrals the idea was already firm: an "uneven number" of mallets hanging on a wheel might make it turn of itself. In about 1640 the Marquess of Worcester probably did demonstrate such a wheel "fourteen foot over" and bearing 40 50-pound weights on levers to Charles I at the Tower of London.

(Inertia is impressive, and flywheels were almost unknown.) He gave a brief account of the wheel in his *Century of Inventions*, under the deadpan rubric *An Advantageous Change of Centres*. Water mills contrived to pump water up, subsequently to fall back down on the wheel, and a windmill-bellows cycle were drawn and sometimes constructed. There were skeptics. Bishop Wilkins wrote in 1648 that he "could scarce forebear, with Archimedes, to cry out 'Eureka!'" when he first had the waterwheel idea, but that experience and trial convinced him that the "stream, though multiplied, will not be of force enough to turn about the screw." Simon Stevinus used the unbalanced chain of balls running around an inclined plane to derive the equilibrium of nonparallel forces by invoking the impossibility of perpetual motion. "A wonder, and yet no wonder," he wrote. Nevertheless, in 1730 the best-known volumes of mechanisms still showed the perpetual cyclical machines, and frauds began to appear about then in various royal precincts. Hopeful patents continued to pour out. The first British patent for perpetual motion was granted in 1635, and there were 600 or more issued up to 1903. Most were Victorian in epoch, and the topic was discussed in the skeptical pages of *Scientific American* during the Yankee inventors' heyday.

Mere mechanisms came to lack mystery, and innovators, such as Jean Bernoulli, Robert Boyle and Sir William Congreve in their time, began to invoke capillarity (Congreve had weighted chains pressing unequally on wet sponges), asymmetries of buoyancy, magnetism, eventually motors and generators wired head to tail.

Enter the day of public frauds. Philadelphia housed two of them. The first, in about 1813, was displayed by one Charles Redheffer. "Incontestably a perpetual self-moving principle," it deployed a big gear driven by a small pinion. A clever young man noticed that these meshing gears had become worn on the wrong faces: power was coming in by way of the supposed output. Redheffer took his device to New York (but only after the ingenious Philadelphians had made up and showed him their own perpetual-motion machine. Driven by a hidden clock spring, it remains a masterpiece of indirection with little weights sliding on inclined planes, arranged so that the inner clockwork could not drive the wheels unless the pressure of the weights was present). In New York it was the redoubtable Robert Fulton who exclaimed as he entered the showroom, "Why, this is a crank motion!" He noticed the rhythm of an unseen hand, hardly to be expected from perpetual movers. Fulton knocked away some light wood braces that were there apparently to steady the machine. A catgut belt drive was revealed that led to "an old man with a long beard" turning the power crank in an attic room.

Some 50 years later John W. Keely, a Philadelphia enterpriser with a cool head but little education, sold shares in his "hydro-pneumatic-pulsating-vacu-engine" to thousands of Gilded Age speculators, who received a fine picture of it on their stock certificates. That engine drew "etheric force" from a thimbleful of water. The firm made millions from stock sales but sold not one joule of energy. After eight or 10 years of high living Keely was without support. The newspaper account of his struggles in poverty attracted a woman, newly widowed by the death of her wealthy husband, who became his benefactress. The Keely engine revived, now "vibratory" and calculated to take a ship across the Atlantic on a gallon of water. Until 1896 the issue was contested, in spite of the fact that skeptics had noticed hollow wires—represented as being solid—in nearly every piece of apparatus in Keely's laboratory. These were compressed-air supplies, people guessed, and so they turned out to be. After Keely's death, examination of his house revealed air ducts, moving magnets, shafts and hydraulic-pressure sources, all hidden in the walls and driven by a strong, silent spring motor in the basement.

There is active in southern California today a well-financed chemical-engineering project for releasing hydrogen fuel from water without cost in energy. Certainly the hydrogen is there; we all await the results.

Self-delusion is more disarmingly wholehearted than fraud. In 1918 an expert commission set up by act of Congress undertook official study of the project of an honest man, Garabed Giragossian. He had stirred the entire country, particularly the press, with his public offer: he asked only searching and expert scrutiny when the time should come for him to present the American people with his new scheme for free energy—perpetual motion at last. He had gone direct to Congress because he doubted the protection of the Patent Office. His invention was the fly-wheel! He saw that he could run his wheel, once it was started, with a 1/20-horsepower motor but that it delivered 10 measured horsepower every time it was braked rapidly to rest. Utterly honest, he had never grasped the difference between energy and power.

The book enters a few whimsical bypaths of interest. A clock made in the 1760's was powered by variations of atmospheric pressure, which induced small but reliable motions of the column of a barometer to wind up the weights. Mr. Cox's Perpetual Motion, a handsome cynosure in its time, did in fact run well on the bounty of the atmosphere for a lifetime; it stands mute today in the Victoria and Albert Museum, its heavy mercury load long since removed, a noble ruin. Ord-Hume can take some comfort from the fact that a well-known Swiss firm now makes a line of handsome and practical mantel clocks with the same never-wind virtue but with an aneroid chamber rather than a mercury column. In an Oxford laboratory today (we see its photograph) there is an electric chime run by two dry voltaic piles, potted in sulfur in 1840. The minute current still flows to strike the bells a few times a second, except when the humidity is too high.

The striker ball is wearing visibly, and below it lies "a tiny but ominous pile of metallic dust." Was this not the forerunner of modern low-power integrated circuitry?

There is good humor, generally careful history and physical sense in this well-illustrated nontechnical book by a British aeronautical engineer. Not every analysis is quite to the point, but there are many good ones. It is hard to forget Ord-Hume's own encounter in 1958 with a touching elderly Londoner who had made in his little flat a wonderful new aircraft engine that ran reliably at high power without any fuel. The author's natural question was might he see it? The polite reply was even more reasonable. Of course, it had been working just out there in the hall for weeks, but the inventor could not make it stop, and so the other tenants had insisted that he disassemble it completely to end the tiresome noise!

(November 1977)

Ultrapurity: Methods and Techniques
Edited by Morris Zief and Robert Speights

Once the concept of chemical purity had to be wholly constructive: a sample was only as pure as you knew how to make it. Nowadays we have an absolute standard, almost Platonic; a volume of space that contains only repeated modules of one single molecular structure, or of one repeated lattice unit, with all nuclear species of a single isotopic nature, is a pure sample. Such a sample scarcely exists; this technical symposium surveys the 20-year history of ever closer approaches to the ultimate. The contributors are English, German and American; they represent university and government research centers and the specialized preparative industries from which the best reagents come. The treatment is at a fully technical level, but the topic is so rich in ingenuity and understanding that it deserves some attention from many readers, certainly from teachers and students of chemistry at almost any level.

The alchemy of World War II, dealing with intensely toxic and scrupulously purified new radioactive elements, began the modern trends. The key idea then was to handle materials dust-free, for the protection both of the sample and of the worker. No sample is pure if it contains dust specks drawn from the air, even though they are insoluble and often slip past the ordinary analyst. The filters developed by the Manhattan project and its successors are still the standard: they are elaborate structures of submicron glass fibers. The individual filters are tested by measuring the passage of a carefully controlled organic smoke of known particle size. An approved filter catches 99.97 percent of the .3-micron particles of the smoke. Build the ceiling of the laboratory entirely of such filters, use a perforated grating for a floor and ventilate the room with a vertical draft of air, moving straight from ceiling to floor in smooth parallel flow at about 100 feet per minute. Now you should have a tolerably dust-free room, one with fewer than 100 particles as large as half a micron in diameter per cubic foot. It is routinely achieved, although not without painstaking attention to detail.

Ultrapure substances approach being the "universal solvent," not because of their high corrosiveness but because the almost inevitable small reaction with the container walls is ruinous to purity. The semiconductor industry must produce the purest of products, because the tiny mass of electrons and holes that course through their samples is disturbed by very slight impurities indeed. The chemical apparatus the industry uses is therefore mostly made of vitreous silica, purified silica sand or quartz crystal, electrically fused, with various surface treatments. For the highest grades of such material the silica is prepared artificially by oxidizing some pure silicon compound. This hard, clear, inert glass is perhaps the most broadly resistant engineering material commercially available. If you store acid or water in a small silica flask, you can expect one part per million of silica in solution in 10 years. In a good bottle of resistant normal glass the effect is 10 times faster. For a trace contaminant such as iron there is not much difference between silica and glass, but for a leachable component of glass—sodium—the difference is a factor of 100,000. Ultrapure water is surprisingly reactive; it attacks pure gum rubber "quite severely." Yet the ideal bottle for such water has been found. It is ice! The water is stored cold enough to promote "the formation of ice from pure water around the walls of a vessel." (The expert writing on the preparation of ultrapure water has the reassuring name of Verity C. Smith.)

The initial preparation of pure substances is of course highly specific to the substance. Nearly a dozen classes are treated here: water, alkali metals and their halides, organic solvents, proteins and more. Parts per billion of contaminants give the broad range of practical analysis today, whether for special impurities or for insoluble particulates. Preparation under an inert atmosphere or in a vacuum can remove even gaseous contaminants, which are generally hard to exclude.

This book is expensive in spite of its composition by typewriter; those in the trade are likely to find themselves directly repaid, but these technical chapters are also full of surprisingly broad insights for any browser with a concern for the nature of matter.

(April 1973)

The Periodic Table
By *Primo Levi*
Translated from the Italian by Raymond Rosenthal

Neither a chemical treatise nor an autobiography, this book is a set of 20 brief chapters of lapidary recollection ordered in time. They are bound with two short science-fiction romances and an essay on the odyssey of an atom of carbon, rather resembling a piece of T. H. Huxley's that has been given a contemporary sensibility. The rare quality of Levi's ideas and their compact expression earn this volume a place on the small shelf where stand the few books that serve to successfully express the self-examination of any life lived in or close to science. Those books include H. G. Wells's *Tono-Bungay*, a couple of the novels of Hans Otto Storm and C. P. Snow, that grotesque masterpiece *Gravity's Rainbow* and very likely the covertly artful *Double Helix*. Their common matter is the daily joys and sorrows, the indelible perceptions and the shared experiences, the community, real and vicarious, the rich lode of ready metaphor, the entire emotional cast of a mind at home in the laboratory. This text exhibits at large the clarity of the Alpine foothills, although the author cannot disguise an endearing old romance with philosophy.

Dr. Levi is by the most superficial account a "factory chemist" with three or four decades of experience in the paint and varnish industry of Turin. But he is also a literary figure of high distinction, earned by two earlier memoirs. Those books had a focal spot that was burning hot: Auschwitz. Levi, chemist, poet, philosopher, acute judge of the most diverse personalities and a writer of controlled intensity, was an ill-prepared partisan in the Piedmont, thereafter an inmate and a survivor of this factory of death. The well-planned furnaces of that place are not much seen in this book, although the strong moral distillate Levi condensed during his years of survival pervades these lucid, witty and in the end loving pages.

It is more of a service to excerpt so charged a work of art than to offer a critique at second hand. Remember that each chapter of the book is given the name of a chemical element, whose presence, real or metaphorical, informs the episode.

Try an early, poignant one, about zinc. "They make tubs out of it for laundry . . . [the metal] is gray and its salts are colorless . . . not toxic, nor does it produce striking chromatic reactions; in short, it is a boring metal." There is one saving detail. The metal, so yielding to acid, obstinately resists attack whenever it is sufficiently pure. Which philosophical conclusion is a thoughtful young man supposed to draw? "The praise of purity . . . I discarded . . . disgustingly moralistic. . . . The praise of impurity, which gives rise to changes, in other words, to life . . . I lingered to consider. . . . For the wheel to turn . . . diversity, the grain of salt and mustard are needed: Fascism does not want them, forbids them . . . ; it wants everybody to be the same, and you are not." Linked to his classmates by the "small zinc bridge," the shy student preparing zinc sulfate, knowing himself an impurity of the new regime, becomes "incomparably audacious." He walks home, arm in arm with a girl for the first time, with modest, pale Rita, who cooked the selfsame dish of acid in the same hood. She was no "grain of mustard" but a reserved young woman, for whom "the university was not at all the temple of Knowledge . . . [but] a difficult path which led to a degree, a job, and regular pay."

Consider nickel. Levi was unemployed, a new graduate but half-proscribed. He is engaged to work in an isolated asbestos mine in the mountains where a scheme has been hatched to extract nickel, precious in wartime, from the ample tailings. "I fell in love with my work from the very first day . . . nothing more at that stage than quantitative analysis of rock samples: attack with hydrofluoric acid, down comes iron with ammonia, down comes nickel (how little! a pinch of red sediment) with dimethylgloxyime . . . always the same, every blessed day. . . . But stimulating and new was another sensation: the sample to be analyzed was no longer . . . a materialized quiz: it was a piece of rock, the earth's entrail, torn . . . by the explosive's force; and on the basis of the daily data . . . little by little was born a map, the portrait of the subterranean veins. For the first time after seventeen years of schoolwork, of Greek verbs and the history of the Peloponnesian War, the things I had learned were beginning to be useful to me."

Try a comic sample, called after nitrogen. The time is the hardscrabble postwar years in Turin, Levi and his partner are eking out a living as manufacturing chemists, precariously set up in father's apartment. "Four resistors of 1,000 watts connected illegally upstream to the meter heat their reactor." A tough cash customer comes for a few kilos of alloxan, a red true stain suited for a new line of indelible lipstick, a compound hard to find in the market.

The library of the Chemical Institute is visited, by no means a simple matter. Alloxan is there in the books. "Here is its portrait. . . . It is a pretty structure, isn't it? It makes you think of something solid, stable, well linked. . . . From the *Zentralblatt* I ricocheted to *Beilstein*, an equally monumental encyclopedia. . . . The sole accessible preparation was the oldest . . . an oxidizing demolition of uric acid." Rare in the excreta of human and mammal, uric acid is 50 percent of bird waste. These creatures are frugal of water, able to dispose of their waste nitrogen not in dilute solution but in solid form. Gold from dung, cosmetic from excrement: the task "warmed my heart like a return to the origins, when alchemists extracted phosphorus from urine." The starting material was not cheap; the canny farmers had long sold their chicken dung for fertilizer at a high price, even if it had been gleaned by the hard work of the customer, and even if it was no fit raw material for the chemist—a crude mix of dung, earth, stone and chicken lice. Home a kilo came anyway on the bicycle carrier rack.

But in Turin an exhibition of snakes had just opened. Reptiles void pellets that are 90 percent uric acid. What an idea! "Out of the question, not even a gram," the exhibitors replied. Python pellets are very scanty, worth their weight in gold and long pledged by contract to the pharmaceutical companies. A few days yielded no alloxan from the well-sifted chicken dung either. "All I got were foul vapors, boredom, humiliation, and a black and murky liquid. . . . The shit remained shit, and the alloxan and its resonant name remained a resonant name. . . . Best to return among the colorless but safe schemes of inorganic chemistry."

End back in university days, with a chapter called iron after a young student, blacksmiths' kin, who seemed made of iron. (He became the first man of one Piedmontese Military Command to be killed fighting in the Resistance.) The class they shared was the classical qualitative analysis, with a challenging unknown sample daily. "The previous lab, where I had tackled zinc, seemed an infantile exercise to us now, similar to when as children we had played at cooking. . . . Not here: here the affair had turned serious, the confrontation with Mother-Matter, our hostile mother, was tougher and closer. At two in the afternoon, Professor D . . . handed each of us precisely one gram of a certain powder. . . . Report in writing, like a police report . . . doubts and hesitations were not admissible: it was each time a choice, a deliberation, a mature and responsible undertaking, for which Fascism had not prepared us, and from which emanated a good smell, dry and clean."

The book "is—or would have liked to be—a micro-history, the history of a trade and its defeats, victories, and miseries, such as everyone wants to tell" who has reached the age when "art ceases to be long." It became even more, a gift to those, young or old, who share in the legacy of man-the-maker and seek the boon of self-understanding. High praise is due the translator: not one phrase rings false.

(February 1985)

QED: The Strange Theory of Light and Matter
By Richard P. Feynman

The bowman knew that light traveled in a straight line whereas his arrow arched in flight. Any mirror broke that rule, although the ray bounce on reflection was orderly and simple enough. The steepening of the ray as light passed from air into denser mediums such as water or glass went a step beyond. The savants could derive all those rules from a single claim, that light traveled along the path of least time. Soon enough there were contradictory findings, narrow slits that spread light broadly and thin films that diffracted light into dazzling colors. No ray scheme at all would work. Mighty Newton himself could not apply his model of corpuscles with any consistency. Only cancellation and reinforcement of waves interfering along many paths could save the phenomena, and the full wave theory, eventually based on Maxwell's fields, ruled serenely.

It was not to last. Wave theories too were done in, by weak light. Radiophysics—a tide of the feeblest of photons, detected only in the aggregate—remains almost pure wave physics; a change in the frequency produces real trouble. For visible colors every photon detector "makes equally loud clicks as the light gets dimmer," although the photon clicks come less and less often. Light seems irretrievably dual, corpuscle and wave at once.

That puzzle has been resolved in exquisite practice, if not in words, since 1929, by the theory we call quantum electrodynamics, QED, the triumphant prototype of quantum field theories. Now, in four conversational and breezy chapters, with many diagrams and a great deal of qualitative geometric argument, Richard Feynman, who himself gave the theory its most useful and powerful form, undertakes without one equation to explain QED to the generality of readers.

We pay for our present unity of wave and particle by a single grand enforced retreat. All we now try to calculate is the relative probability of photon detection in space and time. We abjure exact predictions. "Yet science has not collapsed." For now the QED rule is general; it brooks no exceptions within all the phenomena of light. It subsumes the entire past, the ray paths and least time, colored films, spreading waves and equal clicks; it governs long-wave radio and ultrashort gamma rays with an equal hand.

Feynman shows that all you have to do to find the probabilities required is to draw and combine a vast family of spinning arrows. They are so numerous because they are sent every which way the light can possibly travel, not just along paths we might expect from a ray model. Each arrow spins uniformly, like the hand of a stopwatch, as it flies along. The rate of turning is proportional to the frequency of the light an arrow represents, 36,000 full turns per inch of path for red light. Combining is done simply by hooking the head of each contributing arrow at any point of detection to the tail of the next arrow until the final resultant arrow has been found.

The arrows start out with length proportional to the square root of the source intensity in their direction, color by color. They shrink as they spin and fly, their length dwindling proportionately to the distance traveled. The resultant composite arrow that takes account of every possible path to any point determines the outcome. The relative probability that a photon will be detected then and there is measured by the square of the length of the resultant arrow at any point, once again reckoning color by color. The weakest and the strongest light are treated in exactly the same way, whatever the frequency.

It is wonderful to follow the construction of arrows appropriate to simple reflection of monochromatic light at a plane mirror. There is no initial concern for equal angles of reflection; the arrows are let fly from the source in any direction that can reach any part of the mirror. But now the combinations are decisive. Most parts of a uniform mirror are not important reflectors, for the combining arrows that come from them point in many directions and add up to little. The bulk of the probability comes in fact from the expected region of reflection close to the equal-angle path, where the arrows are almost fully aligned. The process is not a case of empty cancellation: scrape the mirror coating away just in the places where the contributing arrows have a bias for one direction, and reflection then occurs at an unexpected angle, strong for only one color of light. The mirror has become a diffraction grating, "and it works like a charm." No weighty weapon of mathematics has been used, only a little school geometry and close argument.

The last two chapters go deeper, although they are less detailed. The paradox of interference patterns formed by photons that fall one by one on a screen behind two narrow slits is worked out in a clear way, even to a footnote on the effect of extra detectors that seek out which slit has the photon. We learn how to draw the famous Feynman diagrams, with their electron-photon junctions and their weird and wonderful embroidery of possible interchanges.

There is a secure guarantee of sanity: the electron charge is small, so that the more intricate the diagram is, the greater is the number of junctions along any sequence of alternatives in space and time, and the smaller is the diagram's contribution to the possible interchanges. Simple processes dominate.

The proud inventor tells us of the current state of computation of one fundamental property, the magnetic moment of an electron. That property demands at least one junction, one interaction between field and electron: the electron must, like a compass needle, heed at least one photon to represent the aligning magnetic field. The supercomputers are hard at work (in 1985) taking account of all paths possible that have eight extra junctions, 10,000 diagrams with some 500 choices each. Their total effect is evidently minute, but the experts are after high precision. That result should be precise well beyond the ninth decimal place, for which agreement with experiment is now good. (We miss an account of how it is possible to make such an elegant measurement, perhaps the most precise in all physics; the key to the work is that the moment can be expressed as a ratio of resonance frequencies.)

It is a little sobering that although these fundamental interactions can be splendidly mastered within the step-by-step framework, the scheme cannot yield results for all familiar quantum problems. Any process that requires a very large number of electron-photon interactions, for instance the stationary energy levels of electrons electrostatically bound into atoms, is not suited to the method. This limitation hardly casts a shadow on the theory, for it has been shown that the classical field theory does arise exactly from the diagram framework in the right limit. It certainly does, however, ensure continued use of a variety of descriptive schemes by theorists following differing lines of inquiry.

A final brief chapter includes an overview of the current extensions of quantum field theory into the domain of the quarks. Here are indeed "loose ends" (the chapter is so titled). There are fresh tables and blunt remarks here, not the closer argument that is possible in the simplest case of photons and electrons. Feynman does not glove his opinions; he cheerfully concedes messes and mix-ups in theories beyond QED, although he offers a prognosis of hope.

"Why are all the theories of physics so similar in their structure?" Our guide offers three explanations. It may be that physicists can only think of "the same damn thing, over and over," and have not yet found their errors. It may also be that Nature herself is repetitive. Or perhaps all our theories are aspects of one deeper picture, the grand final theory that has caught many minds. A fourth answer occurs to a reader. The questions we ask by experiment are certainly limited, for example by the averaging over space and time that every instrument must carry out. Perhaps almost every deep structure gives similar answers to the repetitive and approximate questions that so far are all we can ask.

Like a magician, Feynman enjoys misdirecting us with his inimitably slangy patter. Over and over he explains how absurd this theory is. And yet is it? It is unexpected, to be sure, but no more so than least time or waves in coupled electric and magnetic fields. Probably he is joking; in fact, he has here made his QED remarkably sensible, almost Q.E.D. The mathematically fluent will recognize well-known functions and integral methods here in playful geometric disguise, and will accept the treatment of spinless photons and electrons as a stand-in for technically more intricate reality. Students of physical science need to read this little book.

The adroit book-midwifery of Feynman's musical friend Ralph Leighton should once again be acknowledged; so should the Alix G. Mautner Memorial Lectures at U.C.L.A., which have their origin in a friendship that goes back to Feynman and Mautner's Far Rockaway years. William Stanton has graced this entire lighthearted enterprise of original pedagogy with his lovely jacket photograph of interference colors.

(October 1986)

Sport Science: Physical Laws and Optimum Performance
By Peter J. Brancazio

A basketball flies at low speed toward the hoop, feeling little effect from air drag. Fit for the simple analysis of projectile motion dear to introductory physics, its flight parabola is a cinch to calculate. Our guide here is a Brooklyn College professor with a physics textbook to his credit, who has long been a serious if wistful aspirant to excellence on the court, where he plays a few times a week all year round. He well knows why and how to compute the entire family of parabolas that link the hand to the hoop, the low-angle line-drive shot no less than the high rainbow one.

Which is best? Everyone admires the cool shooter with a soft touch, the player who uses the economical minimum of force to drop the ball in. The problem is subtler: that minimum-speed trajectory is also the one with the widest tolerance for error in the angle of launch, seven times greater than the error allowed to the flattest trajectory. After 20 years of mediocre line-drive shots our aging physicist-forward improved his performance dramatically once he understood the virtues of the right arch. Practice, with a friend or a coach to the side to help judge the height of the arch, will lead to success, based on "the way it looks and the way it feels." The arched shot calls for an exquisite touch, but it is plainly wise to cluster your long trial efforts around the right optimum.

This engaging book is actually not a how-to-do-it, although because it seeks a rationale for every technique it treats, it can help any serious athlete who has not gone beyond its modest scope. It is instead a volume to satisfy curiosity: how sports work, a book simple and timely enough for television viewers of the summer Olympics and the brightly lighted night baseball diamonds. It deals only briefly with muscle mechanisms and the kinematic evolution of running records. It has nothing much to say about the operations research of sports or the statistical choice of competitive tactics. The focus is closely on matter in motion: bodies, balls and bats, and the resisting medium they traverse. The reader is taken almost at once into the introductory physics of forces and torques, of moment of inertia and center of gravity, of energy and power. The treatment is concrete, so that the stereotypes of the elementary physics texts, all those ladders and falling stones, are replaced with point and freshness by examples that play a natural role on the athletic field.

Only the last chapters go beyond freshman topics; they offer a clear introduction to drag and lift forces in air and in water, treated offscreen, so to speak, by the author's home computer. His results are freely cited, but the book never demands from the reader much mathematical proficiency. Seventeen boxes present sequestered equations and numerical results, from unit conversions to terminal speeds in air. The agreeable way in which "customary units" — miles per hour, say — are employed, like the attractive pages on which commonplace Aristotelian intuitions are gently transformed into working Newtonian dynamics, are the mark of the able and experienced teacher.

The quantitative study of collisions first caught up the savants in good King Charles's golden days, although the modern beginner in physics is likely to be set the same questions. Colliding protons work at the frontier of physics, but little laboratory blocks sliding on their low-friction track are unmitigated pedagogy. Let a bat collide with a ball and the outcome becomes important to many more observers. A couple of dozen pages consider this urgent matter. All the parameters take on meaning. The ball's coefficient of restitution is itself prescribed by high baseball law: "The rebound . . . shall be 54.6 percent of the initial velocity, with a tolerance of ±3.2 percent." Soccer balls are livelier; tennis balls are deader. A good description is given of the bat-ball encounter, including some discussion of the effective mass to be ascribed to the player's hand grip.

Is it better to use a fast but light bat or a slower but heavier one? An early study of bat and ball collisions set an optimum mass much below the weights of bats actually in service. The problem is over-constrained; the best choice for ball speed is a long, thin, light bat. When the batter is at the plate, this choice is out, because such a bat has so small a hitting surface that few batters will risk it. The long, light fungo bat with which the coach hits practice fly balls to his distant outfielders is one realization of the best bat mass, but the coach has only to hit a ball he himself has tossed lightly into the air. The mighty Babe had wrists strong enough to swing a bat with weight half again the big-league norm, to magnificent effect.

Nowadays the aluminum bat has taken over amateur play in schools and colleges. It is indestructible, whereas wood bats often break. Direct experiment shows that the aluminum bat adds 10 percent to the length of a line drive. Moreover, the hollow metal bat ends the tight coupling between weight, moment of inertia, length and striking surface, freeing the batter to roam a parameter space undreamed of in the old days of ash. The statistics in the college leagues bear clear testimony to the new bat; batting averages are way up, and earned runs too. There is rough justice here. The golfer, the hockey player, the cricket batsman and the racquet wielders are all armed with flat striking surfaces. Only in baseball must the batter confront a fast-flying sphere with a circular cylinder. Making a hit is one of the most difficult routine plays in any sport; even the finest batters succeed only about one time in three. So far professional baseball will admit only the traditional wood bat. In the big leagues the war between pitcher and hitter is waged under arms control.

Air is the medium of most sports. The 16-pound iron shot can ignore air drag, which can shorten its flight only by a few inches out of 70 feet. Of the dozen balls whose terminal velocities are tabulated here, only those of golf, baseball and football enter often on long flight paths where aerodynamic effects shape the play. Professor Brancazio has computed drag effects rather simply, using plausible drag coefficients in a trial-and-error fashion to fit experience. Lift is even more complicated, particularly when it arises from spin. The low launch angle of a long drive in golf is a consequence of the high backspin-induced lift. A golf ball just off the driver head may well be spinning at 8,000 revolutions per minute. What are hook and slice but axes of spin slightly askew?

The dimples on the golf ball induce a turbulent boundary layer. In the prevailing regime of flight they decrease drag by reducing the size of the wake. At the same time the lift is increased. The dimpled ball flies better when it is well struck, but it also tends to hook and slice more easily. A golf ball with dimples on an equatorial band only, leaving the poles smooth, is a duffer's compromise. It is said that it curves much less often and falls short by only 10 percent.

It is baseball that "lives and dies" by the curved flight of a spinning ball in air. Wind-tunnel studies have shown there is a significant lateral deflecting force on a baseball even when it is not spinning. The origin of this force is the unsymmetrical wake induced by the raised seams on the surface of the ball. A very slow rotation can lead to a varying wake and a rather erratic flight: the magic of the knuckleball and the black magic of the spitball. There remains reasonable doubt whether or not the fast ball hops or the curve ball breaks. What is at issue is not the fact of curvature, of course, but the sharpness of those departures.

Both perspective effects and increased deflection with time cause the curvature to increase as the ball approaches the batter. Ballplayers say a good overhand curve looks as though the ball is "falling off a table." No smooth increase in curvature fills the bill. Perhaps the witnesses are overwrought. It is possible, however, that the stability regime of the wake is affected by the changing orientation of the seams. We admire the aerodynamic control of men such as Hoyt Wilhelm, an "outstanding knuckleballer" who pitched with success in the major leagues until he was 49; a noisy wake can bring unpredictable perturbations even to a ball thrown at modest speed by an old arm.

This informally written volume and its references also open a substantial recent literature of theory and experiment on the physics of the crawl stroke and cricket, of karate strikes and the angular momentum of divers in the air, of the "sweet spot" and the wonderful soaring flight of that massive Frisbee the discus, and much more. This is a fine place to begin the analysis; surely the end of these rich applications of physics lies well over the fence and far away.

(July 1984)

Phänomena
Edited by Georg Müller

The Book of Phänomena
A paperbound supplement with selected texts in English translation

In summer the wooded shores of Zurich's blue lake are cool and inviting. Across a few acres of that lakeshore there blossomed in the season of 1984 a remarkable garden. It is no longer there, but this engaging book documents in German text (the supplement helps readers of English) and many colorful pictures the short life of an "exhibition about phenomena and the riddles of the environment."

The largest flower there was a delightful multistory bamboo tower, 120 tons of the big stalks prepared in Kunming (Zurich's sister city in China) and then erected and artfully lashed into secure place by a Kunming delegation that would not deign to use any nails or screws. (Wood intermediate floors held on steel bedplates marred the purity of design, but they fulfilled local regulations and made the structure as useful as it was eye-catching.)

The spirit of Phänomena is clear enough from the 100 windwheels, resembling clustered white daisies a yard across, that spin in the breeze along every edge of the tower. Stairs and ramps led up, and smooth-lined chutes sloped down. Like this tower, the entire exposition joined playfulness to a varied invocation of the appearances of the world, often accompanied by apt auxiliary examples bringing understanding to the fingertips.

Gravity? A steel tower even higher than the six-story bamboo offering from the People's Republic of China is traversed by a superelevator whose floor consists of an open mesh. There are weights to hold and scales to step on as you brave accelerations of one-fourth of gravity up and down that provide an approach to weightlessness followed a few seconds later by a knee-bending load. (Commonplace highrise express elevators reach accelerations of one-tenth of gravity.) For a somehow opposite sensation, and an equally valuable exposure to physics, try the thrilling bicycle ride along the high wire, a safety net below. The feat could be managed here without practice and with only a modest amount of daring, since this bicycle carried a heavy counterweight six feet below the wire that assured stability to every novice circus cyclist. Messrs. Coriolis and Foucault and Euler were invoked (mainly anonymously) with spinning chairs and tables that made opportunities for tangible transfers of angular momentum.

Fluid flow? Admire a huge water bell, its 15-foot hemisphere of droplets shimmering above the lake surface, with a number of hand-size versions nearby to help tease out how it works. Add a six-foot water-vortex cone, a spinning wonder held captive in a glass cylinder for steady-state inspection. Smaller and more analytical, a long tank holds at bench height a glycerine solution doped with aluminum powder, in which turbulent flow is slowed and made visible around any barrier you drag along. There is a hydraulic computer, its fluidic oscillators and amplifiers open to view and manipulation. Flettner rotors and airfoil sections sail up a fan-sent breeze, and a one-ton granite sphere spins under the hand within a closely fitted opening lubricated only by the water of a natural spring.

There is a wheeled cart to ride as it jets ahead on rails, the impulse provided by bowling balls that roll backward off the car down a sloping track. A pendulous suspension bridge repays the wary pedestrian with safe but scary motion; a massive pendulum bob hanging beyond reach can be set grandly swinging by many feeble pulls on a slender thread—if the rhythm of repetition is resonant, but not otherwise. There are real, colorful minerals and crystals, including huge points of crystalline quartz, to admire and to gauge by hand; there are mock crystals made by mutually repelling bar magnets, held in tubes that themselves float in air flowing under pressure out of a much-perforated tabletop. Ride a cage hung from a tripod; it avoids the central vertical position because a big magnet in the floor abhors a similar one in the moving cage. (The magnets own up to 800 kilograms of distaste.)

Eye and ear are not forgotten. These displays were mostly sheltered within a few strikingly tensioned tents. Item: A facing pair of sound mirrors offer an open-air whisper circuit, and there is an echo tube one sound-second long. Item: A big geodetic dome is fashioned of mirror facets, so that those who wander within dwell for a while in a multiple kaleidoscope. Item: Heliostat-captured sunbeams are led within one room on a merry chase among mirrors and prisms. In another room 144 tuned tubes, long and short, hang from the ceiling; struck by a rod in the visitor's hand, they utter a spectrum for the ear that is subtle in its selection of overtones.

There were about 250 exhibits more, as small in scale as playful chromatography on filter paper (carried out for the pleasure of seeing the colored drops spread) or as large as a fiberglass parabola, 10 meters in diameter, collecting solar energy. The full book includes them all, and more: mathematics, illusions, mime, an innovative restaurant with Kunming chefs. . . .

Since 1968 the Zürcher Forum has organized hundreds of concerts, readings, exhibitions and days of celebration to win new friends for art and culture among the entire population of the city and the canton. Georg Müller conceived and then, over three years, built up this lively zoo of the phenomena of the world: the very ground of art and science, of our very life. Intended for the wide public, it could not have succeeded without widespread collaboration among engineering firms and skilled craftsmen, university scientists and ingenious designers and inventors, not to mention those construction teams from Yunnan, the masters of bamboo. A page or two on the budget of this enviable and solvent enterprise would have helped us understand it better. Swiss fiscal reticence?

It was bold to plant so fine a museum as one season's flower. Will other cities try it in their own way? The springs of this style are explicitly given; they are the Deutsches Museum of Munich and the Exploratorium of San Francisco. Many of the lakeside exhibits are to be seen now in the Exploratorium in similar form. Quite a few museums of science share in part the approach pioneered by the late Frank Oppenheimer, one that grows out of science itself: genuinely working displays, direct rather than symbolic, participatory rather than didactic, and openly hopeful of widely shared joy and understanding.

(September 1985)

V

Kingdoms of Life

The diversity of life past and present is sampled, and some behavior recounted. We watch the octupus hunting its prey, study the grim society that throngs the termite nest and tease out the mechanics of animal motion.

Five Kingdoms: An Illustrated Guide to the Phyla of Life on Earth

By Lynn Margulis and Karlene V. Schwartz

When Linnaeus published his *System of Nature* he brought boundless classificatory energy to the mapping of three natural kingdoms: the animal, the plant and the mineral. The image has passed into metaphor. In this disciplined and fascinating "catalog of the world's living diversity" the term has a narrow biological meaning: a kingdom is simply the largest category of related living forms. The scheme of the five kingdoms of life used here was developed by the late Robert H. Whittaker, a Cornell ecologist, to reflect appropriately the newer recognition of the profound importance of the host of forms that cannot be regarded as plants or as animals. The oldest of the kingdoms on the earth is the Monera: microbial, usually unicellular forms whose DNA message is not wound onto any proteinaceous chromosomal scrolls. That parts the Monera from all other forms of life; all other cells have chromosomes fit for some more or less complicated ballet of division. The more familiar groupings hold generally multicellular forms: societies of individually larger and more complex cells, all within the three familiar kingdoms, each characterized by a recognizable macroscopic way of life. Fungi are absorbers, Plantae are producers and Animalia are pursuers of nutrient molecules.

The fifth kingdom, necessarily a ragbag since it is defined by exclusion, includes all those forms that have large cells and true nuclei but do not proceed with developmental elaboration as the members of the more familiar kingdoms do. Its variety is wide, although its members are all aquatic, from austerely simple single-cell plankton up to giant kelp. Other authors bent on consistency have carved up to 20 kingdoms out of this domain. Here it is one empire. It has been tagged by a name the Greeks might disown as barbarous: Protoctista. (These Boston biologist authors have their reasons, but the term may not endure.)

This much is mere framework, indispensable but by now familiar to the student of any introductory biology text. What is here is a sparkling string of pictured marvels, examples from about 90 great divisions next under the five kingdoms, each division a broad class of living classes. The category was called a phylum (the Greek for tribe) by Ernst Haeckel a century ago. It includes perhaps 40 phyla that have long been recognized and are widely agreed on, but the authors have added considerably to the list, proposing new phyla to hold many forms of microbial life not widely known. Indeed, such oddities are often half-lost among the bewildering specializations within a study that cannot neglect the botany of the Namibian desert, the sea lilies of the dark Pacific floor, the limestones of the pyramids and the kidney parasites of the octopus.

Naturally microbial life must be characterized more by metabolic style than by visible form; biochemistry is the key. Each phylum is presented by a careful account of its nature and occurrence, amounting to a tentative justification for every category, and a photograph is shown, if possible of the living form, always supplemented by careful annotated diagrams of the structures visible and hidden. A few phyla muster only a handful of known living species; one phylum holds half a million. Arrows on a drawing (a choice among five stock scenes is made) point out the typical habitats of each group. Some phyla are treated more extensively; for our own, the Chordata, the pages display close cousins, a salamander, a sea peach and a swan.

For each kingdom there is offered an illustrated family tree of the descent of the phyla described; necessarily tentative for most of the material, it is full of interest for the reader, particularly because a careful summary of the ideas behind the judgments is given. "Each taxonomy is a theory about the creatures it classifies," we are reminded in a graceful foreword by Stephen Jay Gould. This is not a simple catalogue but a catalogue raisoné; we touch not mere variety but a seamless web, the most exquisite and intricate fabric in all the world's weaving. The book is source for innocent and expert alike. Not its conclusions but its factual premises, the diverse organisms we see in these images, make it irrefutable. That is what life has become here on one planet; about how it happened we still have much to learn.

Middle-earth and the tigers of our dreams are fictions less strange than this tapestry. Take Pelomyxa, a freshwater cell a fifth of a millimeter long. This little gathered bag has been studied mostly from the muddy bottom of a pond in Oxford, where long ago the discarded carcasses of elephants were thrown by those who prepared exhibits for the University Museum. It has a well-enclosed nucleus but almost none of the complex organelles found in other nucleated cells, no mitochondria, no chromatin, no Golgi bodies, no. . . . It harbors two distinct types of bacterial symbionts that it seems to feed with its lactic acid waste. They may functionally replace the lacking mitochondria.

Or consider Trichoplax, "the simplest of animals." Without tissues or organs, head or tail, it looks like an outsize amoeba, formless and undirected in its motion, except that it keeps topside up. It consists of thousands of cells in two layers; it can divide by mere fission or arise out of an egg, although no fertilization has yet been seen. The beast was discovered in the seawater aquarium of landlocked Graz in Austria a century ago; few have ever seen it who have not searched for it carefully in seawater from Plymouth to the Red Sea.

Here is a tiny spine-studded drifting sphere of the sea, an acantharian, whose radially symmetrical skeleton startlingly consists of crystalline rods of strontium sulfate. Here too are the nitrogen-fixing bacteria; without their enzyme, with an uncommon molybdenum or vanadium atom enclosed, we would all starve. Here are the slime molds; those that form stalks and fruit from a host of aggregating big amoebalike cells; those that thrust up their flowerlike reproductive stages from flat multinucleate masses of protoplasm, mobile only by differential growth; those that send up a similar fruited stalk after the convocation of a vast quorum of tiny bacterial cells, all nucleus-free. Here are the spoon worms, at home from the abyss to tropical shores, which occupy a U-tube burrow a few feet long, ever pumping seawater in a life that is a paradigm of one-way flow.

This gallery begins with the smallest cellular forms, the lipid-walled bacteria (grouped perhaps too simply together), from those that dwell in Yellowstone hot springs to those that are pathogens for a strange pneumonia in human beings and their domesticates. (Viruses, even smaller, are not included; noncellular, they are mere genetic recipes and are not alive.) The pictures close with the lovely purple aster of New England meadows. A thousand genera of organisms are listed at the end in a helpful directory with such common names as exist, each assigned to the right phylum. An indispensable glossary is not forgotten; the nomenclature of these curious forms and habits is a formidable pseudo-Hellenic tongue. There is no other comparable guide to the winding path of organic evolution overall; the work is imaginative and yet circumstantial, a terse visual index to the living library of 10 million species that time has compiled in the script of molecular helixes.

(April 1982)

Illuminations: A Bestiary
By Rosamund Wolff Purcell and Stephen Jay Gould

"The only overarching theme of a bestiary is diversity." That high theme is doubly pursued here: we follow it the first time through eloquent still-life images by Rosamund Purcell, who fills out a most generous alphabet, some 70 photographs of specimens from Albatross to Zozymus, the diversity of 600 million years of evolution expressed in organic form. The second diversity we recognize is that of human culture: this artist's glowing work has been complemented picture by picture by an essay-caption out of science, the work of paleontologist Stephen Gould, some 40 half-page pieces nicely freed of jargon, pointed, personal and as illuminating as the joint title promises.

No forest or field appears; not one of these photographs is taken from life. The lighting is natural, like all the animals here, but it is conceded that nature is here only in part. These are animal fragments, forms of emphasis, deletion or wear, all drawn from the storehouses of specimens that crowd the private research wings of the big old museums: the dry bones of Minerva's owl posed against the skeletal pages of a ruined book, the viper bottled fangless in alcohol, the nail-pierced cluster of huge Goliath beetles, the striped pelt of a Grevy's zebra, the eyespots of pinned moths, the molars of a rhinoceros in the shape of the Greek letter pi, the vascular labyrinths of prepared squirrel monkeys. Such is the rich taxonomic ore long mined and refined into our evolutionary biology.

For a museum specimen, death makes not an end but a beginning. Life is only the first layer to be dissected away among many that may then be removed. That perception justified this discerning artist errant as she intruded with her camera and tripod into the hushed aisles reserved for cabinets, calipers and learned curators.

The unity of the disciplines crystallizes out slowly until, with the pattern of a fossil shrimp in the fine-grained Solnhofen limestone, its branched intricacy retained ever since the Jurassic, "art and science meet . . . in the most palpable way." That smooth stone was once an ooze so fine that it could harden without damage to the most delicate tissues. The waters there were at the same time so deep and still that they lacked the oxygen that promotes organic decay, for decay is an active process, not merely the spontaneous work of time. Scientists found in that stone the most prized of fossil evidence, while for artists the same rock became the medium of "the world's great lithographs, including . . . the best illustrations of organisms."

Any enduring collection, however well ordered, itself comes to evoke the chanciness of fossilization. One superbly lighted and harmonious composition shows the deliberate traces of the photographer's finger across the dusty glass cover that protects four curiously banded eggs of the glossy ibis. The scientist reflects: "I once opened a drawer in an old part of our collections. The contents had been dumped and sheepishly piled back in disarray. . . . I found a note, also encrusted by the universal patina. It was dated 1861, and contained . . . an apology . . . penned by a terrified student lest the intense and temperamental boss of the museum, Louis Agassiz himself, discover such a calamity without appropriate documentation. Agassiz, obviously, never opened the drawer. The student, Nathaniel Southgate Shaler, went on to become a famous scientist. The dust still rains and reigns."

A pair of photographs show details of the jaws of two whales. "Yet, for color and form alone, we might be viewing America's . . . desert at 30,000 feet over Arizona." That ambiguity is one of scale. Yet all life is rigorously modular, truly mason's work, and the ubiquitous atomic modules have a fixed size, never changed under the hammer of evolutionary time. "When I understood science far less well than I do today," Gould recalls, "I used to get annoyed at . . . professional talks. The speaker would show a slide, often quite beautiful . . . and someone would interrupt by shouting: 'What's the scale?' 'How crass and narrow-minded,' I used to say to myself. . . . Now I understand the deep sense behind such a question."

This bestiary's artist could indeed wish to exploit such a profound ambiguity. A frank scale bar next to the image, even a numerical statement in the caption, might be held crass. But her scientist partner nodded in neglecting to offer us even a tabular summary of object sizes, placed diffidently in the end matter. What's the scale, Steve?

A deeply felt celebration of diversity in word and image, this intimate collaboration is dedicated to Agassiz' Museum of Comparative Zoology at Harvard. Specimens were sought not only there but in Washington, Dublin, Leiden and Copenhagen, all famous and dusty treasuries of this kind of probing into life after death. Shadowy among the bright pages of this entirely modern volume a reader glimpses a rapt and ancient scene, a shaman dancing entranced, shaking her rattle of bear claws. We perforce share life and death with every other animal species, but the symbolic sharing of insight is ours virtually alone.

(February 1987)

Tropical Nature
By Adrian Forsyth and Kenneth Miyata
Illustrations by Sarah Landry

The Various Contrivances by which Orchids are Fertilised by Insects
By Charles Darwin

Our northern forest floor is carpeted for a footsore hiker: soft deep loams fragrant with humus and springy duff under the trees feel easy underfoot. In the tropical rain forest, where winter never comes, walking is harder. There the litter is thin, typically a couple of inches in typical forests; decay is simply too swift under year-long steady moist incubation. A single good scrape of the boot will disclose the pallid mat of fungal mycelia that dwell in the soil, a lowly root symbiont of the towering trees. The heavy leaching at the rain-drenched surface would carry away all the soluble minerals if that mat did not catch and recycle key ions.

Those mycorrhizal associations live a fast biochemical life. As in an automobile plant in Japan, the steady state of production maintains a frugal inventory: things are used right away. Even the lush green canopy above, where the solar input is made, is not quantitatively as rich a store as it is in the boreal forest by summer. But it is in those leaves on high, and most of all in the great supporting cellulose cylinders of the tree stems, whether erect or new-fallen, that the main stores reside, the essential atoms and the light-derived chemical free energy for all the life of the forest.

"Consider the sloth of the sloth," write the authors of *Tropical Nature*, the first of these two books. That proverbial beast is genuinely lethargic; its metabolism runs at about half the norm for mammals of its size. It is a slow, steady grazer on tree leaves. Herbivores of the forest understory are rare; grass and herbs do not grow in that deep shade. A sloth ranges little; over months one individual may feed within only a few dozen big trees. A sloth prudently avoids the ground, where most carnivores prowl. In its leafy canopy it is hard to see; its fur is camouflaged, greened by algal growth. Its fecal pellets are small, hard and infrequent, as befits an animal that must live high overhead where water is hard to come by. Yet it does not drop the pellets "the easy way" from above. No, the beast laboriously descends each week from its high tree, pokes a hole in the ground at the base of the tree with its stubby tail and carefully buries its scat. The howler monkeys, which range far in the same forests and browse on many of the same leaves, defecate freely from the treetops. The agile monkeys also venture most reluctantly to the ground, even though the watchful eyes of the entire howler band are at the service of any single member. The solitary sloth has no sentinels.

Why? It turns out that a sloth not only dwells within a small set of trees but also spends disproportionate amounts of time grazing in a single tree. One or two sloths in a tree can take as much as a fifth of the annual product of that tree in the course of their deliberate grazing. If they dropped their pellets from 100 feet up, it is easy to believe the stuff would scatter widely as it fell through the vines and branches below. The single sustaining tree could not much benefit from the recycling of the sloth's nutrient. The sloth's feces may return about half of the nutrient to the tree roots. It is a long-term investment by the sloth tribe through a risky and exacting husbandry of the resource, one that is less important to the wide-ranging howler monkey. The scenario is untested, but the authors "like to believe that in the arduous, dangerous descent of the sloth there is a metaphor."

We who saunter in parks and gardens notice easily that plants protect themselves against animals that eat them by visible structures such as spines and thorns. Animals that live by gathering, from our sapient ancestors to Baird's tapir, the largest herbivore in the New World Tropics, learn well that the chief defenses stoutly erected by plants are molecular. Hallucinogens are the innovations not of "clandestine Berkeley chemists" but of fungi and plants seeking cheap ways of discouraging small mammalian herbivores. If 13 seeds of a morning glory can cause wild hallucinations in a man with a body weight of 70 kilograms, consider what a single seed is apt to do to a mouse with the same neurochemistry.

But the powerful alkaloids are expensive for plants, particularly in the nitrogen-short Tropics. A plant that colonizes the neighborhood of tree falls, where for a few years sunlight reaches the ground, may sacrifice chemical defenses for fast growth. It has no time to spare. A balsa tree will grow rapidly toward a gap in the canopy, its leaves pocked with insect-chewed holes, four-tenths of the leaf area gone.

The tapestry of the forest bears such an intricate design that plant-animal interaction can on occasion reverse the chemical conflict. A striking example is the relation between certain colorful bees and fragrant orchids. Male orchid bees visit and pollinate a variety of orchids, but these nonsocial bees have no use for the pollen they carry away and the flowers offer them no nutrient nectar. To summon the bee species the flowers manufacture a mix of fragrances, often rather simple aromatic chemicals. The bees build up a store of varied scents kept in specialized leg pockets. Once the mix is right, the perfumer becomes irresistible. He does not, however, attract the wanted female, as they might have planned it in Paris. No, the sweet-smelling bee gathers a small crowd of males of his species, which buzz and flitter around their beau. Then in some favorable spot of sunlight the bright, dancing aggregation draws from far around those orchid-bee females for which the entire elaborate scheme has coadaptively come to be.

In 17 chapters, each a brief essay on tropical nature observed, these two young field biologists have made a model of contemporary natural history, cheerfully speculative, concerned as much with large pattern as with diversity, chemically informed, thoroughly ecological and Darwinian to the core. Most of the chapters were not jointly written, but their book is nonetheless a whole. They have for a dozen years visited one of "the most complex biological communities that exist," the neotropical rain forest, particularly in Costa Rica and in Amazonian Ecuador. The book is based on what they saw and tasted and heard there, although it is by no means only a journal. They know and call on the relevant specialized literature of today and yesterday, although never technically, but the work is not a textbook either. Its epigraphs are drawn from pop songs as well as from William Blake; the style is of our years, although the authors warmly praise and well employ their great Victorian predecessors.

The larger issues, like the reasons for the tropical diversity they celebrate, are examined, but large answers will remain tentative until that living fabric is more intimately known. Each chapter opens with a handsome drawing of some organism from the chapter text. The authors supply an appendix for the beginner, with knowing advice on how to make your own trip to these remarkable forests, from the choice of tours to toilet paper (always travel with a roll) and clothing (do not bring much). It is sad to learn that Kenneth Miyata drowned last fall in a rapid of the Big Horn River, the galley proofs of this fine book unseen on his desk at home.

The paperback reissue of Darwin's first published book after his *Origin* (the reprint is actually that of the second edition of 1877) brings the reader to the same kind of detailed example, to repeat the title: the various contrivances by which orchids are fertilized by insects. The argument is founded on evolutionary inference, drawn mainly from homology and observed function, and tested experimentally. We see it here as it looked in the vigorous youth of evolutionary science. The contesting explanations of the day seem frivolous: "to complete the scheme of nature," say. Darwin's work, pushing a flower hinge with a fingertip or some dangling filament with a human hair, or placing small bees within a flower cavity to watch their escape, is entirely different. There are no appeals to final causes or ideal schemes, only, as Michael T. Ghiselin writes in his foreword, "reconstructed history and laws of nature."

As in all historiography, successful reconstructions are tentative but wonderfully fruitful. It was Darwin who first found those remarkable devices of the orchid. Contrivances is an apt term, although it may have had a certain allusive irony for those who first saw the title. One orchid manages to paste a pollen mass onto the right part of the right bee, to be removed by a well-placed sticky cleft when the bee in time visits the right female flower. So different are the male and female blossoms of the orchid genus *Catasetum*, intricately formed to carry out the vital implantation and removal, that they were regarded as distinct genera until they were found growing on a single plant. The question Darwin puts, as do his powerful modern colleagues, is always: What can have happened to bring about the state we uncover by a close look?

(July 1984)

Bumblebee Economics
By Bernd Heinrich

It might be anywhere in the temperate U.S. where morning sunlight falls full on some moist meadow. A shadowed woodland is not far off, and nearby too may be a quiet pond, where beavers silently glide. In the spring a flycatcher calls; later on stands of high-bush blueberry and jewelweed come to decorate the spot. Insistent little furry aerial forms in orange and black dart among the blossoms. The simple sense of leisure is our own sunny reverie; here we are watching the work of a hard-pressed economy. Bumblebees (there are 50 species over the U.S. and Canada, all neatly painted in color in an identification key useful in the field) have been inlaid within the complex of tundra life for tens of millions of years by the deftest of invisible hands. Found now in all kinds of open areas — field, roadside and mountaintop — bumblebees are best adapted to the flora of the slowly changing bogs that mark the cool woodlands, relicts of the ancient tundra.

The free energy that drives this urgent economy is held in tiny droplets of a few milligrams of nectar within a myriad of blossoms dotted over the landscape. The bumblebee must visit these, flying in cool air effectively enough for the foraging investment to return an energy profit, with allowance for the indispensable moiety of protein, fats and the like that the flower pollen offers for forming capital: new bees. To this end bees of the genus *Bombus* have evolved a powerful thermoregulatory system; their furry muscle engine remains above 30 degrees Celsius, running even in a snowstorm, whereas almost all other bees are not able to forage at air temperatures below 16 degrees. Engine losses, kept under elaborate circulatory and nervous control, warm the engine itself and the nest as well.

The bumblebee is a flying machine with a power of about a fiftieth of a watt. On a cold morning it develops as much power again in heat; in midsummer the heat is only the minimal loss. Foraging is usually done at full speed, blossom to blossom, engines always revved up for ready flight, for time is — one almost says — money. Time is heat loss in a short season, and profit is in fast foraging. Hovering costs too much to do often, and walking about on big flowering panicles of goldenrod is a strategy most commonly followed by the drones, which have no obligations to the babes at home. Large loads and long flight paths cost little compared with the cost of lost foraging time.

Bumblebees dwell in colonies of a few hundred, often with many queens as well as many workers, the village demographics changing in response to food supply, established by feedback loops as yet unknown.

One queen early in the spring starts it all, typically in some abandoned field-mouse nest, warm and snug in the ground, lined by its original builder with delicate fibrous insulation. In contrast to this nectar pioneer the honeybee swarm, a creature originally of the Old World Tropics, is a "big corporation that goes after the big markets." Honeybees recruit entire flights of foragers to a bonanza, using a dance language; bumblebees are individualist foragers, without communications. The honeybee cities have a huge communal storage for a population of tens of thousands. Honeybee life is plainly adapted to tropical windfalls, some large banana inflorescence loaded with pounds of nectar over a few square feet. The bumblebee is matched to a Temperate Zone scatter of open flowers, species following species during an upland summer. ("A bumblebee colony has a more individualistic cottage-industry approach. It thrives by living hand to mouth, exploiting small, scattered energy sources that in most cases can be taken up by single workers operating individually.") Human beings have domesticated the honeybee to orchard and cropland; the bumblebee remains wild because it thrives on fields where no plow has upset the best-laid plans of the field mouse. The fields of red clover in crop rotation are nonetheless fertilized by bumblebees, a princely gift to the farmer.

The data in this book sample the state of the science, not merely the work of Professor Heinrich. Two of his own recent results do, however, go far to strengthen his thesis. They were secured by novel techniques. An electronic system developed in his Berkeley group was able to serve as a time clock for bumblebee workers, identifying single bees and recording their times in and out, with their overall weight. Tiny tags weighing one milligram held microwave resonant circuits, each of which rang to a particular frequency from a wideband transmitter. A scanning receiver recorded the pip and thus the worker's card number, a form of micro-Taylorism. In another facet of this diverse work Heinrich found that the free-flying bumblebee (six minutes aloft in a temperature-controlled room before capture and thermal probe) showed a temperature change of only some five degrees C. when the air temperature changed 25 degrees. This demonstrated thermostability had been missed in earlier work relying on tethered bees as test animals; the tethered bee does not need to work all out to stay at speed; it has no direct perception of its thoracic temperature, and it is cooled by the ambient air.

What about the bumblebee's coevolutionary partner, the flower, for which the economics of the bee is a system of mating? The book devotes a couple of chapters to such questions, as various as the species are numerous, for example the mutuality of design of the corolla of the desert willow and the daily behavior of the bee. The entire study is not only a model of the adaptive systems within the ecological world, a model as rich in questions as it is in answers, but also an example of good popular exposition. Jargon is at a minimum, sharp metaphor and simple estimates form integral parts of the argument; not even the clear quantitative graphs are necessary for understanding, although they and the rest of the illustrations do enhance it. There is a Maine ambience in this displaced New Englander's writing; every chapter bears an epigraph, often one from a New England poet. The book is itself a concentrate of goodness. Not least is the indirect light it casts on human beings, that single species so swift to change and so varied in social structure that its diverse patterns of behavior worldwide can hardly be the work of the same invisible slow forces that have exquisitely sorted the genes of the bumblebees throughout the Cenozoic.

(January 1980)

The Insect Societies
By *Edward O. Wilson*

An insect colony is a "diffuse organism," "an animal that forages ameba-like over fixed territories" with its million tiny mouths. The African driver ant is the giant of such "superorganisms": a carnivore weighing more than 20 kilograms, with 20 million mouths and stings, patrolling tens of acres of bush. "It still does not match up to the lurid stories told about it. After all, the swarm can only cover about a meter of ground every three minutes. Any competent bush mouse, not to mention man or elephant, can step aside and contemplate the whole grass-roots frenzy at leisure, an object less of menace than of strangeness and wonder, the culmination of an evolutionary story as different from that of mammals as it is possible to conceive in this world."

Forty-five years ago the American myrmecologist William Morton Wheeler wrote a volume with a very similar title, the fruit of his lifetime study of ants. His eloquent descriptions and his extraordinarily compendious knowledge made his book a classic for the general scientific reader, a classic whose honorable place the volume reviewed here will surely come to hold. Wilson is less eloquent than the Edwardian Wheeler, and the growth of the subject forbids that air of encyclopedic completeness that was easier long ago.

Wilson writes with personal warmth and flair, in a tone of remarkable clarity and candor and with a breadth and depth of method and understanding that Wheeler's generation could only dream of. The superorganism was the "mirage [that] drew us to a point on the horizon," writes Wilson. No new holistic concept now replaces that earlier mystique. Analogies—particularly those from information theory—are still valuable, but the goal of the experimentalist today is to gain such a thorough and adroit piecemeal analysis that the insect colony and its full behavior will one day be open to his reconstruction, so to speak, in vitro. He will be able to fix caste artificially, making a worker or a queen from a larva at will, to elicit behavior as complex as brood care by artificially presented chemical and acoustic signals, to simulate nest-building using only those elements of behavior observed in individual workers. That goal is not yet close, but it is grand enough, and together with the genetic explanation of each trait it represents the "exciting modern substitute for the superorganism concept."

How like an organism the colony is, particularly in today's language of information and control, can be made out from two examples drawn from the rich store in this large and attractive volume. There is an alpine species of blackish-brown woodland ant that is host to an extreme social parasite, a second tiny species of ant. The parasite species has no workers at all; its queens are little degenerate riders on the back of the big host queens throughout almost all their lives. The intruder queens exude an attractant for the host workers, which feed and care for them and their offspring, which in turn are all males and queens. The host queens live and even lay eggs, but now none of those eggs ever develop into sexual forms. The colony continues, new workers are born, forage, tend and die, but the progeny of the colony is that of the parasite, not of the host. The parasite queens mate at home and remain there, or fly off to seduce another host nest. The entire system has been seized and turned to the genetic purposes of the parasite, which has for itself no "metabolic" means at all. The result is analogous to a cell infected with a virus. The virus enters the host cell, dwells within its genetic apparatus and maintains its metabolic activity, and the product of that generation is not another cell but an alien swarm of virus particles.

Take the problem of caste. Termites supply one example. In a typical lower termite species the newly hatched larva is potentially capable of developing into either a reproductive form or a soldier. What happens depends on the schedule on which the growing larva receives amounts of two competing hormones, the molting and the juvenile hormones common to insects. These hormone secretions are under external chemical control by the substances called pheromones, which pass from insect to insect during the constant interchange of fluids by contact among termites. The details of caste are complex, and they differ widely among species, but if one may generalize a little prematurely, it appears that individuals are capable genetically of entering any caste (allowing for sexual bimorphism); what in fact they become is determined by a complex set of stimuli, environmental and biochemical, that statistically and impersonally reflect the needs of the nest. When one active queen is present, for example, other queens often do not appear. An army-ant worker is "loyal" to the nest, and it will not join any other column of marching ants of the same species. Take the queen away for some hours and the workers can emigrate and will be welcome. The entire affair parallels the development of tissues from cells. Any embryo cell of a carrot can make a whole carrot, for example, if it is taken early enough and suitably treated. The cell, like the insect larva, inherits not a specific form but an entire program, which can be variously called up under a complex set of contingencies.

The key to true sociability in ants, bees and wasps is "altruism between sisters." The workers are sisters, and they care tenderly for their younger sisters, forswearing any offspring of their own. W. D. Hamilton put forward eight years ago a brilliant explanation of the evolution of sociability "so simple and starkly mechanical that my own first reaction," Wilson writes, "was to reject it out of hand." The audacious theory simply assumes that an altruistic trait can evolve only if the sacrifice of fitness by an individual is quantitatively more than compensated for by an increase in the fitness of some of its relatives. The right genes will persist and increase in frequency only if the rate of reproduction of its sisters is more than doubled by the sacrifice of its own progeny, whereas the rate of reproduction of half sisters would need to be more than quadrupled, and so on.

Now, in the Hymenoptera, which includes bees, ants and wasps, males donate all their genes to each daughter, because the males are homozygous. Females, however, give only half of their genes to any offspring, because their genes occur in diploid pairs. Therefore bee sisters, say, share on the average three-quarters of their genes but a mother shares only half of her genes with her own daughter. Bee sisters are thus closer kin than bee mothers and daughters. Daughters, then, favor survival of their own genes more by caring for their younger sisters than by giving equal care to their own offspring! Such species should tend to become social. Among social insects only the termites have a genetic system different from that curious scheme. The case is not open and shut; a full fascinating chapter of Wilson's book is given over to tests of this marvelously simple and powerful idea.

Social behavior has other preconditions. Manipulation of objects for nest-building or brood care requires some special organs, and mothers must be to some degree in contact with their living young. Many arthropods are potentially social; some spiders even live communally in a great web nest, but each mother lays her own eggs in her own case, and there is no social altruism. One spider species in Mexico, reported only a year or two ago, does seem to construct a common egg sac for many females. Spider biology may still hold surprises. Termites, which are biologically "social cockroaches," may have first formed their societies on quite another basis. They depend for the digestion of the wood cellulose they eat on certain symbiotic intestinal microorganisms. These symbionts must be passed from old to young by anal feeding, which implies at least some social behavior. Termite societies began as feeding communities, and it may be that they evolved full social care of the brood only later.

It is impossible even at length to convey the full range of Wilson's book, which is magisterially at home among mathematical, paleontological, genetic, ecological and biochemical arguments. Biology is here unified, and in a context of no small philosophical depth. Even demography is not absent: worker honeybees live about a month in summer; they die mainly when they become old foragers, usually in flying accidents or from predators. Most insects suffer the highest mortality in their youth. Humans share the bee mortality curve. There are other lessons for human society. "The worst enemies of social insects are other social insects."

It seems, however, that the sluggard need not look so earnestly to the ant. Although ants and honeybees never play, they are idle about half of the time even in peak seasons. Perhaps the army of the underemployed is reserved for various emergencies, fanning to cool the nest, fighting off intruders and the like. Draw what lessons you can; this is a book for rumination.

(September 1972)

The Desert Locust
By Stanley Baron

"And Moses stretched forth his rod over the land of Egypt, and the Lord brought an east wind upon the land all that day, and all that night; and when it was morning, the east wind brought the locusts. . . . For they covered the face of the whole earth, so that the land was darkened; and they did eat every herb of the land, and all the fruit of the trees which the hail had left: and there remained not any green thing in the trees, or in the herbs of the field, through all the land of Egypt." So it is told in Exodus, of a time 3,500 years ago, and so it has been ever since, absent the rod. "Out of sixty-one years since 1910, some forty have been plague years" somewhere in the vast range of the desert locust. That species, *Schistocerca gregaria*, a big hard-skinned winged grasshopper, has no area of permanent outbreak. It is uniquely adapted to the chances of desert life; like men in the desert, it is nomadic, opportunist, following the wind and the rain, explosively expansive whenever conditions suit. (A year's rainfall in the central Sahara — 1.6 inches — may come within one hour!) Its range is that empire of rock and sand of which the Sahara is the biggest province; the Red Sea is only a firebreak in a varied desert that stretches across Africa and Asia from the Atlantic surf to the valley of the Ganges, and north from Lake Chad to the Zagros Mountains on the Anatolian border: an area nearly four times that of the U.S.

A major swarm of these metallic black-and-yellow locusts can shadow an area of 500 square kilometers or more, their layers up to a kilometer deep. There will be fully 10^{10} finger-length insects in such a swarm, a flying mass of 50,000 or 100,000 tons. From a distance the swarm looks like the streaked smoke of a bush fire, pillars of locusts here and there rising in the convection currents like dust devils. From above one often sees "an intense and unmistakable glitter caused by reflections from the wings." A swarm can fly 3,000 miles overland, normally in 10-hour daily flights at airspeeds of only a few miles an hour. The locusts hold reserves of fat adequate even for overseas flights (up to 17 hours by wind-tunnel tests). The Canary Islands are well within their range, and around the Red Sea "so often has the despairing farmer seen locusts apparently flying in from the sea that many Arabians believe that they originate in the stomachs of whales."

This fascinating eyewitness account is written with verve by a skillful travel writer who personally followed the campaigns against the desert locust carried out by the Food and Agriculture Organization of the United Nations in the empty quarters of the desert where locusts breed, among the oases and the cultivated margins where they bring ruin to hard-pressed farmers and in the laboratories in London where the latest tactics for this 10,000-year war are devised. As a travel book alone its narrative would be diverting and impressive. Consider the little party south of Tamanrasset early in 1966, some seven men in three UN Landrovers. Three were young Algerian "locust prospectors." One was a gifted Tuareg desert guide, full-veiled, tall, "a whipcord of a man" who knew every furrow of the runoffs and the "date and duration of every rainfall within his own lifetime and those of his father and grandfather" for a range of 500 miles, beyond which "the world ceased to exist for him." Then there were the zoology professor from Algiers, grown gray in 40 years' study of desert life, and the writer. "We had been going some hours . . . when faint specks . . . began to take shape as a file of fifty or sixty camels head to tail. . . . We pulled up . . . and waited. The caravan came on steadily . . . for no caravan stops for a chance encounter. Camels fight, entangle their linked ropes and displace their loads at the slightest opportunity. The Tuareg leader, on foot, marched ahead . . . while eight of his companions . . . detached themselves to greet us. They were evidently well known to [our guide], whom they welcomed warmly yet with a kind of formal politeness, accompanied by much handshaking all round. Where were they bound for? To Timbuktu, twenty days' march away."

Around such tales, with plenty of daring low-altitude flying in light aircraft amidst the swarms of locusts, Baron builds a clear account of his war. It is truly a war, waged in behalf of the hard work and bread of millions, by a coalition of 42 nations through the UN with field stations, radio links, trucks, aircraft, stores of insecticides and skilled teams of combatants who must know the enemy, the land and the farmers for whom they fight. The locust is in recession now; it has been proved controllable by present knowledge, at least while men work together across the national boundaries so little visible down the long wadis of the desert.

The cycle of the insect is extraordinary. The species is found in two phases: the solitary and the gregarious. For a long time its generations may go by with the insect remaining small, harmless, never concentrating, just another green grasshopper. In the swarming phase it is larger, stronger, migratory, gregarious, yellow-uniformed. The phase change was first seen in 1929; until then the two forms were held to be distinct species. The change may go in either direction. Whereas desert plants have the ability to thrive in suspended animation, ready to germinate and blossom once the dry wadi springs to life after about an inch of rain, the locust cannot quite do that; it must move on once its swarms have fed on the local green. It seems probable that somewhere one of two events must occur. Either a set of solitary insects has the good fortune to multiply, by successful hatching, to a density large enough to trigger the phase change or a swarm beaten back by events remains gregarious in some remote spot, lays its eggs synchronously and so finds success. In either case the immature hoppers hatch out in numbers, march together using up food and fly in a swarm to seek their fortune. They fly downwind, and it has become pretty plain that the wind systems gather them along the long, seasonally shifting line of the great intertropical front, where the desert rains are favored. It is not only in poetry that the Koran speaks of locusts as "the teeth of the wind." Three fortunate hatchings and the swarm is a plague, growing tenfold in each generation, some four to six months to a generation. Disturbances cause the hoppers to become more gregarious, for example a disturbing antelope or camel herd, come from nowhere to seek out the greening wadi. Even the desert incense, the aromatic terpenes of the shrubs that yield frankincense and myrrh, can trigger egg-laying, anticipating the rains. The hoppers hatch a couple of weeks later, just as the rains come. (The shrubs can become fragrant before the rains, perhaps because the overcast skies result in lower temperature underground.) South of Tamanrasset in 1967 there was what may have been the first witnessed rise of a plague originating from solitary insects.

There are misgivings even in this tale of a moral war. The insecticides kill more than locusts. Although the governor may rejoice in the dead locusts, the local people mourn their dead goats. In the long run there will be too much dieldrin used over and over again in the same wadis. The locusts are themselves part of the chancy life of the desert. We need a more specific insecticide, even if it costs more to develop than the market can pay for. There is work for radar, new aerial cameras, even satellites. It should be recalled that the entire decade of hopeful effort, leaving behind a few plagues well fought, an organization in reserve, the locusts dormant and a solid basis of knowledge, cost the UN about the same as a couple of the supersonic fighter-bombers they make in St. Louis.

(November 1972)

Octopus: Physiology and Behaviour of an Advanced Invertebrate
By M. J. Wells

When the great reptiles ruled the land, certain timorous hairy creatures found a niche in their shadow. Step by slow step ways of life began that owed more to adaptability than to offensive and defensive weaponry, more to neuroelectronics than to bulk. As the world changed, the mammals, less specialized than their reptilian contemporaries, rose to dominate in their turn, their rule resting more on some kind of plan than on large teeth and armor. The least specialized of the little mammals were the diurnal primates. With clever hands and eyes they sought their varied food, stayed out of the way of big trouble and came one day to rule by insight.

But long before any reptile trod the ground the sea was quick with life. Before the Devonian all that sea life was invertebrate and the cephalopods were its masters. Their spiral shells fill the museums as the animals themselves filled the seas, first of all large free-swimming forms, with "very possibly a virtual immunity from attack by creatures other than their own kind." The sutures on fossil ammonite shells show a progressive increase in complexity. A likely account can be given for this: the animals with their gas-filled chambers had to move to deeper water, and the developing shell is fighting off implosion. The shallows had seen the entry of a new and swifter form of life, fishes and reptiles, our distant vertebrate forebears. They drove the big coiled mollusks out of the coastal waters, and the physics of depth set a severe limit on the seaward retreat. The era of such cephalopods is over; only the chambered nautilus remains, as a heavily armored scavenger on the slopes of coral reefs.

One devious road remained to the molluscan kind. Lightly built cephalopods appeared, the coiled shell reduced to a simple internal stiffener; they reinvaded the shallow waters, rich in simpler prey. These new cephalopods themselves rely on tactics rather than armor. They are exceptionally well equipped with sensory input and computing systems, capable of cunning concealment and of a close watch on their world, successful competitors in coastal waters. "The result is a mollusk that a primate can recognize as a fellow creature." It is *Octopus vulgaris*, the common octopus, the subject of this wonderful book.

A technical treatise with room both for the evidence and for a valuable overall summary of basic octopus anatomy and physiology, the volume devotes about two-thirds of its space to octopus behavior, to the animal's sight and touch, to its learning style, to its extraordinary control of color and pattern (and not enough to its jet propulsion). The story comes mainly out of careful laboratory experience but is told with sensitivity to the conditions of free life. Dr. Wells is a member of the famed group around J. Z. Young that has so long and meticulously studied the octopus, mostly at the Zoological Station in Naples. Wells has himself watched the octopus and has set tasks for it over 20 years; his text is knowing, personal and admiring but never indulgent.

An octopus watches you, comes close to be fed, runs away from mistreatment and develops a clear individuality of habit and attitude; it seems "a sort of aquatic dog or cat." But of course it is not that kind of animal at all. To us it is profoundly alien; even though it is unmistakably convergent on a recognizable way of life, that way has been elaborated from an entirely different ground plan.

The octopus hatches from one egg of the 150,000 its mother laid down in one week. She tends her eggs constantly with jets and eddies of water, and she rarely leaves them in order to take food. Emaciated, she dies shortly after they hatch. The males too leave off eating not long after mating, lose weight and die. Octopus society seems confined to combat (the loser is often eaten) and copulation; they appear to live out most of their two-year span solitary in the sea. The limit on all octopus activity is set by the scarcity of circulating blood oxygen. Mollusks lack that subtle device of oxygen-binding iron hemoglobin wrapped in corpuscles, a biochemical patent held by the vertebrate line. Their circulating coppery hemocyanin is simply not as good by a factor of three, even though their viscous blood is loaded with the protein and three hearts are at work keeping blood pressure high.

The individual octopus hatches as a vulnerable member of the plankton, a mere eighth of an inch long. In a month or so the happy few survivors settle to the bottom, already looking rather adult but weighing only a gram, and grow pretty steadily up to five or 10 kilograms. They dine on fine seafood, mostly crabs and lobsters they have searched out in the crannies where those hardshells hide, seized with a jet-propelled pounce, taken in batches held in a web of arms back to a rocky lair, paralyzed by a special central-nervous-system poison, broken apart and finally cleaned out neatly.

Octopus emotions are skin-deep, signaled by a rich repertory of patterns, blushings and palings. An animal pushing back another in fight or in love turns a uniform dark red. But they are above all cool customers. They avoid peaks. They perform steadily at a plateau level but often fall back to a sleepy rest. It takes a long time for an octopus to recover from minor exercise; digestion is an all-day matter. The male heart skips a beat with every spermatophore ejaculation during copulation but without any change in heart rate or amplitude. ("Octopuses take these things very calmly.") They feel no imperative to maintain the internal furnace. A mammal long kept from food ventures on peaks and excesses of behavior to take any meal; it is hungry, we say out of empathy. Not the octopus; when crabs are scarce, it resigns itself to long watchful inactivity until one day the supply improves. That is what cool calculation would teach, but we and our warm kind are less objective; we must eat often to keep the fires of metabolism lighted.

The octopus is remarkable to look at. Its powers of camouflage are all but incredible, matching and varying colors and even textures (it can change at once from smooth to prickly by extending papillae in the skin) with what could be called art. It can in a flash change from a "dark brown glowering creature to a pale ghost," foiling any searcher's plan, and can top that tactic by producing a dark decoy, a life-size puff of mucus-bound ink moving out as the beast itself jets away in the opposite direction. The octopus skin holds a couple of million tiny sacs of pigment, which can be locally spread under central control (but open-loop, with no direct nervous feedback) from almost invisible points out to large spots of color. The spots span a color range from black through brown to red and pale yellow. All the marvelous blues and greens in the octopus palette (colorplates here prove their functional presence) are passively won, with the use of opaque white pigment spots and broad-band mirror spots as well.

But "all the available evidence suggests that *Octopus* is color-blind." What the animal does is match most exquisitely the overall reflected intensity of the background. A blinded octopus no longer can do it and even loses most of the complex, long-lasting patterns a normal octopus can show. The flickering chromatophores often seen in the living octopus attest to the real difficulty of this subtle procedure mediated only by visual feedback; one is led close to the idea of conscious control.

If the solitary octopus had culture, it would rest on vision. The animal manipulates the world poorly. It has no way of relating its arm positions to the touch information richly provided by its myriad suckers. It cannot scan; it can detect texture but not shape, size or weight. For an octopus that has been trained to distinguish a cube from a sphere, the cube is better matched by a narrow rod than by a cube with rounded corners. Although the arms of an octopus stiffen to handle increased weight, the animal apparently cannot sense that muscle change; no octopus has yet learned to distinguish between two objects that differ only in weight.

Here is intelligence in a soft body; with no fixed reference frame of joints the octopus has never developed the sense of bodily position, in principle available to it by a mighty task of integration. The octopus cannot put one stone on top of another, it learns to pull levers with great difficulty, it is poor at learning mazes. A newly blinded octopus at first sits touchingly huddled in its arms and after a week takes up a position on the wall or floor of its tank, its arms outstretched, feeling all the surfaces of the tank as much as it can with its suckers. These are minds even more visual than our own.

The last two chapters of the book describe at length the long efforts to localize and analyze function in the octopus brain. The approach is to train the animal to tasks after making such lesions as splitting the brain or removing various lobes. Specialized function is clear enough, but there is a long way to go before evolving a convincing analysis of this ancient computer: a few tens of millions of neurons in a gram of brain and a few more grams of widely diffused gangliated cables serving the blood vessels, the skin organs and the arms. One is all but led to declare that the proper study of neurophysiological mankind is octopus. Can we know our primate selves before we know this cold little forerunner?

(September 1978)

East African Mammals: An Atlas of Evolution in Africa, Volume I
By Jonathan Kingdon

This singularly handsome book is visually without a peer among many years of publishers' output in science. The designer, Tagelsir Ahmed, has given us a volume of the right size and weight, with generous margins and paper that is neither slickly whitened nor blurringly rough. He has justly fulfilled the terms of the work. The book is the work of an artist-scientist; "the drawings and maps are a fundamental part," and the "prime stimulus for the drawings . . . has been the contemplation of physical beauty in mammals; this is a reward in itself."

Our reward is the hundreds of maps and pencil sketches in an entire gamut of styles, and a number of striking pages of paintings in color, like so many designs by artists of the School of Paris. Across many a page climb and crawl and posture dozens of quick-drawn pottos or pangolins, reminding the reader of the sketchbooks of the old masters. There are fine-lined and careful representations of the bony skeleton of man and gorilla, detailed studies of musculature (even one overlay), marginal drawings and softened renderings of the silky-haired colobus monkey, skulls, faces and sequenced drawings of the jump of a galago, like a strip of motion-picture film. There is a silhouette of the bridge across the Firth of Forth, to compare with the skeletons of quadrupeds. There are small, elegant renderings of the trees of savanna and thicket, of hardpan and multistoried rain forest, like old engravings of cities seen from the waterfront. One can look at chromosomes and electrophoresis patterns of the serum proteins in man and chimpanzee, and coordinate nets with primate-skull profiles superposed on the warp. The "red, white and blue" genital display of the vervet monkey and the white nose and red tail of other forms are presented in comparison studies, with the aim of tracing the origins of these striking signal schemes. Maps abound, informed with the personal graphic alphabet of one sensitive draftsman-artist, mapping the range of a band of 80 chimpanzees or the human population of all East Africa compared with the prevalence of the tsetse fly and the reliability of 20 annual inches of rain.

Kingdon has a clear grand aim: he seeks to make an agreeable, broad and complete inventory and introduction to all the mammalian species of East Africa, the region where a million years or so ago our own species emerged among a rich and diverse mammalian fauna. This volume, the first of three, is largely concerned with the primates (including *Homo* and other hominids) "and the peculiar interest their habits excite." Since it is the first volume, it has a set of introductory chapters as background, treating the vegetation and the general environment, the perspective of the long past of geologic time and the foundations of the anatomy of mammals. The author is caught up in the life of field and zoo—"I have kept [the Zanzibar galagos] over long periods"—but he is no stranger to the talk, books and journals of mammalogists. Indeed, it is the very catholicity of the content of his graphics, with his ability to subtly match style and content, that gives his book its unique beauty. There is a bibliography of some 600 titles.

Primates are the stars of Volume I, but the anteaters, the aardvark and the dugong complete the work. Was the Egyptian god Set a tube-snouted aardvark, devouring the moon each month? Will the giant pangolin survive? This beast, feeding on the termites whose mounds it rips open, is threatened by the "purveyor of charms." The overlapping horny scales, a specialized protective armor that may make up a third of the weight of the animal, are popular love charms among the women of Buganda. Bury one suitably under a man's doorstep and he is "incapable of denying his woman's wishes and he will, under the influence of this scale, buy her new dresses or indulge any other of her desires; naturally these are popular charms." A whole pangolin skin is worth a small fortune.

This is a work of analysis, the pencil seeking "to extract from the complex whole some limited coherent pattern" for the mind and the eye. Because the author is an artist he delights the eye; because he is a scientist he goes beyond form and the present to tease out the origins, context and interpretation of form. The second volume will cover the little animals of East Africa, which are the least known; the third volume will treat the large mammals of the region, with a special effort to bring out information relevant to the eventual use of those showy large ungulates as meat-yielders for man. The work as a whole is a luxurious wonder for both the possessor and the user.

(February 1972)

Mechanics and Energetics of Animal Locomotion
Edited by R. McN. Alexander and G. Goldspink

Pedal Power: In Work, Leisure, and Transportation
Edited by James C. McCullagh

Every animal that moves has the analogue of an engine, an electronic control system and a specific dynamical mechanism for converting internal energy into the appropriate motion. Two decades ago the work of the late Professor Sir James Gray and his school outlined the problems and teased out just how the forces that move each creature arise from its interaction with the environment. *Mechanics and Energetics of Animal Locomotion* is a compendium, tightly packed with results and brief analyses and rich in its references, of the work of a group of British and American investigators, a comprehensive summary of what we know. Our view is based on a much deeper understanding of muscle itself, on big gains in neurophysiology (particularly in insects), on physiological measurements made possible by wind or water tunnels and on performance analysis and field tests carried out at the level of detail of quantitative engineering design.

The engine is of course muscle, fueled by ATP (except for the fast contractions of certain tiny creatures such as *Stentor,* where a calcium potential gives rise to tension directly). One chapter surveys the intricate design of muscle and its force and work relations seen as a function of rates and lengths. A second chapter details the molecular mechanisms of muscle motion and fuel supply; a third reviews the prime mover's energy economy. One point is basic and is emphasized anew: muscles stretched while still developing tension (doing negative work, like the muscles of a man walking downstairs) consume much less fuel. A. V. Hill once demonstrated this to the Royal Society. A slight woman pedaling to slow down easily resisted the best efforts of a "large healthy male athlete" doing the positive work on their coupled ergometers.

This perception is a key to much natural design. The fast-beating wings of a mosquito would consume much negative work even at this big discount rate, but elastic hinges (made of a special protein super-rubber) mean that no such work is done. The wings resonate, more or less; the muscles do not work against the inertial forces but only against the air (working a trifle more to make up for the lack of total perfection in the elastic material). How the neural controls manage it is now pretty clear. The wing muscles contract in response mainly to their own stretch; infrequent neuron impulses merely keep them in an activated state. A hopping kangaroo shows similar elastic savings. The jump of the flea is a spring-catapulted feat, wound up by slow muscle contraction and suddenly released. Muscle fiber could not react swiftly enough on a flea scale, even though there are fast muscle fibers and slow ones. Many muscles contain more than one type of fiber, each reaching its optimum efficiency at a different rate of contraction, "as it were, a two- or three-geared system."

The gait of the cockroach has been studied in detail and is described here in the context of many patterns of loping quadrupeds: duty factors of the several feet, stability and favored speeds of gait-pattern shift. There is even a hopeful block diagram of the neural circuitry that might underlie the gait, with an input block marked "Command to walk" (a roach thought?). Archy would have liked it.

If it walks, runs, trots, crawls or burrows, there is some account of its dynamics, neatly done. A careful mechanical treatment in dimensionless terms by R. McN. Alexander of the University of Leeds helps one understand the effects of scale. Swimming (along with rowing and jet propulsion in water) is discussed in depth; so is flight, from hovering through gliding and soaring to fast flapping. There is a report of C. J. Pennycuick with his data on East African vultures and storks, collected as the investigator and the birds flew around together under the same cumulus cloud a few years ago. (He occupied a small motorized glider.) A bumblebee lies a little off the mean hovering curves, with a fast beat and small wings for its size, but there is no doubt of the basis of its flight design; we understand it mainly from the brilliant work of the late Torkel Weis-Fogh. (Professor Alexander gives us the review chapters on flight and swimming that Weis-Fogh did not live to prepare.)

Fishes have three ways to avoid sinking to the bottom. Hydrofoil-like fins work, given continuous swimming; low-density compounds such as squalene can balance off the denser tissue; a gas-filled swim bladder is energetically a better idea — maybe. Slow swimmers in fact do better with the light low-density compounds, but fast swimming speeds favor the active-lift scheme (all that extra volume makes for extra drag, which is serious at higher speeds). The gas bladder is best of all, but it takes chemical work to keep it at the ambient pressure; only big fish can afford to maintain a costly gas bubble at depth. The final chapter deals with single cells and their motion through a sticky world. Amoeba cytoplasm sets tough problems in rheology, but it is there that the motion of these "lobose carnivores" is to be sought.

This work is a particularly neat example of British bookmaking, although it is expensive for its modest size. There are many drawings; nearly all the other pictures are electron micrographs. It is a rich lode of physics and engineering, and an up-to-date road map to a big literature of wonderful freshness and ingenuity, in the high tradition of the physiologists of golden Bloomsbury times.

Only *Homo sapiens* has the muscle-driven wheel, which is celebrated in *Pedal Power*, a big paperback. David G. Wilson, a spry M.I.T. mechanical engineer, can be seen almost any day skimming the Cambridge streets in his own redesigned recumbent bicycle (lie back and enjoy the ride); he says it is safer, more efficient and more comfortable. Here we read of historical and modern pedicabs, bicycles with outriggers to ride the rails, pedal boats and lathes and a neat design for a homemade anchored bike to power kitchen, shop and garden tasks (or even television) while you exercise for 20 minutes. The theme is in the title: this is the best means of coupling the muscles of the human thigh and back to yield usable rotary power, at the rate of an easy tenth of a horsepower — or more for spurts and from athletes.

The work is at once practical and philosophical, not to say here and there rather hortatory; it offers information at many levels yet by no means offends simple economic man. We can do a lot more with pedals, even where food is dearer than petroleum. Stuart S. Wilson of Oxford outlines useful ways to harness pedal power in the context of the Third World, where power lines and refineries are distant. "Perhaps an interface between East and West is the bicycle, the machine which makes us all brothers and sisters."

(April 1978)

VI

Gunpowder and Beyond

Our century has been marked by war and warlike forebodings, but may end closer to peace. These books begin with medieval gunpowder and go on to machines now at watch from orbit. Some authors look at both sides of the dilemma, at both armorer and peaceable artisan.

Science and Civilisation in China, Volume 5, Chemistry and Chemistry Technology, Part 7. Military Technology: The Gunpowder Epic

By Joseph Needham

With the collaboration of Ho Ping-Yü, Lu Gwei-Djen, and Wang Ling

"This volume has been 43 years in the gestating" since one summer evening when the talk turned to the history of gunpowder and a very old printed passage was found and copied out. Dr. Needham and a few senior Chinese historians had been evacuated after some adventures to a "delightful little town" in Szechuan. The young Wang Ling was there too, and he made the matter his lifelong study. The first draft of this sparkling fire fountain of learning was lighted by Dr. Ho; by now all four authors have had a hand in the book.

This is a story of power, power both as swift release of energy and as enforcement of the will of the state. On page 4 a chart diagrams the entire development, a current that flows from Byzantium to Cape Canaveral. The medieval Chinese fire drug would come to depose the feudal lords of distant Europe; in 1449 the artillery train of the king of France toured the castles held by the English in Normandy to batter them down one by one "at the rate of five a month." In China the same stuff, employed in the widest variety of weapons for five centuries, had essentially no effect on the age-old bureaucratic structure, which held no castles and fielded no armored cavalry. Like printing in China, gunpowder made no revolution there; like the Chinese compass, gunpowder in the end equipped the overseas barbarians who would for a while humiliate the descendants of its early inventors.

In summary of this thick volume we address mainly the engineering history of the first chemical explosive. Fire flies with the arrows of war out of the deepest archaic past. The natural seepage of petroleum was a major resource, found in many places and used widely for military incendiaries. The coming of the first big change, the formidable Greek fire itself, can be dated with some precision. It depended on the discovery of distillation to produce a low-boiling hydrocarbon fraction: naphtha, a kind of kerosene or petrol — free-flowing, volatile, most inflammable. The blazing stuff was pumped over enemy craft in the sea fight that saved Byzantium from Arab attack in the late seventh century. The defending ships were called siphon bearers: behind iron shields their Greek seamen worked rumbling bronze flame-thrower pumps. The technique made its way to China, along with the fire oil itself, through the sea trade of the Arab merchants into southeastern Asia. By the year 1000 or so flame-thrower pumps were government issue in the Chinese armies.

Meanwhile the Taoist alchemists, seeking not death but the elixir of life, had from the third century or so received sulfur and of course carbonaceous substances into their masteries of the furnace. But the singular key to gunpowder was of course its internal oxidant saltpeter, or potassium nitrate. There is a long history of Chinese alchemical experimentation with the natural decomposition products of organic material, nitrates recent or ancient, and a slow rise of the recognition and preparation of increasingly pure saltpeter. By 850 or 900 the chemistry and its product were well understood. After 1200 the Arab chemists would call the stuff "Chinese snow."

The first loud, clear report of the sudden deflagration of the triple mix, saltpeter, sulfur and carbon, is heard in an entirely nonmilitary context. Among dozens of procedures against which the responsible Taoist adept is warned, a famous book of the Tao canon, probably from before 900, records that some people who had heated together sulfur, realgar and saltpeter with honey had been burned in hands and face "and even the whole house burned down." The internal oxidant was at work.

The weapons makers enter slowly. The usual Chinese term relates gunpowder to medicine or alchemy; it is called fire drug. In English the name is military from the start, powder for guns. Contemporary texts — not fully clear to a reader — suggest its first military use as a slow-match igniter for Greek fire in China in about 920. Pretty soon it is certainly used on its own in incendiary bolts and arrows, wrapped up and lighted behind the arrowhead to set a fire that is hard to extinguish. There is a description and a picture, although much later, of this "fiery pomegranate shot from a bow." Next comes the gunpowder flamethrower, its burning gases erupting from a bamboo tube — a fire lance. Such arms are still clearly seen in photographs of passenger junks of the 1930's, mounted for defense against pirates in the South China seas.

If gases flow fiercely out, why not projectiles along with them? Now the fire tubes hold sand and broken porcelain, and even human feces and other materials hopefully deemed to be toxic, all of which spurt out with the rushing flame. Next, the true explosive. (Of course the powder recipe steadily changes; the texts confirm that.) By the 1100's they have made a higher-nitrate mixture, enclosed in a weak container of bamboo; a loud bang is its main effect. A picture shows this "thunderclap bomb." Progress is swift; by 1230 or so the Chin Tatars stoutly defended Khaifêng from the powerful Mongols. The only weapons the Mongol soldiers feared were the flying-fire spears (big fire lances) and the thunder-crash bombs. Those bombs, the oldest true explosive devices, were gunpowder-loaded cast-iron shells two inches thick, shaped like bottle gourds. It was a famous defense, although it could not save the city or the dynasty.

Then comes the true propellant. For a long time the fiery gases drag out only ill-fitted scraps of all kinds. But in the end they propel well-made balls and arrows with gaskets (wads) that begin to occlude the opening; the true gun was born, first of all in bamboo and finally in metal. The evolution is intricate, but by about 1290 the species has clearly appeared. An eight-pound bronze hand bombard has been excavated in Manchuria, without a date but with excellent supporting ages derived from the archaeology and from local texts. The oldest gun, it must go back to just before 1290.

The first illustration of a gun in Europe is dated 1327. The picture seems clear: judging by the comments of Roger Bacon and the response of the arsenals, Europe eagerly seized on the villainous saltpeter between about 1270 and 1310 or so, as soon as the long Chinese development reached the artillery stage.

How was gunpowder brought to far-off Europe? There is a closing piece full of surmises bolstered by what evidence there is: yellow-haired Norsemen from Novgorod, Arab military engineers in China, learned friars and Nestorians, an Italian merchant colony in Tabriz? By the start of the 1300's "the bell had rung . . . and the Western world was set upon the fateful road" that led to small arms, artillery, heat engines and space travel. The mandarinate, however experienced, soon proved no match for the fervor of Europe, of its investors, its inventors, its kings and its sects. Before 1650 the busiest and most celebrated of the cannon founders in Peking itself were two Jesuit fathers.

(July 1987)

Military and Civilian Pyrotechnics
By Herbert Ellern

Here is an expert's account of a living technology — up to date, coherent and personal. Pyrotechnics is much older and much more conspicuous than its present economic scale would suggest. For this author pyrotechnics can no longer be fireworks alone; he defines it as the technology of the use of the heat and other products from the mainly nonexplosive exothermic reactions of solids. The core of the industry is the safety match; the 400 or 500 billion matches made each year in the U.S. exceed by tenfold the value of all fireworks production. Matches are treated here both historically and technically, although with little attention to the purely mechanical side of their mass production. The safety match has no secret formula; its successful manufacture is based on skillful management of the process, on maintaining uniformity in the face of small changes in materials and external conditions. The key is in details such as the use of the best hide glue ("Peter Cooper Grade IIa extra with foaming properties"); other binders can form a hardened skin over the pyrotechnic material, and the match explodes instead of burning smoothly. Good glue solidifies quickly and reversibly on mere cooling, without need for evaporation.

The dual title goes with a rather tough-minded text, rich in references to devices with names such as the "Mark 1 Smoke Pot (HC)." The duality lies deep in the material itself: the toy percussion cap and the old-fashioned gravel-filled fireworks torpedo are made with Armstrong's mixture: potassium chlorate and red phosphorus mixed wet with a starchy binder. Mixed with ether the same stuff can be loaded into larger containers and evaporated to dryness. Then it is a "formidable antipersonnel mine" that is exploded by slight pressure. The same reaction is the ingenious basis of the safety match. There the phosphorus is in the striker and the chlorate is in the head. (It is a "most fascinating . . . solid reaction.") The subtlety of a reliable safety match is made quite clear, if only qualitatively. The fuel is the glue, there are necessary catalysts, particle size is controlled and a sintered residue is designed in.

A special chapter by an English semipro, Rev. Ronald Lancaster, discusses fireworks for pleasure. That industry is too small to afford much research, unlike the military side. Fireworks history is divided into periods by the materials available: first black powder alone, with movement and propulsion the aim; then the rise of chlorates and pure chemicals in general, leading to the glories of color; next the bright light given by aluminum and magnesium and finally titanium. (A high output of white light depends on high energy release and on a very refractory solid oxide.) There are formulas for all the favorite fireworks: Roman candles, sparklers, Bengal lights, fountains and stars. Potassium chlorate, metal powders and the special ions for color pretty much span the field. The great Tokyo family Marutamaya launches paper shells full of marvelous colored stars 1,000 feet into the air from mortars a yard in diameter.

Tear gas? Orthochlorobenzal malononitrile, the irritant, is made up in sugared pellets. These are embedded in a mixture of nitrocellulose, chlorate and sugar. The reaction disperses the stuff as a distressing aerosol. (Chemical Mace is a nonpyrotechnic liquid dispersion of very fine particles.) The great flashes used to illuminate the terrain for night photography from high altitude call for a mixture of atomized aluminum (uniform grains 20 microns in diameter) with perchlorate and barium nitrate. A very large flash uses 100 kilograms of the mixture and yields for some milliseconds the luminous power of a few million garden flood lamps. Somehow this work, in which intelligence enlivens a technical and even esoteric topic, is a microcosm; within it death and delight stand very close. Even so special a technology can imply an epoch.

(April 1969)

Giving up the Gun: Japan's Reversion to the Sword, 1543 – 1879
By Noel Perrin

In 1543 a Chinese trading vessel anchored in the small harbor of Tanegashima Island, 20 miles south of Kyushu, the southernmost big island of Japan. Three of the tough crew, rovers and adventurers, were Portuguese seamen, the first Europeans known to reach Japan. Two of them had harquebuses; the moment the feudal master of the island saw one of these foreigners bring down a duck, "the gun enters Japanese history." Lord Tokitaka began lessons in shooting, and within the month he had bought the two guns at a princely price in gold, 30 years' fair wages for a workingman. The day of the purchase Tokitaka set his chief swordsmith to copying the weapons.

Japan was in the midst of her bloody century of feudal wars. Her craftsmen in iron and steel, her armorers, were perhaps the most skilled in the world; Japan was a leading exporter to all Asia of swords, pikes and armor. The country was populous, having six times the head count of contemporaneous England. The island was fertile soil, and the gun took root. True, the imported matchlocks did not catch on at once; the harvest was slow. Within a generation, however, the matchlock had been naturalized, refined, enlarged in caliber and muzzle energy and even fitted with rainproofing devices of Japanese design (shown here in one of the many delightful prints). The gunsmiths had been both inventive and busy; their improved product was no longer rare.

The great Lord Oda, who was to begin the unification of the nation, had as a young commander praised the spear as "the weapon on which to rely in battle." In 1575, however, he appeared at the terrible Battle of Nagashino, at the head of his army of 38,000 men, 10,000 of whom bore matchlocks. The men were unchivalrously concealed behind breastworks across a river; they held their fire until the time came to shoot "in volleys of a thousand." Bullets ended the noble samurai charge. Oda's gunpowder infantry tactics had been a brilliant success; within a few months after Nagashino two cannon, the first Japanese-made artillery, were test-fired for him, bronze two-pounders. Oda's matchlock corps at Nagashino had enlisted many young farmers, even though specially trained samurai knights stiffened it. "It was a shock to everyone to find out that a farmer with a gun could kill the toughest samurai so readily." Skill had been transferred back to the gunsmith from the soldier and up to his commander.

But in 1853 when Commodore Perry anchored his black ships in Tokyo Bay, the gunports of his flagship showed 64-pounder cannon and some even a little bigger. The shogun's samurai harbor defense manned cannon cast before 1620, six- and eight-pounders. One order of magnitude and more separated the arms of the barbarians from those of the men of honor. Firearms R&D had come to a full stop in Japan before its craftsmen had ever gone to flintlocks, say by 1650. Japan had plenty of flint, plenty of skilled artisans and a number of late Dutch prototypes. By then, however, they had simply lost interest in guns, except for the maintenance of an archaic coast defense. The lesson of Nagashino had been well absorbed. Once the feudal lords were brought securely under the unifying rule of the Tokugawas the newly centralized state began slowly and cleverly to undo the nation's firearms industry. Senior gunsmiths were promoted to samurai and converted to swordmakers. The scattered provincial gunmakers were required to move to either of two centers of the industry, and by 1607 they had all been assembled. They found only a dribble of orders from the central government and a salary paid them even if no guns were made. The land was at peace, the gun trade was reduced to a symbol: a few hundred matchlocks a year for almost a century (with some exceptions) in a country counting half a million sword-bearing warriors. Politics was in command; the technology of war had to obey.

The author, a Dartmouth English professor, has drawn much material from scholarly Japanese sources available to him in special translation. He has collected a striking set of illustrations, and his brief, readable text is full of helpful and often surprising comparisons with the history of Europe most readers know much better. The reasons behind this parable are many; certainly the most important one is the geopolitical status of the Empire of Japan, so long isolated from foreign entry by the sea and the Divine Wind. Two rebellions serve to accent the account. In 1637 the last effort of outlawed Christian Japan to reclaim freedom was the rising at Shimabara. Both sides then were armed with guns; the outnumbered rebels were killed to the last man. Long afterward, once the black ships had come and gone, a strong faction of the samurai, nearly one in 10 of them, joined in counterrevolution against the modernizing Meiji Emperor. In 1877 it was patrician swordsmen against peasant soldiers in Frenchified uniforms, with rebuilt matchlocks and some new rifles. After the decisive battle the scattered rebels yielded a few small firearms, mainly antique matchlocks, and a mound of captured swords rising "at least 10 feet from the ground." The march of military Japan was once again in melancholy step with the warlike West. Today's Japan, however, has at least proscribed war by nuclear fire.

(July 1981)

Thinkers and Tinkers: Early American Men of Science
By Silvio A. Bedini

World Armaments and Disarmament: SIPRI Yearbook 1975
Stockholm International Peace Research Institute

It is now 200 years since the English colonies precariously planted up and down the Atlantic coast became "of Right . . . Free and Independent States," but the history of those colonies was itself not much shorter than two centuries by the time of the first Glorious Fourth. They were initially settled in the same half-century in which Gilbert, Galileo and Pascal were placing the cornerstones of modern science, and they grew through the times of Newton and Watt.

There were a few Colonial scientists of distinction, in the end even one or two of preeminence; Franklin was recognized in his day as the equal of any electrician of Europe. A string of well-known naturalists richly reported the life forms of the New World. There was a third branch, humbler in purpose and scope and yet numbering men of energy, originality and skill who are chronicled and celebrated by this apt and interesting volume. They were the "mathematical practitioners," those who aimed at the practical, everyday application of optics, of geometry from trigonometry to conics and of the techniques of engraving, dividing and lens grinding—all new. They made the maps and the plates, marked the boundaries, conned the ships on coast and ocean, used compass and vernier; they understood projections, orbit elements and the measurement of time. Land surveyors, mapmakers, navigators and the rest, along with the small firms that made the instruments indispensable to those tasks and the teachers who wrote the books and recruited such men from a farming population, are Bedini's actors. He claims no comprehensive work. Their number is too great, their individual acts are too small; their memory is fragmented among the few instruments and maps that survive, the proud advertisements they once placed in the contemporary press, the local archives and provincial publications that hold the scattered material. This lively book is an overview, a valuable guide to the literature and an interesting photographic museum of their work. About a fourth of the photographs come from the great collection in the National Museum of History and Technology of the Smithsonian Institution in Washington, where the author serves as deputy director.

The book has 18 chapters and is mainly a brief, well-documented chronological narrative of the several periods of British North America, with an occasional more thematic chapter. The practical sciences were perforce based on English precept and practice. The Colonials were untrained, but they proved themselves equal to the task of self-improvement, adapting the methods and devices of London and Bristol to their own needs.

One case is the mariner's sextant. The precision angle-measurer in most general use at sea from the middle of the 18th century up to our day, it is a direct minor modification of Hadley's octant. It was in 1731 that John Hadley published his ingenious design of an accurate device to bring a directly viewed star into visual coincidence with a mirror image of, say, the horizon. In the previous year, however, a model of that same device had been successfully tested by a skipper out of Philadelphia for a young self-taught glazier-plumber-inventor of that city, Thomas Godfrey. (Ben Franklin, printer, had once taken lodgings with the Godfreys.) The English gentleman-inventor was anticipated by the Colonial artisan. An alternative design by Hadley proved more practical in one detail, and so to Hadley went the patent, the sales, the eponym and the popular acclaim. Historians today quite generally regard the credit as shared. "It often happens that the true author . . . lose the credit thereof and from age to age it passes to the name of another. Thus it happened heretofore to Columbus and many others; and this also has happened to a native of Philadelphia." So complained *American Magazine and Monthly Chronicle* in 1758.

The Colonial artisan-enterprisers formed no guilds, sought few specializations. They worked in any material suited to their ends, whereas the bigger instrument trade over in London split into branches of workers in brass and workers in wood. Indeed, brass was hard to get, a British monopoly based on English zinc carbonate and Welsh copper. Quadrants were made in Boston and New London of carefully pieced tropical hardwoods from the West Indies, particularly "green ebony" (Jamaican granadilla wood), close-grained and well protected by its natural oils against the sea air and salt water that made iron or New England black walnut or fruitwoods less desirable. Brass production did not begin in Connecticut until the 1830's.

A revolution required maps. General Washington reminded the Congress in 1777 that "a good Geographer to Survey the Roads and take Sketches of the Country where the Army is to Act would be extremely useful." The British had plenty of good maps and a corps of engineer officers and draftsmen trained in the Tower of London. Robert Erskine was appointed Geographer-Surveyor of the Continental Army within 10 days after Washington's letter. Before Erskine's untimely death in 1780 he and his corps of surveyors had made about 130 maps, mostly rough plane-table products. He reported in 1780: "In short, from the Surveys made . . . I could form a pretty accurate Map of the four States of Pennsylvania, New Jersey, New York and Connecticut." These were in the end compiled on a grid based on a prime meridian at New York City.

The new nation needed maps and careful bounds for orderly expansion. The disputed boundary between Lord Baltimore's colony and that of William Penn had been fixed carefully on the ground a generation earlier (with errors verified in this century at only two or three degrees) by a pair of imported English experts, Charles Mason and Jeremiah Dixon, who brought along English instruments of unusual sophistication. By Thomas Jefferson's presidency a zenith sector like theirs (but made by two Americans, David Rittenhouse and Andrew Ellicott) was fixing the boundaries down south and "in the western Country" beyond Buffalo. Americans did not look back; they were feisty and confident and their skills increased with their own high self-estimate. Joseph Pope, an ambitious and learned clockmaker of Boston, spent years building an ornate outsided orrery more than six feet in diameter, perhaps "the most elaborate piece of scientific apparatus constructed in America up to that time." A state lottery was held in Massachusetts to raise money so that Harvard might gain the touted marvel. There it still is, a flashy gilt-and-mahogany lemon so poorly designed that it never worked.

"What may we not expect from this harmony between the sciences and government!" wrote Benjamin Rush. "Methinks I see canals cut, rivers once impassable rendered navigable, bridges erected, and roads improved, to facilitate the exportation of grain. I see the banks of our rivers vying in fruitfulness with banks of the river of Egypt. I behold our farmers nobles, our merchants princes."

Dr. Rush was farsighted; it has all come to be true. The ironies of history nonetheless bar any simple pride in our princely merchants and noble farmers. In the South Bronx or out at Pine Ridge, to name only unarguable examples, the dreams of the Yankee Enlightenment seem hollow. It is facile to blame that on thinkers and tinkers, one might maintain. But the 10,000 elegant single-axis gyros precessing slowly in the underground silos or in sleek tubes undersea are the handiwork of the manifest inheritors of those mathematical practitioners, now to be found in clean rooms from Newport Beach to Rocky Flats and Cambridge. Together with their counterparts between the Neva and the Pacific they hold the world uneasy hostage. The facts behind the ceaseless growth of more formidable weapons are yearly reviewed by the analysts of the

Stockholm International Peace Research Institute (SIPRI), mainly on the basis of material from newspapers, the aerospace trade journals and official Government documents. They present this material in book form: a more or less unique study of the largest of all high-technology industries, worldwide.

This year's issue, which reviews the race up to the end of 1974, signals the advent of a new country, India, as the latest nuclear entrant and also marks the clear rise of a counterforce strategy by the hundred-armed U.S. Technically the most novel chapter is an account of reconnaissance satellites. The analysis "suggests that a ground resolution of 15 cm is feasible." Working from private observations (apparently made by the students and staff of an English grammar school), the report maps the ground tracks of Russian and U.S. satellites during the Cyprus conflict and at about the time of the Indian nuclear test. The conclusion is drawn that satellites are now maneuvered from the ground to monitor crisis areas "as a matter of routine" by both powers. The volume contains much information, technical, military and legal. The words of SIPRI's director, Frank Barnaby, are cogent: the big powers must expect more proliferation until they "show by their actions that they see no utility in nuclear weapons. . . . The only way is to reduce their nuclear arsenals." What can the Tricentennial expect?

(July 1976)

Gyroscopic Theory, Design, and Instrumentation
By Walter Wrigley, Walter M. Hollister and William G. Denhard

About as costly and as numerous as Rolls-Royces, there spin all over the earth and the seas, at 10,000 or 20,000 turns per minute, the two-inch beryllium rotors that are the heart of the elegant navigational gyroscopes built in clusters into every guided missile the great powers have, into their space vehicles and—in less elite versions—into the instrument panels of aircraft. This engineering text, complete with explicit problems but a little lacking in candor about performance and dimensions, is intended as a one-term course for senior or early graduate students. It does not have much to say about the navigational system as a whole, the electronics of servomechanisms and computers that makes the gyroscope sensors useful, but it presents the theory of the gyroscope (and the simpler accelerometer) from the general equations, through the linearized approximations that describe the useful case, the choices taken now and in the past by a generation of designers, and the intricate testing procedures. The familiar aircraft instruments are included, as is the ship's gyrocompass, mainly for their theory; the center of interest is the modern strapped-down single-degree-of-freedom floated integrating gyroscope — the working state of this high art until lasers or electrostatically suspended grains or something else proves acceptable. In this device the rotor is driven magnetically on a superb ball-bearing axis. (The tolerances are specified to five or 10 microinches.) The rotor is housed in a float also made of the light, strong metal beryllium. That float is buoyed up by a bath of a syrupy fluorocarbon liquid, which takes the weight and inertial load off the transverse output axis on which the floating rotor housing can so delicately turn. That axis, whose remarkably small motions represent the output of the gyroscope, is damped by the fluid, which kills the oscillations dear to gyroscopic theory. In some ways this is the key idea. There are no bearings on the output axis. Alternating-current magnetic suspensions center the output axis fully, so that in normal operation it does not even touch. The axis direction is servo-controlled by the computing circuits, which step by step, every fraction of a millisecond, pulse torque into the gyroscope to compensate for its tiny deviations, and keep algebraic count of what they do. Thus the device integrates motion and leads the vehicle to the target, given six separate integrators, a known starting point and a built-in gravity model. The output axis is not likely to turn through more than a fraction of a minute of arc at any time; such motions are submicroscopic. The power leads are carefully designed linear spring devices. The entire can is temperature-controlled for exact buoyancy and fixed sizes; it is magnetically shielded, made with press fits designed in advance to 20 microinches or less and sealed with special adhesives. The top spins in helium in its precise way for the few years of its working life, provided that it has been put together in an ultraclean atmosphere, checked for dust specks with a microscope (a few micrograms of extra weight is too much) and designed and built by a team whose experience is reflected in the curves showing the steady evolution of lifetime and performance over the past 20 years.

Such virtuosity in the paths of Newton, Maxwell, Whitworth and the metallurgists is genuinely remarkable. No matching wisdom in saving these gems of gyroscopes from being vaporized someday, along with our cities, is to be found in any current text.

(March 1970)

Think Tanks
By Paul Dickson

Out of the Douglas Aircraft Company
by the Army Air Forces, RAND was born at Santa Monica in the months
after World War II. The first charge to the organization (it is still the
contract that pays half of the bills) was for "'a program of study and
research on the broad subject of intercontinental warfare other than
surface. . . . '" A fanatically sectarian college without students, wary of
critics, privy to ambitious air generals, RAND (for Research ANd Development) has spun out the theoretical base for the arms race, and has devised,
or at least justified, most of the gambits of the Strategic Air Command,
from refueling, hardening and fail-safe to how best to split the fallout
between our old enemy Red China and our old friend Japan. It has often
revealed real insight: as early as 1946 RAND saw the magic that would
attend the first artificial satellite, and later RAND people foresaw and
indeed developed much of the conceptual design of satellite reconnaissance. But its strategic policy innovations, whether they arose more from
the sober calculations of Albert Wohlstetter or more from the apocalyptic
world view of Secretary of Defense James V. Forrestal, have rationalized
the arms race ever since 1951. RAND largely sees the nation's problem as
lying in the grim fact of Russian nuclear weapons. It may well be, however,
that RAND itself is more the problem than the solution.

Dickson, a young free-lance writer who has made his excellent journalist's report mainly out of visits and interviews and rather less from the
documentary record, sums up RAND today: "It has by its own admission
fallen behind in perceiving and acting to solve the major problems facing
the nation. It is now trying to catch up, and without question a new RAND
is developing. . . . Its once single-minded concern will soon become just
one of many concerns about national security in the broadest, nonmilitary
sense of the term. If RAND cannot make that conversion, then it knows it
might as well go out of business." Perhaps it could start making type-
writers, he adds, embroidering an old jape about RAND's name and public
image. But can the B-52 ever change its spots?

Mother RAND has many children, some born before her. There are
"at least 17,000 research entities" in the U.S. today, from the Hale Obser-
vatories to the dog-food-company laboratories. About 600 of them are
think tanks. These are here defined as multidisciplinary R&D groups,
closely coupled to industry, government or public purpose, whose output
is not directed toward science and technology so much as toward analytical matter "relevant to people who make policy," from admirals to mere
voters. About 75 think tanks are contract adjuncts to Government agen-

cies, like RAND; another dozen or so live within the Government itself, like the Army's Institute for Land Combat; 200 are nonprofit enterprises, like the Stanford Research Institute; 300 more simply think for profit as *condottieri* of the brain. A handful of them, like the Institute for Policy Studies — the left end of the think-tank continuum — work and publish for a point of view they hold as the public good.

A couple of dozen ubiquitous think-tank acronyms are explained in a glossary that closes the book. Most of this readable volume is devoted to narratives of what in fact goes on at 10 or 15 of these lettered places. At the Institute for Land Combat they plan and game out wars of the future, doing with computer just what everyone believed the Prussian general staff was doing long ago with pencil and paper. In an Alexandria office building not far from the Pentagon they have thought up some 145 wars that might plausibly involve the U.S. One example is a desert war in North Africa with the U.S., Libya, Tunisia, Italy and West Germany fighting Algeria, the United Arab Republic and the U.S.S.R.

The Hudson Institute was founded by RAND heretics who left the sunny purlieus of Santa Monica in the name of the engaging legendary prophet Herman Kahn, half-droll and half-dread, to whom they still impute their most colorful irresponsibilities. The place is described factually, if somewhat implausibly, in one chapter. One of its recent specialties is the "flying think tank." Its teams flew and thought over Angola for 10 days in four light planes. Two volumes of papers came out of this incontrovertible overview (which was too high to see any fighting). Some specific ideas include damming the Congo, creating a wine industry, organizing safaris with "black hunters" and setting up a Mountie-like all-black elite border patrol that would always get its man. This report to a Portuguese manufacturer, complete with detailed scenarios, cost $100,000. It included a paper ascribed to Kahn himself. The prophet was not, of course, physically with the team on high. He dwells in still thinner air. Hudson has dropped most of the old operations-research tradition, with its heavy computing and rich tables of real or as-if data. The members of the Hudson Institute "often boast that its computing power is, with a gesture to the head, 'all up here.'" Somehow this "politically Rightist" ideological fiction factory finds apt clients. ABM and Vietnamization have had Hudsonian inputs.

The genre is still wider. There is room for the corporate study around Mr. Nader and the dissenting policy thought around Drs. Raskin and Waskow, just as for the semidetached Brookings Institution. There is the R&D supermarket of Arthur D. Little, where once they made a real silk purse — you can see it today in the Smithsonian — out of 100 pounds of sows' ears. That low yield hardly disposes of the adage, but it somehow seems to be the most unifying comment one can make on this typically

American phenomenon, a collective but constrained search for reason applied in our competitive and corporate society.

(July 1972)

Deep Black: Space Espionage and National Security
By William E. Burrows

Not even a black hole can manage to remain entirely invisible. In this volume full of satisfying and documented detail a responsible and savvy journalist has fitted together patches and fragments of published information and informed opinion to depict the nature of overhead reconnaissance today. The portfolio of relevant images he offers is capped by a sunlit orbital photograph of the first large Soviet aircraft carrier, under construction on the Black Sea, made by the video imagers of the satellite *Keyhole-11* in the summer of 1984. The view at 500 oblique miles is sharp and informative: it is the look of a shipyard seen from a light plane passing a mile or so away. We owe the image to the London editors of *Jane's;* the American naval analyst who unofficially supplied it to them has since been convicted and is awaiting judgment on appeal. The technical manual for that satellite had been sold earlier by a Central Intelligence Agency employee to Soviet intelligence for $3,000, a bargain price (although it is notorious that early editions of such manuals are often badly written).

Suite 4C-956, part of an Air Force province in the Pentagon, houses the headquarters of the National Reconnaissance Office (NRO), "responsible," since its formation in August, 1960, "for the design, development, and procurement of all U.S. reconnaissance satellites and for their management once in orbit." Its input includes dollars—up to five billion of them during 1985—and policy guidance from a couple of boards; the director of the CIA is also a prominent influence. The U.S.A.F. and the CIA share this high task somewhat uneasily, troubled by memories of "all-out tribal warfare" in the distant past: targeting and analysis are no easy mirrorfellows, particularly when information confers more power than a handful of Cayman bankbooks.

The NRO is to be found again at the Big Blue Cube in Sunnyvale, Calif., from which all U.S. military satellites are controlled, and also in El Segundo, where not the Red Army but the contractors are monitored. The chief systems contractors to the NRO are Lockheed and TRW; they head a long parade of other high-technology firms.

The NRO is a little short of assets these days, "blind in one eye" after the *Challenger* disaster and two other launch failures. Its single deployed *Keyhole-11*, the sixth of its design, has been working overtime. Usually there have been a pair in low polar orbit overflying everywhere, one in the morning, one in the afternoon. This *KH-11* was launched in December of 1984; on the record such a craft serves for 1,000 or 1,2000 days. Its two-meter mirror and infrared scanner feed a package of sensors, in particular a CCD (charge-coupled device) mosaic of high resolution, as well as an array of special-purpose detectors including a photomultiplier for night views. The satellite propagates its digitized data by relay satellites to Fort Belvoir, and there the downlink is completed.

The admirable images are seen in "real time." Within an hour of their capture they are available by courtesy in the Oval Office. Less honored images are interpreted in a variety of places; each user seems to prefer its own eyes, or programs. Nowadays the images are enhanced, transformed and even routinely monitored by computer. The machines can detect changes and report them. Stereo views are made and multiband analyses can be run. The National Photographic Interpretation Center, a window-less beige warehouse on M Street S.E. with plenty of air conditioning, was once the seat of the unified eagle-eyed watchers of Cuban-crisis days but now is probably a lending library of digital images pored over by cool, sedulous Crays.

KH-11, the fifth generation in its lineage, if formidable. Its resolution must be about two to four inches, not quite good enough to read license plates. Its datalink bandwidth matches the quality of the films so daringly dropped from orbit by *KH-4* in 1962.

What of *KH-12*? A Lockheed design, it was tightly integrated with the shuttle for launch and resupply. It is a heavy platform, 20 tons when full. It has plenty of its own fuel, hydrazine, for wide maneuverability. Four satellites are intended to serve at the same time, two for night and two for day. The sensors will be improved, as usual, and there is a grandiose plan to deliver real-time images to commanders in the field. Tactical imagery will flow along a chair of seven *Milstar* relay satellites, hardened, encrypted, jamproofed and highly maneuverable, not only to Washington but also "straight off the bird" to the theater staff. When costs rise, you broaden the market.

Soviet orbiters bring film back by returning to the earth; such craft are relatives of the manned *Soyuz*. The Soviets launch one such vehicle routinely every couple of weeks, and when events suggest it, one every few days. Their style is that of the assembly line: each device delivers relatively low performance, but each is simpler, less expensive, adaptable and quickly replaced. The impression is that since 1984 the craft have also been able to transmit digital images in real time. The most impressive Soviet satellites are aimed at the blue-water U.S. Navy. These include radar

satellites powered by small nuclear reactors—one fell on Canada years
ago—and paired passive trackers of radar and radio from the fleet. These
are fitted with ion microthrusters to allow minute control of orbit altitude, so that a target's shifting position can be triangulated.

There are air breathers in plenty overhead. The stealthy "blackbirds"
of Beale Air Force Base in California, Lockheed SR-71 aircraft, fly everywhere, staging in Okinawa and England. They are no strangers to Nicara-
guan seaports at low altitude. In more developed regions of the world
their cameras, side-looking radar and electronic monitors move at Mach
3+ 100,000 feet up. They are only first within a large and complex
system. The narrative of overhead reconnaissance from aircraft is the topic
of almost half of the text. The crises entrained by the downings of U-2's
over Sverdlovsk and Cuba and the involvement of an RC-135 flying
toward Sakhalin in the tragedy of a Korean Air Lines 747 are recounted.
Those Tupolev four-engine Bears photographed seasonally off the East
Coast bound for Cuba are the visible Soviet counterparts. The text treats
undersea information gathering briefly but well.

This is an up-to-date, thoughtful, nontechnical, factual study of a
topic that lies behind much of the news. Although the actions in this arena
are hostile, even warlike, they continue by tacit consent. This state of
affairs may even hold the promise of a world were armed forces can also
be reliably reduced by consent. The new French commercial system, SPOT,
offers pictures with a resolution of 10 meters in black and white, and
multiband images as well. Their CCD's blur the boundary between civil
and military observation from space; they may help to keep the NRO, SAC
and the others "honest." A SPOT photograph reproduced here clearly
shows the Semipalatinsk nuclear test site in the summer of 1986; it has lain
fallow for almost two years, although tunnels are being readied. The
world is open enough; we can see what we need to see. "To cast doubt on
the process itself by falsely labeling national technical means of verification as inadequate is to subvert reason to the basest political posturing."
In orbit, war and peace fly together. The carrying of physical conflict into
space is a danger just ahead.

(May 1987)

VII

Earth, Sea and Sky

Certain sciences of the field — in particular pale-ontology, geology, astronomy of the solar system and of the deep sky — have thrived by generous gifts from modern technology. Here a small but delightful view is opened on a number of such marvelous successes.

Krakatau 1883: The Volcanic Eruption and Its Effects
By Tom Simkin and Richard S. Fiske

Sunsets, Twilights, and Evening Skies
By Aden and Marjorie Meinel

When the hush-hush technical library was deviously assembled for wartime Los Alamos, two titles were included by the witty librarians that might have brushed the limits of discretion. One was the science fiction novel *Krakatit*, by the Czech novelist Karel Čapek, who imagined a chemist hero capable of coaxing explosive reactions out of almost any raw material. The title celebrates the chemist's most alarming compound, for which he became the cynosure and pawn of governments. The other title was a matter-of-fact, although sumptuous, 1888 volume of the Royal Society, which carried its expert committee's compilation of material on the Krakatau eruption itself. There is no doubt that the eruption, with its catastrophic loss of life, its physical effects noticed worldwide and its full accounting by unprecedentedly prompt stories in the press, borne everywhere by the new cable links, caught the imagination of a generation.

The centennial of Krakatau was last year. Two scholarly young volcanologists have here compiled a modern version of that 1888 tome out of London. They offer us an exemplary treatment: documented, comprehensive, fascinating, beautiful, even cheap. The bargain volume consists of a useful introduction and concise chronology, then a hundred pages of eyewitness accounts, half in terror and half in wonder, a first translation into English (done by E. M. and A. F. Koster van Groos and J. A. Nelen) of much of the monograph prepared by the prescient leader of the official on-the-spot investigation sent in seven weeks afterward by the government of the Dutch East Indies, and an anthology of scientific papers about Krakatau.

The cited papers cover the geology, the prodigious waves radiated the world around through air and sea, the visual atmospheric phenomena seen for once in a blue moon, the plausible effect on climate and the slow, steady return of life to the wrecked and denuded island. The papers span a century of interpretation, and they are eloquent witness to the blend of truth and error in science at any one epoch. The young mining engineer Rogier D. M. Verbeek, who led the official investigation, had sought the services of a photographer. That specialist objected to a long field trip, and in his place was sent "the sergeant-major draughtsman P. B. Schreuders." Schreuders' paintings, done with the aid of the camera lucida, were reproduced for publication by the new process of chromolithography; they supply vivid evocations of the scenes. (The most important single view, that of the cliffed ruin of the half cone as seen from the sea, was reproduced in the November 1983 issue of this magazine; here there are many more views as well.)

Since the geology has recently been described in *Scientific American* and the strange atmospheric effects are covered in the second book reviewed here, it is the waves we shall cite to sample the science reported in the first book. Death's chief minister was the fearful tsunamis. On the sloping coasts in the area the sea rose as high as 40 meters and more, carrying one warship inland for miles and sweeping prosperous market towns clean of their green groves and paddy, leaving them melancholy featureless tidal flats. For weeks the inland people toiled to burn or bury the corpses cast up here and there in heaps. As far away as San Francisco and even in the English Channel the tide gauges showed Krakatau-timed trains of waves inches high. The dynamics, however, did not fit well: those little waves had come too fast from the Sunda Straits, and in some instances any sea path seemed implausibly circuitous.

A fine paper of 20 years ago (by Frank Press and David G. Harkrider, who were then at the California Institute of Technology) goes far toward a solution of the century-old riddle. That small distant effect was not the sea wave direct but a secondary sea disturbance driven by the shocked atmosphere. (The sound of "distant roars of heavy guns" was reliably reported from an island 3,000 miles away, after four hours of sound transit time.) There are modes of vibration of the entire atmosphere that nearly match the phase velocity of the long waves in the deepest seas. It is these air modes that jumped over land barriers to reexcite local sea waves one way or another, with unexpected amplitude and speed. And the anxiety about the fearful substance krakatite is not quite stilled: Simkin and Fiske estimate that a surface explosion "of about 100 to 150 megatons would produce pressure pulses equivalent to those observed from Krakatau."

The Meinels are an astronomical couple from Tucson, well known at many a mountain dome around the world. To their professional work, now centered on the exploitation of solar energy, they have for two decades added an open-eyed study of sunset phenomena. They report it all here delightfully "in the old fashion, when science was open to every reader," the fascinating facts told in personal stories and as tales from friends. Catastrophe apart, their book, aglow with dozens of color plates of fiery sunsets, stilled by the purple vault of desert nights, echoes and explains the puzzled witness of those Krakatau-painted sunsets a century ago.

Their subject is vista. Narrow valleys and lowering rainclouds are not the places to look; long, low horizons and clear desert air are needed. The scale is set by the layered spheres of the earth and its atmosphere; the

quantum clarity of the air molecules allows the effects of dust and droplets to shine out. The book begins with the geometry of sunset and its
physics, made plain in diagram and graph. The green flash is given a
chapter of its own; the most agreeable novelty is a simple sketch and
account of how a triangular shadow converges to the horizon at sunset
and sunrise to an observer watching from a mountaintop. That triangle
does not depend on the shape of the mountain but is the necessary
consequence of the set of shadow forms converging by perspective to a
single highest point: the shadow point of the observer. Just as we stand
always at the top of our world — the highest surface point along our own
vertical radius — so do we stand at the tip of our mountain's shadow
pyramid.

The most original part of this delightful book is volcano watching,
albeit at a big distance. The dusts and aerosols from the eruptions did not
stop, of course, with old Krakatau but continue still. Here are sunsets of
recent decades colored by Agung and El Chichón and El Fuego and the
rest, with the explanation of what you see and why. Some of the interpretation calls for rather more gear than a keen eye and a clock, but a good
start can be made with what every viewer sees. The brilliant crimsons of
post-Agung sunsets disappeared in half a year, as had those of Krakatau.
No one was surprised; the dust had simply settled out. But a century ago,
as they did in the late 1960's, the enhanced sunsets unexpectedly recurred
in the fall and winter for some years. The reappearances bore the mark of
high aerosol layers: a sharp upper edge to the glow, together with spectral
details. More is going on than a simple settling of dust.

It seems probable that the stratospheric aerosol is in fact droplets of
sulfuric acid (they have been found on the windshields of the high-flying
U-2's) generated not by dust but by sulfur dioxide ejected by the volcano.
That reagent slowly diffuses upward, reacting finally with the ozone layer
to form the acid droplets. The abundance of the droplets is under the
control of the seasonal response of ozone formation to the insolation of
the high atmosphere. Acid droplets re-form season after season until most
of the gas is used up. Blue suns and emerald green moons are not just
centennial memories either: in northern China the effect is not infrequent,
as dust borne by winds from the distant loess of the Gobi fills the skies to
provide a complex example of angle- and color-dependent light scattering.

The night sky draws the Meinels' attention as well. In the dark are
subtler glows: the aurora, high clouds of artificial and natural origin,
effects of interplanetary dust in the plane of the ecliptic, odd visitors (such
as asteroids and comets) and city lights. All of these are briefly introduced
for the benefit of would-be watchers of the skies. Other worlds are not
neglected; for twilight glory, though, the earth remains the "best of all the
planets," at least while it enjoys a climate that allows clear air. It seems
probable that cloudy skies were general during epochs as warm and rainy

as the Mesozoic; the swampy earth of the coal beds was no planet for sky watchers. The Meinels aptly chose the psalmist to close in eloquence their engaging and enthusiastic book: "The dawn and the sunset shout for joy!"
(March 1984)

The Burgess Shale
By Harry B. Whittington

The unexpected bones of our own ancestors lie quietly in Olduvai Gorge; the first of all the birds left unique impressions of its plumage in the satiny limestone of Solnhafen. This persuasive and visual little book by an authoritative University of Cambridge paleontologist takes the reader to another fossil site richer, if less intimate, than Olduvai, to see the marks of creatures stranger, if humbler, than *Archeopteryx*.

A few miles west of the tourist-filled meadows at Lake Louise in the Canadian Rockies, a certain Mount Burgess looks across to a steep ridge. Halfway up that ridge—the scene is pictured in the book—an area of fine-grained dark shale is exposed. It was named the Burgess Shale in about 1909 by Charles D. Walcott, newly the secretary of the Smithsonian Institution. The Burgess yields no trace of bone or feather; those are biochemical inventions that came much too late to have entered the 540 million years of storage here. But it is a wide window on Cambrian life in the sea—the dry land was yet unquickened—that we find nowhere else.

Walcott was not only a scientific administrator of talent but also a brilliant and untiring field-worker. He was a world authority on the Cambrian System, whose rocks he searched out and split during more than 50 years. His greatest discovery, the Burgess Shale repository, was made with his wife. They paused to split just one more loose block of shale, and before them shone silvery images against the dark rock; they dubbed the intricate filmy creatures "lace crabs."

Walcott returned the next summer with his two sons. The three patiently searched the slope high above the place where the loose block had been found, until they came on the narrow band rich in fossils. Summer after summer they came back to pry at that rock. During eight years of work—Walcott was 67 the last year he spent at the site—their excavation removed a six-foot layer from an area the size of a narrow garden. From that shale came 60,000 fossils, including 15,000 thumb-size lace crabs, formally *Marrella splendens*. They are much more abundant in this fauna than any of the trilobites, the forms that typically characterize the Cambrian.

Harry B. Whittington's compact book is a model of concise exposition and presentation of the evidence. The reader will see 100 photographs, drawings and models of the animals of the Burgess, all carefully marked for scale, many exhaustively described. The gallery makes a curious impression on a reader who is no marine biologist. Unfamiliar enough, these varied soft-bodied organisms, spiny, tentacled or segmented, would attract anyone spotting them in a rock pool, but they would come to a casual stroller as no grand surprise.

Yet the expert paleontologists, from Walcott to today, betray surprise. The very names they gave stand witness: *Hallucigenia, Anomalocaris,* . . . *inexpectans,* . . . *dubia,* . . . *rara.* . . . The reason is plain: inconsistent architecture. Take *Hallucigenia.* You and I look at its inch-long print with interest. The little animal stands on seven pairs of pointed spines, and its back bears a set of tentacles. Its head is only vaguely known. It looks like an unusual but plausible enough small scavenger of the shallow sea floor, but to the author "it would be difficult to imagine an animal as bizarre." Walcott thought it a strange kind of worm; the moderns, who know 40 prints of it, some from the 1930's, see that it is a puzzle, without clear affinities, without any basis for higher classification. Seven spines? There are a couple of dozen such forms, most possessing a variety of traits that are plausible in themselves but are so strange in combination that the overall assemblage cannot be placed in any large group now known, whether continuing or extinct.

These are creatures from another world of time, the seas of half a billion years ago. Among their kind they are neither primitive nor simple. They played subtle and well-adapted roles in a highly organized ecology; some of those roles can be made out clearly today by their diverse means of feeding, for example. Their strangeness consists only in that they neither left descendants nor followed the architecture of more fortunate forms that did. The reasons for their extinction could be manifold, even chancy. We have every reason to regard these creatures as a fair sample of their time and place, reminders that evolution is an ongoing experiment on a large scale, its many repeated runs far more numerous than our capricious samples.

How did this unique paleontologists' paradise come about? That account is the most fascinating part of the narrative. There is no space to follow the arguments in detail; moreover, the geological diagrams here are indispensable for clarity. The conclusions derive from the work of a wonderful little international expedition to the Burgess, sent there in 1966 by the Geological Survey of Canada, Whittington among them.

What they untangled was context. Walcott's fauna are so strange because nowhere else were so many soft-bodied Cambrian creatures preserved. Within the past few years, though, a number of other sites have turned up, some only a few miles from the original quarry, some as far distant as Utah, that yielded a few specimens resembling the Burgess Shale creatures. What happened undersea on Mount Burgess long ago was that a small section of a sloping mud fringe around a Cambrian reef (a limestone structure, too early to have been the work of the polyps that build modern coral) suddenly slumped. The turbulent mud carried down with it the creatures of a shallow, oxygenated, well-lighted patch of sea bottom below the high reef wall, burying them no great distance away in a quieter, muddier bottom where seawater circulation was poor and the oxygen sparse.

All these circumstances can be pretty well inferred from the details of the rocky context, examined for miles around, and from the key fossils themselves. They are preserved as mineralized film (best photographed in ultraviolet) lacking original hard parts, compacted and flattened tenfold during their long mineralization. The microdrill the moderns use to dissect the fossils makes it plain that the animal had been tumbled and infiltrated with fine mud before its compaction; mineral grains still separate the delicate layers of the fossil itself. So constrained an event is evidently rare. Without some version of it we would find no well-preserved soft-bodied animals, even though they were dominant in that time and place.

The largest animal of the Cambrian swam there too, a formidable if soft-bodied hunter, particularly of the still-unhardened large trilobite species of the time, all forms known only from the Burgess Shale. The monster was about 20 inches long. It undulated its way close to the bottom. Up front it bore a hardened but not mineralized ring jaw and a single pair of strong spined limbs it could dangle to probe for and then seize its crawling prey. Isolated parts of the predator were known earlier, but the whole creature has been assembled, understood and restored only very recently by the author and a colleague, Derek E. G. Briggs. Any daring scuba diver on Cambrian holiday from another star would have been delighted to spear such a prime trophy, unclassifiable in any phylum we know.

(May 1986)

The Mediterranean Was a Desert:
A Voyage of the *Glomar Challenger*
By Kenneth J. Hsü

The evidence that glaciers once covered much of central Europe, not to mention North America, is overwhelming. The idea is now a commonplace; every schoolchild learns it, if only from the comic strips. About 10 million cubic kilometers of the mineral ice were added to cap Europe alone over the past million years. The first insight into that preposterous past came from the Swiss peasants who lived where a thoughtful person could see almost in one glance both the moraines and boulders at the living glacier edge and their counterparts mysteriously strewn down along the pleasant valley where no glacier had ever been known to intrude. The geologists who incredulously verified that picture and extended it step by step a century and a half ago needed no equipment beyond stout shoes and perhaps an alpenstock and a hammer.

This personal account, its first draft written on shipboard, tells a parallel story but a modern one. A similar if somewhat smaller volume of the mineral water was not added but removed from the map of Europe about five million years back. The central wine-dark sea, where Odysseus made his finally happy voyage, was then a desert, a "deep, dry, hot hellhole," its wide basin three kilometers below sea level, the seat of whirlwinds stirring red painted deserts, of transient briny lakes and of long river-cut canyons. Ken Hsü first found clear evidence for this picture (by now of course much elaborated) on the morning of August 24, 1970, watching his partner, Bill Ryan, another young shipboard sedimentologist, working up the sand-and-gravel sample they had collected during the long sleepless night before. The gravel held gypsum, an evaporative residue of seawater, along with two or three other components typical of the gravelly outwash from a long-eroded bed formed in a dried-up salt lake. A keen eye, a wash bucket and a hot plate were all the laboratory equipment needed to disclose the ancient desert that is the only plausible source.

No one, however, had ever seen or walked out those beds of gravel that furnished the illuminating little sample. It was fished out of two kilometers of sea off the Barcelona coast, held in a core barrel that had drilled deep into the ooze of the sea floor until it had struck a harder surface below, long recognized solely by its ubiquitous echo reflection up to the sounding ships, now disclosed as desert floor. The bright flash of inference was in the lofty tradition of field geology back to Louis Agassiz and James Hutton; the tools were no longer the traditional ones but the very epitome of big science, heavy investment and teamwork on a grand scale.

A hammer can loosen a sample from a rock wall by hand. A collector underseas needs much more, an entire ship dedicated to deep-sea drilling. Such a ship was the *Glomar Challenger* (now ignominiously idle, awaiting a buyer), sponsored by the National Science Foundation, sailing on the 13th drilling cruise out of the 80-odd legs of its career of deep-sea drilling. The product of Texas offshore-oil technology, with an assist from the shadowy world of technical intelligence, it was the concrete embodiment of that half-dream and half-spoof, the abandoned Mohole proposal of the

1950's, out of whose failure blossomed the ship's dynamical positioning scheme. That keeps the unmoored drilling vessel aligned to some 50 meters' accuracy above the drill hole kilometers below, trimming its position by sensing and responding to acoustic beacons set on the bottom.

It is no beauty, this slow-steaming ship of 11,000 tons, with a 60-meter drilling tower, a foredeck piled high with 10 kilometers of big steel drill pipes and a "moon pool" opened midships to pass the drill string and its bulky attachments. It can nonetheless support 500 tons of drill pipe, to bore into rock a kilometer below the ocean floor through a seven-kilometer layer of seawater. It has done something like that 500 times, in all the oceans except the Arctic, over its dozen years of service.

For two months in 1970 direct responsibility for 15 drill holes of its expensive mission (put the operating cost at $1 million per month at sea, and $100 million or so of 1968 dollars to build it) was shared by Hsü and Ryan, who had just finished his Ph.D. The wiseacres complained, with some show of reason, that the unique ship had been placed in the hands of "a student and an amateur." Those two co-chief scientists were, however, well up to their heavy task of supplying relevance to the ship's work, day after costly, tedious day.

The book is a personal and candid chronicle of Hsü's Leg 13, a tale of garbled radio messages, stubborn management, elated success, grim failure, shipboard intrigue and loyal and delighted colleagues. The cast of characters includes the captain and his crew, who knew both the sea and the demands of shore on the vessel; the drilling crew, roughnecks, tool pushers and their supervisors, who knew how to manhandle the rig and how to manage its surprising encounters with the rock far below; the half-dozen scientists who were "the 'decoding' section," and the long-haired young marine scientists and technicians from the Scripps Institution, who staffed the shipboard laboratories. The geophysical laboratory had to characterize and store the precious cores, ready for X-ray and mass-spectrometric analysis; the micropaleontological laboratory peered expertly at the tiny fossils that make possible stratigraphic dating, "the Foram-, Rad- and Nanno- team," as they signed their parting ditty.

There were 69 people aboard, "a big, happy, quarreling family in a small oasis, isolated from reality," insecurely led by what they found, their novice leaders acutely aware of the costs of their golden opportunities. Every time the drill stuck or the satellite position electronics (finding its first use outside the navies) went bad there began a new hour of tense decision. The lucky campaign of Leg 13 nonetheless sailed to success, to end in two months, rotating to shore its leaders and boarding others to man a new drilling cruise in another ocean.

One feature of the voyage is curious. The leg was nearly canceled by the planners because earlier seismic exploration of that sea floor had revealed abundant salt domes with strong promise of gas and oil. The industry was glad enough to have such a powerful exploration crew at work, particularly one it did not have to pay for. The National Science Foundation advisers, in an era of $3 oil and new ecological concerns, took quite the opposite view. A find would probably be too deep to be of any benefit, and it could pollute the seas. By imperative command from the heights above, the drill had to avoid broaching any submarine gas or oil. Worse than a sticking drill or a lost bottom assembly was the strong scent of gasoline in a core; get out of there!

There is now, of course, much more evidence than those early flakes of gypsum. The cores brought up samples of algal stromatolites, signs of shallow-water growth in the sun, and of "chicken-wire anhydrite," a wispy distribution of dark carbonates in a white matrix of calcium sulfate, long taken as a signature of arid coastal flats in the borehole studies of petroleum geologists. By now the carefully archived half of core 124, left undisturbed in the first shipboard studies, has been painstakingly peeled. Eight or 10 cycles can be traced, one above another; the laminations follow in regular succession, first the fines of a lake bottom, signaled as brackish by the unusual diatoms found, then layers more disturbed as the lake shallowed and the bottom felt the winds, then the surface algal growth, then the final aridity shown by the chicken-wire anhydrite. The cycle repeated as seawater entered anew or the next lake overflowed; for a million years or so that was the history of a random spot on the Great Mediterranean Desert.

The case is hard to doubt. All plausible alternatives stand excluded. The micropaleontologist Maria Cita of the University of Milan, one of the shipboard specialists to support the early insights of the cruise, has by now helped to piece together the chronology of the salinity crisis of that time, when the marine organisms almost vanished from the cores. Today whatever evaporating seawater there gets briny and hence denser can escape out into the Atlantic, flowing deep below the surface of the Strait of Gibraltar. In the Miocene, however, Gibraltar was a huge dam between the Mediterranean and the Atlantic. The waters got steadily saltier in the hot sun; only a dwarf microfauna survived. Suddenly the dam broke and the great basin was refilled over a falls a thousand times grander than Niagara, taking perhaps centuries.

The microfauna of the modern Mediterranean does not resemble its Miocene predecessors; it is more like the Atlantic fauna. The animals are immigrants, not natives. The old plankton families are gone, lost in the salt. The Rhone and the Nile cut deep gorges into the dry valley, long drowned; there are many others. The caves and the karst lands of the coasts are now understandable; they were highlands draining into a low desert. In 1975 the *Glomar Challenger* returned to drill again deep below Mare Nostrum. This time the cruise was "more somber and more difficult." The cores probed deeper and tapped earlier times, revealing a deep-sea environment for at least 15 million years before the desert epoch. The catastrophe of desiccation has left its residue of rich potash deposit, the last salts to crystallize out of the brine, just where they ought to be, in the deep Ionian basin. Then came a series of lakes fed by the reorganized streams of Europe, captured out of the north by that vast yawning valley.

Not everyone is convinced. Like the glaciers, this is a story hard to accept. Now, however, we take the ice for granted. "Cita gets excited sometimes when her colleagues do not listen to her." One of these days "Cita's last tormenter" will fall quiet, and the desert of the Mediterranean will be held as gospel truth. Then in the megayear fullness of time, if our species somehow makes it, it will all happen again. The Strait is shoaling up as the plates compress the basin. Once again there will be an isthmus at Gibraltar. Cannes will become a highlands resort for the desert roughnecks winning the oil from all those salt domes southward, and the more adventuresome tourists will price dory trips down the twisting gorge of the Nile and camel caravans to the mountains of Malta.

Kenneth Hsü is professor of geology at the Swiss Federal Institute of Technology now, and no amateur. But his warmth, good humor and candid manner remain much as they must have been when he spent all those days and nights forward in the noisy little driller's shack just starboard of the tower. The plentiful photographs, maps and bottom profiles are evocative and helpful. This is a winning account of a sunny and serendipitous quest after deep secrets, of youth and insight and simplicity amid worldly tangles, and not least a "testimonial to a friendship born at sea."

(September 1983)

Islands
By H. W. Menard

First, find your island. Just how to do so is the topic of the fresh opening chapter of this final delightful work by the late author, distinguished marine geologist at Scripps whose handful of popular books are treasures for the general reader. Who else would begin with a clever piece of operations research that discloses pretty convincingly from the number of unexpected islands found per ship per decade that the islands of the Pacific were come on by the European explorers quite at random? The Polynesian discovery, itself probably made both by chance and by voyages of design, was "pigs, chickens, and all . . . the greatest maritime feat in human history."

In exploration it is not a small achievement to do "as well as pure chance." Striking photographs help us to grasp the circumstances at sea. One picture shows the orographic clouds that stand high every day as a white beacon over Palau; another shows the formidable cliffs of St. Helena, one of the islands called ironbound, that is, circled by towering cliffs beset by great breakers. That island stood high enough to have been spotted in 1502 at a distance by mariners tacking far eastward to seek favorable tradewinds.

The last chapter treats just as freshly the question of how life including human cultures reaches islands. The weapons of World War II were not able to end the long lives of the atolls, although combat littered the blue lagoons and white beaches with rusting bits of heavy equipment. Even thermonuclear tests make only small if lasting changes; an islet or two has gone into vapor, but the atolls "looked little the worse for wear."

Oceanic islands (not Long Island or even Ireland) are both interesting and important to geology and biology because they are in effect small, rather new, laboratorylike samples, near enough both in isolation and in uniformity. Young Darwin first glimpsed something of evolution in the strange limited fauna of the Galápagos, and he came to his famous inference about coral atolls from the charts alone, because they were simple enough to show the work of "a single geological factor — subsidence." In the same spirit, H. W. Menard uses the islands, high and low, to draw out and to apply the insights of plate tectonics, both in worldwide comparisons and statistics and in such regional patterns as the long line of the volcanic Hawaiian Islands and their submerged cousins. He builds in this inductive way the most understandable survey of that theory to be found in the popular literature. Eye-catching support from maps, graphs and photographs is a large part of his success. Here are the islands of the world: Iceland, Bouvet, Tahiti, the Canaries, Réunion and dozens more, pictured and discussed not merely as varied specimens of beauty and curiosity but as instances of a single grand process.

One dramatic page compares the silhouettes of tiny landlubber volcanoes such as Vesuvius with Mauna Loa and other great marine shield volcanoes. A spreading sea floor contracts and sinks slowly as it cools, so that across the Pacific volcanoes subside steadily. By a model calculation it becomes plain that mere random outpouring of volcanic material at the present observed rate could have built the islands we now see on the Pacific plate, scattering them sensibly according to the age of the crust they stand on.

It is the Hawaiian Islands that best expose the life course of an oceanic volcano. The first stage is youth, the fluid outpouring that built the great smooth shields of Hawaii. The second stage is old age; a stiffer lava pours out a modest "warty cover" onto the smooth shield. Then follows long inactivity and with it deep erosion; in a brief rebirth a small dramatic feature such as Diamond Head can appear to adorn the long-cold shield with a finial cliff or two.

The simplest regularity is the steady aging of the islands of the Hawaiian group in sequence as one passes along the line of islands toward the northwest, as the crustal plate is dragged over a virtually stationary hot plume that wells up from below. Modern potassium-argon dating yields a plot of age versus distance from Kilauea that makes the point at once. Yet the exercise confirms what is implicit in facts determined in 1927, when the geologist Chester K. Wentworth dated the islands from fieldwork on erosion. (Menard has recalculated the case with more modern maps, to find an even closer fit.) Begin with an island of volcanic rock modeled to the original smooth shield form and wear it away to the present volume as mapped. The valleys and ridges along steep green once conical slopes are famous now, bedecked by waterfalls. Hawaii is high, smooth, still active and half a million years above water; distant Kauai's knife-edge ridges and steep headlands are 10 times older. That spectacular relief, dear to the tourist brochures, is not a sign of any special processes of erosion but merely of steady rainfall and conical shape. Wentworth even found one place where he could calibrate his relative measure of erosion time island by island. On Lanai the trunks of the old kiawe trees on the shore were buried up to a meter deep. The volume of sediment removed upslope could be estimated, and it was recorded that the foreign forest species had been introduced in 1837. The result fits the current radiometric ages within a factor of two. But at the time no one noticed Wentworth's powerful argument for seafloor motion.

Wise with hindsight from magnetic stripes and midocean ridges, we can now almost watch the Pacific plate moving by, all the way to the last long-submerged seamount of the Emperor Guyots up by the Aleutians. We even see the big plate shift direction; the rising hot plume anchored deep in the still core of the convection cell far below the ocean floor left its prints on the crust in the form of the island chain. The book ends with a few wondering paragraphs: Do the plants and animals that have survived and changed for 100 million years on this line of shifting islands show any signs of their long migration up the volcanic steps of a down escalator?

(January 1988)

Earth at Night
By Woodruff T. Sullivan, III
A poster map, 23 by 35 inches

Night as Frontier: Colonizing the World after Dark
By Murray Melbin

The dark night sky is a sphere whose surface the lights of the stars define. Within that sphere is another, also marked in light: the surface of the earth at night. This unique poster map presents the night earth—not the night sky—on a Mercator projection, as a mosaic of carefully assembled actual nighttime scans. The images were made by two Defense Meteorological Satellite Program birds that orbit pole to pole, one near the shadow terminator around dawn and dusk, the other near the noon-midnight line, both 500 miles up.

Woody Sullivan is a radio astronomer with a keen interest in the idea of viewing our planet (and others) from afar. He has laid out these images into a world map with positional errors of only a few percent. Transmitted from orbit as digitized images of strips 1,800 miles by two miles, the scans were made by a photodiode sensitive to the entire visible range of color and the near infrared. They are reconstructed strip by strip into photographs by laser scan. The DMSP system and its striking yield were described in this magazine [see "Nighttime Images of the Earth from Space," by Thomas A. Croft; SCIENTIFIC AMERICAN, July, 1978]. The poster is the coherent composition of 40 DMSP photographs into a world map, adjusting for scale, exposure, moonlight and various small distortions. The poster is darkly beautiful, glittering in form and in meaning. To separate black land from black seas Sullivan calls on the clever graphic device of marking the empty oceans with a matte pencil striping that ends sharply at continental outlines.

The continents and islands blaze most unevenly with light. Three kinds of light are shown, all the work of our cunning species. The most familiar white areas are the populous cities whose denizens wake by night. Recognizably patterned areas shine from the Rhine-Ruhr, the south of England, the American Northeast, the Punjab, Rio de Janeiro and São Paulo, Japan east and west. Small maps in the margin neatly index about 180 identifiable cities large and small, from Fairbanks across the world to far Christchurch.

Then there is the light of the rural poor; these are not the dim lamps of the villages but the burning fields of shifting cultivators, the fires of herdsmen clearing their dry grasslands, the woodland set on fire to gain new fields. They all appear here in a distinct texture, less solidly overexposed. They glow from the Malagasy Republic to the Sahel, and from the highlands of Burma, Thailand and Laos. In years of scan some places never were freed enough from cloud cover to see; southwestern Africa and South China are thus abnormally dark, and many islands are missing.

The third kind of light is flame seriously overexposed. Its nature can be surmised at once from the bright patches that fill the desert shores of the Persian Gulf. There no one farms wide fields and few cattle graze, but the light from the Gulf rivals the brightest metropolitan centers on the earth: we are seeing the tall fiery flares of waste natural gas. These luminous genies stalk the Surgut gas fields along the Ob north of Omsk, the tropical island of Sulawesi, the delta of the Niger and the North Sea beyond the Shetlands.

Finally, strings and alignments mark out particular features such as the Nile, the Ohio, the Yellow River and the Trans-Siberian railroad. A dozen spots in a straight line not explained by the usual atlases join Madras to the bright patch of Delhi. All these lights must be centers of population that are arrayed along rivers or rail lines or perhaps are simply brightened by the megawatt bounty of a high-power line nearby. A single densely packed page of text comes with the poster to suggest still more that the eye may find and the imagination grasp in this marvelous (and inexpensive) view of the constellations of humanity.

Who is it that wakes by night among us five billion diurnal primates? City dwellers have long pushed back the night through the provision of artificial lights, which clear no stubble but make possible the activities of the urbanized. Murray Melbin is a sociologist at Boston University who documents his insight in a charming and persuasive book. Once the lands have been occupied and the spatial frontier comes to an end, human activities grow to fill a new temporal regime. Midnight and beyond are still a frontier. Few Americans dwell there, although urban life has long ago advanced well past sunset; prime time has been thickly settled and is no longer an adventuresome territory.

The cartography is tentative. A national census was taken on the American night frontier in May, 1980. About 30 million people were up and about after midnight; by the small hours between 3:00 and 5:00 A.M. the count had dropped to 10 million. That scant 5 percent represents the core of incessancy, the worldwide spread of purposeful social wakefulness that never stops. Fewer than four million were wage earners at regular work. More than four million were patrons of public establishments, stopping, say, for meals or fuel. Most of these seemed to have been on the way somewhere, perhaps home; a million and a half more were in transit by private automobile. It is a restless frontier.

Three schedules of the world of work and play are clear. The first one is ruled by daylight. The second is the spread of everyday life over the boundaries of natural light. Fishermen, bakers and wholesale markets traditionally start early to prepare for the morning; at night the metabolism of every city now turns largely rejuvenative — to cleaning, repair, waste removal, maintenance, revelry and recreation. The third schedule is newer: it is the rule of the incessant organization explicitly at work around the clock, partly in response to telecommunications that can relate the distant sunlit world to local night.

Incessancy is still an open frontier. The White House, the chemical plants, the powerhouses, the international airports, the newspapers, the hospitals and the shops to serve their people work around the clock. Yet the Marine guards at the U.S. Embassy in Moscow and the operators at Bhopal and Chernobyl do not seem to have included the heads of those enterprises. Leadership is still largely single and diurnal; the night duty officer is junior. But the trend is clear. At Three Mile Island the staff knew what to do in their predawn crisis: they awakened the plant manager himself. "Incessance had arrived."

On the streets of Boston in 1974 the researchers asked for directions, sought open shops to count friendly comments and proposed interviews to a large sample right around the clock. The night people unmistakably treated one another in a friendlier way than is common among day dwellers. This is the hospitality of the frontier; people there are bound by a sense of common vulnerability to random risk. The people of the night see themselves as suited to a special niche, as pioneers. "In a well-established society there is less adversity and less good will than at the precarious edge of human settlement."

We seem slowly to be becoming more wakeful. "Reared in the changed environment, our children will take incessance for granted," and the midnight satellites of the future will record more light everywhere. Or perhaps not; a prosperous future will have to waste less fuel than we do.

(July 1987)

Giant Meteorites
By E. L. Krinov
Translated by J. S. Romankiewicz
Edited by M. M. Beynon

At 7:17 local time on the morning of June 30, 1908, in the remote Yenisei taiga, not far from the fur-trading post of Vanovara, a gigantic meteorite fell. A couple of hundred miles to the southeast toward Lake Baikal a boy in the forest heard "in the northwest what sounded like gunfire repeated at intervals at least ten times," and wondered. This book is the work of that boy, become a lifelong student of meteoritics and sometime Scientific Secretary of the Committee on Meteorites of the Academy of Sciences of the U.S.S.R. His book tells the story of the great Tunguska fall, of the Arizona meteor crater, of the Sikhote-Aline shower in 1947 in the Soviet Far East, and briefly describes a dozen other known or suspected star-wounds on the earth. Krinov is more at home with mineral analysis and orbit calculations than he is with the hydrodynamics of shock, and his volume is therefore not the final word on the ancient craters and their formation, but on what he reports in full there can hardly be a more helpful or detailed treatise.

Krinov tells of the Arizona crater, where in 1876 a cowboy named Mathias Armijo found the first fragment of iron. The mineralogist A. E. Foote analyzed samples of the iron later, and after a visit in 1891 plainly concluded, but did not publish, that this was a meteor crater. The point came into dispute; in 1903 Daniel M. Barringer bought the land in the belief that it was in fact a meteor crater, and that the huge metal mass might still be there. Half a century of scientific work has made it all but certain that Barringer was correct about the initial fall, some 20,000 years ago, yet wrong about the residual mass. There is not much metal left in the crater; most of it went up as vapor in the fall and came down in the thousands of tons of tiny magnetic particles that lie in the Arizona desert for miles around.

The Tunguska fall is even more elusive. Since it knocked down the forest of larch and hemlock for 20 kilometers, was heard 800 miles away, marked seismic records half a world away and made barographic disturbances to be followed twice around the world, it might be expected to have left a fine large crater. There is no such crater, in spite of early false reports. The whole story points more and more clearly, as Krinov recounts it, to an object exploding kilometers above the ground, with a burst of radiant heat and a gigantic bang, but no crater. No one was killed; perhaps some flour stores of the Evenki hunters were burned, and some reindeer were certainly frightened. No radioactivity is known, and no large fragments, although again some microscopic globules of iron and silicate bear their witness. The night skies after the fall were extraordinarily bright from Edinburgh to the Crimea; one could read small print at midnight. The story points to the fall of something like a small comet, all ices and dust, with a tail stretching out toward the North Atlantic. Such is Krinov's view.

The history of knowledge of the Tunguska fall is the history of Russia and the U.S.S.R. in this century. No expedition to the site was mounted until the mineralogist L. A. Kulik managed to travel there in 1927, after the long travail of Czarist Russia and the final establishment of the Soviet state. He led several expeditions, poorly equipped, brave, earnest. On the second expedition the men were troubled by food shortages and scurvy. They had to wire back to Leningrad for more funds. No air photography was attempted until 1930; the first successful air mapping was done in 1938, by a flier named Petrov. Both Petrov and Kulik died at the hands of the Germans in the first year of the war.

The 1947 expedition was different. While the Sikote-Aline fall was less energetic than the Tunguska by a couple of orders of magnitude, the search could be mounted now with real power. Four expeditions went to the scene in as many years; they included air photography and magnetic surveying and even the making of a documentary film, and this time a detachment of engineer troops helped with logistics and earth-moving. There is change on earth as well as in the heavens.

If one estimates the energy release of the Arizona fall, or of the Tunguska event, they come out by chance remarkably similar, in the neighborhood of 10 or 20 megatons TNT equivalent, to use a unit familiar in other contexts. Both artificial craters and airbursts are well known.

This book is a real contribution to the literature of the science; its firsthand quality, its sense of time-spanning and of human growth give it a special interest. A few missing scales and an occasional mishap, such as the statement that Meteor Crater lies just south of "railway line 66," attest to its remarkable history: it was written in Russian by its distinguished senior author and first published in English in this translation.

(April 1967)

Exploring the Southern Sky: A Pictorial Atlas from the European Southern Observatory
By Svend Laustsen, Claus Madsen and Richard M. West

Nearby Galaxies Atlas
By R. Brent Tully and J. Richard Fisher

The Sky at Many Wavelengths
By Christine Jones and William Forman
Eleven color slides in folder

To celebrate "the extraordinary beauty of the southern sky" and to offer a sense of what it is they do, three Danish optical astronomers at the European Southern Observatory have spread a treasury of images over the big pages of this picture book. The domes and dorms and airstrip of the ESO station in the high Atacama Desert in Chile make up a solitary little mountain town that spreads over its treeless saddle at an altitude of 8,000 feet. The air is remarkably clear, stable and dry—two inches of rain a year—right for big telescopes and small, and for the large submillimeter-band radio dish just put in use.

Because the dazzling center of the Milky Way passes directly overhead, the black night blazes with clouds of stars. These latitudes offer the
best view inward toward the center of our own city of stars, the Galaxy,
and at the same time a fine view outward to the celestial suburbs we call
the Magellanic Clouds. The ESO's outpost at La Silla serves close to half of
the world's astronomers, particularly those from its eight member countries. Fourteen telescopes are now at work, the largest a fine 140-inch, a
dozen years past its first light.

The big photographs are fresh and very well documented. This is a
run of vintage seasons for southern skywatchers; we are shown what they
saw of Comet Halley in 1986, particularly its changing gas tail, in quite
fine views. Comet West (found by the third author in 1976), trailing its
multiple dust tails, was far brighter and more colorful; it has fled back into
space and will not be seen again for a million years. Thanks to the authors'
energy their intricate atlas shares in the February 1987 sensation: Supernova 1987A. No supernova has flared in such close proximity for 300
years. The star floats in the bar of the Large Magellanic Cloud, shown here
in before-and-after color shots, amidst an entire gallery of bright red
emission nebulas and a superposed foam of bubbles, probably the rem-
nants of other spent supernovas from the distant past, with which our
visible guest star is somehow involved.

The Milky Way is, as it ought to be, the centerpiece of this atlas. A
bonus inclusion consists of a yard-long panorama of the full circle of the
Milky Way, assembled from eight photographs of the sky made with a
small, guided wide-angle camera. Some of the pictures were shot from La
Palma in the Canary Islands, some from the La Silla station. The authors
offer a guided tour of the disk, commenting on many features of the
Galaxy, which they amplify through deep and detailed photographs of the
regions. Three big, exciting pages, for instance, show rich fields at the very
center of the Galaxy. One field is viewed through a heavy overcast, much
intervening dust, right in front of the distant hub, whose presence is
revealed by radio and infrared emissions. In adjoining fields the clouds
dwindle, until myriads of stars offer evidence that we are looking beyond
the dust, to see the far-off edge of the great starry central bulge of the
Galaxy. Here is that wonderful optical window found long ago by Walter
Baade, a dust-free opening through which he could study stars that are
nearly 10 times as close to the galactic center as the sun is.

External galaxies are also presented: there is a bright little smooth-
textured elliptical galaxy, apparently now the center of a big flat disk of
stars like that of a spiral galaxy, and a stunning view of the famous
colliding pair in Corvus, the ones with long, starry antennas.

One small picture in pseudocolor is genuinely instructive. It shows a
galaxy in two views made by a sensitive electronic imager, a CCD. In one
view a red filter was used, and the image is printed in red. The other view

used a blue filter. Superposed, the images show a galaxy in blue, decorated with dozens of fuzzy red spots, distributed mainly along the inner edges of its spiral arms, where brilliant young stars light up clouds of atomic hydrogen. Two nearby fields are expertly chosen to make a dramatic contrast. In one we look out to the empty depths of the sky, far from the Milky Way band. Only a few foreground stars are seen, along with a sparse array of distant galaxies; it is a grand void. A slight shift of direction fills the field of view with a nearby cluster of diverse galaxies in the constellation Fornax. The next page magnifies one of those small galaxy images into a detailed and colorful pinwheel.

The second atlas is pure cartography: it presents only large, clear maps that sum up the long optical and radio study of our extragalactic neighborhood. The first maps (all are the handwork of Jane J. Eckelman of Manoa Mapworks, Honolulu) plot with care the place in the sky of about 2,400 galaxies. They appear as circles, triangles, squares in black, blue, red and other colors, each galaxy coded for its apparent size, type and red shift. The band of the Milky Way is nearly devoid of external galaxies, of course, since its dust hides the background. The cap of the south galactic pole discloses a local void; there are relatively few nearby galaxies out that way. Northward toward the crowded Virgo Cluster the galaxies abound.

R. Brent Tully is an optical astronomer at Hawaii, J. Richard Fisher a radio astronomer at Green Bank. They have jointly pioneered powerful techniques for measuring galactic distances. The first set of maps, close to the data, are two-dimensional. They are simply projections onto the sky of clouds, clusters, spurs, voids. They do, however, make possible recognition of correlations in space: similar red shift can be taken as a mark of similarity in distance.

The authors name a couple of dozen evident groupings among these nearby galaxies, then undertake a bolder task. They pass from two dimensions and the red-shift hint to a full three-dimensional model. The maps in space begin with a map showing only colored dots on the sky's plane: the starting point. Now the red shift is taken seriously as being proportional to distance in space. The ambiguity introduced by internal motions within groups is recognized by demanding that groups remain usually rounded in space, without the bias of elongation in the line of sight. By plate 21 there is a composite of composites. We see a set of colorful smoothed contour maps, pools and coarse filaments of galaxies in space, plotting in greens, yellows and reds the density of galaxies on the sky. What comes out is the local supercluster: two thick layers, galaxies by the thousands, the larger layer to the north, the smaller to the south, of the plane of the Milky Way.

The projection used to set forth these dissected three-dimensional views from vantages far from home is less self-centered. It is based on the flattened local supercluster, recognized and described to a generally doubting community during the 1960's and 1970's by Antoinette and Gerard de Vaucouleurs of the University of Texas. Today that structure has been made the cornerstone; its principal plane holds the Virgo Cluster and the Local Group. The geometry of this inner neighborhood, nominally a quarter of a billion light-years across, is viewed this way and that in projections of a dozen bricklike domains. Two final maps extend tentatively and incompletely to superclusters at a tenfold distance. For readers who like to know just where they are and who make a genuine effort at visualization, this is a remarkably imaginative presentation. A separate catalogue volume presents a compilation of the galaxy data. To cite the authors: "Enough of words. The maps are more eloquent."

The third of these visual explorations is the work of two astronomers, Christine Jones and William Forman, who look more steadily with detectors in orbit than with eye at night. The authors have chosen the familiar 35-millimeter projection slide rather than the printed page as their medium. They have compiled from the contemporary research literature up-to-date and reliable charts. The maps present in comparable format first the entire sky in a careful painting as a keen and patient eye sees it, with the Milky Way as visible backbone; then the sky is rendered as it appears to all our newer senses. Those novel panoramas are shown as color-coded whole-sky maps made at wavelengths no eye can see: broadband radio, two distinct radio line emissions, two views in the far infrared, two more by X ray and one by gamma rays. (For that most energetic of well-explored radiation bands, the entire map was compiled from 200,000 photons, each one individually counted.) Last comes the deepest sky of all, the relict microwave glow of the big flash. An auxiliary slide shows which radiation from all spectral regions can pierce the atmosphere. This set opens wide today's windows on the universe (neutrino astronomy has yet to begin any map of the sky); of course, the tale is too rich to exhaust in the helpful few pages that accompany the slides.

(January 1988)

VIII

Technologies High and Low

From the wheel itself—and why it did not form old Damascus as it did ancient Rome—to the nature and use of the silicon chip and the minutely divided circle, these books look at some fascinations of technology old and new, and do not omit the aesthetic use that it has sometimes wonderfully served.

The Camel and the Wheel
By Richard W. Bulliet

The Wheelwright's Shop
By George Sturt

The labyrinth of the *casbah* is a commonplace thrill to travelers struck by the intricately winding streets, steep and narrow alleys, quaint stairs and culs-de-sac that nucleate most old cities from Fez to Kabul. Moreover, until recently the building and upkeep of surfaced roads outside the city was not usually taken as a serious task by the indigenous governments of North Africa and the Middle East. Used to the rectilinear city plans of the Roman world, convinced that road building was a chief task of the state, scholars have sought deep within Islam some inner reason for this fancied deficiency of public order.

The witty, reflective argument of *The Camel and the Wheel* explains the facts by a surprising proposition. The economics of bulk transport in a dry climate favors the pack camel over the wheeled vehicle drawn by ox or horse. Heavy oxcarts hauled the city's goods from remotest antiquity until about the fifth century, after which the camel took over until the days of Otto and Benz. The level, straight streets of the Frankish world gave the carters access for heavy loads to all points in the city, once the streets were made wide enough to admit one rigid axle, or even two passing. But if the surefooted camel alone serves your town, you have no need for squared corners, wide streets or gentle grades. Local considerations, from wind protection to the direction of shade, from high habitation density to easy defense, take over; narrow, curving ways, little street markets and steep, changing grades were all incorporated efficiently into the medieval cities of Islam. It was no philosophical mystery; economic rationality determined. After all, Mecca itself, holiest of Islamic cities, is built with straight streets — a design older than camel transport.

The support of this proposition is manifold, drawing from art and archaeology, old texts and new, camel husbandry, anthropological studies, linguistic forms. The doubter must look at the photograph of a line of pack camels, haughty and graceful under heavy loads, swinging past a bemired horse cart on a bad Chinese road. The changeover was made wherever camels could be effectively bred to yield their competitive edge over wheeled transport, a matter of fully 20 percent. The camel is faster and stronger, its pack-saddle is cheaper than a wagon, its driver is more easily shared among half a dozen animals. Domestication of the camel had taken place very much earlier, probably in southern Arabia and the eastern horn of Africa. The ancient overland trade in "frankincense and myrrh" brought the nomad's camel to the desert borders of the settled lands of Syria and Mesopotamia by the seventh century B.C., but nearly 1,000 years passed before the creaky oxcarts of the ancient Middle East gave way to the silent caravan. It was a social transformation that did it: the sway of "the camel-borne warrior mounted upon a North Arabian saddle." The Arab nomads who bred camels and understood them became the cultured and powerful sovereigns of all Islam. Once the camel was available its productivity was telling, and along the narrow ways of the camel a wheel-less society grew. Camel-mounted field artillery, fired from the back of the couched animal, existed in the Persian army well into the 19th century, and that same army, without wheels or roads for loads exceeding the camel's standard quarter ton, "carried unformed metal on camelback to the scene of battle and there cast it into siege guns." What counts to a prosperous and well-governed wheelless state in an arid region is not road surfacing; it is bridges, caravanserais and police protection for the traveler. (Compare, *passim*, *The Thousand and One Nights*.)

The book excels in its remarkable levelheadedness and its critical and candid writing. The esoteric topic has often attracted—as the biblio-graphical essay and the notes here fully demonstrate—not mere enthusi-asts but true zealots. Professor Bulliet, a Berkeley Arabist, escapes from the trap and recognizes fully the danger of one-sided explanations and easy correlations. His critical stance is of interest to historians of technol-ogy and to students of social change in general. The nature of the camel lies at the base of the argument, of course. The reader will learn that camels store not water but heat; they tolerate both remarkable increases of body temperature and severe water loss, their desert endurance coming from both traits; no sweat for camels!

The era of the pack camel is near its end, done in by that other energy gift of the Arabian Gulf. But camel efficiency, evolved by nature and by human insight in that climatic region, may yet reveal the camel in the role of meat producer, "and the disdainful expression on its face will ever call to mind the past era when the camel was superior to man's proud inven-tion, the wheel."

Precisely how the wheel could be the everyday load-bearer of an agricultural economy in the south of England is the burden of George Sturt's classic and beautiful evocation (first published 50 years ago) of the craftsmen he knew in Surrey in the 1880's, plying a trade in blacksmith's iron and in the elm, ash, bone-hard beech and stout oak of the local woodlands. That trade—making wagons, carts, plows and barrows—was itself the adaptive growth of six centuries or more, a matured folk craft whose hardworking, low-paid, unlettered but skilled and subtle journey-men and masters knew their way from collective experience and tradition alone, without so much as a single calculation. Rules and gauges were used, mostly undivided, but no computations entered, not even in the pricing of the goods, which often went for "less than the mere iron and timber. . . . They never knew. . . . These matters . . . were settled by guess work, not by calculation." Over the unchanging generations errors would even out and a reasonable charge emerged, but change came very hard. The keen drawshave deftly broke every corner of each squared timber and reduced each shaft and "pillar" until it looked right. "A man skillful with the draw-shave enjoyed this work, lingering over it like an artist." It was not decoration, however; its vital object was to lighten the horse's load, and the corner-shaving removed an eighth of the dead weight of the wagon timbers. Every longitudinal piece of a wagon was slightly curved, following ancient wood patterns long stored in the shop. The timber was not steam-bent; rather it was chosen for its natural curves. ("How accurately woodland nature seemed to know the shape of moving horses.")

Across this detailed account of the demanding love of hand for work Sturt paints the picture of social relations in such a shop, where the working man found deep pride, "that satisfaction which of old . . . streamed into their muscles all day long from close contact with iron, timber, clay, wind and wave, horsestrength."

(February 1976)

The World Railway System
By Bernard de Fontgalland

M. de Fontgalland, Honorary Secretary General of the International Union of Railways, is a philosopher of the ringing rail. In this brief, lucid volume he sums up railway principles, technology, operations, marketing and management in an account both warmed by long-time engagement and cooled by a candid and systematic mind. And he does not shrink to apply his insights to the concrete.

His best and longest chapter outlines the railway macrosystems in place, those internationally linked steel nets that bear the passengers and freight of most of the world. The longest stretch now open to a single railway vehicle (with occasional car ferries, four changes of gauge and plenty of paperwork) extends from Algeciras in Morocco 10,000 miles across Europe, Siberia and China to Ho Chi Minh City. Container traffic is heavy from Japan by way of the U.S.S.R. to Europe and the Middle East. Since 1950 the Soviet railways have woven a "real spider's web, centred on

Moscow," a network over which sleepers and block trains roll to almost all the capitals of Europe and to the east as far as Beijing and Pyongyang. The Soviet railways have built a large fleet of smaller rolling stock, particularly passenger cars, to meet the less generous width and height clearances standard in Europe. The main border stations have equipment for changing the bogies (wheels) to accommodate the track gauge; the delay is no more than that required for customs formalities. "Such a huge system cannot be immune to political upheavals." In the early 1980's there were enforced stops at borders in the Middle East and in Korea.

A railway is a "birail with rail-wheel guidance by flanges under the body of the vehicle." Monorails, from the beginning to the ambitious magnetically suspended cars of our day, have never solved the problem of safe switching. The track defines a one-dimensional geometry; switching is a choice of left or right, and any section must either be free or occupied. Thus railways are logically binary, Boolean and naturally computerizable. The real operational time unit of modern railways, the built-in clock rate, is about 10 seconds. For a century that unit was a minute, since all important operations were once largely or entirely manual, for instance coupling, switching, signaling and writing and issuing train orders. In the past 20 years the pace has quickened; general automation and modern telecommunications have become key parts of the economic renaissance of many national railways. Overall the steel-steel contact of wheel on rail rules; although still noisy, the low-loss and weatherproof properties of this technology remain excellent, particularly if the rail is welded. Power can be supplied by diesel engines, by central generators (now installed on about one-eighth of the world's track, half of them producing the more modern a.c.) or even by coal-fueled steam engines.

The original railways hauled coal in block trains that consisted of a single chain of cars, shuttling unmodified from mine to mill. Such specialized heavy transport from siding to siding remains important and economical; some dedicated cargo trains haul 20,000 tons gross per train, two kilometers of high-capacity ore cars rolling at 50 kilometers per hour. The other limit is the high-speed passenger train, the Paris–South East express or the Hikari from Tokyo to Hikata, fliers that achieve a schedule speed (counting stops and slowdowns) only 20 percent below their top speed of 300 kilometers per hour along the rails. The basis of this performance is the dedication of the system in both space and time to these awesome conveyances: freight and ordinary passenger trains are either kept off the new priority line entirely or limited to late-night travel. A two-track line with two-way signals, using each track in either direction as needed, can safely handle about 300 trains in 24 hours.

Rolling stock is a heavy investment, and its efficient use is a key goal of operations. Fast passenger trains, like jet aircraft, can make many trips; the multiple-unit electric trains of the Shinkansen log half a million kilometers a year. The commercial freightcar duty cycle rarely amounts to a twelfth of that hard use; the consequences are high cost, a need for lots of storage track and often charges for delays in unloading cars at their destinations. The block trains can do much better, even though they usually clank emptily back to the dock or the mine.

The world's railways divide into four species. Japan and the Netherlands, small countries with very high population density, give priority to passenger traffic. Freight runs only at night; intercity passenger service using advanced technology approaches the usual frequency and performance of metropolitan commuter lines. Three big young countries of the New World, with spotty population distribution and long hauls for raw materials, give rail priority instead to freight. The U.S., Canada and Brazil all have market economies, in which substantial public investment has been made in excellent roadways and air transport. Their technology and operations favor freight traffic; "some passenger trains are tolerated, but their quality of service is mediocre if not poor. However some densely populated corridors do offer good quality passenger service."

Between the two extremes come the "traditional" railways. For them supply has difficulty in keeping up with demand, and there is not much interest in specialized high performance at the expense of global capacity. Private automobiles are of limited use, either perforce because of low income or by decision of a centrally planned economy. These systems carry both passengers and freight across the large distances of India, China, eastern Europe and the U.S.S.R. Their networks account for most of the world's rail traffic.

Over only an eighth of the world's total trackage the railways of the U.S.S.R. handle more than half of the world's traffic; they do so within a continental expanse that is marked by gentle relief and bathed in extremes of climate. There are few small rail lines, but the still growing main lines are five or 10 times more heavily used than those of western Europe or the U.S. Overall speeds are not above 70 kilometers per hour; the fastest service over the "straight, flat route" between Moscow and Leningrad, the chief cities, "runs at 93 km/h." Yet along the vast distances of the Trans-Siberian the freight trains proceed at 10- or 15-minute intervals, linked by radio, following automated signals; as they traverse the deep boreal forests their performance is not much different from that achieved outside peak hours on the central suburban lines of other railways. Twenty passenger trains a day run across the Urals as far as Lake Baikal. Although Aeroflot is vigorous aloft, the train remains an essential of intercity travel for Soviet passengers. Soviet rail passenger-miles total 10 to 20 times the U.S. Amtrak output, a volume nearly as large as that of all western Europe.

The fourth railway species is the "sophisticated" linked system in the larger countries of western Europe. Those railways are national enterprises, but they must survive in a market economy, "adapted to double sector operation," by maximizing quality of service. They generally have sufficient technical capacity to offer passengers both high speed and serious attention, and yet they haul freight well.

What of the future? Brazil is a land that always promises; if 200 million people are there by the century's end, with a large long-haul trade in raw materials, the high-speed railway should flourish. An uncrossed stretch of desert in southern Iran alone isolates the busy railways of the subcontinent of southern Asia (India's system is 10 times larger than the railways of Pakistan and Bangladesh) from the Eurasian macronet. There is an optimistic plan to close that final gap by the end of the century, to join two-thirds of the world's population into "the tricontinental megasystem," a through train possible from London to Calcutta. A tunnel under the English Channel would transform land transport in Europe, particularly if smaller links under the Oresund and by bridge to Sicily complement it. In Japan they are about to complete a submarine tunnel of Channel length, to unite their southern islands by express rail. The North American future of rail remains problematical. The twin transcontinental Canadian railways remain healthier than the beset system south of the border, caught between an ideal of public service and market competition in the Serengeti of the automobile.

The author names the heroes of modern railway management; "great railwaymen" include Louis Armand, Boris Pavlovich Beshehev and Hideo Shima. Theirs is a kind of generalship that achieves victories of peace: we ought to pay homage to France's leader for a new automation, to the Soviet Union's for a new internationalism and to Japan's for a new modern standard of technology and service. But it is geography and the economic system that in fact "articulate the activity of every mode of transport." The top decision maker, the "number one" who "directs an enterprise often classed among the most important in his country," cannot decide on expenditure, for two-thirds of that goes for staff with guaranteed employment, nor on revenue, for fares are controlled, nor on network structure, nor on the volume of investments. Yet the role crowns any manager's career, civil service or private sector; what remains is all the same a real job.

This is a real book too, a personal systems analysis of unusual spirit and penetration. It was first written in French and then, it appears, put into succinct and flexible English by its author *extraordinaire*.

(October 1985)

Handling the Big Jets
By D. P. Davies

"Airline flying really is money for old rope most of the time; but when things get hairy *then* you earn your pay." This cheerful, analytic, wonderfully knowing book by the chief test pilot of the U.K. Airworthiness Authority is aimed at the thoughtful professional pilot who wants preparation for the worst at the level not only of the what and the how but also of the why. A technically alert jet passenger will find it rewarding even if he is no engineer but simply a reader able to follow graphs and the conclusions they imply past a somewhat daunting barrier of acronyms and symbols of art (which are most of the time made clear by a careful glossary). No question of it: the flight deck of that plane is not only a gleaming display of instruments but also the workplace of a crew that operates a complex system by more than rote and feel.

The text begins with an account of why jets are different. They carry more momentum, much more than piston planes in both factors: weight and speed. The biggest civil jet, the 747C, has a maximum takeoff weight of about 350 metric tons. (That mass changes in flight by a factor of up to two as fuel burns!) The jet turbines give a comparatively small mass of air a much greater steady acceleration than the large propeller engines did. The turbines are powerful, reliable, efficient and cool, but they make no slipstream to give extra lift and they can change speed only gradually. The big control surfaces and high airspeeds demand servo-powered controls, and so artificial-feel feedback systems are necessary. They work well; a good one is "so good that the pilot has no indication that there is a servo system between him and the surface." A total feel-failure is bad news, but it is "a most remote possibility." The 747 controls, for example, are praised here in the most effective way, with a foldout sheet bearing the flow chart of the four separate hydraulic control systems. In that area the well-engineered 747 is "an order better in terms of redundancy and failure survival than any current airworthiness level would require." Civil jets are designed to the double-failure standard more or less across the board.

The clean form of the jet-transport wing — thin, swept back and not unusually long — means that it offers poor lift at low speeds. At low speed the drag actually increases faster than the lift as the speed decreases, and "the aeroplane will quietly slide up the back end of the drag curve." That is the reason for the elaborate system of leading-edge and trailing-edge flaps, more often seen through the cabin windows than by the officers up front. The high-performance swept wing and the high-set tail plane and rear engines can lead to a nose-up superstall (carefully explained here with many graphs and drawings and a simple formula), from which at best an extremely large loss in height is bound to occur. ("It cannot be put too strongly. Whatever you do, *don't stall the aeroplane.*")

Unable to provide enough natural aerodynamic stability and timely prestall warning behavior, the jet designers have built prevention into the controls. Some pilots "cannot stand the thought of a stick pusher," but pushers are generally in use, they work well and they confer virtually

"immaculate stalling qualities." One such system is described and dia-
grammed. The sensor is a duplicated set of vanes in the airstream near the
wing. Reliably powered by nitrogen stored under high pressure, the system
responds promptly to a change in flow, shakes the stick to warn the pilot,
blows a strident klaxon and in due time pushes the stick strongly forward,
nosing the aircraft down sharply. The design is biased strongly toward not
pushing when pushing is not required. The reason is that erroneous
operation would put the airplane at clear risk of nosing right into the
runway during those 10 seconds of approach when the plane is between
about 120 feet high (too low to allow pilot countermeasures) and 10 feet
high (when the penalty is only a hard landing). The overall probability of
such a mishap is about one in 36 million approaches. "This we just have to
live with. The problem is far less than the normal risk of an accident
resulting from any single cause."

Jets "lift off" ("come unstuck" in British English, according to the
little English-American aviation phrasebook included here) at high speeds.
That means a lot of energy wasted by transfer to any water, snow or slush
on the runway. The matter is discussed in interesting detail. Runway
conditions, like severe weather aloft, require a captain to understand and
to decide, unaided by designer or ground control. Crude measurements of
the depth and density of the runway slush and of the speed costs of drag
are the elements that shape his decision. Thus is tested command character, the ability to make the essential quick response to a complex problem
with the data uncertain and the stakes high. A commander has the choice:
he can delay or divert. Let the competitors care for themselves. ("If you
should bust something, the fact that someone else got away with it a few
minutes before or after will be little consolation.")

Severe weather aloft is the final test of designer and pilot. The jets are
designed to withstand gust speeds at altitude that are rather reduced from
their low-level values, walking the prudent line between speeds high
enough to avoid stalling and low enough so that all parts of the plane can
withstand the gust forces. "Inspired estimations" for the limits, made by
structures experts on the basis of World War II experience, remain valid;
all recent flight-recorder results support their choices: vertical gust speeds
of 45 miles per hour (corrected for air density) are still the design standard.
Turbulence can cause gross upsets, knocking out the main altitude indica-
tors. Here too the prepared and prudent captain earns his pay. "*The
inverted dive* will be obvious by all the loose equipment flying around the
flight deck"; the remedy is to roll 180 degrees, and promptly.

What else can happen? Consider hail. There can be severe damage
when the stones are more than two inches in diameter; that condition is
encountered by some unfortunate aircraft worldwide about four times a
year. One should not fly under thunderstorms. "When the awful battering
starts, there is no means of establishing the size of the hail." One should

not turn away from that assault if one hits it suddenly; the "quickest way out is straight on." The cabin may suddenly decompress. Then to the other problems is added the cloud-chamber effect, as the quickly oversaturated air of the cabin and flight deck becomes a dense cloud. It is not serious—if you expect it.

Here is what can happen (Davies is reporting on what a pilot called the most violent jolt "in over 20,000 hours of flying"): "I felt . . . a buffeting . . . one might expect to encounter sitting on the end of a huge tuning fork that had been struck violently. Not an instrument on any panel was readable . . . white blurs against their dark background. . . . Briefcases, manuals, ashtrays, suitcases, pencils, cigarettes, flashlights flying about like unguided missiles. . . . My seat belt was tight . . . briefcase was on the ceiling. . . . We acted in unison applying as much force as we could gather to roll aileron control to the left. . . . The air smoothed out and we gently leveled off at between 1,400–1,500 feet."

Chief Pilot Davies is truly a man for all seasons. One comes away with a new respect for jet captains and crews. They need the famous seat-of-the-pants experience and reflexes, and no less the stout heart of command. This book, accessible to the nonspecialist, makes it evident how much they depend as well on a personal enthusiasm for the job that ensures a variety of rational processes of analysis that are carried out in thought, well in advance of that next engine failure or turbulent cloud.

(July 1976)

The Art of Electronics
By Paul Horowitz and Winfield Hill

The computer is so salient now that we associate the very idea with those word-and-symbol processors that take in our names and put out our paychecks, or those that respond to our mathematical queries. The same technology is also commonplace in the laboratory, where is skeptically queries and senses the world, more of Hume than of Plato. We know about the pulsars as we know about feature recognition in neurons of the cerebral cortex: some well-formed configuration of transistor circuitry has told us.

This volume, avoiding both the lee shore of excessive handbook detail and the windy tack of cookbook oversimplification, is a basic navigator's guide to laboratory electronics as it is today. It is meant for serious study, hands on the oscilloscope probe, for those who would go on to carry out experimental research in just about any branch of science or technology. It omits all theory that is less useful than it is conventional for students, to aim straight at the art of circuit design; it is roughly quantitative, studiously analytical, full of clever circuits and sharp insights, but with a surprising minimum of mathematics. The style is wry and casual, almost deprecatory, the very speech of the laboratory. The depth is genuine, as is the richness of examples, data and apt tricks. There is an indispensable introduction to the Anglo-American electronics culture: data sheets, magazines, how to recognize a mystery chip, which firms supply a "nice selection of transformers and quick delivery," even how to avoid mislabeled counterfeit integrated circuits.

It takes until the third chapter to reach the sovereign idea of feedback, past a chapter on the current-voltage foundations of circuit theory and one on discrete transistor circuits (made workably simple, with solid-state physics just about ignored). Feedback is introduced by way of operational amplifiers, those clever packages of a score of transistors and resistors that act as very-high-gain differential direct-current amplifiers and are never used without external feedback. The initial treatment is based on an idealized set of rules, in fact the limiting case of feedback with infinite open-loop gain. The fundamental gain equation itself enters only after 35 pages of powerful and quite understandable examples.

This scheme of making maximum use of the insights of simple approximations described in words, and introducing more formal design only after understanding has gained real headway, is the pedagogical core of this original treatment. Filter design, for example, is treated in the same nonmathematical, estimational fashion, with tables and charts but with barely a whisper of the intricacies of poles in the complex plane and the Chebyshev polynomials. Yet broad understanding is never sacrificed along with the formulas.

Half of the text treats analogue and half treats digital. We approach the digital magic in the same sensible way, first with arrays of gates alone and their logic. Only then do we step into the realm of sequential logic, where output depends not only on input but also on history: the same basis as mind. Modest entry here is made by way of the basic flip-flop, two simple cross-fed NAND gates. After some additional work on analogue-digital interfaces and on noise (including the intriguing digital pseudo-random noise schemes) there is a long look at minicomputers and their software and then at a microprocessor and how to feed, teach and control it. The problems of power supplies, of precision and even of construction are not forgotten, with mechanical and thermal attention from the breadboard up.

The last chapter, perhaps the most readable one for someone not engaged in laboratory work itself, is a fine overview of measurement. It explains a variety of transducers for sensing the world, the wonderful precision with which we can handle frequency and time, and the power of some ingenious schemes, such as lock-in detectors and signal averaging, that can all be seen as ways to narrow the detection bandwidth.

A dozen appendixes give instructions for the use of the oscilloscope, for drawing diagrams neatly and for finding data sheets, a math review and the necessary color codes. The volume is a nice match of the conceptual and the practical, produced by a pragmatic Harvard physicist, widely known for his electronics flair, and an engineer from the demanding redoubts of Route 128.

(April 1981)

Dividing, Ruling and Mask-making
By D. F. Horne

"He had great faith in instruments, and I do not think it naturally occurred to him to doubt the accuracy of a scale. . . . He was astonished when we found that one of his micrometers differed from the other." So wrote Francis Darwin of his father, Charles Darwin. This volume is devoted to the justification of our faith in the elegant and exacting industry that forms and calibrates the linear and circular scales that fix the settings of machine tools, theodolites and levels. These in their turn determine the fit, size and shape of most of our engineering products, large and small. Today's best production practice routinely reaches an accuracy of a quarter of a micrometer (formerly a micron). This volume surveys the techniques by embedding within a clear and expert general account rather detailed excerpts from actual manufacturer's directions for the use of a wide variety of special instruments and procedures. It is well illustrated with many diagrams and photographs of real setups.

The classical products are mainly sets of lines on stainless steel or on glass, either ruled directly with a sharp diamond edge or etched through a "resist" that has been made by ruling or by photochemistry. Evaporated metal can also be deposited through the resist. The widest contemporary extension of these arts is the one covered in the third term in the title: the remarkable technology of making integrated circuits. There calibration is of little importance, but high precision is nonetheless needed for the proper and precise registry of half a dozen layers (resistive, conductive and carrier-diffusing) that are placed on a silicon semiconductor base to yield the complex arrays of minute circuit elements — smaller and denser each year — that are the works of pocket calculators and guided missiles. Such patterns come to resemble molecular biology more than they do the uniform crystalline divisions of setting circles and micrometers (the instrument, not the unit).

Calibration occupies one chapter, fascinating to the general reader. Slip (or block) gauges are fundamental in the precision machine shop. They must be finished well enough so that they can be "wrung" together, or to special flat steel surfaces, with allowance made for wringing thickness, which amounts to a quarter of a microinch. One clever instrument uses four different wavelengths of the mercury-vapor lamp to give a kind of optical vernier reading of gauge thickness, without counting many interference fringes. Air pressure, temperature and humidity must be corrected for, and the gauges can be checked to a microinch. A standard meter bar (made of a steel alloy less noble than the platinum-iridium prototype in Paris) is still the basis for calibration of steel tapes and scales. The fiducial lines are engraved on the crossbar of the H-section standard, cleverly arranged to be in the neutral axis of the beam, where length does not change with small bending. The firm of V.E.B. (formerly Carl Zeiss) Jena has found a neat extension of that idea. Transparent glass scales have advantages (they give strong signals when they are scanned photoelectrically for fast calibration at many scale points, and the polished surfaces are consistently good), but it is not practical to form a glass H section in one piece. The optical wits at Jena have found a cross section, a carefully computed but simple trapezoidal shape, such that rulings made on the lower glass surface but viewed from above through the thickness of glass are seen in virtual image at the unbending mechanical neutral axis inside the solid glass.

The future seems to lie closer to laser interferometry. Electronic counting of fringes (with heterodyne techniques) and stable wavelengths give such instruments remarkable powers. One is described here: a Hewlett-Packard device based on a helium-neon laser, which can accommodate itself to calibrating 200-foot lengths with one-microinch resolution. Beam alignment might be a limit in use, but the narrow beam makes such errors minimal in the hands of an alert operator. There are even correcting thumbwheels for feeding in ambient air conditions in order to get standardized results on the digital display; they affect only the fourth digit and beyond. With a cube-corner reflector and a beam-bender one can fully survey a near-flat area. Here is displayed one such map, with half a dozen profiles running across a yard-long granite surface plate, accuracy in the microinch range. This is virtuoso work in the tool shop.

Here is the contemporary standard of circle division too. No official bar need be consulted for it; every circle has its own million-plus seconds of arc. The trick is equal division. The Moore Special Tool Company of Bridgeport, Conn., will supply you with a small-angle divider to calibrate circles to $1/10$ second of arc at any position. (A test certificate shown here gives corrections to the nominal at the level of a few hundredths of a second of arc.) The heart of this classically inspired instrument (developed about 1960) is a pair of identical steel "face gears," each of which is about eight inches in diameter and has 1,440 identical V-shaped teeth. The two gears mesh well, of course. Once the teeth are engaged they are mutually locked. Then they are disengaged, the gears are rotated a finite number of teeth and are once again brought in contact. Thus a definite angle is stepped off, a quarter of a degree per tooth. High precision arises from the averaging effect of all those teeth in mesh at once; each gear has been mutually lapped against its mate by such engaging and disengaging motions, with random rotations, through long hours of lapping with increasingly fine abrasives. Finally the gear teeth are mutually run in for still more hours of random repetition while they are clean and dry. Interpolation between quarter-degree steps is made by a fine-pitch micrometer screw with a dial and a vernier, its flat end carefully held in contact with the main index. It need work linearly over only a fortieth of an inch, and it is adjusted to agree with the result of a single-tooth increment.

Auxiliary arts are treated too: the making of the wide variety of optical graticules, with their lettering and scales, that we so often look through or see projected; the preparation of diamond cutting edges; the cleaning of glass; the evaporation of metal layers, and more. The arcana of diffraction gratings are laid out in a long chapter. Some gratings are ruled directly by great interferometer-controlled ruling engines; some are made from a fine master screw thread by casting cylindrical plastic replicas and splitting them, a surprisingly accurate technique developed at the National Physical Laboratory in England. The design of clean rooms is sketched, with examples. The usual ceiling-to-floor clean airflow was not good enough for the Moore Special Tool Company because the temperature of the air in such a flow pattern tends to stratify horizontally: the room is dust-free but is thermally unsuited for precision work in steel. The company added air intakes at a number of levels and temperature-control of the floor.

Horne is no stranger to this industry. He is the developer of a new device — now called the Nikon I C (integrated circuit) Printer — that produces microimages optically, without making contact with the base semiconductor slice. (The device is aligned automatically to a few micrometers and its sharp images are projected across a gap of up to tens of micrometers, preventing contamination and damage to the mask or the slice itself.) A wide-ranging chapter on metrological history, from Pharaoh's forearm to Maudslay and Johansson, has been supplied by a colleague of Horne's at Hilger and Watts, Ltd, Mrs. C. E. Arregger.

The volume was first to be called simply *Dividing and Ruling*. That sounded too political, and so the third noun, *Mask-making*, was added. It does not help: modern states behave in ways that pun on the matter-of-fact activities of that remarkable tradition of manufacture, a fusion of the graphic arts with the precision of the optical laboratory.

(January 1976)

From Art to Science: Seventy-Two Objects Illustrating the Nature of Discovery
By Cyril Stanley Smith

A Search for Structure: Selected Essays on Science, Art and History
By Cyril Stanley Smith

The first of these two celebratory volumes brings the reader some ripened and colorful fruit out of a lifetime's insight and taste. In 1978 Cyril Stanley Smith and Jon Eklúnd chose 72 objects for exhibition both in Washington and in Cambridge, Mass. The objects range from a sample of ocher simulating an Upper Paleolithic pigment to masterpieces of the potter, the weaver, the armorer, the artist and the scientist. Most of them are strikingly presented in fine color plates, and the viewer is "expected first to become lost in simple enjoyment of their beauty." They also serve, however, to document a summary of the properties of materials as one after another new potential has engaged artists, artisans and at last analysts over the entire history of our species.

The evidence is presented in seven sections, each section with a brief evocation of what the mind can tell the eye about how those delights came to be. Each object is itself the topic of a specific paragraph; the exhibition (with one entire dimension, alas, lacking) is here on paper. A few of the displays may serve to encourage entry. An Attic vase, the famous red-and-black ware from Lekythos in about 500 B.C., stands gracefully before the viewer. The deeper story is plain. The red and the black alike are visual consequences of the iron present in the fine-grained potter's clay. That much is well known; it is the fact that both remained black during the main firing that is less familiar except to the experts. Then, toward the end of the firing, the atmosphere of the kiln became oxidizing. The painted pattern reddened, as oxygen diffused into the matrix to change the ferrous ions to ferric. The areas that remained black had a small addition of alkaline flux; their surface was slightly vitreous. There the oxidation was slowed; the adept kiln worker had to know just how long to fire. A check on this model is now opened to the observant viewer: at a sharp break along the profile of the vase, the glaze, "being very thin, is turning red."

A section on the discovery of acids brings together a carnelian bead from old Harappa on the Indus, an etched seashell from Snaketown Pueblo in Arizona, a copper-plate etching from the hand of Rembrandt van Rijn, and a marvel of a Damascus blade, its watery pattern visible only after etching. Here too is a pre-Columbian crocodile, figured in tumbaga, a gold-copper alloy carefully corroded by a preparation of weathered ferric sulfate hydrate (the mineral sample is also shown) to achieve "depletion gilding." The baser metal was removed from a thin layer to leave the outer surface pure gleaming gold.

A section on crystals shows a jade disk, a crust of decorative calcite crystals, the actual wood stacked-ball crystal models made by William Hyde Wollaston around 1820, a meteorite, a sword guard and the pattern formed by the dendritic crystals that grow as a small antimony ingot solidifies and shrinks, known to the alchemists and to Isaac Newton as the mystical Star of Antimony. Professor Smith remarks that the Linnaean classifications of the 18th century included the mineral kingdom, noting "that the variation between individuals was much greater than among animals. (How different from the modern view, which emphasizes the unalterable internal symmetry of the crystal lattice rather than the external accidents of growth!)"

For the second of these books Professor Smith selected 14 of his papers, some quite long, as being of interest to the general reader. Out of the nearly 200 papers he has published, starting with an undergraduate one on copper welding in 1926, "not one has survived from the period of professional work as an industrial metallurgist." There are, however, some four dozen of those in the complete bibliographic list. The bibliography also alone points to wartime experience, when Smith directed the brilliant group at Los Alamos that performed the plainly alchemical feat of mastering on demand the preparation and fabrication of a brand-new element, the metal plutonium.

Half a dozen book-long works are perforce omitted, a couple of them interesting monographs on the history and historiography of metallurgy, a few others admirable translations of classical texts on the history of materials. One misses the neat little study of the famous brass plate alleged to have been left north of San Francisco Bay by Francis Drake. The object yielded up to a few minutes of caliper work the damning information that everywhere its thickness held to within a few mils of standard modern specs, a performance quite impossible for brass founders in Queen Bess's day.

Three of the longer papers will suffice to test the lot. The first, from 1952, is the most original piece of scientific material in the corpus. An exercise in applied topology, its discussion of the shapes of metal grains in the context of Pablo Picasso, fat tissue, soap froth and glass is a deep pleasure and a piece of powerful mathematics. Its chief result is the demonstration that five-sided faces of contact are to be expected to dominate all cellular arrays governed by surface-tension forces. They do in the real world, the integers seeking in vain to manifest the optimal statistical rule: between 5.10 and 5.14 edges per face.

Here very probably lies the innermost rationale of the decimal system; our five fingers reflect some such pathway within an ancient cluster of embryonic cells. These relations exemplify what has become a chief theme for Smith: there is profound interaction among the several scales of any complex and growing structure. In the metal-grain example the rigorous but quite general rule of topology that binds all networks, regular or irregular, is in a kind of struggle with the boundary forces, which seek as best they can locally to reach energy minimums at every surface.

A long essay bears the modest title "Metallurgical Footnotes to the History of Art." It is a wonderful stroll led by a master through half a dozen traditions that have given rise to objects of the highest virtu, east and west. Beads, pots, bells, swords, cups, armor and jewelry are closely observed and knowingly perceived. One closing remark may open up the future to a view still deeper than the one we now have: the "balance between local and regional requirements," like the metal grains regarded in a topological mode, may please the eye because our perceptual mechanisms themselves have a similar hierarchy, either in space or in response times or in both.

This entire topic has been carried to the point of philosophical generality in Professor Smith's most recent papers in print. One briefer essay treats of art, invention and technology, all interwound. It argues strongly for study of the past, taking the testimony of things no less carefully than that of books. This tendency is now a winning one in the history of technology, in some part after Smith's example. Here is the wonderful insight (although it is found in many another form) that for any novelty not utterly simple (the bookish historian often lets mere names obscure this decisive detail) necessity cannot be the mother of invention but only of improvement. The first venture along an uncertain path to a new material, device or process is too halting to carry a useful burden. It is free curiosity and aesthetic enjoyment that can better afford the risk of innovation.

Any metallurgist named Smith has heard his fill of wordplay. Around Cyril Smith, however, the ambience of inquiry is so strong that it seemed a good idea to look up the old word. It proved to be worthwhile: the Middle English manuscripts called by the title of Smith that elderly man who once fled with a young wife and her babe into Egypt. Now, they did not think that Joseph of Nazareth was a forge worker; he was a good workman, handy with tools, *faber* in the Latin texts. The old meaning is apt for this Smith too, a man equally at home with his hand on the microscope or above the etching bath, pondering a subtle vellum manuscript or a complicated phase diagram, a scientist, a reflective craftsman, a scholar, a teacher and a connoisseur. "All my early interests were narrow, pretty much confined to experimental science. I had not a single University course that was not directly technical in content. . . . One can learn without being taught."

In 1931 the American Brass Company's young research leader on new copper alloys (with a staff of two) married a student of English social history. Alice Kimball Smith is now the perceptive historian of the scientists' movement in America around the control of nuclear energy. One can learn in many ways. "From beginning to end I have been a simple metallurgist," he wrote recently, "using metals and their structure as a kind of inverted touchstone to assay all things."

(September 1981)

Structures, or Why Things Don't Fall Down
By J. E. Gordon

Why Buildings Stand Up: The Strength of Architecture
By Mario Salvadori

Fry a sausage and nearly always the steamy, swelling interior cracks open the skin along the length, almost never across it. That result follows directly from one of the simplest practical formulas of the mechanics of stress in a material. The cheap but heavy gas cylinder in the garage and the elegantly optimized spherical oxygen bottles of spacecraft bear out the same mechanical truism. The taut rigging and flattened Dacron sails of the tensely constructed racing yacht contrast acutely with the partitioned sails of a Chinese junk, which bulge between supports to adjust pressure curvature, the stress on the sail remaining roughly constant as the wind freshens. Bats are rigged on

Chinese-junk lines, and they pay a small price in aerodynamic costs; so probably did the big pelagic pterodactyls.

Still more striking energy containment lies deep in living forms. A constant-stress biological membrane, with its stress-strain curve running horizontally across the graph, must resemble a soap film. Such membranes can support stress only if they are formed as spheres or part spheres: bubble trains, like a segmented worm. But a tube or a pipe, the cylinders that transport essential stuffs throughout the kingdom of larger life forms, like our own vital arterial plumbing, cannot function with constant stress. "The circumferential stress is ineluctably twice the axial stress," and so the stress-strain curve of the walls of tubing must slope upward to accommodate the doubled stress. Rubbery elastomers indeed can work, but their stress-strain curves are S-shaped; they are therefore unstable at high strains, blowing out into local bubbles like a snake that has eaten a football. A kitchen observation has led to the logic of the deadly aneurysm.

A fuller analysis demonstrates that a material that is stable under fluid pressure even at high strains must show a stress-strain curve that is rather flat at first but then rises steeply. Very often found in living organisms is a composite tissue whose soft matrix (the protein elastin), almost as yielding as a surface-tension film, is reinforced by a felted mat of the stiffer protein collagen. The collagen fibers come taut only after much extension, to provide the increased resistance needed at high strain. It is the tough collagen in muscle that cooking breaks down to tenderer gelatin at a temperature below that which destroys elastin (enough to restore "one's faith in the beneficence of Providence").

Leave soft materials; consider stone. Men have built well in heavy brick and stone from earliest times. The crushing of well-baked bricks by the sheer dead weight of the walls towering above them sets a very grand limit indeed: the Tower of Babel could have been raised two kilometers high with parallel walls, even higher if it had tapered like a mountain. (The tallest actual masonry structures indeed rise half as high as modern steel towers.) The real limit is evident; we all learned it playing with blocks. Block walls do not crush but fall down from lack of stability. They fall sideways. Masonry cannot withstand any tension; tensioned joints crack and gape. Then, if the wall thickness still bearing weight dwindles any more, the uptilted block will eventually rock around an outside edge; the wall tips upward and out and collapses utterly. Masonry design is a matter of arranging things so that the lines of thrust from the weight above remain well within the lower walls. Mere weight is not the issue; cathedral walls actually gained stability from the massive pinnacles and sculptured saints added to their top. Fortunately structures that fail not by breakage but from such geometrical instability can be scaled up proportionately both from models and from previous experience.

The cathedral builders had plenty of experience. The audacity and beauty of those transparent, pierced, lofty walls, their necessary supports artfully flying outside the structure, is superb. The style ended at Beauvais; there the stone tower reached an incredible 500 feet above the still incomplete nave. It failed in 1573 and was never rebuilt. The Gothic impetus was spent; the schools for the skilled tradesmen had died out, with the lore perhaps not fully mastered. After all, 350 years had passed since the beginning of construction at Beauvais. The epoch had changed; as Beauvais was dying, the masters of the Renaissance were proudly building in a new way. The death of St. Peter's at Beauvais came as St. Peter's in Rome grew in heavy-domed triumph.

Today we still gather ceremonially, although often for a secular sacrament around the playing field, under marvelous composite inverted domes. The current Madison Square Garden (there have been three) is one of those, a dish roof made of a thin concrete slab held on tensed cables. The web of radial cables (modern steel cables easily support 10 times the stress found safe for the wrought-iron chains of 19th-century bridges, some of which are still in faithful service) acts to compress their concrete ring support on the outer building wall and also to extend the inner steel anchor ring at the center of the roof. The slabs for the tight roof can be thin (usually only a couple of inches) because the concrete merely spans the small distance between the cables. The entire structure can be erected without any expensive scaffolding.

The dish roof was made practical within the past 25 years by the pioneer design of the Uruguayan engineer Leonel Viera. He had the happy idea of loading the roof with brick ballast before joining the slabs with a good mortar. Once the slab had set, the ballast was removed, having tensed the cables within the solid concrete. Thus stiffened, the roof no longer responded much to wind gusts — as had earlier, lightly loaded roofs held by flexible cables. The pre-stressed, stiff, cable-held light concrete dish (there are now other ways to achieve it) can span 400 or even 500 feet easily. We can expect better materials still, and can "dream of dish roofs . . . under which hundreds of thousands of people gather for the enhancement of their deepest experiences."

The paragraphs above conflate two rich and readable books. J. E. Gordon, the author of *Structures*, is professor of materials science at the University of Reading, with a background in Glasgow naval architecture, in yachting and in aircraft design. His book is much the more wide-ranging. Its tables of strengths and moduli include not only brick and steel and wood but also a few dozen other substances, from eggshell membrane to diamond. Gordon presents his topic in four parts. He begins with a careful account of the meaning and history of the ideas of stress and strain, goes on to cover modern fracture mechanics (that is, the energy considerations of crack propagation) and then structures of all kinds in tension and in compression, and finally pays due attention to more complicated stress patterns such as bending (and, unexpectedly, bias-cut dressmaking, à la Mlle Vionnet of Paris in the 1920's, complete with period fashion illustrations). His style is personal, witty and ironic, with a good deal of wordplay and much attention to apt epigraphs from Kipling.

Mario Salvadori is a widely known architectural engineer at Columbia University; his writing is lucid, hopeful and direct. His gaze is tightly fixed on buildings. *Why Buildings Stand Up* discusses the principles of stress analysis without formulas, although at a less physical level than Gordon's book. It includes chapter after chapter sketching the design and history of famous structures from the Pyramids to the Brooklyn Bridge, the Eiffel Tower and the wonderful works of Pier Luigi Nervi in reinforced concrete (even a beautiful sailing ketch). Salvadori's title is accurate, but Gordon treats many topics entirely apart from gravity.

Both men offer strongly stated views on the relations between aesthetics and technology. Salvadori argues for the naturalness of design that reveals structure, although with due concern for novel experience. Gordon disdains austerity and hopes for lots of ornament: "Let there be figureheads . . . crinolines . . . flags." Both books are lasting additions to the slim stock of readable works on structure and form; the Gordon book is a find for the scientific reader at large, the Salvadori for the reader who is caught up in the roofs and bridges of all the world.

(April 1984)

Science and Civilisation in China
By Joseph Needham

Volume 5, Chemistry and Chemistry Technology, Part 1: Paper and Printing
By Tsien Tsuen-Hsuin

Two billion of us are literate in one or more of the languages of the earth. Each day we readers enjoy on the average a quantity of new hard copy sufficient to fill an area 10 to 20 times the size of this page. Nearly all of that text and image appears on white paper in ink derived from carbon black. For 1,000 years it was imprinted by a flat surface cut of the desired form in relief as a mirror image.

All three essentials, paper, ink and letterpress, are well-known Chinese inventions. Here is an up-to-date account of their history, the newest addition to the splendid shelf that began to appear under Joseph Needham's signature a generation ago and that continues to please and inform readers, now with a little help from his learned friends throughout the world. Professor Tsien Tsuen-Hsuin is an eminent authority on the matter who has enjoyed a long sinological career at the University of Chicago; his book continues the enterprise in the high comparative style established by Needham. A couple of hundred illustrations, fine footnotes (as a rule less ambitious than Needham's most magisterial asides) and grand bibliographies from East and West buttress the text.

Of the elements of printing, paper came first. Writing is much older. In China it appeared on the scapulas of oxen and the carapaces of tortoises. Stone, clay, wood slips, palm leaves, woven silk and split sheepskin then became widely used mediums. Paper is a matted sheet of fibers taken from water suspension onto a fine screen. It was the ability to unite random linear fibers provided by the disintegration of plant tissues or by textile scraps into a new dimensionality, large flat sheets, that gave paper economic advantage over all its predecessors. Those included natural laminar materials from the stems of the sedge papyrus and from many woody sources of pounded bark. Cellulose-rich fibers are required for good bonding (there are now synthetic exceptions to this rule); no paper is made from silk fiber, although some may be added to give luster. The best natural sources are those without much binding substance that are high in yield of long cellulose fibers.

The oldest specimen of paper we have — it is shown here — was found near Xi'an. Manufactured in the second century B.C., probably from hempen rags, it was coarse paper used for packing bronze mirrors. The official histories of the Eastern Han concur in celebrating the eunuch Cai Lun as the inventor of paper for writing, centuries later, in about A.D. 100. The historians observe that silk was too costly and bamboo slips too heavy. It may be that what Cai hit on was using fresh fibers from tree bark and hemp plant instead of fibers from secondhand textiles. By Cai's time better papers are indeed found in use for writing.

The handicraft grew steadily, in villages near streams and by wooded hillsides (fuel for boiling the raw plant material was important). One by one new fiber sources were tapped. At first hemp and cotton were used, but they were too valuable in textile production; their rags are a limited if superior source. Then came the slow-growing climbing rattan; by A.D. 986 a scholar could lament satirically that worthless writers were killing off the rattan with their millions of words. He was right. The paper mulberry shrub and the young bamboo have been cultivated ever since in most parts of China as the main fiber sources for handcrafted paper. Of course, pulped wood fibers are now the dominant source for the industrial process everywhere.

The oldest paper known was used for careful wrapping. Today too only about four-tenths of the paper made worldwide is intended to receive ink. Old China also used handmade paper variously; paper currency, "flying money," began to supplement coins about 1,000 years ago, and everyone knows of China's ubiquitous paper lanterns, kites, fans, umbrellas, windows and screens. Funeral offerings simulated worldly wealth in paper. Paper effigies of caparisoned horses, camels, servants, armor and money "in great quantities" were, according to Marco Polo, all burned along with the dead man. Less familiar are light paper armor, practical for foot soldiers in difficult terrain, and decorated wallpaper. The latter touch, which caught on for good in Europe earlier than 1700, was regarded in China at the time as being in rather low taste. Nevertheless, one photograph here shows a delightfully intricate round geometric design, the oldest paper-cut known, found recently in Xinjiang. It was made in the fifth or sixth century. A few pages later we see the proverbial paper tiger itself, satisfyingly striped and toothy but hardly frightening.

The humblest and most intimate use is also old; literary sources are primly silent, but in the sixth century a scholar, Yan Zhitui, wrote for his household: "I dare not use for toilet purposes" paper bearing the names of sages. An Arab traveler of the ninth century, accustomed to meticulous ablutions, was offended by what he regarded as the careless Chinese habit. Toilet paper was made cheaply in very large quantities from rice straw; in 1393 the imperial court alone bought 750,000 newspaper-size sheets, reserving a special quality for the imperial family. At the other end of the aesthetic axis, we encounter the small, reddish notepaper designed by the ninth-century courtesan-poet Xue Tao. Made of hibiscus skin mixed with the powdered petals of hibiscus, it remained in vogue for many centuries.

Paper led to printing. Hand copying of manuscript onto silk and paper was well known. Seal cutting on wood blocks of inscriptions in mirror image, sometimes consisting of as many as 100 characters, was certainly a forerunner; so was the wide use of inked paper squeezes or rubbings made from ample carved inscriptions on bronze and stone. The astonishing Mountain of Stone grotto in Hebei has preserved for a dozen centuries 7,000 steles, each 30 meters in height, bearing in all four million words of the Buddhist canon carved in relief. The complex ideographs meant accurate copying by hand was costly and difficult. Yet both the standardization of Confucian texts needed for national civil service examinations and the zeal of believers enjoined to multiply repetition of the powerful formulas of Buddhist sutras provided motive enough for the development of printing.

We hold sure evidence of the consequences. In 1966 a miniature scroll two inches wide printed from a dozen 20-inch-long wood blocks was found in southeast Korea. It is the oldest printed document known. The text is a Buddhist sutra done into Chinese. A known translation made by a monk of Chang-An (now Xi'an), the temple construction itself and the form of certain new characters place the date of production early in the eighth century. Only slightly later is the famous A.D. 764 edition of a million copies of brief prayers from the same sutra. They were placed by order of the empress Shōtoku in 10 Japanese temples; each printed charm was stored in a tiny wood pagoda. Many copies and some of the pagodas still exist; one is shown in an illustration. Although the edition of one million was certainly printed, it cannot be established from what material the blocks were cut. These examples produced outside China follow exactly the detailed methods of all subsequent Chinese printing. It can hardly be doubted that printing had begun somewhat earlier within China, had followed the widening usage of Chinese characters and had finally spread beyond that symbolic frontier.

The art flourished. Sir Aurel Stein found in the monastery at Dunhuang as long ago as 1907 what is still the oldest complete printed book we know, a five-meter paper scroll of the *Diamond Sutra*. Its colophon dates it "reverently . . . for universal distribution" on the 15th day of the fourth month of A.D. 868. Its frontispiece showing the Buddha and his disciple and its rather refined printing are eloquent. Although the Bible of Johann Gutenberg would not appear for six centuries, there are quite a few printed Buddhist texts known to be only a little younger than this sutra.

The craftsmen and the craft of Chinese bookmaking are described here in some detail: the calligrapher whose nimble brush put the information on fine paper, pasted ink side down to the smoothed fruitwood block; the skillful engravers who then cut away with their elegant arsenal of chisels and gouges all surface that was not black; the printer who inked the block with a horsehair brush, pressed the paper to the inked surface and brushed a pad lightly over the back. By the Ming time, Matteo Ricci reckoned that in a day's work a skilled printer produced 1,500 double-page sheets. The engraving process was proofread at four stages; inlaid local corrections to the block are commonplace. Page format and binding have long since been standardized, and they support a fine trade jargon, adorned by such terms as elephant trunk and book ear, applied to the functional features of the traditional paperbound, thin Chinese book.

The 81,258 magnolia wood blocks carved on both sides to print the *Tripitaka Koreana*, which was completed in the year 1251, are still neatly shelved in southern Korea. They capture the flavor of the golden age of Chinese bookmaking during that period, the Song dynasty. Such grand canons were rare, but there were a great many widely used secular works and many private printers as fine as those of the state and the monasteries. By the year 1500 some 20 million books had been printed in Europe, copies of perhaps 10,000 or 15,000 titles. From that period China yields registers of 50,000 titles, half a million distinct, thin volumes. It seems likely that until about 1700 it was text in Chinese that could be read from the majority of the world's printed pages.

Of course, we associate movable type, not whole-page blocks, with Gutenberg. Such type suits well the alphabetical languages of Europe. Yet Gutenberg holds no priority even on movable type. Earthenware type for individual characters was certainly made and used in China in about 1050. The contemporaneous scholar-scientist Shen Kuo tells us about it in terse detail. "If one were to print only two or three copies, this method would be neither simple nor easy. But for printing hundreds or thousands of copies, it was marvelously quick." A font in a Western language needs about 100 species of type; given a few thousand individual pieces, any spread can be set. A full Chinese font requires from 2,000 to 400,000 pieces, including the necessary repetitions. The hardworking early compositor could put most characters within arm's reach only by the use of a number of big lazy Susans. Eventually he was kept on the run. In about 1300 the characters of a Chinese font were arranged by their rhyme.

Type was made from wood, from enamel and from bronze in China before the European invention of printing. Korean prints made use of cast bronze type as early as 1234. The impetus came from the book by Shen Kuo; therefore it seems possible such type may have been used earlier. There are extant pages printed from cast bronze type in Korea in 1403, 50 years before the German success. A book or two were printed there with movable wood type even earlier. In Korea the casting of type derived from the casting of coins. The character was cut in beechwood; the die was pressed into a clay mold, which was baked and used to cast the bronze. The type was finished by polishing. In premodern China lead was not used for type.

Historical queries crowd into the mind, and Tsien has addressed them soberly. Paper clearly entered Europe from China by way of Samarkand, Baghdad and Damascus by means of Arab intermediaries. The oldest European paper manuscript known comes from 10th-century Spain. By 1150 Arab and Jewish papermakers there were manufacturing an excellent product from flax.

Printing took three or four centuries more to appear, although for a century before any type was set by Gutenberg many products were printed from wood blocks: textiles, playing cards, religious images and even block books. All of these have earlier Chinese counterparts; yet there is no clear evidence one way or another for the diffusion even of the notion of movable type for text from the world of 10,000 characters to the world of the short Latin alphabet along the river Main.

Even more striking is the contrasting impact of printing on the two worlds. Printing on paper is democratic, we traditionally hold; much cheaper than hand copying on scarcer surfaces, it reaches many more readers. It fed a great expansion of learning in Europe, characterized by national diversity and social mobility. At the same time, printing guarantees authentic spread of a central text (and figures), and easy multiplication enables many to ponder the same canonical truths. In Europe print capped deep change within a century or two; in China it shared for 1,000 years the punctuated stability of a unified culture.

This fascinating book is a worthy updating of its celebrated predecessor of 60 years ago, *The Invention of Printing in China and Its Spread Westward*, by T. F. Carter, revised in 1955 by L. Carrington Goodrich. Let us offer the courtesy of the last words to an Elizabethan versifier, old Thomas Churchyard: "Though parchment duer a greater time and space,/ Yet can it not put paper out of place: / For paper, still, [from] man to man doth go, / When parchment comes in few men's hands you knowe."

(May 1986)

Energy in China's Modernization: Advances and Limitations
By Vaclav Smil

Not so long ago any penetrating appraisal of current economic and environmental affairs in China was something like archaeology—based, as Professor Smil puts it, on the piecing together of many "shards of information" into shadowy larger shapes of reality. No longer. This penetrating, friendly if critical book by a geographer from the University of Manitoba draws on a wealth of detailed Chinese publications, largely from the 1980's. The task is now to find pattern in the flood of consistent new data, and he succeeds admirably.

The daily necessities for a billion people are dauntingly diverse. Widespread changes in their energy supply and consumption are of necessity intricate, often marked by surprises, missteps, even paradox. China is in part one of the large, modernizing industrial states, with some 200 million people living more or less by city ways. But around them are 800 million villagers, more than a third of them adults hard at work on the land. It is no small achievement that China is able to feed its people — one-fifth of humankind with access to only one-fifteenth of all cultivated land — with a calorie supply per person not much below Japan's. Of course, there are plenty of ill-fed people still: a tenth of the population, mainly in interior provinces.

What is most striking is that the Chinese countryside lives by coal as well as by sun-grown grain. Coal provides two-thirds of the country's ammonia-based fertilizer, the nitrogen fixed in a large number of small and inefficient synthesis plants. The rest of the essential commercial nitrogen is produced in large, efficient new plants (provided by the U.S. firm M. W. Kellogg) fueled by natural gas. The famous recycling of organic wastes, including night soil, still goes cannily on as it always has, but now that turnaround can supply at most a fourth of all the nitrogen applied to the crops. (Much comes as well from the symbiotic microorganisms of the rice paddy.)

The overall outcome is unexpected: the energy supplied for agricultural production to each hectare of cultivated land in China is double the amount supplied in the U.S. It is about the same as that of prosperous France, although only a fourth of what prevails in the land-poor Netherlands. The reasons are plain: fertilizer is heavily used in China, and mechanical power too is essential for extensive irrigation by pumped water. Mechanization of fieldwork is still minimal. Only about a fifth of all the energy brought to the farm goes to build or to fuel farm machinery, tractors or trucks. Yet the populous countryside is seriously energy-short. About half a billion people lack fuel to stay warm or to cook three hot meals a day during the cold seasons. When in winter the housewives of one county in cold Gansu "face the stoves, tears come to their eyes."

These hardworking people endure the bitter energy crisis of the world's poor: not the lack of gasoline but the scarcity of fuelwood. For rural China even the term fuelwood is a kind of euphemism. Four-fifths of household energy in the Chinese village is gained by burning biomass, all right. But about half of that fuel is from crop residues, the cereal straws, stalks and vines from the fields. The other half is from the woods: branches, twigs, roots, needles and bark raked from the woodland floor, even dried sod and grass tufts lugged home in the back baskets of women and children, some 20 pounds per household per day. (Biogas from wastes and cattle dung furnishes a few percent.)

It is here that a simplistic evaluation of energy efficiency on the farm as the ratio of fossil-energy subsidy to photosynthetic gain loses touch with reality. Even the frugal winter-pinched households of village China consume three or four times more fuel energy for daily living than is spent on their fields, the fuel burned at low efficiency in traditional stoves. Long-range hope rests in growing food with less human labor on the land. What country people most need in the near term, along with the extensive spread of high-efficiency household stoves (some clever new models are shown here), is above all "the greatest possible extension of private fuel-wood lots."

China's abundant coal is mined by the largest corps of underground workers in the world, two or 2.5 million miners at the coal face, working mostly in small, local, shallow mines and open pits with shovel, pickaxe and barrow—a simple handcraft, arduous and often risky, with open flames instead of enclosed safety lamps. It is a big mine of this class that can manage to ship a single truckload of coal per day. The mean yield per shift below-ground is about what it was in late-Victorian Britain. Only the U.S. now rivals China for overall coal production, and our tonnage is won with less than a tenth as many miners. Half of Chinese coal is the quality product of a few large mechanized state mines, but the rest of it is the raw, dusty and unsorted yield of 50,000 country mines, more of which are being opened every day. For it is coal that drives Chinese railroads and Chinese industry, rural and centralized production alike; two-thirds of all the energy used in China comes from coal.

The rivers of China plunge from the roof of the world down to the crowded coastal valleys and lowlands. No other country has so much hydropower potential. Here too experience has brought surprise, in some ways the reverse of the story of coal. Some 70,000 small hydro plants dot the countryside. This appropriate technology is based on cheap, effective turbines, made available in 80 varieties for placement in any irrigation ditch or stream. This development is an internationally acclaimed success that surely rests in part on China's "unmatched ancient tradition of hydraulic engineering."

On the other hand, the grandest of the Sino-Soviet hydro schemes of the 1960's, a giant dam in the rocky gorge of the Three Gates, below the big bend where at last the Yellow River leaves the easily eroded loess, has miscarried. Its basin was silt-filled within a few years, and the headwaters backed up to dangerous flood stage. The dam had to be pierced to let the river flow free; the high hopes for Sanmenxia ended in "a low head run-of-the-river plant," its power capacity cut sixfold, with no potential for flood control. The fearful passage of the Gates has had no pity on human effort since grain first traveled the river in the days of Han.

There are lofty plans afoot: coal-slurry pipelines to take some of the heavy burden of coal off the railway system, where it is the bulk of all cargo; modern open-cast coal mines to fuel power plants right at the mine mouth, sited along the rich coal seams of Shanxi at a density that will match that of the Ruhr or the valleys of the Ohio-Pennsylvania border. Expensive French-licensed nuclear reactors will soon be coming on-line, and new major hydropower schemes, including the largest power plant in the world, are rising now within the Three Gorges of the Yangtze, China's largest river.

Nothing comes easy. The health of land and air will be at multiple risk, both in the shadow of the big projects and in the path of the undirected "coal rush" of ambitious peasant miners. China must and will grow richer, although more slowly than hopeful planners reckon. Efficiency in every detail is needed — say more diesel trucks, and cheap sedans for road-bound officials instead of expensive four-wheel-drive vehicles. Frugality, productivity and prompt attention to externalities are as important as ambitious plans.

The thematic maps, the careful tables and graphs, rough estimates from first principles used to explain and test the data, and a lively sense of each activity in its context give this model of a book its authority and interest. Over the years the author has prepared half a dozen expert volumes, several of them studies of China, others ranging beyond that land. (His provocative worldwide survey, *Energy-Food-Environment*, appeared in 1987 under the imprint of the Oxford University Press.) Certainly no one's prophecy in these high matters will always prove right, but Smil's sober treatments seem a mark against which other views should be tested. He does not usually share the highest hopes or cry the loudest alarms; for him Rome was not built, nor did it fall, in a day.

The epigraph he cites—and then caps—is from Master Meng, eloquent apostle of Confucius. It hints at Smil's unfailingly humane concern for China's prospects and our own: "'If you do not interfere with the busy seasons in the fields, then there will be more grain than the people can eat; . . . if hatchets and axes are permitted in the forests . . . only in the proper seasons, then there will be more timber than they can use. . . . When the aged wear silk and eat meat and the masses are neither cold nor hungry, it is impossible for their prince not to be a true king.' Would Deng Xiaoping disagree?"

(March 1989)

Whole Earth Catalog: Access to Tools
Portola Institute

On the heavy paper cover of this large newsprint brochure there appears, true to the name, the whole earth photographed in color from a synchronous satellite. The 60 inside pages list and discuss, in a kind of reasoned and personal set of reviews, with copious facsimile citations and illustrations, many books, services and materials, all of which are easily gained by mail. The *Whole Earth Catalog* is more a pointer than a seller, as it engagingly says, although the institute will accept orders for many items listed.

The document is good reading: it assembles the input and output channels of a strangely attractive contemporary subculture, that of the dissenter and reformer who seeks to construct a philosophical, personal and economic refuge from this curious industrial society. The philosophy is the appealing one of "understanding whole systems"—from Buckminster Fuller and D'Arcy Wentworth Thompson to the famous children's book of Kees Boeke (the universe seen in 40 order-of-magnitude jumps). The economics is consistent: it includes domes for houses (both their established study and their improvised construction—"the crystallographic theory and junkyard practice"), mushrooms, beekeeping, teepees, village technology and campcraft. There is, for example, an attachment for converting your chain saw to a one-man lumber mill, a knowing account of the best kerosene lamps ("Coleman lamps are terrible—they hiss and clank and blind you, just like civilization") and information about automobile repair data, consumer guides, extrication of Government documents, discount houses and the better mail-order suppliers of camping gear, radio parts, optical components—even art reproductions. The best educational reform and popular science are devotedly included, with a catholic spread of taste. Most of the reviews are from readers and users themselves; the catalogue solicits more, for which a small payment is offered. The personal side is conservationist, rural and iconoclastic; the books of Yoga and Tantra are here, with the journal of the Modern Utopians. Just as in the wider society, there is a strong component of the irrational and the indulgent, more from the supplement, which contains the letters of readers, than from the more disciplined rebelliousness of the editors. There is a good stock of a few Anglo-Saxon words, and some touching visual exhibits of drug-induced mental deterioration. Yet even this ugly side of the subculture is more benign, one can argue, than the cancers of war and cruelty, which proliferate in the publications of our straight world and which are completely absent here.

(June 1969)

How to Wrap Five Eggs: Japanese Design in Traditional Packaging
By Hideyuki Oka

The Japanese sensibly trade by fives and tens, not by the dozen. When the farmers of one prefecture sell half a ten of eggs, they wrap them in a kind of cage tied out of rice straw, the eggs held tangent one above the other, gleaming through the three strands of the wrapping. There follow page by page in this beautiful and loving book 200-odd full-page photographs, some in color, of how specific packages, mainly holding good things to eat, are made here and there in Japan, and were made before the rise of blister packs or vinyl squeeze bottles. All the packages were taken from a 1964 national exhibition arranged by the devoted author for the commercial artists of Japan. They fall into classes: those that are merely wrapped in simple and honest beauty by rural sellers — true folk packages — and those from cities such as Nara, or great centers such as Tokyo or Kyoto, where a special shop has, sometimes for centuries, packaged its wares in a triumph of wood, white coopering or pottery.

To leaf these pages with any interest in how things are done is to spend a heartwarming hour. The objects are beautiful and right; they combine homely materials — straw, paper, bamboo, cloth, earthenware — in the Japanese way. They do not stay wholly within the low-key mode of Japanese country folk; they show very often the colorful, strong, clamoring look of the eager shopkeeper. Here is a hand-cut wooden box, copied from the style of a box used for an individual gold coin in feudal times, marked with bold black hand-brushed characters and a faint carmine seal, holding toothpicks. A few pages on you see a warm, rough pottery jar, held closed by an end-cut slab of wood, fastened by a purple cord across a twisted vine handle. It contains a special soy pickle, and of course it is kept for later use.

The author is no pessimist. He sees, unlike the American designer George Nelson, who writes an enamored but gloomy foreword, that we can have hope, we can still work. "If the craftsmen and 'designers' of old Japan could create beauty with *their* materials, are we today to accept defeat when faced with *ours?*" If our technology is ever to lift and not to depress the spirit, we need to face this question squarely. We need to learn to pay for the luxury of good looks, of honest work, of detail outside the commonplace, of time-honored excellence in small things. The Japanese have always understood — at least until now — that it is better to splurge some, to have rare extravagances, than it is to face every day the mediocrity of mere expanding G.N.P. or the shoddy fad. The machine and the artist can meet the artisan's challenge; it is the managers and their clients who raise our doubts. Packages, in this particular year, are certainly not the most important issue on our minds, but these utter a sharp comment.

(*July 1968*)

The Nature and Art of Workmanship
By David Pye

This little paperback, only 60 pages of text and another 30 of carefully captioned photographs, is the work of the Professor of Furniture Design at the Royal College of Art in London. His eye is naturally out for the quality of work in wood, and half of the photographs are of wood objects, but the rest span the range from sail canvas to beer can and computer module. It would be an error to try to enlarge much on the message of a book this crisp and thoughtful, but some remarks are called for. Altogether it is as penetrating an account of the aesthetics of what humans make as has been seen for a good many years, and it deserves a wide readership.

Such work rests on the validity of nice distinctions. Professor Pye begins with the sharp comment that design can be symbolically conveyed, whereas workmanship cannot. "On the workman's decision depends a great part of the quality of our environment." The designer prepares the score, the workman performs the music. Workmanship is of two kinds: the workmanship of risk and the workmanship of certainty. In the first the result is not predetermined but depends heavily on the maker; the quality of the second kind is fixed in advance, by jig or tool bed, die or punch. To separate hand and power tools is no useful way of division and to distinguish mass production from one by one is also a false division. Indeed, little is really done "by hand"; how can we exclude from the machine category the brace and bit, the potter's wheel and the hand loom? Writing with a pen is perhaps the commonest handwork that remains.

Nor can "rough" and "precise" be helpful dividers; rough work is often excellent, fully achieved, beautiful. Pye uses instead "regulated" and "free." Regulated work admits of no disparity between idea and achievement; when there are evident disparities, the work is called free. Both modes, risk and certainty, can, of course, achieve high regulation. The workman regulates risk by his dexterity, his gradualness and the use of jigs and forms. The workman of certainty usually gains regulation immediately; in this kind of production high regulation is today almost inevitable, although it is not logically required. So far the distinctions named are on the side of production. They seem helpful and knowing.

The key to Professor Pye's argument lies on the side of the user, the viewer, the perceiver. It is based on what he calls diversity. The intrinsic limitations of human vision and touch leave — under any circumstances of distance, lighting or size — some unresolved and indistinguishable elements of any object. It is these that generally determine surface — through texture, reflections, gloss, luster and the rest. A surface looks tinny or leathery because we recognize by experience the particular scale and range of the unseen tiny undulations and deviations from flatness of the surfaces. The workmanship of risk can deal masterfully with these matters; "surface quality in man-made things comes of workmanship." Even a careful microfinish specification of surface roughness brings the designer little visual gain; he cannot hope to specify an entire surface, as complex as the Alps, with a number or two or even a root-mean-square average. Meanwhile the designer for the workmanship of certainty must continue to learn about the quality and potential of materials from the best works made by the craftsmen of risk.

"Four things are going wrong." One is the present inability of the workmanship of certainty to predetermine the diversity that makes surface; only in woven synthetic fibers and in the use of transparent and translucent plastics is there so far any sign of design success in diversity. Computer-controlled machine tools might begin to introduce regulated diversity but they have not done so yet. Another is the bad workmanship of risk in the assembly of objects made with high regulation, as in carelessly fitted millwork doors. Still another: The best of the regulated workmanship of risk requires so much time that it is dying of its high cost, although it still contributes unique qualities to our environment, for example the finest cabinetmaking. Finally, free workmanship is dwindling too (if less speedily).

The last three problems can be met by specific changes—through education, cooperation, deliberate support, or perhaps by amateurs who will work more for love than for money. The handmade gun and the handmade viola bow are examples of the finest regulated workmanship of risk today, and they are not in danger of neglect. Free workmanship too can be preserved; the Japanese packaging crafts give a splendid example. It is up to high technology and perceptual science, however, to solve the first problem. There are no matters of bread and butter, but we well know we do not live by bread alone.

No one who reads this book will again throw away a beer can with indifference. The slight buckling of the surface gives it an element of free workmanship, and the raw, direct edges do not clash with its low surface polish. "Anyone accustomed to doing regulated work by the workmanship of risk must feel something of a pang at throwing such a thing away, for to make it by the workmanship of risk would be an intensely difficult and very long job."

(May 1974)

Christo: Running Fence, Sonoma and Marin Counties, California 1972–76

Narrative text by David Bourdon
Photographs by Gianfranco Gorgoni
Chronicle by Calvin Tomkins

The inception is brilliantly documented. "RUNNING FENCE project for the West Coast. Woven synthetic fabric forming Fence, attached to an upper steel cable and to 20 feet high poles, spaced 60 to 80 feet, running 18 to 20 miles, from the Pacific Ocean towards Inland, through the Landscape, over the crest of the Hills, into a small City, along and across the Highways, county and dirt roads." The pencil-and-crayon drawing of the concept over the typed label "Christo, October 1972" is convincing; the long sweep of the curtain over the tawny, rolling lands and then out of sight along the ridgeline is a pretty good representation of the reality, which began to grow in two counties in the summer of 1976. In the end it stretched out of Bodega Bay 24.5 miles across the landscape, from noon of September 10 until its complete removal on October 23, 1976. Christo Javacheff and his wife Jeanne-Claude, the principals of the Running Fence Corporation, had finished what they set out to do. They created a beautiful work of art, both visual and social, another Christo project of his uniquely playful and aesthetic engineering.

The money? Working capital came from the cosponsors, museums and collectors, who were solicited with the proposal in 1973 and were offered a hefty discount off the market price on some drawing or collage by Christo. The bottom line came to about $3 million, most of it for materials and labor, construction vehicles and legal, engineering and insurance fees. The physical fence was some 2,000 big panels of woven nylon fabric (surplus from early projects for air bags in automobiles, and a bargain). Each pure white panel was 18 by 68 feet and weighed less than 60 pounds. A panel was fitted on all four sides with grommets, to hang on hooks from steel cable spanning steel posts each 18 feet high (plus three feet belowground).

Those posts did not stand in concrete footings; each was supported vertically by a pair of "shoe angles," bolted steel L beams that kept the post from sinking. Guy cables braced the posts laterally; a single long, tapered panel ran from the beach down into the sea, where it was strongly anchored. There were a few special panels with archways cut to pass a road or free a parking lot here and there. Ninety miles of cable was used. "At the end of the viewing period, the anchors were driven below plow level; all holes were backfilled with sand and reseeded with grass." All other materials were removed and given to the ranchers whose land the fence had crossed; the county experts inspected the entire site with approval, and on December 14 the Sonoma County Landmarks Commission designated Pole No. 7–33 as Historic Landmark No. 24.

This book, made in the luxurious and handsome manner of well-illustrated presentations of the work of an artist or an architect, records the project. It begins with the chronology of events, includes an adroit essay on the entire tale and continues with documents, drawings, letters, invoices, reports, calculations, hearings. There is even a page-size sample of the fabric itself. The last half of the big volume mainly presents color photographs of the fence both in construction and during the time of viewing, seen as a work of art, flame-touched by the sunset, filled delicately by the wind, a mark of hand and mind across the land, evocative of drapery, regattas and the Great Wall of China.

The engineering was modest but real. There were desert tests of poles and fittings, and plenty of worry about the seagoing end. The route was crucial; it was laid out by the artist himself, who walked the fence line for three weeks in the fall of 1974. He carried a bag of wood stakes, and he dropped one every few hundred feet for the crew that followed. They hammered in the stakes at the future post intervals of 62 feet; the stakes and posts were numbered and the terrain was recorded. The route was not traveled sequentially; Christo worked rather with the landholders at their convenience, with concern for their livestock and their vehicles. Sharp curves were structurally difficult (nine feet offset from pole to pole was the maximum without special anchors). Christo made frequent revisions as the surveyors and the contractor came along his original zigzagging trail.

The 50-odd landholders along the line were natural proponents of the work. Indeed, they were won over first by the personal sincerity of the Christos and then by the audacity and beauty of the task. The 60 skilled professional hard hats who worked at driving anchors, laying cable and erecting poles enjoyed the project, and so did the 360 extras, the young men and women who were taken on for fabric-panel installation in late August. For them, many caught up in the counterculture way of life, the hard, sharp work and the beauty it created made a little epiphany.

There were plenty of opponents, including even artists, together with scientists, certain conservationists and resident squares. The corporation employed nine lawyers, and in the end they satisfied 15 governmental agencies, from both the counties and the state, with highway, fish and game, forest, water quality, land and coastal jurisdictions. One transgression of the laws marked this project: the permit to use the coastal section was granted by the regional division, but an appeal against it was taken to the statewide commission. That appeal meant the automatic revocation of the permit, and fatal delay. Christo boldly went ahead; the application for an injunction sought by the commission to uphold its powers against this vulnerable, delightful and entirely transient project was carefully read by a wise judge with his blind eye. He set his hearing weeks later; by then the fence had flowered and gone. "I completely work within American system by being illegal, like everyone else," Christo said. "And no make-believe, remember. We challenge, and we pay the consequences."

This volume is a fine record for anyone who wants to see into how things are done in our society, how the world works, both the newer world of environmental-impact reports and the older world of wire, wild flowers and wind. It lacks only one thing: it has no visual report of the death of the fence, which is surely part of its life. If you would enjoy your share of this contribution to the G.N.W.B. (the gross national wellbeing), seek out this expensive volume. Let the artist lower the curtain: he was watching a quarter mile of cloth rippling in the moving air. "'Look there, Ted,' he said, his voice rising in excitement. 'See how it describes the wind.'"

(July 1980)

IX

The Staff of Life

By bread we live, though not by bread alone.
These books outline a few ways in which the
symbiosis between humankind and plants has determined the way we live, now and yesterday, for
good and for bad.

Wheat: Botany, Cultivation, and Utilization

By R. F. Peterson

A carbonized spikelet of a hulled variety of wheat is perfectly imprinted on baked clay in material excavated in Iraq at Jarmo, a village where men already gained their strength by feeding on the seeds of wheat. That was about 6700 B.C.; today all over the world outside the Tropics men tend each year about 10^{14} individual wheat plants, mainly of the species *Triticum aestivum*, a species that itself arose in a wheat field in western Asia some 3,000 years ago. This substantial volume is a general account of wheat, taking up the plant itself, its genetics and physiology, its varieties, breeding and diseases; it gives a broad treatment of cultivation, from seed preparation to sowing, of weed and insect control, harvesting and threshing; finally it describes use, from storage, nutrient content and milling to baking, spaghetti-extrusion and international trade. The pictorial matter is fascinating: the Jarmo spikelet is here, and color photographs of grains of many varieties. The chromosome configurations of the several "species" are shown, as are the external look of the ears of almost 100 varieties. Here are the broad flatlands with the golden meadows stretching for miles, or traversed all night by a dozen combines in echelon. There are grain elevators in the Crimea and the Transvaal, and red wheat in great heaps on the ground during a bumper year in Alberta. There is a funerary model from the Old Kingdom of Egypt, showing the wheat being ground and the baker tending his fire. Next to it are modern automatic ovens, producing some 100,000 loaves a day.

Most U.S. wheat is hard red winter wheat, sown in the fall, when it forms a strong root system and sends up its early-branching leaves. On the dry plains the plowman no longer encourages a layer of dust (once thought to check water loss through evaporation, a practice that itself encouraged the dust bowl) but uses a cultivator whose blades work mainly below the surface. Most fertilizer is applied at sowing time.

The next spring the field grows, with that special promising green, and the wheat grower sprays for control of broad-leaved weeds by 2,4-D and of wild oats by a specific called barban. Chinch bug, hopper, Hessian fly and their like he attacks with more sprays, even by airplane. (The crop is still not won without bloodshed: accidents to crop-dusting pilots are frequent.) He reaps and threshes all at once with the direct combine, a self-propelled machine that cuts the stems, parts grain from the chaff, stores the grain in its tank and blows the chaff and the cuttings out into the field. In 1829, even before the use of the hand cradle, one acre of wheat required 46 man-hours for harvesting, consisting in 14 for cutting by sickle, five for hand-binding, 13 for threshing with the flail, 10 for winnowing with rod and fan, and a little more. With the combine it takes half an hour. On this fact we who dwell in cities depend. By 1896 the total had already dropped to three hours; the 19th century set the pace.

Wheat seeds mainly contain starch, but their protein is important both as a nutrient and as a substance indispensable to the formation of small bubbles in the dough, which makes wheat and rye the only true bread-making grains. Heating before grinding denatures the proteins and prevents the evolution of gas. Bread eaters do not parch the grain; they probably stopped doing so, in order to turn the flatbread into the leavened, sometime in the fourth millennium B.C., a turn of events perhaps not unconnected with the spread of *T. aestivum*. Palatable bread requires only flour, water and yeast; salt is usually held essential for its savor. (It is not easy to speak of this topic without echoes of the Bible.)

The longevity of the fertile wheat seed is surprising: "By adjusting all factors to [an] optimum, it will be possible to keep wheat seed viable for as long as 100 years." The occasional assertion that wheats from ancient Egyptian storage pits and tombs has germinated is flatly denied. The authentic seeds show no germination whatever; "they are hard, dry, brittle and lifeless."

Ergot is a minor disease of wheat, although it is a major one of rye. Its black, powdery spore bodies replace entire grains in the wheat ear. We are protected statistically against the grave symptoms of ergot poisoning: the price of wheat containing even a few such bodies is lower. Dilution saves us in an era of mass production; formerly we depended on the good offices of a watchful miller. (Nowadays the ergot alkaloids are elaborately modified into LSD and supplied separately.) Our greatest competitor for the wheat is probably the stem rust, a fungus found in many races on all continents. It has a complex life cycle, requiring alternate infection of wheat or grass stems and the barberry bush. Resistant varieties of wheat are the main weapon against rust, and the task of keeping ahead of the mutating races of the rust is literally endless. Chemical control is a promising backup procedure. The major losses to stored grain come not from rats and mice but from small beetles and weevils. Such insects can develop even in very dry conditions; their respiration produces enough water vapor to promote the growth of molds and other fungi. These spread rapidly, their metabolism releasing much heat. This is the main cause of grain spoilage. The grain needs checking from time to time for moisture and temperature rise. The biology of all these events has an air of thermodynamic inevitability. The wheat is a microcosm of history, of biology, of trade, of invention.

The author of this admirable work is a specialist in cereal rusts from the Agriculture Research Station in Winnipeg. He has tried to make a book that expresses his experience and wisdom as well as library gleanings.

It is a book aimed at "readers seeking a broad view" and not at specialists, nor at giving practical directions. He has fully succeeded. There is one curious lack: beer, intimately related to bread since the time of Ur, is nowhere mentioned, nor is malt whisky. Recipes and statistics are given for cakes but not for ale.

(February 1967)

Food in Chinese Culture: Anthropological and Historical Perspectives
Edited by K. C. Chang

In Peking dialect to have lost one's job is to have *ta p'o le fan wan*, broken the rice bowl. The bowl of *fan* is indeed the center of every Chinese meal, as it has been for four or five millenniums. But "rice" is too narrow a translation, since *fan* is in fact any staple food made from grain: rice, steamed breads of wheat, millet or maize flour, pancakes, noodles. Each diner has his own portion of *fan*. To "assist" the *fan* every meal should have some *ts'ai*, selections from the overwhelming, flexible variety of dishes of cooked meats, fish and vegetables, those products of "the art of mixture," cut into small morsels and served for the entire table, to be shared through personal selection, often with individual sauces. Chopsticks are usual, and have been common for 3,000 or 4,000 years. The kitchen always has a cauldron for *ts'ai*, a steamer or boiler for *fan*; the dual principle defines a Chinese meal even more sharply than the familiar ingredients from Chinese farm, field or stream.

That dual scheme is found in the invariable paired utensils in Han digs, in famous Chou texts of Homeric age and every day at a couple of hundred million family tables. The miraculous infant "Lord Millet" began to wail, says the ancient poem; his baby voice was very loud, but soon he showed the people the husbandry of the yellow crop, which "failed nowhere, it grew thick." The Chinese food style is truly an agricultural style. Some wild tribes on their marches ate no *fan* and some other barbarians took uncooked meat, but to be fully Chinese meant and still means eating grain food and cooked morsels, *fan-ts'ai*. Even in the dumplings and filled buns that may appear to mix the grain with its staple meat-and-vegetable accompaniment, the *fan* and *ts'ai* are not mixed but rather put together, the wrapping distinct around the filling.

Eight lively and learned chapters present an informal descriptive history of food in China, dynasty by dynasty, drawing on archaeological, literary, graphic and scientific evidence, seasoned with a good deal of personal experience in contemporary China north and south. The second aim is to interpret the rich material as a part of cultural history, probing the social and ritual implications in a pioneering way that is far from mature but full of interest. The final chapter (by E. N. Anderson, Jr., and Marja L. Anderson of the University of California at Riverside) draws a conclusion of remarkable force. The authors first show persuasively what everyone would concede, that the everyday Chinese cuisine is a "minimax game" making efficient use of land and sun. What then of the festival meals in their variety and splendor? Only here is *fan* made secondary to *ts'ai*, and here too the result is adaptive. Nothing is wasted: the pigs and chickens have converted scraps into high-quality protein, and the production of diverse crops and foodstuffs is encouraged by the habit of feasting.

The shared community essential to Chinese life is given tangible expression by the social use of enjoyable food. In China today this experience is more and more widely shared. The polarization of the past—the many hungry, the elegant few—is dwindling, and the old structures of holiday enjoyment remain as public goods. The *ts'ai* dishes are today less expensive but more numerous. Indeed, it is attractive to foresee the future in a world of limited resources, where in any country the scheme of life will not be some wasteful and mediocre hamburger every day but a frugal everyday diet set lower on the food chain and punctuated by a variety of socially sanctioned and highly enjoyable special occasions, yet economical overall. In 1972 Peking one couple of authors enjoyed not only "the best Peking duck we had ever tasted" but also "separate little dishes of sautéed duck's kidneys, sautéed duck's liver and intestines, deep-fried duck's tongue, salt-fried duck's pancreas, smoked duck's brain, and eggs steamed with duck fat."

Here are a few tidbits from this artful mixture of comment. The recent find of the remarkably well-sealed Han tombs (the lady of the Marquis of Tai died in about 160 B.C., but her grave goods and her body are wonderfully preserved) has fully verified the texts. In the tomb many bamboo slips bear meticulous recipes (distinguishing the use of dog flank and liver and of beef lips and tongue). Fermented darkened soybeans came in then, and perhaps bean curd; the great discovery, flowing out of new large-scale grinding technology, was "noodle food" based on wheat flour, attributed by a writer in the third century A.D. to the "invention of the common people."

The T'ang, a time of well-being, an era of cosmopolitanism and intercourse with foreign lands, may perhaps have seen Chinese invention of distilled spirits, which is usually ascribed to the physicians of Salerno in Italy at about the same epoch. In the Sung, a period of population growth, we know that early-maturing rice was introduced from the region of present-day Vietnam, relieving famine by making possible a second crop and by spreading rice culture to the drier uplands. Tea drinking reached the entire population and sugarcane began to be cultivated widely. China grew and prospered; in the Ming there was iced storage, and refrigerated barges plied the Grand Canal carrying fresh fruit and fresh shad. The 17th century saw new species from America come to nourish many Chinese; maize, peanuts, sweet potatoes (but never widely the white potato) and of course tobacco became major crops, as they still are.

The volume cites gourmets in many eras, one of them of such refinement that he included in the rice water the dew collected from flowers, although the dew from garden roses was too strong in flavor and could not be recommended! Such a pose is far from the honest "classic fare of the everyday Chinese world." In China today a huge bowl of rice, a dollop of bean curd, a dish of cabbage (fresh in season, otherwise pickled), some flavor from fermented soybean and a little rapeseed oil to stir-fry the greens constitute a square meal. The diet has "quality, variety and a nutritional effectiveness" and is able to sustain "more people per acre than any other diet on earth," at least beyond laboratory scale. And New Year's and someone's wedding are sure to come.

(February 1978)

Snack Food Technology
By Samuel A. Matz, Ph.D.

Popcorn has been an American foodstuff at least since the ancient deposits in Bat Cave, which were in place 4,000 years ago. The attractive, convenient, crisp white puffs expand from the unique kernel, which bursts sharply when it is heated at atmospheric pressure. Hundreds of square miles of good Corn Belt farmland are planted to this crop and about as much again grows in home gardens. It is no traditional area of husbandry: some 30 years ago the volume expansion of a good grade of popcorn was about 26 to one, whereas the expansion of the hybrids patiently bred at Purdue and Iowa State is now as much as 40 to one. (This seems a benign enough change: the producer cuts his costs and the consumer of a fixed volume ingests fewer calories!)

Popcorn and potato chips, baked wheaten pretzels and crackers and bits of cornmeal dough extruded at high temperature and pressure so that they puff into a variety of forms for subsequent drying—those are the chief American snacks. Peanuts and other nut meats are popular (P. T. Barnum brought roasted peanuts in the shell to New York in 1870); even pickled pigs' feet and beef jerky are well known, if rather restricted in appeal. The big volume, however, is in starchy foodstuffs that are crisped, coated with oil, flavored primarily with salt and marketed to be eaten out of the hand. Insofar as French-fried potatoes and a dozen other savory temptations eaten avidly in the marketplace and the home the world over fit this description, it must be a mark of some quite general human indulgence.

This coolly technical book is devoted to the snack-food industry in the U.S., and in particular to packaged snacks to be eaten cold, between regular meals. It treats systematically the ingredients, equipment and processes required to produce the entire wide range of snacks, together with packaging and even the development of novelties. The aim is to introduce the reader to the quite substantial periodical and patent literature. The general reader will not find it all of equal interest, but the picture the book conveys is engrossing: from the pH of vanilla wafers to the tradition of secrecy in the pretzel trade. ("The production of pretzels is more of an art than a science.")

For example, a special pretzel salt from a particular salt dome of the Louisiana coast has the peculiar characteristic that "it breaks up into uniformly flat, rectangular-shaped particles upon crushing." A photograph is presented in evidence. Such granules adhere particularly well to the smooth, hard pretzel surface, and the natural salt impurities add a note of "huskiness." Pretzel-twisting machines are not described in detail; stick pretzels can be made with almost any flour, but "the flour used in twisted pretzels is very critical."

The slice of peeled potato from one millimeter to two millimeters thick that is fried to become the natural potato chip is generally acceptable only if its color after frying is golden rather than dark brown. The slice is darkened by the presence of reducing sugars that react with cellular amino acids. Potatoes ought therefore to be stored near room temperature so as to slow the accumulation of the sugars; the lower the temperature is, the more rapidly the unwanted sugars form. The apparent packed bulk density of the thin, bent plates of fried potato we call chips is less than a twentieth of their true density, and so the packing and shipping are substantially controlled by that loose, bulky fit. In 1971 the ingenious A. L. Liepa patented a scheme for simulating potato chips by rolling out thin sheets of quite solid dough in which reconstituted dehydrated potatoes play a major role, with support from cereals and other additives. Carefully cut pieces are held in a saddle shape by molds during the frying process. Such mashed-potato chips stack neatly in a shipping cylinder as Pringles (the registered trademark of the makers, Procter & Gamble) at an apparent density three times greater than conventional chips, and they now enjoy commercial success. It is a clear victory of geometry over substance. The oil layer of the fried snack is a source of serious problems because the limit to the shelf life of such foods is set by rancid taste, which develops from the slow oxidation of double carbon bonds in the oils. The reaction is catalyzed by light and by trace amounts of metal ions, particularly copper. No copper, bronze, brass or Monel metal is allowed to touch the fat; equipment surfaces are preferably of welded stainless steel; the empty space at the top of tanks of oil is filled with nitrogen. Expensive products such as nut meats are packed in a vacuum or are held under refrigeration. Opaque pigmented plastic films are almost universal in food pouches; moisture loss and light leak are fought with composite bagging materials and sometimes with a layer of aluminum foil.

The oils favored in order to avoid rancidity are the saturated ones, which are perhaps the least healthful. The fried snack foods are prepared with hydrogenated soybean or cottonseed oils. Coconut oil is widely used for spray fat, as on the familiar unsweetened but rich round crackers. That oil is based mostly on lauric acid, which is highly saturated but has a rather low melting point; the main carbon chain is short, only 12 atoms long instead of the 18 or 20 of the commonest fatty acids. Antioxidant additives are incorporated to fight rancidity; they include such unexpected snack ingredients as tertiary butylhydroquinone (TBHQ). The Food and Drug Administration allows only 200 parts per million of fat and oil for such constituents, whose side effects the book does not mention.

The mechanical engineering of all this slicing and extruding and frying and packing is described here quite clearly, with a good many references to specific manufacturers. If you want to start up a corn-puff product line, expect to spend some $60,000 before installation in order to turn out 300 pounds of cheese curls per hour. You will own an auger feeder for the cornmeal mix, a pressurized collet machine with a water-cooled die head to turn out the puffs, a conveyor that feeds the puffs steadily to the drying oven, plenty of hot air and another transfer belt that drops the dried curls into the tumbler where they are coated with oil and cheese powder. Pumps and blenders are required too. The packaging machinery is extra. A cheese curl of quality will run about 60 percent cornmeal collets, 25 percent oil and from 10 to 12 percent cheese powder (mostly a spray-dried emulsion of cheddar, well salted and with added color).

Flavors are the product of quite a distinct industry, since synthetic flavors call for a heavy investment in sophisticated analytical techniques before the flavor can be caught. Snack foods generally depend on rather few and simple flavorings. As a response to attacks on snack foods as "empty calories," the present trend is to enrich them with supplemental nutrients. Vitamins are useful in such small amounts that it is not difficult to add them, but effective amounts of minerals are hard to include without "textural and visual defects," which are apparent with, say, half a gram of tricalcium phosphate per portion. Protein can be added—with care—in the form of defatted soy flour, which may constitute up to 15 or 20 percent of the protein of the cornmeal puff. Pure amino acid supplements are possible, but they are tricky and not cheap. The only fat required in the human diet, arachidonic acid or its linoleic acid precursor, is needed mainly for infants; there is little indication for adding it to the fatty snack foods.

The technology laid out here is rather disarming. The snack-food technologist is trying to please, and by and large he takes no part in fraud or deception. That the result is not very praiseworthy seems to reflect on grander problems, from the motives and scale of U.S. production to the uses of leisure, to television commercials and on to the social role of youth and who knows what profundities of depth psychology. Popcorn will be munched, one expects, as long as maize grows. Close-packed potato chips and TBHQ antioxidant appear more transient; there will be ebb and flow in the salience of the junk-food junkies. Sugar and cigarettes belong to other and gloomier chapters.

(August 1976)

Fertilizer in America: From Waste Recycling to Resource Exploitation
By Richard A. Wines

Fertilizer Technology and Use, Third Edition
Edited by O. P. Engelstad

By 1850 New York had for a generation been the largest city in the country; it was the bustling commercial and manufacturing center we glimpse in the pages of Melville and Whitman. The hay to power its horses, the fresh produce on its tables and the fuelwood for its fires came from the intensively worked farms of nearby Queens and Nassau counties, celebrated among the "gardens of America."

The newly cleared lands of America could be farmed for about a century on the nutrients stored in the soil under vanished forest, and so the task of replenishment could be postponed. European observers were astonished that the pioneer farmers could universally neglect this arduous and traditional rite. Perhaps the first macronutrient to be missed from most soils is phosphorus, then nitrogen and finally potassium. By about 1800 the long-worked farms of the settled East began to show loss of yield just as the urban markets started to grow. From the 1830's on the farm journals praised the virtues of composts and manures along with the rotation of crops.

Near the city there was no way to rebuild the soil from the farm's own resources, as a self-sufficient landholder might hope to do. Long Island farmers sold off half of their hay to keep city traffic on the move and would not even allot many acres to pasture livestock, because fresh produce was so much in demand. They were therefore obliged to look outside the farm for other sources of plant nutrients to restore their sandy soils. The sea at hand offered inedible but plentiful alewives, horseshoe crabs and seaweed. These were liberally spread along the furrows, with many other organic expedients as well, all of them bulky, wet, dilute and heavy materials, demanding plenty of labor.

Yet plainly New York City "was a veritable manure factory." A great ecocycle was set turning across the East River before 1840; the very boats and trains that took out the farmer's cash products returned bearing stable manure from dray horses and horsecar teams, ashes from spent city fires, ground bones from the busy slaughterhouses, even odorous street sweepings. The best farmers now were held to be those who bought the most manure. The nutrient cycle was regarded as being closed not farmyard by prudent farmyard but through an intricate maze of technical and market provisions for gathering organic fertilizer of whatever kind in the city and doling it back to the farms.

Yes, New Yorkers tapped the most obvious urban source as well: night soil. Every night the honey buckets were carted off from a multitude of privies and cesspools to the wharves, where in less frugal mood the stuff would be dumped forthwith; a foul mess perpetually surrounded Manhattan. But for two decades a company whose long sheds adjoined the Hackensack River contracted for its boats to receive a portion of that municipal bounty, which it transformed into an unoffending dry powder mainly by mixing in plenty of peat. It was no success; the acclaimed poudrette they touted and sold was too dilute to return much nutrient value to the farm.

Enter guano (the word comes from the Incas, and its agricultural use in Peru is 2,000 years old). By 1845, barely five years after the first barrels of guano were sold in Liverpool, a "perfect mania" was abroad in the U.S. as well for this most powerful of natural manures: guano enough to bring a strong crop response required less weight spread on the land, compared with usual manures, by one or even two orders of magnitude.

The stuff was first collected from three islets washed by the Humboldt Current 10 miles off the arid coast south of Lima. It is the conse-

quence of an almost unique natural setting: up-welling nutrient-rich cold
waters blossom with plankton to nourish great schools of fish, colonies of
gregarious seabirds batten on the fish and the utterly rainless regime allows
the droppings of the replete birds to heap up over the centuries, all soluble
ingredients still in place.

Year after year the Chincha Islands yielded up entire sea cliffs of
guano (some of the layers were 200 feet deep) to a rotating fleet of
merchantmen that waited by the hundreds to load the fertilizer. Ten
million tons had been taken to Europe and North America in 30 years.
Although they were sought, no such profitable sources of guano were ever
found except along that same coast. (Smaller quantities were harvested in
the analogous cold current off southwestern Africa.) The speculative
frenzy led to bizarre claims and rapacious deeds around many a scattered
island. Some 70 guano islands in the Pacific and the Caribbean were
claimed for the U.S. before 1880. Many islands were claimed twice; some
were quite imaginary. In the end American guano fever left us such
enduring tiny dependencies as Swan, Howland and Baker.

Seabird guano was in due course shipped from many places far from
Peru, but it was always more or less rain-leached; soluble nitrates were low
and the less soluble phosphates were high. The substitute fertilizer was
nonetheless commercially useful, although on a smaller scale. Almost
odorless, inorganic, concentrated, the phosphatic guano prepared the
farmers for more change still.

This surprising chapter of technological history is at once outrageous
and subtle. For Richard Wines it becomes a persuasive story of evolutionary preadaptation. Phosphate rock was found in South Carolina in 1867. It
was so well received that by 1880 its production was an order of magnitude greater than all imported phosphatic guanos. Yet phosphate rock
would never have been so rapidly adopted if the system of the farmers, the
market, the transport, the periodicals, the farming practices and all the rest
had not evolved step by step toward use of a mineral-like concentrate
from afar. For such an evolution to unfold, the old conception of a cycle
closed on the farm itself—the land sustained through hard work using
familiar barnyard manures and farmyard composts—had to be broken.

Superphosphates, pulverized bone treated with acid to render it soluble and hence more available to plant roots, were proposed by the eminent
Justus Liebig, if rather unemphatically. By the 1870's many American
entrepreneurs were offering mixed fertilizers of useful grade. They were 2
or 3 percent nitrogen, 6 to 8 percent soluble phosphoric acid and (imported from Germany) about 2 percent potash. Gross adulteration had
been ended by law and by the producers. Even the analyses on the bag
were credible.

A map derived from the 1880 census shows general use of commercial fertilizer in the counties of the Eastern Seaboard to be heaviest around

the major cities, from Boston to Norfolk. In the South its use was widespread as well, more as a short-term solution to the labor and credit problems of postwar agriculture than as the outcome of a long history of soil improvement. Fertilizer began to move inland during the same decade; in the Finger Lakes the wheat farmers of the time all applied it, although it is reported to have had no appeal whatever for farmers in Ohio, Wisconsin and Kansas. Their time was to come. In America 100 years ago "the fertilizer industry had evolved to its modern shape."

Today fertilizers can be said to feed rather more than a billion human beings the world around. After growing steadily for the past 20 years, production has reached a plateau of about 50 pounds per person per year, about half of it nitrogen. Production is also shifting from the developed countries, old seat of the chemical industries, to the developing ones, in particular to those that possess the raw materials.

A rough sketch of the industry at present looks like this. Everywhere atmospheric nitrogen is fixed as ammonia, at high pressure under catalysis, in plants that are thoroughly modernized but still depend on the reactions Fritz Haber developed at Karlsruhe before World War I. Ammonium phosphates supply the majority of the phosphorus; potassium is spread as the chloride. Nitrogen fixation requires plenty of energy. It is done most cheaply with natural gas, which also provides the needed hydrogen. The big natural gas fields are beginning to attract the nitrogen-fixation plants, although right now China and the U.S.S.R. outfix the rest of the world. Phosphates are strip-mined from sedimentary rock outcrops. Their dominant deposits are those in the southeastern U.S. and in Morocco. Sulfuric acid treatment yields phosphoric acid, which is then ammoniated. The potassium salt is mined underground, mostly in Saskatchewan and in the Ukraine; it is freed from sodium chloride by an ingenious froth-flotation process.

The experts assembled by the Soil Science Society have prepared an ample text and reference volume. About half of the book treats of the production, marketing and use of each major fertilizer type. The rest touches a wide spectrum of technical topics.

A general reader is caught by more than one surprise. There is a pipeline net that brings liquid anhydrous ammonia from the Gulf Coast north to the corn and soybean belt. The largest of these lines joins synthesis plants in the Louisiana delta to a fan of terminals that spreads from Indiana to Nebraska. There railroad tank cars and tank trucks load up with a million tons of ammonia each year and deliver their cargo to the fields.

Nowadays sulfate-laden rainwater is acid rain. Yet the contribution rainfall makes to the sulfur needs of crops (the element is absorbed as sulfate ion) has always been important; increased use of prepared fertilizers low in sulfur impurities coupled with high hopes of cleaner air implies that more attention should be paid to this nutrient. Here and there in the U.S. and Canada overt signs of sulfur deficiency in crops are seen. Although natural sulfate sources are complex, the balance sheets clearly show a net loss of sulfur sent off with the crops. Some good seems to be blowing in that ill wind.

Yet modern farming continues the strategy of leaving as little as possible to nature. Those circular fields under center-pivot sprinkler irrigation now gain fertilizer along with water; new measuring and mixing systems make the scheme efficient. New minimal soil-working techniques, the chisel plow and no-till planting, show some waste of fertilizer nitrogen after such shallow application. Still, crop yield does not decrease with no-till farming: other advantages of the technique compensate for the loss of nitrogen.

Even in the well-fertilized agriculture of the U.S. the bacterial symbionts of legumes, crop residues and animal manures return a little more nitrogen to the croplands than fertilizer does. Sewage sludge—the night soil of an industrialized society—supplies little of the need. (If all of it were returned to the land, it could contribute only 1 or 2 percent.) The nutrient cycle will remain open until the genetic engineers can contrive a nitrogen-fixing symbiosis for our major crops.

(January 1987)

Harvest of the Palm: Ecological Change in Eastern Indonesia
By James J. Fox

"It is not unusual on Roti to come upon an entire family dining regally from the contents of a couple of lontar [palm leaf] buckets, one containing five or six liters of sweet palm juice, the other brimfull of salty, slimy, slightly sour strands of green seaweed." These people drink more meals than they eat; that palm-sugar solution is their sucrose-rich staple.

The lontar fan-leaf palm (*Borassus sundaicus* Beccari) is a massive single stem two or three feet in diameter that soars straight up to a height of 90 feet, bearing high a crown of great leaves. It blossoms twice a year for a generation; at each blossoming the sweet sap can be made, by the right cut across the bud, to flow copiously for a couple of months. The yield can be astonishing: a good tree provides the skilled tapper with 300 or 400 liters of sweet juice per year containing a measured 15 to 17 percent of sucrose. Half a dozen such trees yield the calories of an acre of wetland rice. In season the juice is drunk directly, but it can be stored by cooking to a dark thick syrup or even to hard sugar.

On this extraordinary base (the trees grow wild almost everywhere on Roti) the rocky, poorly watered island supports a population density that here and there reaches the high values typical of wetland rice regions. Like all well-fed peoples the 75,000 islanders (a small cluster of islands nearby share the culture) are not limited to their staple. They grow some rice and maize and also fish, and a main protein source is the pig. A materials-flow sheet would be a delight (what do the pigs eat besides syrup?), but the book does not report any quantitative nutritional data.

The lontar has its relatives (often of the same species) in lands all the way from the two shores of South India through Burma, Thailand and Indochina and across Indonesia. Almost everywhere else the trees do not give sweet juice, only a raffish fermented product, soured or alcoholic or strongly flavored with lime or some other substance to inhibit swift fermentation as the juice collects in the heat of the day. On Roti the islanders harvest sweet juice without additives by collecting it twice a day, in the early morning and in the afternoon, and by scrupulously putting it only in clean, fresh receptacles.

It seems that the Rotinese came to their island long before they were a palm-tapping people. Initially they tapped the palm casually to eke out a grain grower's living. Eventually they perfected the elegant process of today. The men tap trees for a living, having given up the hardscrabble swidden grain farming of neighboring—and poorer—islands. There is a poem about a clan founder: "Tapping lontar twice a day/Comes from Dou-Danga. . . ." With Dou-Danga they entered the sweet life.

There can be no doubt that is the kind of life it is. The Rotinese are proud and confident; they are prosperous and are even spreading their complex subsistence culture to other islands in direct competition with more familiar husbandry, some of it introduced by the Dutch. Theirs is no relict culture, either. They have long distilled gin and practiced law; Rotinese are found throughout Indonesian life, from pillars of the establishment to leading Communists in exile. They adopted the Malay language long ago as a literary and unifying tongue, the better to deal with the colonial power. (Malay in a modern form is now the official language of the Republic.) Their schools are Malay and so is their Bible, but these litigious, talkative islanders stoutly maintain their many ministates and dialect differences in the mother tongue.

Fox is at pains to make it clear that this is in no way the automatic work of the generous palm, even accepting the genius of Dou-Danga. The islanders' geography made them not worth economic invasion, yet they were assaulted for strategic advantage. They learned early that Christianity, education and having neither plantation lands nor much taxable crop all made for a workable accommodation with their rulers. Half of the volume discusses such matters, far from sugar and syrup, and we are promised an entire volume on the political tradition of their state. The author submits plenty of near-parallels to prove his case. The palm offered opportunity, and the Rotinese seized it over a period of centuries. Their neighbors on the island of Savu made a different world of the same strands.

The rajas and a tapper on his way up the tree alike wear the elegant textiles of these islands, yarn-dyed woven figures of world-famous intricacy. One can hope for more volumes, on both the history and the material culture—and the public health—of these people who live by strong, sweet draughts.

(March 1978)

Sweetness and Power: The Place of Sugar in Modern History
By Sidney W. Mintz

Perhaps three-fourths of the people of the world today still depend for their nutrition on a single starchy staple, a complex plant carbohydrate yielded by potato or rice or maize or millet. Along with it they count on some of a wide variety of sauces, stews and relishes, viewed not quite as food but as food's essential helper. It has been so among sedentary peoples as far back as we have evidence: utensils specialized for cooking rice and its helpers are found in pre-dynastic Chinese graves. One ethnographer cited here, Audrey Richards, evokes the meaning of a true staple. Richards studied the Bemba, whose staple food was a glutinous paste of millet, always taken with a savory and slippery sauce. She would watch people enjoy four or five roasted ears of maize, only to hear them exclaim later: "Alas, we are dying of hunger. We have not had a bite to eat all day."

The modern world no longer adheres to this ancient pattern, even among its poorest classes. We hardly have a staple food. Compared with the norms of history our diet is as exotic as the milk and blood taken by the Masai or the blubber and caribou venison that nourish Inuit hunters. We Americans consume fewer total carbohydrates today than we did in 1910; a sharp increase in fats has made up most of the difference. At present sweeteners supply most of the carbohydrate calories Americans consume. In TR's time flour was virtually a staple, and sugar contributed one-third as much as flour. (A true staple provides the people of a peasant countryside with considerably more than half of their calories, up to 80 or 90 percent.)

This novel work is economic history, as seen and elaborated by an anthropologist of analytic penetration, learning and wit. Sidney W. Mintz is alert to the role of class and implicit power and observes their effect with well-controlled indignation. Now professor at Johns Hopkins, he did his first field work decades ago among the hardworking Puerto Ricans of a cane-field village. He has generalized that experience in this book, not by any field work (yet) but through wide reading in the library.

The domination of working life in the "sugar islands" from Cyprus to Barbados and Fiji by this tropical crop out of India is a phenomenon one clear millennium old. Sugar has long been a plantation crop, initially cultivated by slave labor. Its place in the formative centuries of European imperial power, especially for the British, is plain. "Sugar . . . has been one of the massive demographic forces in world history. Because of it, literally millions of enslaved Africans reached the New World, particularly the American South, the Caribbean and its littorals. . . . It was sugar that sent East Indians to Natal and the Orange Free State, sugar that carried them to Mauritius and Fiji. Sugar brought a dozen different ethnic groups in staggering succession to Hawaii, and sugar still moves people about the Caribbean."

But all that is production: sucrose viewed from the supply side, from below, from overseas. What about the demand up in the metropolis? How is it that a medicine, an exotic spice, a decoration at the feasts of the Elizabethan nobility could come to be a major national source of calories? "A rarity in 1650, a luxury in 1750, sugar had been transformed into a virtual necessity by 1850." First of all had come the bitter stimulant tea, sweetened with white sugar (or its refined syrup, golden treacle), its use spreading group by group from the well-to-do of the city down the social rungs to the rural poor.

Sugar was ubiquitous by 1850, although still at the fringe of the diet — a couple of percent of dietary energy. It added quickly won taste to help out staple bread. With the triumph of industrial capital the planter's claim to special prices and profits withered. The slaves were set free, and sugar from productive mechanized plantations became a dominant Victorian source of cheap calories. By 1900 it supplied nearly one-sixth of all English calories (an eightfold rise in a century), surely more among working-class women and children, who shared unequally in the family's scanty fats and meats.

The focus of inquiry is really that second rise in demand. Tea and two lumps at each meal are enough to make up the first climb to ubiquity. To climb the next power of 10 from flavor fringe to calorie core requires half a cup a day. That hot cuppa won't do it; there must be jam with our daily bread, marmalade, sweet biscuits, custard sauce, sweetened condensed milk, candies and chocolate, and on good evenings a nice treacle pudding. All these appeared, and much more, along with new industries to serve the buoyant demand of consumers who earned an increasing amount of money and found themselves free to choose.

Of course the only choices they could make were among a sharply constrained set of unsolicited new options. Daily life changed; the population grew apace; more working people were ready to work harder to earn more and to consume more; their time became money and their money became goods. The nation turned urban, time-conscious, organized—in short, "modern." Tea and biscuits provisioned each clock-timed work break; more factory laborers ate away from home and returned to an evening meal that in good times ended with a newly conventional course, the sweet (in American English, dessert). Not to be forgotten is the caloric efficiency of tropical cane. Sugar cane yields edible calories per season per acre at a rate four times that of a potato crop. The British worker in the steam-driven mills got more and more tea, tobacco and sugar for less and less work as the decades passed. "No wonder the rich and powerful liked it so much, and no wonder the poor learned to love it."

We still love it, rich and poor, with differences. The family meal with its shared menu is giving way to prepared food individually chosen and to eating out; we witness the decline of mealtime as an everyday ritual for kin groups. (All those trends promote inexpensive, fast-eaten sugar.) The week's round of Friday fish and Sunday chicken has long been broken. The tradition of seasons that once brought "bock beer, shad, fresh dill, and new potatoes, each in its turn, turkey twice a year, and fruit cake with hard sauce at New Year's, survives only on sufferance, finessed by turkey burgers, year-round bock beer, and other modern wonders." One sample among middleclass families suggested that an average consumer had 20 "contacts" with food in one day: "gastro-anomie," punned the French sociologist Claude Fischler. The consumer's free choice might now be "between a Big Mac and a Gino's chicken leg in a 30-minute lunch hour." (Both have some sugar, even without recalling the sugared beverage that goes along.) Evidently that free choice itself hardly matters, but the defining constraints are so full of implication that they themselves characterize our society.

The modern chronic shortage is not of food but of time. Our vastly productive new technologies paradoxically ensure that most individuals feel they have "less time, rather than more." Should we be surprised at that, Mintz asks, when "those who run a society so bent on 'discovering' new consumption needs will have little interest in finding time for their satisfaction"? Most of the notable tendencies in eating in America can be found growing thriftily in the other two worlds as well, even to Coca-Cola and its congeners. Plainly a fine book lies in the one closing chapter that attends to the contemporary.

In the nature of so deep-going a critique, its claims are not proved; perhaps they are not now provable. They are fascinating efforts at ordering incomplete information of a diverse kind, an order that in the end illuminates "what being a person means . . . the history of ourselves." A measure of the book's success is our strong desire to read on; questions crowd the mind.

What about sugar in peasant India, its original home? Or the traditional sucrose staple of the palm-growing people of the Indonesian island Roti? We need more modern comparisons; France is not enough. Why, for instance, does Iceland lead the world in sugar consumption per head? How could it be that many developed lands, once fearful of wartime shortages of sugar, have for a century subsidized an alternate onshore source of sucrose from the sugar beet? Will the enzymatically treated cornstarch sweetener continue its displacement of sucrose in soft drinks and processed foods?

A reader comes away a little puzzled but much wiser. The argument that links sugar uniquely to the economic interests of a decisive class is not quite persuasive. One suspects that the high-gain feedback loops of industrial capitalism could amplify any little tinkle of predilection into a roar of mass consumption, even if there were no cane to be grown. Like the three bittersweet sources of caffeine, like addictive tobacco, sucrose must have some subtle druglike quality, some satisfying rush of glucose, or whatever the physiology may be. It is a versatile foodstuff that is marginally a drug, offering the economic potential of large dosages long tolerated.

The extensive footnotes are as stimulating as the unexpected illustrations: the frontispiece is William Blake's engraving of three young women, white Europe supported by black Africa and red America. Oddly, the index contains no entry for Coca-Cola, although that important substance is of course discussed in several places.

(September 1985)

The Last Great Subsistence Crisis in the Western World
By John D. Post

Famine and Human Development: The Dutch Hunger Winter of 1944/45
By Zena Stein, Mervyn Susser, Gerhard Saenger and Francis Marolla

Bourbon and Hapsburg had won; Napoleon was on St. Helena. In this early summer of the year 1816 the Belgians were preparing to celebrate the first anniversary of Waterloo. But there was something wrong in the very look and feel of the summer sun. A New York physician wrote: "The human eye could thus, during the long days, gaze on the great luminary . . . deprived of its dazzling splendour and radiance; . . . numerous dark spots were discovered on its face, without the help of telescopic . . . glasses." Many thought those sunspots were significant, but others noted the long twilights, a blue moon, blood red sunsets. Far from the Atlantic world the volcano of Tomboro 200 miles east of Bali had erupted in 1815, killing tens of thousands by explosion and ashfall. Hundreds of cubic kilometers of dust entered the air to spread around the world in the dustiest eruption of three centuries (three times the dust of Krakatoa in 1883).

The year 1816 would be the year without a summer. The data are clear enough: Milan, Geneva, Paris, Salem—at each station the mean temperatures were down from the years before, without any exceptions for the months of June through September, by some four to eight degrees Fahrenheit. Professor Dewey of Williams College summed up the year: "Frosts are extremely rare here in either of the summer months; but this year there was frost in each of them. . . . June 6th . . . snowed several times. . . . July 9th, frost, which killed parts of cucumbers. August 22nd, cucumbers killed. . . . Very little Indian corn became ripe in the region."

The result was famine, one not matched in the Western world since that time and certainly the worst since the year 1710. The author, an economic historian at Northeastern University, paints a careful picture of economic distress and its political and social consequences across all Europe. That unsettled postwar world was ill-prepared for so disastrous a harvest. Grain prices nearly doubled in 1816 and 1817 in a dozen European markets (and in the U.S.), and in not one was there an appreciable decrease. Many starved in Hungary and even in Switzerland, where the price of bread rose four- or fivefold compared with 1814 levels. Interior New England suffered heavily; in Vermont farm families lived on hedgehogs and boiled nettles.

Not all the hungry were resigned. Strikes had not yet become the mode, but everywhere there were demonstrations outside bakers' shops, looting and rioting, and vagrant bands often attacked farm granaries. In Suffolk they carried a flag inscribed "Bread or Blood." There was extensive rioting in Brussels on the second anniversary of Waterloo. A mass German emigration was set off: "Whole multitudes of emigrants with their families" went down the Rhine to the Dutch ports and on to America; others went to Russia. "A sort of stampede took place from cold, desolate, worn-out New England to this land of promise." The writer was referring to Ohio.

Actually "the old biological regime" had already been shattered everywhere in Europe. Population was steadily on the rise; we are not quite sure why. High peaks in mortality had been the usual consequence of subsistence crises up to the second half of the 18th century; the deaths in hungry years offset the years of growth. The famine of 1816–17 was the last of those continental peaks; death rates rose all over Europe, most steeply in Switzerland, Italy and the Carpathians. In 1710, the previous great crisis, mortality had been enormous from pestilence, particularly plague. This time typhus took some toll, notably in East London and among the Swiss and the Irish, but plague was unimportant. The author contends that plague had left European cities largely because of structural change, from fire-prone wood and shingle walls and roofs to brick and stone. In the 18th century most of the ports of western Europe had become fireproof, and thus also inhospitable to the black house rat. It was not lack of food directly but social turbulence that had formerly linked famine and pestilence.

Good weather and low grain prices returned by 1820, but the volcano had pulled the trigger of history. Governments moved to the right all over Europe. Political repression grew (but so too did the prosaic but positive administrative programs that have ever since tempered the challenge of scarce grain to the life of the poor in Europe). By 1819 the dust from the distant crater had touched off a bizarre foreshadowing of Europe's deepest tragedy. The culpable students of Bavaria began a campaign of disorder that ended in violent anti-Semitic riots all over Germany and as far away as Copenhagen, "to the taunting cry of Hep-Hep," an obscure phrase followed by "Jude verreck" ("Jew, drop dead"). The military put an end to these "outbreaks of the vulgar masses," as Prince Metternich saw them. Once such outbreaks appear, he argued, "no security exists, for the same thing could arise again at any moment and over any other matter."

It is four decades since that "same thing" arose again in its most terrible array, now as state policy. One of its smaller cruelties was a famine induced in the populous and well-run cities of western Holland — Amsterdam, Rotterdam, The Hague and others — by the deliberate act of the Occupying Authority and the Wehrmacht. It was 1944, late in their day; the Allied forces had driven for the Rhine bridges without success. The Dutch rail workers brought all rail traffic to a stop as soon as the battle began in late September. In reprisal all transport to the big Dutch cities, including food supplies, was embargoed by the Germans. When water traffic was allowed as a concession in November, an early freeze prevented the barges from moving. "By that time the acute food shortage had become a famine." That half of the Dutch people who lived in the western towns suffered true famine until liberation in May, although rural people had eaten well enough all over the country. But the embargoed cities starved. "The ordinary person . . . consumed in two or three days all that was given for the whole week."

By January hospitals were filled with the starving. Nurses and physicians worked day and night without extra rations. A slice of bread and a tea substitute was their breakfast; two potatoes and some watery sauce was lunch; dinner was one or two slices of bread and a plate of soup. Special starvation hospitals were opened in February. People dropped in the streets; the old ones, who could not roam in search of food, stayed in bed and died, out of sight of the doctors. The mortality figures show 10,000 dead from hunger. One graph tells the story: a deep notch appears in the plot of the monthly food ration. That notch is the bite of the long hunger winter.

Why dwell on such a mournful story? People starved in greater numbers in gallant Leningrad and in the camps all over the greater Reich. But this calm, meticulous, well-written book turns the famine into a heroic large-scale experiment on human development. This starving population was in no way in disorder. The births and the deaths were meticulously recorded as usual. In 1971 and 1972 these authors checked up. They took 2,000 birth records at random among all the birth registers of the famine city of Amsterdam (and of a control city in the south). The names they chose were those of baby boys. In his 19th year each of them would come to be examined medically and psychologically by the doctors of the draft board, under a uniform and well-recorded protocol. In the validation sample 3 percent had died and 2 percent had emigrated, and there were the expected 3 percent of legal exemptions from the draft. In all, 97 percent of the births of the preceding generation were either represented by induction medical records or lost to known channels. The missing names were distributed through the lists randomly.

About 40,000 people were exposed to prenatal famine. The coded tapes of the Dutch military hold the data, the best large-scale survey we have of the health of mature people who were exposed to famine before birth. The controls were less than perfect. They are twofold: comparisons in time (among individuals born before, during and after that famine winter) and in place (with those born in southern cities not held by the Germans). History provides no well-managed laboratories. The control cities no less than the famine ones were literally decimated—one in every 10 babies dead—by a mysterious epidemic in the summer of 1945. But the controls retain enough leverage to show, for instance, that babies born to mothers who were hungry during the last trimester of pregnancy were small ones. This result is fortified by a quite elaborate set of analyses, testing multiple correlations between the size of rations and hospital measurements. The significance of the best results is better than 1,000 to one.

From this nutritional experiment carried out on pregnant women that bitter winter the authors (a team of epidemiologists at the Columbia University College of Physicians and Surgeons) have woven their compact, explicit, table-filled book, a model of perception and of honesty. They begin with reflective accounts of the biological and social questions they might face, they devise tentative models for the correlations they turn up, they put forward extra little tests, subdivided samples and controls to tease out the meaning of the data in their study. The message they bring is on the whole a welcome one. In this brief description of the work the message is summed without the evidence that gives it strength. It is the evidence that is the burden of the report, a statistical study whose findings lead to strong conclusions. Hunger cuts the birthrate and the size of infants. The poor suffered most. But overall there is one unequivocal finding. Among the young men reaching 19 who had been born to women exposed to famine no detectable effect was found on mental performance, physical stature or health, with one exception: there was a larger percentage of rare congenital anomalies of the central nervous system, such as cerebral palsy. Above some nutritional threshold, at least, the mother protects her fetus.

The senior authors have pursued their studies of the origins of public health from the ghettos of Johannesburg to those of Manhattan. They have "exploited the collective woe of a whole people" in search of hope for the future. From the Dutch famine they can now make plain that one winter's cruelty is largely reversible. But what of the myriads of infants born to poorly nourished mothers who remain poorly nourished during a lifetime of poverty thereafter? Hunger did not leave the West with the dust of Tomboro.

(July 1977)

X

Health

The rearing of infants, epidemic and malignant disease, all the understandings and mysteries of medicine, have served to allot life and death. These books examine a few cases of importance, from the recent suppression of smallpox to our yet-unrelieved fear of cancer.

Breasts, Bottles and Babies: A History of Infant Feeding
By Valerie A. Fildes

The nail test was set down by Pliny the Elder. You put a drop of the milk on your thumbnail; the right stuff spreads gently and retains its form when rocked a little. "Milk which runs off immediately is watery, whereas milk that stays together like honey . . . is thick." Such objective perceptual clues represent the model of conscious intervention by human beings into the subtly adaptive biochemical system through which mothers feed infants, a system human beings largely share with the entire mammalian class. It is daunting how often reasonable inferences from our partial knowledge have proved damaging in practice.

This chunky volume combs the past for every kind of clue to how infants were fed and why during the preindustrial centuries of Europe, from the first printed medical books in about 1500 to about 1800; its story ends before the era of 19th-century science, nutrition from Liebig and infection control from Pasteur. A general introduction touches on the universal issues from Sumer to Galen, Avicenna and the Ayurvedic writings, partly because the theories of Renaissance medicine in Europe drew heavily on the ancients. The feeding of infants is followed from maternal breast-feeding through wet-nursing to mixed feeding, hand-feeding and on to weaning; the text stays close to its sources, but it never accepts their quirks uncritically.

The thoughtful comparative lists and small-sample statistics that effectively support the lively text (mostly from the safe enclosure of a long appendix) begin with the old writers. In a model of historical exposition the force of argument grows as information increases.

In many parts of the world it is held that the mother's first milk, called colostrum, which persists for three or four days after delivery, is a bad substance. It does not pass Pliny's test. The artists show us what was done: a print portrays a nurse feeding the newborn with a spoon (honey and oil were popular and are mentioned in the Old Testament), and a Tintoretto shows a woman offering the newborn St. John her breast while the mother rests in bed. Before 1673 all writers condemn colostrum as harmful: it was a tradition. The change in ideas began in Paris with an influential work that did not recommend colostrum but did report that some people thought it was useful. Medical author after author modifies the old stance: the stuff is not harmful, and it may do some good. By 1748 William Cadogan boldly recommends that no infant be given anything by mouth before it is put to the breast; harm will come to any child who is denied colostrum.

A dual feedback loop had been noted. The purging of the dark greenish meconium from the newborn intestine is aided by early suckling. And milk fever, with a high mortality, arises a few days after delivery in many mothers who do not breast-feed. The residual milk serves as a focus for infection, which is often made worse by clumsy efforts to remove the milk. Early breast-feeding reduced milk fever to unimportance.

Today it is recognized that maternal antibodies supplied in colostrom protect the infant against infection for about six weeks. A table of infant mortality (up to one year) shows a steep fall among English ducal families after 1750, and parish records confirm the idea that much of this fall was realized during the first month of life. Neither improvements in midwifery, recourse to cow's milk, better nutrition nor any other hypothesis yet proposed fits the evidence (that the gain was registered in early survival) as well as a turn to breast-feeding does.

Subtler still, mothers who breast-feed immediately after giving birth have a stronger emotional bond to an infant than those who may not even see the child for days, and who must then learn how to give suck with distended breasts. It is argued that the concept of the special nature of infants and children, with explicit concern for their welfare, began in Britain in this period. "The change in neonatal feeding practices cannot be disregarded as one factor in the change of attitude of British society towards its children."

Jump to the other end of infancy: weaning. What is the age of weaning? Here Dr. Fildes offers much original material. First of all, three kinds of weaning age are found in books: the age recommended by a sagacious author, the age said to be common among the people and the age at which children were actually being weaned. The ancient sources — Galen or the Bible or Maimonides — tend to agree on two or three years. (One individual wet-nursing contract in Roman Egypt stipulated 16 months.) The medical books of the 16th and 17th centuries follow the old authors, but factual ages can be found at least for a sample of known, named children. For instance, the six little ones of John Dee, scryer and scientist at court to Elizabeth I, were put to a wet nurse. Their median age of weaning was 14 months. Almost the same median age is given for the five breast-fed children of a clergyman in the mid-17th century. The median remains the same for more than 40 named children of the author's sample — the largest yet published — in confirmation.

The picture is coherent. The upper- and middle-class women who had depended on a wet nurse during the earlier period, were largely breast-feeding by the 18th century. Hand-feeding had become practical and socially acceptable. Whereas earlier the children had been weaned at an age when they could share the diet of the family, in the late 18th century they were weaned while still without teeth, to take milk mixtures from feeding vessels. Some 50 formulas are listed here, the paps and panadas of three centuries: flour, bread, milk, broth.

There is a clear risk in today's world as before. Breast milk, from the mother or from a wet nurse, is a good and pure food. Anything less direct — as the preparer of sterile foodstuffs knows — carries the danger of acute gastrointestinal infection. "The errors in infant nutrition made during industrialisation of western societies are being repeated today. Even though we have the knowledge, . . . the infant mortality in the Third-World societies today is identical to that of 18th-century London: up to 70 percent of infants did not survive to their second birthday."

(August 1987)

The Causes of Cancer: Quantitative Estimates of Avoidable Risks of Cancer in the United States Today

By Richard Doll and Richard Peto

At the request of the Office of Technology Assessment two British epidemiologists here estimate the avoidable risks of cancer in the U.S. today. Theirs is the "black box" approach of the discipline: widespread long-time studies of sizable human populations. "Humans feed themselves, house themselves and arrange their own medical care at no cost to the epidemiologist." Human response to any exposure is exactly what we want, not some overdosed white rat's. How much the experimenter's control is lacking in such spontaneous data is all too clear. It is arguably the worst of methods, but it is all we are likely to have, the only game in town.

The basic ideas are not new; it is detailed sifting of the tables that can persuade. The avoidability of most cancer rests on the fact that worldwide cancers vary in incidence specifically site by site, by one or two orders of magnitude from Iran to Nigeria, or from California to Japan. The implication is clear: we might come to face only the minimal risk at every site, although that can certainly not happen by chance. It is pretty clear there is no built-in overall rate that simply shifts sites from country to country. The statistics argue against it, and specific exposures that much increase a given type of cancer do not reduce the risk of other types. Nor is the main effect genetic: migrants change their cancers with their residence. It is somehow embedded in the way we live. Of course, no meaningful numbers can be presented without close attention to age distributions; cancer increases at most sites along with age.

The study explicitly considers a dozen avoidable causes in the practical sense, from tobacco and alcohol through diet, food additives, occupation, pollution and on to unknown agencies. Each is examined at length against the abundant but still far from adequate literature. The conclusions are well supported, although these workers do not fail to warn against complacency. The numbers must be kept under scrutiny; there is a great deal we do not know, and here what we do not know can hurt us.

This report appeared in a technical journal in the middle of 1981; it confirms the only two earlier studies (one of them for Britain) the authors know of. Although several dozen types of cancer are reported, more than half of all U.S. cancer deaths result from cancer of the lung, the breast or the colon. That is the central social fact. The chief causes of cancer in the U.S. today are also few: tobacco and food. The tobacco factor is ascribed to smoking, particularly of tarry cigarettes. Each year there die from lung cancer more Americans who would have survived if no Americans had ever smoked than the nation lost in all the years of the war in Vietnam plus the annual deaths in automobile accidents.

That heavy risk is strongly increased by exposure to cigarette smoke in the first decade of adult life. (Young smokers — it is particularly sad that the habit has grown in the 1970's most rapidly among young women — are at serious risk; persuade them to stop!) Details matter; Americans leave longer stubs unburned than the British, as one of the authors can testify from the experience of his early teens, when he scavenged "the Southampton docks for smokable stubs discarded by sailors of various nations." Matters are therefore improving under our new knowledge (which we owe to Sir Richard Doll more than to any other person) but too slowly.

Diet is in principle even more important and almost as modifiable. Here, however, we cannot act with much effect, because we do not know what in the U.S. diet causes the relatively high rate of cancers at half a dozen sites, such as the colon, the breast, the gall bladder and the pancreas. (Stomach cancers are on the decline.) Any number of tantalizing hints are at hand. Underfed mice are sleek, active and long-lived; they have about half the rate of cancers at the major sites. Breast cancer is correlated with consumption of milk, colon cancers with meat. Colorectal cancers are inversely related to a healthy population of certain intestinal bacteria that feed on particular components of dietary fiber, the pentose polymers. The powerful carcinogens our body makes from nitrites in the diet do not show any clear effect, although a test meal of both bacon and spinach resulted in the production of plenty of the hazardous compounds.

There is much more to argue about, but the outcome is that we have good reason to blame the stuff we eat (and how much of it and when) for a third of the avoidable U.S. cancer deaths. But it is not the food additives,

not the butter yellow, not the saccharin, not the nitrites, not the antioxi-
dants. Additives can be estimated to contribute "a token proportion"
below 1 percent. It is not hair dyes and not the pill. Nor is it the
carcinogens poured out in increasing amounts by industry and transport;
the total effect of all pollution cannot be much above 5 percent for air,
water or food. There the most uncertain single component appears to be
from the halogenated impurities in drinking water. Industrial output as a
whole, medical practices, occupational hazards, ionizing and solar radiation, infection by viruses known and unknown may together contribute
20 percent of the avoidable risk. Another 5 percent takes ample account
of the indirect effects of infection, such as that of hepatitis on liver cancer.

These estimates are rough, some almost speculative, and Doll and
Peto allow for a wide range of error. Still, it remains their conclusion that
smoking and some unknown attributes of our diet are the dominant
entryways of avoidable fatal cancers, two-thirds of them all. Cancer is not
increasing in America, save for lung cancer, clearly the result of increased
cigarette use, and for an uncommon form of skin cancer, plausibly (but
speculatively) related to increased exposure of bare skin to the sun by
those who are not already tanned by steady outdoor work. That overall
constancy is a gross argument against attributing much new risk to the
flood of novel materials with which our smokestacks and our workplaces
assault us; detailed examination confirms that view.

Doll and Peto single out several Government, industrial and private
publications that have disagreed with them over the past few years; their
critique of those publications seems cogent, both as a matter of explicit
argument and as gauged by the concurrence of other studies. They go so
far as to characterize one Federal report as written for "political rather
than scientific purposes" and another private set of studies as done by
"people who wish to emphasize the importance of occupational factors."
Overestimates by a factor of 10 follow, they say, from reliance not on
observed fatalities but on broad extrapolations from studies of incidence
under acute exposure. In one instance the nasal-sinus cancers projected
from moderate occupational exposure to nickel would have caused 10
times as many deaths as the national total that was reported.

This is of course no brief for greed or carelessness in the shop, the
causes of numerous preventable cruel poisonings of workers and other
citizens. It is rather to offer perspective; our experience has not been as
bad as our fears. But if we are to progress, we need to know more as well
as to act more wisely. These authors recommend a long-term epidemiolog-
ical investment. Perhaps we can persuade a few hundred thousand healthy
people to contribute blood and fecal samples to a bank, along with
detailed answers to an open-ended questionnaire on food, smoking,
drinking, work, residence, reproductive history, drugs and the like. Epidemiologists could study a set of such samples for speculative inquiry once

death from a particular cause took any class of donors. We have a steadily increasing ability to find significant factors in stored blood. Naturally a national index of causes of death would be needed as well; such an index is not available today across the barriers of state record keeping and expense and of our increasing concern with privacy. There are some five or 10 years of life expectancy to be gained by civil victory over avoidable cancers; if we can keep the nuclear peace, we should one day be able to claim that worthwhile trophy for public health.

(April 1982)

Epidemic and Peace: 1918
By Alfred W. Crosby, Jr.

The flu was not even a reportable disease in that spring of 1918. True, there were a lot of cases of the grippe going around, and rather more people died than had been expected. There was certainly something odd about it: in the few postmortems the pathologists did they saw but could not understand an unusual widespread edema and hemorrhage in the lungs. Like the war of that terrible year, this malady preferred young adult victims: the curve of mortality against age was shaped like a W, with the central peak between 20 and 30, instead of the familiar U, with respiratory death claiming only the very young and the very old.

The epidemic seems to have begun in the U.S. It spread around the world within four months, killing relatively few, but those few were mainly young adults. In May of 1918, 10 percent of the men of the British Grand Fleet at Scapa Flow were down with it. By July the docks of Manila in the Philippines were crippled, with three-fourths of the longshoremen down. Although people called it the Spanish influenza, it had not originated in that neutral country. But the eight million Spanish who fell ill were freely written about, whereas within the belligerent states of Europe and America war censorship minimized the reporting.

It was a pandemic, all right, but a mild one, claiming its dead in the tens of thousands, although there must have been many thousands of brief illnesses for every death. The old physician's saw—"Quite a Godsend! Everybody ill, nobody dying"—did not quite fit this new flu, but no one yet felt the error. American public health was robust; Equitable Life had its best year. But in the midst of the lightly regarded pandemic a new virus had appeared, and "some 1.5 million American adults who were most perfectly qualified to cultivate" it were in the military camps, traveling freely, dispatched across the sea within six months in the fastest migration known up to that time.

The little RNA coils in their spiky protein jackets changed slightly sometime during the latter part of August, 1918. At Brest in France the American Expeditionary Force had its chief port. At Freetown in the British African colony of Sierra Leone troop transports took on coal to break the long haul to British ports from Australia. At Boston the First Naval District played an important, although not a dominant, part in training and shipping Yanks over there. By the end of September the war had flared into the American offensive of the Meuse-Argonne, and the "Spanish influenza" had become deadly. In Sierra Leone one person in 30 of the entire population had died, in Brest there were thousands dead, French and Americans alike, and in Boston there was panic.

As the fall and winter progressed the disease spread from the Aleutians to Calcutta. (By May of 1919 it had ebbed everywhere.) This graphic volume details the American experience, region by region, in camp and on shipboard, and supplies at least a broad narrative for the world as a whole. The October draft call in the U.S. was canceled, although General Pershing wanted more men. Philadelphia was the worst-hit city in the East: of its two million citizens more than 12,000 were dead of the flu and its concomitant pneumonia by the middle of November, against a macabre background of military embalmers and a price-controlled quick-coffin industry.

San Francisco had its turn, forewarned. There the first peak of deaths had passed by the middle of November; the city was hit less hard than the East, and it felt that its civic unity had stopped the flu as once it had flouted the earthquake. In public places most San Franciscans wore the gauze face masks much urged by the authorities. The Armistice arrived like a performance in the theater of the absurd: "Bonfires blazed up on [the] hills, all the whistles and sirens in town let loose. . . . Many had cow bells, . . . and everyone, except the infamous slackers, had a mask on. [There were] tens of thousands of deliriously happy, dancing, singing, masked celebrants." Then the flu returned for Christmas, although it was only about half as bad. Masking became an embattled political issue; it meant "the stilling of song in the throats of singers." The proponents of masks were even threatened by a bomb. It appears that masks had no measurable effect; Stockton, Calif., where masking was faithfully practiced, fared no better than Boston, which had taken no control measures.

Dr. Crosby judges the American cities generously. They could do little of value against the flu. No one knew how. The public-health institutions were not at all equal to the challenge. The social structure nonetheless proved itself fit, in spite of inequity, slums and drifters. The flu actually brought to the U.S. a kind of social cohesion: Americans lent one another a helping hand. "When everyone in the nation had a fever and aching muscles or personally knew someone who had, Americans did by and large act as if they were all, if not brothers and sisters, at least cousins."

The terrifying plague infected more than 25 percent of the U.S. population. It seems probable that at least that fraction of the world population was infected. A conservative estimate of the excess of respiratory deaths in the U.S., with the rates of 1915 as a base line, comes to about 550,000 in a period of 10 months. The fatality rate was thus about 2 percent. The usual world figure is 21 million dead, but it is "probably a gross underestimation." That many may well have died on the Indian subcontinent alone; the mortality there in October of 1918 was "without parallel in the history of disease."

Yet the dying does not bulk large in the American mind. It has inspired no awe; the Black Death means more to us — or did until the Fort Dix death early this past spring. Of the six best-selling college textbooks of American history only one even mentions it. Stein, Dos Passos, Fitzgerald, Hemingway and Faulkner barely allude to it. Only Thomas Wolfe and Katherine Anne Porter recognize the killer in his terrible dignity. Porter's *Pale Horse, Pale Rider* is a masterpiece worthy of the flu. The virus nearly killed her, and it did take her love, a young army lieutenant, Dr. Crosby, who has immersed himself in this strange brief period, sees her novella not only as the interior voyage it is but also as "the most accurate depiction of American society in the fall of 1918 in literature."

Why did the flu not mark the minds of the survivors as it filled the graves? Apparently because the catastrophe was almost entirely a statistical one. Nearly everyone who was infected recovered — 97 or 98 percent. It took few well-known people, since it killed mainly the young. It was relatively evenhanded with town and country, rich and poor. It is remembered not by the collectivities of society, not by journalists, historians or lawgivers but by the atoms of society: individuals. The letters and journals of ordinary people are full of it, and those who lived through it still acknowledge it. The fourth horseman struck freely but at random; anyone who tries to give a logical account of the past is compelled to ignore his blows. "How does one discern the great figures of the mid-twentieth century who never became great because they died of flu in 1918?" Only the rare artist such as Katherine Anne Porter speaks what is silent in the hearts of millions.

The Polynesians, isolated from most infections by the enfolding ocean, suffered worst of all wherever the flu reached. Western Samoa, freshly under New Zealand rule, received no warning. No one radioed from Auckland, where the disease raged, to explain that the ship *Talune* had sailed under quarantine, and her captain did not remind the medical officer on her reaching Apia. Between the arrival of the ship on November 7, 1918, and the end of the year about 20 percent of the Western Samoans died of the flu and its complications. Many of the sick were taken simply by starvation; they had no one to feed or tend them. Fortunately in American Samoa, Commander Poyer, the naval governor, was a man able to draw conclusions from the daily wireless news. He turned back even the mail boat from Western Samoa (which caused the New Zealand officials to break off radio contact with their American counterparts). It is only 40 miles between the two islands, but Poyer called for every Samoan leader to prevent the landing of any boats from the west. The local people created an effective coast patrol of their own. The virus never reached American Samoa. By early 1919 men in Western Samoa would sing, to the tune of "The Star-spangled Banner," a Polynesian lyric that goes in translation: "In Upolu, the island of New Zealand, many are dead/While in Tutuila, the American island, not a one is dead. . . . God in heaven bless the American Governor and Flag." Crosby drily adds, "The like would not be heard again in a colony."

How did the virulent pandemic come about? We do not yet know. Even the molecular virologists, the masters of nucleic acids, cannot say. Indeed, Crosby does not mention RNA. He describes virology from the work of the 1930's, which found the virus, to about 1960. For a virus to be virulent against young adults may be a sign that the generalized immune system of the child has been replaced by a vigorous response to local injury. When the virus spreads over the entire surface of the lungs, the adult response is a massive inflammation; the lungs are overwhelmed by the exuded fluid. Older people react with less vigor locally, and they survive better. But why was the virus so deadly overall? In 1957 a different antigenic strain of the flu pandemic struck out of Asia even more widely. Its world mortality, however, was well under one per 1,000 cases. We have little idea why.

There is one theory, not flawless and not favored today but nonetheless plausible and fruitful. J. S. Koen, a U.S. Government inspector, saw a raging epizootic at the Cedar Rapids Swine Show in October of 1918. The hogs had a new disease: sore muscles and drippy snouts, with much mortality. Koen wrote: "It looked like flu, it presented the identical symptoms of flu, it terminated like flu, and until proved it was not flu, I shall stand by that diagnosis." Ten years later Richard E. Shope, an Iowa virologist at the Rockefeller Institute, took it up. Shope worked for 20 years on the swine flu. He argued that it was a virus infection on top of an endemic respiratory infection of swine caused by a bacterium known as Pfeiffer's bacillus. The flu virus remains latent, like the virus of the fever blister, until it is triggered by cold, wet weather. Then the twice-infected swine show deadly symptoms.

That explains the timing of the epizootic, which occurs only in the fall and the winter. The hog disease explodes without spreading; since its agents are already in place, it is everywhere at once. For Shope the human flu of the spring of 1918 seeded the new virus infection. Then a bacillus —found in most autopsies of victims, and long known as *Haemophilus influenzae*—caused the later pandemic under the stress of bad weather. The trouble with the hypothesis is that the virulent wave started in August, in the hot port of Freetown. Some victims of the Spanish flu had no bacilli in their lungs or throat, and laboratory animals got the flu from the virus alone. But perhaps there is some other form of prepandemic seeding. The flu peaked in Boston and in Bombay in the same week of 1918. Is something latent?

Those six cases at Fort Dix early this year showed the old "footprint in the blood": antigens like those against the swine virus, which are usually found only in people old enough to have had the 1918 flu. The virus itself is still unknown to us. In 1951 some 1918 victims were exhumed on the coast of Alaska in the hope of finding living virus preserved in the icy graves, but it did not appear, even though it was possible to culture some living bacteria from the dead tissues.

Why was the Spanish flu so deadly? Will it come back in some form even to our world of egg-reared vaccines? This winter or the next is likely to make us all somewhat wiser, even though we cannot expect full knowledge. The ecology of pathogenic organisms is a fateful and difficult subject.

(November 1976)

Sudden Infant Death: Patterns, Puzzles and Problems
By Jean Golding, Sylvia Limerick and Aidan Macfarlane

Melloni's Illustrated Medical Dictionary, Second Edition
By Ida Dox, Biagio John Melloni and Gilbert M. Eisner

Three-month-old David's mother is a nurse in her early 30's. He is her third child; happily married to a physician, she does not smoke. Through normal birth she has just mothered a normal, contented baby. At two months he was screened at the health clinic: no abnormality at all. At three months, not long before David was due for his first immunization, she put him in his crib for his afternoon sleep. Warm but not encumbered, he went right to sleep. She heard no sound, but in 30 minutes she went up to check on him. He was very pale; when she picked him up, he was floppy and around his mouth was a blood-tinged froth. She cleared the tiny mouth, phoned for an ambulance and tried resuscitation. Within 10 minutes David was in the hospital, still warm but without breath or heartbeat. The emergency staff gave up after an hour's effort. The postmortem was entirely normal except for some vomit in the infant's upper mouth and airways. Certificate: Sudden Infant Death (SID).

Even during the late 1970's (the most recent data on hand) parents in Bangladesh had to face the fact that there one baby in six would die somehow during the first year. That was the hard experience in the U.S. or the U.K. just a century ago. Today in developed lands total infant mortality has fallen by more than an order of magnitude, to perhaps one infant death per 100 live births. Change continues as health care improves; since 1971 infant mortality in England and Wales has decreased by a factor of almost two.

There lies beneath that falling curve one small component that has remained quite flat over decades. Of each 1,000 live births in modernized lands, 990 infants can be expected to live to their first birthday. Of the 10 who die before that, six do not survive the first month of life, victims of gross errors of growth, mostly either low birth weight (prematurity) or a clear congenital defect. Two or three of the remaining four will die in the hospital, taken there during the first year for some late-detected birth abnormality or with an acute infection that resists treatment. The rest, two or three apparently well babies out of the 1,000, will die unexpectedly nonetheless, mostly in their own cribs, too suddenly to have reached the hospital or even a doctor, bearing no marks or signs, infants "in whom a thorough necropsy examination fails to demonstrate an adequate cause of death."

Taking the U.S. and the U.K. together, about 10,000 families endure such a blow each year. The definition of SID is plainly operational; it implies an autopsy, a degree of expert medical attention hardly to be expected where this faint signal is swamped in the grim noise of abundant infant death, whether in our own past or where the old regime still rules and ill-fed mothers take water from unprotected wells for pining infants. Recognition rests on some 40 studies in conditions of low total infant mortality, some local and some national. They have been carried out in Britain, Canada, the U.S., Australia and New Zealand, in a few countries of western and eastern Europe and in Japan and Israel. Wherever the statistics seem reliable the results are broadly similar; the one clear exception is in Sweden, where two big cities showed a fourfold lower rate for sudden infant death.

Fifteen years ago this column first noted the report of an international conference on the problem. Five such gatherings have convened in the past 25 years to unravel the causes of sudden infant death. The physicians have taken counsel, and yet the mystery remains unsolved.

This recent book by two British epidemiologists and a research pediatrician sums up clearly what is known in a fascinating and humane account, a fine case study in epidemiology and its problems. The small volume presents new data from two recent English surveys, one following up in detail the record of every infant death for a decade in a medically well-tended regional population with 14,000 births per year. The clearest result is the age distribution of these enigmatic deaths. They follow a curve that rises to a peak between eight and 12 weeks and thereafter trails off into a longish tail, a few cases occurring even at the age of two.

Some 600 or 800 papers that seek a cause are referenced here. Of course no single cause may dominate; the problem is after all a form of contemporary ignorance, diagnosis by failure to diagnose. Yet Table 13 lists no fewer than some 30 characteristics of mother and dead infant that show considerable consistency worldwide. These include such factors as the age distribution and the season of the year (deaths increase in winter). Risk is relatively high among infants born to young mothers, particularly those in the lower social classes and those who smoke or use drugs. Male babies and babies whose birth weight is low are also unusually susceptible. It is not hard to conclude that sudden-death infants often have endured "an adverse period *in utero*."

Yet for half of the cases the families were not under economic or social stress, a third of the mothers did not smoke, more than 80 percent of the babies who died were of normal weight; nothing amiss is known.

The failed hypotheses are legion. Breast-feeding does not protect statistically; inhalation of traces of cow's milk by an allergic infant was a popular theory of the 1960's. No antibody differences were found between sudden-death infants and the controls. The same story can be told of protein from mites in house dust. "Gentle battering," infanticide in some form, was a cause ascribed by the Bible, put delicately as accidental overlaying. There are cases of infanticide here; they hit the headlines, but the evidence indicates that they are a numerically unimportant fraction of the whole.

Siblings of dead infants do not seem to be at much greater risk, allowing for social and maternal biases, although there are certainly exceptional cases: one mother of an SID case in the big survey reported here had three other children who died suddenly and unexpectedly. Surviving twins are in fact at higher risk, mainly during the four weeks after the first twin dies; identical twins are not more at risk. Genetics seems to offer little.

The sudden arrest of breathing was suspect—some failure in bioelectronic development?—and gave rise to a special campaign around near-misses, children who had been found alive but blue from lack of breath. Consequently electronic alarms have been devised and installed.

The results do not suggest that the scheme is an answer to SID, although parents who must raise siblings after one sudden death often value this kind of support. None of the 30 infants who eventually died among the more than 9,000 whose breathing movements were studied during the first weeks of life had shown abnormalities. The birth-control pill is not at fault, nor are the usual triple vaccines given infants, nor any other medical drugs, except possibly barbiturates taken during pregnancy.

There are some surprising hypotheses formed by analogy, unlikely and ingenious. Selenium deficiency leads to fatal heart disease among children in China and a kind of sudden infant death among piglets. In New Zealand selenium is low, yet SID is not high. It is true that there the city of Auckland has both more selenium and less SID, but the correlation did not hold elsewhere. Nor is selenium lower in the measured blood of SID infants than it is in the controls. Measurements of a dozen other trace elements, along with a variety of vitamins and hormones, have given no firm results. Overheating (perhaps augmented by fever) has been suspected of somehow causing death by heat stroke. Although febrile convulsions are common in young children, they occur only at ages far beyond the peak of SID.

One father of a sudden-infant-death victim had a "relatively rare" condition that causes a sharp rise of muscle temperature under anesthesia; the disease can cause sudden death among pigs. In 1982 an Australian team reported that five of the 15 parents of sudden infant deaths whose muscle tissue they sampled had the muscular disorder. The second shoe of confirmation has not yet fallen.

The age distribution among babies admitted to the hospital with respiratory syncytial virus (the common virus infection leading to bronchitis and pneumonia) matches the age distribution of SID cases. That virus infects boys more than girls in the same ratio found for SID; it is winter-prevalent, more likely in cities, lowest in better-off families. The match is striking; it is not a negative point that other and less common viruses might show similar patterns. The immune system of the child is in transition, shedding its endowment of maternal immunoglobulins in favor of its own defenses. This event transpires between the age of two and three months, the age peak of SID. Perhaps anaphylactic shock to the sensitized infant in reaction to respiratory virus infection is the pathway to "a proportion" of SID cases, the authors cautiously write.

About half of a modest sample of SID cases do yield small amounts of common viruses. This is a larger fraction than the controls show. Of course, there is no massive viral infection; such a clear finding would have excluded the infant from classification as a sudden infant death. The hypothesis must include some kind of hypersensitivity.

The riddle is still unanswered. Controls are difficult: not many normal children die at a comparable age. In the absence of a standard of comparison erroneous yet plausible hypotheses easily persist. The cause of sudden death in the 1900's was held to be a grossly enlarged thymus. Actually the thymus is normally large in infants, but the "controls" of the day were babies who had died of malnutrition or infection; their thymus glands had shrunk. It took 50 years for those facts to be generally recognized. Misunderstanding and fashion enter today as well. Current tests center on biochemical studies, cases of near-misses and the follow-up of infant siblings.

The logical outcome of advances in medical knowledge is certainly a steadily declining incidence of death "from unknown causes." SID is not as complex as the eventual residual mix of everything unknown. But the age distribution of sudden deaths does differ strongly between those in summer months and those in winter. That suggests we may be on the verge of resolving SID into two differing patterns, perhaps with distinct causes.

Even more than SID's intellectual challenge, even more than the human suffering it brings — both well described in this study — the circumstances pose a deeper riddle yet in our contradictory epoch. If we can struggle so steadily against that half percent of SID, can we not act to relieve the infants of the Third World, who are dying at a dozen times the SID rate from familiar microbial infections we know very well how to prevent? If not we, who? If not now, when? Those are old questions, but they still have bite.

Biagio John Melloni's medical dictionary is recent, legible, neither overpriced nor uncomfortably bulky. Its 26,000 entries are made much more usable by a richness of about a tenth as many apt and well-arranged tables and diagrams, and by illustrations of anatomy at every scale. Size is in general not explicitly marked, although the entries contain the data for objects, such as red cells, not visible without the microscope. The work is for nonspecialists; it tabulates, for instance, all arteries, bones, muscles, nerves and veins by name. The generally useful glossary of the SID book omitted a definition of the suspect respiratory syncytial virus, but that definition and a little context were quickly found in the attractive volume by Melloni — the image expert — and his friends.

(August 1986)

The Balkan Nephropathy
Edited by G. E. W. Wolstenholme and Julie Knight

A pocket-sized book with such a title will remind some readers of hours they spent long ago immersed in tales of intrigue set on the speeding trains and in the ancient towns of that polyglot and diverse heart of Europe. Here again is a mystery unfolding on the shores of the Danube, only now it is not fiction. it is the enigmatic, challenging and tragic account of a one-day international meeting of specialists, held last year by the Ciba Foundation in London to look into the cause of the deaths of thousands of men and women. They were all poor farm people, dwellers in the lowlands near the central reaches of the Danube, stretching 100 kilometers or so above and below the Iron Gate in Romania, Yugoslavia and Bulgaria. The disease is a chronic defect of kidney function, leading in some 10 years to almost certain death by the inability to remove protein breakdown products from the blood. Children do not die of the illness, although recent tests show that some even of them have signs of incipient failure.

The condition seems new. It has been recognized by physicians for a decade, although there are rumors that the few doctors among these hardworking peasants a generation ago also knew it. It might be very old and merely long unrecognized. Clinically the disease resembles lead poisoning (indeed, it is even more like cadmium poisoning, although it is more often fatal) and clearly the first task was to search for these metals in the region. The food — mainly the grain of local fields, with meat served only a couple of times a week — the air, the water, the fertilizer contained no dangerous amounts of these elements. One miller was found who had patched his millstones with solder; his village was being slowly dosed with lead, but he was a special case. Fifteen trace elements have been looked for, but none are found in more than the normal amounts, not even in the tissues of the dead.

Is the disease hereditary? Certainly it afflicts families; whole families have been wiped out by it in the past decade. That is too complete for a dominant gene, and the children of susceptible families who are sent to live in towns, where the disease is not found, escape. One man lost two wives to the condition. He took a third from a far-off village where the disease was unknown. In a few years she too was dead. Lowland villages have the disease; upland ones do not. In one village on the boundary between the affected and the disease-free region 16 percent of those who lived in Lower Glogovac were affected; only 5 percent of those in Upper Glogovac, 50 feet higher, were threatened. "No differences were to be found between the two parts of the village in housing conditions, diet, disposal of waste, customs, occupations, diseases of men and domestic animals, the use of fertilizers, insecticides, pesticides and other chemicals, consumption of alcohol, or in the economic, social and other ecological conditions. The only difference [is] in the water supply and . . . altitude." So far no one has found anything out of the ordinary in the well water.

Is it strange herbs used in the "people's tea"? No; the village schoolteachers collected samples, and they were harmless. Households without this habit were not always safe. Is it a bacterial infection? No unusual antibodies are found. Is it some fungus in the grain or in the soil, perhaps brought in floodwaters? None has been found, although perhaps one will be. Is it the copper stills used to make slivovitz? No; exactly the same are used elsewhere.

The people themselves say particular houses bring the disease. Sometimes the maps bear them out. One entire village has been evacuated and resettled as an experiment; it is still too soon to perceive results.

The World Health Organization and specialists from the U.S.S.R., Denmark, the U.S. and the Balkan countries are all in the field and hard at work. The mystery remains; the killer is at large.

(June 1968)

The Healing Hand: Man and Wound in the Ancient World
By Guido Majno

Only one book of Pliny remains to us. It is a monument to obsessive data-collecting. The author wrote only by night, had books read to him during rubdowns and at table and scolded his friends, "Your interruption has cost us ten lines!" This tireless Roman army officer and civil official collected 20,000 facts from 2,000 volumes by 100 authors in the course of two years, just a few years before his death in A.D. 79 (probably of a heart attack as he approached Vesuvius in eruption). His reputation today is low; he is remembered mainly for the mistakes he repeated. Not here, however. The cheerful scholar, skeptic and medical scientist who has produced this extraordinary volume admires the old fellow greatly and cites almost eight pages of his remarks, grouped by topic, with genuine pleasure. (For example: "Physicians acquire their knowledge from our dangers, making experiments at the cost of our lives" and "There is a marvelous neatness in the titles of Greek books, but when you get inside them, good heavens, what a void!")

Professor Majno even found an unnoticed pearl in Pliny. There is a plain account of the juice of a certain plant that can stanch bleeding and cure cough; it was named *ephedron*. We have known the drug, an analogue of adrenalin, only since its efficacy was reported 50 years ago by a young American at Peking Union Medical College who had tested popular Chinese herbs. (It was the one find of 2,000 samples he examined.) The Mediterranean remedy seems to have been independent of the very old

Chinese tradition. Strangely enough, the drug had been extracted and purified in the 1880's, but it was ignored because at full strength it poisoned the experimental dogs. "Asthmatics went on coughing and wheezing—and all the while it lay written in the books . . . that a gentler, impure decoction of *Ephedra* would have brought them instant relief."

Professor Majno is a pathologist "primarily interested in sick people," a specialist in inflammation. He began to write a historical preface to a monograph, he says, and "the preface took over." We are grateful, if not quite persuaded. There is not much about wounds in the citations from Pliny; throughout the book what is opened up is a lighthearted and yet compelling path toward the pleasures and depths of classical learning. The author is a courageous and catholic amateur of history who delights in inference, an experimenter, a questioner and a cultivated writer of imagination, humor and compassion. He has entered the past over a daunting span of space and time with the best of all preparation: real knowledge of the discipline whose history he teases out. He follows the wound (there is no problem with its diagnosis) from before history through Sumer, Egypt, Greece, China, India, Alexandria and Rome—with no narrow view of what he is seeking. He is as interested in how cuneiform is construed as he is in just what some learned editor concludes about contested phrases; he fears no digression and he nourishes the eye with text facsimiles, diagrams, sketches of his own, experimental results and archaeological and artistic finds—a treasure made coherent out of diversity. Although he does not normally seek primary historical novelty (Pliny's drug aside), his work is above all a delectable lesson in how to know the past. The bibliography is critical and extensive. He has written to or talked with the contending scholars; he explains his own tentative best surmises, and he draws the reader along on a journey over the millenniums, through clinical laboratories and into the libraries at one and the same time.

The volume is as much a delight to view as to reflect on, with 15 color plates, hundreds of figures and such elegancies as marginal sketches to identify the chapters. It would be of little use to summarize this rich summary-history; before the reader sets out for the bookstore or the library it will suffice to sample almost telegraphically a half-dozen points. Most of these remarks stand each for an entire well-knit chapter.

The apes administer first aid along with their more obvious grooming. "Nature does most of the job, while the chimps perform a few helpful gestures . . . *in the pursuit of pleasure.* . . . But to turn to my surgical colleagues: would anyone deny that cleaning up an untidy wound still is, deep down, a pleasure?"

There is a photograph of a hand impression in the late Paleolithic Gargas cave, showing fingers that appear to be chopped short. Missing-joint counts suggest that what is represented is a sign language of bent fingers, not ritual amputation. And yet the sacrifice of fingers among hunting peoples is known.

Powdered malachite and chrysocolla, two lovely blue-green copper minerals, were typically used for Egyptian eye makeup and paint. Here is an ancient carved head so decorated; with it we see a Petri dish test that makes plain the antibiotic effect of the two cosmetic powders. There is a serious function for eye paint; Dioscorides confirmed it. Not for nothing does a fashion endure over five millenniums.

Gaping wounds close to some extent by natural contraction. (One basic mechanism was discovered in the author's Harvard laboratory while he was completing this book: "a good omen.") The contractile tissue draws the closure much more easily when a wound has corners than when it is round; the healing time in rabbits is shortened by a week. Hippocrates was willing to cut to change a circular wound into an oval one; round wounds can heal only by changing shape, and so they are slow to heal and therefore dangerous.

The balm of Gilead was a treatment par excellence for wounds, with "an overtone of salvation." Myrrh is soluble and is a clear-cut bacteriostatic agent. "I conclude that the ancient use of myrrh as a wound drug was fully justified." How did it come to be adopted? First, the resin fills gashes in plants; perhaps that was a clue, conscious or not. Second, wounds used to smell, and so the fragrant resin was welcome. Third, resins never decay in nature; the analogy is real. And best of all, the resins actually helped.

Professor Majno faces up to China (depending of course on scholarly translations) in a brief chapter full of novelty. Readers who recall the Hemingway short stories will be surprised to learn that the Chinese surgeons who made eunuchs, like the unhappy Kansas City kid in the story, took away all the external genitalia. The citation is grim; it describes 1929 practice that cannot have been much easier back in the Han.

Here too is the dread white-hooded cobra and the scheme of Ayurvedic medicine for treating snakebite. The affair is described as the concrete living experience of an ancient doctor on a busy day, not in the abstract codified style of the Sanskrit texts. "Treatments that really treat are so rare in ancient medicine" that the ligature tied above the bite deserves and receives special mention.

The mandibles of a soldier ant are said to be efficacious for clamping a wound; they may have been the first sutures. Majno tried them; see the photograph in color. Indeed, one formicologist (the late T. C. Schneirla) reported that his clothes had been sutured to his skin by the appropriate species. ("I have ceased to doubt about the ancient Hindu sutures.")

There is a loving page about papyrology, that specialty of epigraphy. Police reports and accounts of an enema doctor make intimate the chapter on Alexandria. It is Galen who ends the book. The chapter on him begins with a photograph of the formidable shelf of his works in the only available edition, from the 1830's (admittedly a bit overplayed, since it includes a complete translation from the Greek to Latin). "I must confess that when it came to Galen I broke my own rule: I did *not* read the twenty-two volumes." It is fascinating that medical professors routinely teach that this Greek of the four humors produced a fifth sign of inflammation, that he added to *rubor, tumor, calor* and *dolor* (redness, swelling, heat and pain) another sign: disturbed function. "The concept of a fifth sign is definitely catchy. . . . It sounds like progress." It is not, however, progressive in Galen. He did not even repeat the four cardinal signs of the Roman Celsus: Galen "consumed gallons of Roman ink, but took no notice of anything Roman." It was the great Rudolf Virchow who enunciated the fifth sign in 1858; soon the handbooks and textbooks included the fifth sign as general wisdom, and in 1919 someone ascribed it to Galen! "After Galen, the history of the wound grinds to a halt for at least one thousand years."

A review can only clumsily transmit the feel of this remarkable book. Few indeed are works that so intimately connect past learning with present experience; the volume is itself a kind of healing, uniting in mutual benefit the classicist and the experimenter, the scholar and the general reader.

(June 1976)

The Eradication of Smallpox from India
By R. N. Basu, Z. Jezek and N. A. Ward

Lakshmi, beautiful consort to great Vishnu, is the generous source of prosperity and good fortune. Born in the Ocean of Milk, she has placed her sign in milk. No one who seeks her favor would turn aside any offer of a foamy beaker of milk, set at every good meal in all India. There are less benign deities in the pantheon of the subcontinent. Mother Shitala is represented as a woman of commanding presence, large-eyed and grave. She rides the land past rich and poor on her humble vehicle, the donkey. In her right hand she holds a pitcher of water, in her left a dry broom. On her head she balances with womanly dexterity as Indian as the summer monsoon a basket filled with grain. As she rides she may happen to shake her powerful head. Each grain she spills turns into a smallpox pustule; her marked victim will survive if she cleans away the spilt grain with a swish of water, but if she uses only the dry broom, the pox will take a life. Her temples dot the land; she has been propitiated in painted image whenever in India smallpox has come, surely for thousands of years.

The bounty of Lakshmi is one outcome of the ancient symbiosis between cattlekind and humankind, important in India since the Neolithic. The ugly burden imposed by arbitrary Shitala may well, however, be another element of that same tie between our two mammalian species. It is at least an attractive surmise that variola, the smallpox virus, first came to mankind from the cattle we have so long tended, after some particular modifying genetic event. Smallpox is Old World, unknown in the Americas before Columbus, and deadlier there than all the cannon and cavalry of the conquistadors. It is invariably virulent in man, without any carriers or invisible infection; what you get, you see. That bespeaks the novelty of the parasitism; there has been no time for the evolution of an enduring temperate relation between the virus and the host.

Smallpox needs a sizable population to offer new hosts; otherwise it dies out through the long immunity it confers on those who recover. Hunters might have acquired the new virus from other primates, in which similar pox viruses are known. But hunting bands are small, and their contact with the other primates is very old. Rather, the cowpox vaccine that in the experience of Americans has ended smallpox gets its very name from the gentle milch cow, whence Edward Jenner believed he had taken a mild surrogate for the dread disease. Nowadays it is thought the modern strains of the cowpox vaccinia virus are variants of the human variola virus itself, although they are still harvested in quantity from the skin lesions of inoculated calves or sheep, or from growing chick embryos.

The news is victory. Shitala Mata has decided to hold her head uncommonly steady these days. Across the entire country, from alpine Ladakh up against Tibet to the forested Andaman Islands in tropical seas, not one grain is split. No case of smallpox is to be found in all India. The last-reported smallpox patient there was discharged from the hospital on July 4, 1975; her pocked face confronts the reader. Saiban Bibi, a migrant beggar woman from Bangladesh, developed a fever and a rash "while living on the platform of the Karimganj railway station." Shivering with ague, subsisting for a few days on the tea she could get from the third-class waitingroom stall 10 meters away, she finally walked to the hospital, to enter history.

Polyglot and wonderfully diverse, some 600 million people live under the rule of Delhi, in about 115 million dwellings of every kind. Many millions wander the roads and the streets, pilgrims, migrants, homeless. Thirty years ago some 250,000 cases of smallpox were reported there every year, the majority of all the world's human hosts to variola. There is excellent reason to estimate that the cases were then massively under-reported; it is likely there were more than two million sufferers each year, a fourth of them fatal. A graph shows the cases reported from 1950 on; there are peaks every four to seven years, time to accumulate a pool of new susceptibles "following the high birth rate" in densely populated areas.

In 1961 war was declared on smallpox by India: the National Smallpox Eradication Programme was set in motion. Hopes were high; the U.S.S.R. gave India half a billion doses of its newly developed freeze-dried vaccine. Smallpox remained vigorously endemic. By 1966 there had been half a billion vaccinations, but the case rate had not materially decreased. To be sure, there were many states, particularly in the south, where smallpox was now rare and almost entirely imported from elsewhere. But mass vaccination could never reach all the teeming inhabitants; the disease prospered among the many who were missed.

The Intensified Campaign began in 1973. WHO had fixed on and demonstrated a new worldwide strategy; India was the most challenging theater of the war, particularly the populous Gangetic valley. The plan was powerful. Its base was the sure intelligence that this disease cannot hide; its spread is solely by close, although not necessarily intimate, human contact. Every infection shows up within a couple of weeks, and people can spot the fever with rash every time. True, it takes more skill to distinguish smallpox from other contagious rashes, but in any case the alarm has been sounded. The logistics were favorable; the old liquid vaccine, temperature-sensitive and often nothing but glycerine and dead virus, was no longer in service. Four Indian centers were in full production by 1973, making enough of the new quick-frozen and vacuum-dried vaccine to serve India and four of its neighbors. A central laboratory in Delhi and a WHO laboratory abroad monitored the output against world standards of potency and bacterial sterility.

Finally came the bifurcated needle, the right weapon for the front-line vaccinator. It is sparing of ammunition; a quarter of a cubic centimeter of vaccine could support a long day's work for an energetic young person, more than 100 vaccinations. The take rate was close to 100 percent among primary vaccinees. A vaccinator moving from house to house needs only a vial of diluted freeze-dried vaccine and a plastic tube full of bifurcated needles. With a new vial of vaccine and the same needles, simply boiled after hours to sterilize them, the soldier is armed for another day. "In 20 minutes an untrained worker could be converted into a skilled vaccinator."

The tactical plan was clear, soundly based on epidemiology. Search out every outbreak and then contain it. When the season of disease opened in the spring of 1973, the forces were ready. Their first task was a periodic national search for cases. In each of the nearly 400 administrative districts of India the primary health-center staff was drafted for search, a week per month in endemic states, less in the nonendemic areas. Out they spread, each with a photograph showing a smallpox-affected child, to ask city people and villagers, teachers, mailmen, doctors of ayurvedic medicine and leaders of every kind if they knew of a case of smallpox. The weekly markets were regularly targeted, together with "bus stands, . . . schools, railway stations, tea and betel shops, mosques, temples and migrant camps and brick kilns."

One hundred and fifty thousand people took part in the searches. They did not neglect travelers on the road, dockside, rail platform, forest camp and river island. A typical district includes some 200 villages, about the equivalent urban population in a dozen municipal wards. Once an outbreak was found (any village or ward with one or more cases in the preceding six weeks was defined as an outbreak) it was contained. Came the vaccinators, one full-time person for 20,000 people on the average, and one noncom, an experienced supervisor, for each squad of four. They followed the chain of which the reported case made one link. The people in the nearest houses were all vaccinated, if possible within 24 hours. All other contacts that could be established were followed up for vaccination; if the chain left the district, urgent notice was sent in person or by wire. As long as outbreaks were many, these measures were necessarily minimized. At first only 50 nearby houses could be visited with needles; then as cases dwindled the number of houses grew to 200. Later the entire village was included in the treatment, and finally a 10-mile radius was.

By the end of 1973 the maps show the endemic regions in a clear light. Four populous states held 80,000 cases among them; the rest of the country had only 5,500. In the little-affected areas the campaign could go on the offensive. There house-to-house searches could be undertaken in every village that reported an outbreak, instead of relying on the reports of leaders. Forces concentrated in the worst areas. The local staff was reinforced, often with international epidemiologists and special mobile teams. There was dramatic progress after the monsoon of 1974, yet in the worst places a bitter fight remained. Visitors came too often to affected houses; even patients were found to move from place to place. Now, however, bigger teams of vaccinators could be sent to any outbreak. Local watchmen were hired and posted in pairs at the door on a 24-hour basis. Food was provided for the family within. By the end of 1974 the map shows outbreak dots in only a few dozen districts.

The year of Operation Smallpox Target Zero was 1975. It is the chief pleasure of this well-illustrated, detailed and candid volume that the authors offer persuasive evidence that no smallpox case was left in India after the summer of that year. The argument springs really from continuity. Down the outbreak numbers steadily fall. The workers, no longer vaccinating so much, can post or stencil signs on every school, indeed on 10 or 15 million houses in all India, offering a cash reward for notice of a smallpox case. The reward grows; the payoffs are progressively fewer. The smallpox workers seek cases of fever with rash, and they see plenty of them. But these patients have chickenpox, not smallpox, and the virologists confirm the judgment.

A million cases of fever and rash, mainly chickenpox and measles, were reported in 1975; hundreds of them resulted in death. But the presence of a smallpox vaccination scar, the determination of contact with someone else suffering from another infection or other evidence made it clear that smallpox was not implicated in a single fatal case. In 1972 one district had deliberately concealed its epidemic of more than 1,000 cases. Of course, the event finally came to light, and the "transmission was arrested." The rewards for case notification were extended to reward both the public informant and the health worker who made the first report. In another district chickenpox was the diagnosis for more than a dozen suspected smallpox outbreaks. The verification of the diagnoses was then set into routine operation.

The great steel complex at Jamshedpur became for the month of May, 1974, "the world's greatest exporter of smallpox." The steel towns are prosperous; they attract beggars, transients, poor relations. A third of the third-class passengers at the station were unauthorized, ticketless travelers whom no one tried to stop. Responsibility was diffuse. Once the problem came to light two months of stringent control—barricaded roads, checkpoints, companies asked to deny travel leave to unvaccinated employees and their families—ended the matter. Finally, long after public notice of the last case in India, the coroner's court in Bombay declared after an autopsy that a four-year-old boy had died from "complications of smallpox." That protocol of autopsy was done in secret by the police. Burial was at noon one day. By five in the afternoon the international commission of assessment had asked for exhumation of the body. Fluid was collected from some 50 vesicles. The virus laboratory reported the samples negative for smallpox. The fatal illness was chickenpox; the Bombay coroner was wrong.

The war is won worldwide, at least for a good while. Smallpox is possibly to be found somewhere in the war-torn Horn of Africa; it is under guard in some laboratories and nowhere else as far as is known. In India even the laboratories made their final gesture of peace; all four research centers known to hold variola virus destroyed their stocks. All other medical schools and virus laboratories in India have been checked, and all published literature issuing from India on smallpox has been examined to locate other possible virus workers. There is no known virus left. A tragedy like that of Birmingham—escaped laboratory virus— cannot happen in India. Maybe there is some wild primate vector, although it is not expected. Smallpox has been routed in its ancient home; Shitala Mata will ride head high, unseen forever.

It is a grand triumph. Science, reason, energy and devotion have won. There were of course those who resisted vaccination. Indeed, there is a real risk of death from vaccination (one in about 10 million in Indian circumstances), although those who resist it do not depend on such arguments. Most of the 3 percent of initial resisters were women past 70. Persuasion, tact, the use of local workers, of senior staff or of female team members, particularly in Muslim areas, generally overcame their refusal. In the end resistance had no substantial effect.

After a stringent series of all-India verification surveys an international commission declared India free of smallpox on April 23, 1977. They had good reason. This volume is the required record of the entire campaign; the three authors are themselves veterans of the war, Delhi-based officers of WHO. (They are surely among the group here photographed in handsome T-shirts inscribed Smallpox Zero.) The cost was $95.4 million, the auditors say, with a saving for India of $91 million per year, not costing out bereavement, disfigurement and pain.

Human beings are able to stand united against a virus. Divided by nation, caste and class, they are less able to ameliorate more human problems. Saiban Bibi is immune to smallpox now; one wonders if she is yet immune to sleeping on railway platforms. Still, there rises from these lively pages, with all their maps, forms and graphs, the distant fragrance of rational hope.

(July 1980)

The Modern Rise of Population
By Thomas McKeown

The human population has increased with increasing rapidity since about 1750. A subset much better measured, the population of England and Wales, had risen threefold in the seven centuries from the time of the Domesday Book to 1700. It tripled again by 1851 and has very nearly tripled once more since then. The phenomenon is unique in its scale, duration and continuity. We need to know why, for the sake of our future, if for no other reason. The author, a British demographer of medical background, seeks the answer in this small book of tight argument, first published in 1976. His method is explicitly unhistorical. He proposes to study the problem in the light of present knowledge; what we need to know is not what the physicians of the past thought they were doing but how effective their treatments actually were. Gauging that does not call for the historian's leap into the concepts of the past.

National registers of birth and death supply the first firm data; no effort to repair that lack for earlier times by local records or clever indirect accounts can be relied on. Concordant statistics are provided by Sweden from 1749, France from 1800, England and Wales from 1838 and Ireland from 1871. Birthrates have been falling pretty steadily; allowing for net migration, the population has grown in spite of a lower birthrate. The direct cause of the rise in population is the decline in mortality. For this we have significant detail: the cause of death. The data are again decisive: most of the decline has been due to the reduction of the effects of infectious disease. The decline in deaths from infectious diseases amounted to three-fourths of the total decrease in mortality between 1850 and 1971 (with all rates standardized to the age and sex distribution of 1901). Leading the decline, indeed contributing more than half of it, were airborne infections, including tuberculosis, pneumonia, influenza, scarlet fever and smallpox.

Until about 1900 there was no decrease in infant mortality or in mortality among those over 45; the improvement came through the steady reduction at just those ages where mortality was naturally lowest: the years from two to 45. Tuberculosis was the largest single cause of death in Victorian times; its decline is steady since the first years of registration, a generation before the tubercle bacillus was even identified. Effective treatment began only after World War II, first with streptomycin and then with the BCG vaccine. The detailed consideration of the other important diseases broadly confirms the conclusion: neither treatment nor prophylaxis was the cause of lowered mortality.

Was it reduced exposure? For waterborne diseases the answer is plain; the safety of drinking water, milk and food and the control of sewage made a real difference. For the airborne diseases, however, the reduction of exposure was at most a secondary cause, unimportant before 1900. Even as late as 1950 all adolescents were shown by the tuberculin reaction to have been exposed to tuberculosis; today only a minority bear those immune signs. Was it perhaps a spontaneous reduction in the virulence of the disease? For scarlet fever and influenza such changes are fairly plain, although they are cyclical. Again the uniformity of the effect over a wide variety of disease agents that, like tuberculosis and measles, remain fully infectious today seems to exclude that cause or its counterpart: a selective change in the specific resistance of the human population.

What remains? Argument by exclusion is dangerous, but there are positive grounds for accepting the remaining factor: general health has improved, mainly because of the improvement of the nutritional state of the people. New crops, new seeds, new tools, better farming methods and better transport all resulted in the people's being better fed. Britain fed herself during a trebling of population without substantial imports of food. The improvement in the life expectancy of the aristocrats, docu-

mented along with the overall changes, does not contradict this conclusion. Their minority case can be explained by their reduced exposure, not
offset by the bad conditions of the cities. The lesson of this analysis is easy
to infer. Yet the Birmingham of 1850 is not the Bengal of 1980; the lesson
must not be read too narrowly.

McKeown frequently draws indirect support from animal-population
studies and from what is known of birth and death among human hunting
populations living today. In these matters he has not always found the best
and most recent data, nor is anyone quite sure of the generalizations. At
the worst, however, these questions lie in the background; his central
points are strong, if not yet compelling because of the lack of quantitative
knowledge. It is tempting to draw the conclusions over the span of the
entire human epoch. Hunting peoples achieved a balance with their environment at a low number, by methods that are not quite clear. Agriculture
induced a strong rise in the number of head of human beings and their
livestock. The microbial parasites of the domesticated mammals found a
new host in the inhabitants of the populous new farm villages; infectious
diseases set limits on population once human numbers grew enough to
make the food supply again marginal.

Then in western Europe at the beginning of modern times the chain
was broken: a new agriculture brought new food supplies, disease receded,
population grew apace. This time the growth was limited not by a rise in
deaths but by a permanent drop in the birthrate brought about by the
conditions of the modern nation state. Better water and better food,
preventive medicine, contraception (which reduced the incidence of unre-
ported infanticide) and finally better therapy all now take part in the
balance. Infectious diseases are no longer the captains of the men of death;
even our fears seem different now.

(August 1979)

XI

The Human Past

Our species has its gifted ancestors, more and more entering the light as our finds increase. Then we come to know the few of our contemporaries who keep something of the old ways of living from the yield of the wildlands, and even of their magic still alive around us. Newer cultures appear under the spade, clearer and clearer in all continents. The sharp interactions of new and old bear recounting, by witnesses as well as through old monuments and old books. Some now dream of voyages, even of visitors, to and fro among the stars.

It seems well to end this collection with archeology and its analogues; we need to understand our own changes during the long span of time.

The Hunters or the Hunted? An Introduction to African Cave Taphonomy

By C. K. Brain

"This is a detective story, but a rather odd one. The clues are bones, and the aim of the investigation is to establish the causes of death, but the evidence is ancient and no witnesses survive." Just as unusual is the scrupulous fairness of the narrative. The evidence is placed before the reader at length: there are 70 pages of tables and many pages that are mere lists of numbers, catalogues of the bones under study. The argument is nonetheless clean enough for a verdict, although by the very nature of the topic there can be no certainty.

The scene is the slopes of a river valley in the open limestone country a few dozen miles to the northwest of Johannesburg. The beautiful caves in dolomite there have been visited for many decades, although mining for the lime-burning kilns has from time to time encroached on the caverns. Here and there, sometimes in the rubble left behind by the miners, there are tons of bone-bearing cave breccias, bones in plenty cemented into a kind of concrete. The admissible evidence is the bones; there are about 20,000 of them from at least 1,300 animals. It is tedious work to sort and clean the clues.

The key events took place at the time of passage from our apelike walkabout ancestors, the australopithecines, to the larger-brained tool-making primates usually called *Homo erectus*, members of our own genus. It was a long time ago, maybe a million years, but there are no good dates for the material.

Our detective has a bright record. His method is taphonomy, the study by statistical means not only of the bones that fit into one skeleton but also of the entire assembly of bones found together. It was by this approach that Brain cleared up another suspected crime, in a cave not far away. There the pioneer Raymond A. Dart (his picture is the frontispiece) had unearthed what appeared to be evidence of mass murder. It seemed that the australopithecines there had killed a zoo of other animals, including a few of their own kind. Broken baboon skulls abounded; bone bludgeons were present to explain the damage. The antelope remains included big bones but no tail vertebrae. The tails had not been brought back to the cave, apparent evidence of culture.

The inference was circumstantial and hasty. Brain showed before 1970 that the discarded skeletons of goats killed and eaten in Hottentot settlements today show the same bone distribution. The Hottentots do not sort the bones; it is only that the bones that endure dog chewing and other such processes are the denser and larger ones. The verdict: Not

297

guilty. The early hunters did not sort meat or bone or kill their own kind. The baboons and the occasional hominid were all victims of big carnivores. There remains some doubt; the excavations were never made "with due regard to subtle detail."

The bone accumulations in a dozen caves of the wider region have been sampled. The bone wastes of people, big carnivorous cats, hyenas, owls and porcupines have been examined in the field. Porcupines make gnaw marks; owls collect small bones and deposit them under their roost in the cave mouth. Broken flakes of bone are frequently polished by the feet of animals around a watering place; so it goes. It is detailed attention to clues that is required; the witnesses must be cross-examined.

We come next to the fossil animals of long ago. A fine chapter lists and shows in illustration the animals large and small that lived around the caves. The primates were baboons, ape-men, then men; there are saber-toothed cats, false and true. There is a strange antelope resembling a musk ox, and a hunting form of hyena.

The case is prepared. Now the bones are teased out, identified, counted and sorted by their level in the cave. Among the big bones in two of the caves a clear pattern emerges from the data. There is a sharp change between two levels. In the earlier of the two the bones of the primates, baboon and ape-man, are very frequent. In the later level (it is a pity that no absolute dates are available) we see a switch: primate remains are all but absent, and antelope kind provide the bulk of the bones. (In the third cave there is no strong change seen; the situation remains consistent with the earlier level in the other caves.) The pattern makes good sense in only one way.

The primate bones found in the lower level were not those of animals that had entered voluntarily to die. They were carried in, prey to the carnivores of the lair. it is not clear whether the carnivores were leopards or other species. Possibly an unknown specialized predator on primates was one of the old cats or hyenas, whose skeletons we know but whose habits we can only guess at. It may have been the false sabertooth, a big cat that hunted its prey by stealth. Its powerful teeth would have enabled it to eat all parts of a primate skeleton except the skull.

The case is tentatively solved. "At Sterkfontein, the interface between the top of Member 4 and the bottom of Member 5 represents a time interval crucial in the course of human evolution. During this interval the gracile australopithecines disappeared from the Transvaal scene and the first men appeared. . . . During Member 4 times the cats apparently controlled the Sterkfontein cave, dragging their australopithecine victims into its dark recesses. By Member 5 days, however, the new men not only had evicted the predators, but had taken up residence in the very chamber where their ancestors had been eaten."

The bones give eloquent witness. Were there fire, weapons, speech, clearer thought? We cannot say. But something new tipped the balance for

good, and here we are, a species that, unlike the australopithecines, is truly
threatened only by its own kind.

(February 1982)

Laetoli: A Pliocene Site in Northern Tanzania
Edited by M. D. Leakey and J. M. Harris

Hardly another page in all the
weighty Book of Sediments bears so graphic a text as that found at
Laetoli. It is pressed into a six-inch, level layer of cemented gray volcanic
ash. That stratum lies within a 500-foot-thick succession of volcanic beds,
visible wherever a small river has meandered on its way down to a wide
salt lake on the Serengeti. Here and there over some 30 square miles of the
upland savanna a little stretch of that particular long-lasting layer, harder
than the material above it, is exposed by erosion. Where that has happened "prints are visible on the surface."

The first prints were found in 1976. By now just nine exposures of
the Footprint Tuff have been minutely searched; nearly 10,000 impressions have been counted over a total exposed area of less than an acre.
Nine-tenths of them are small oval marks left by the African hare and the
tiny deerlike dik dik, both animals abundant at this place today, in modern although kindred species. "An elderly Musukuma tracker" helped to
identify the genera of the creatures that left the tracks, although he tried
to fit individuals into living species. Trails were also left by hyena and
ostrich, giraffe and rhino; you can see one or two pawprints of a really big
cat.

The little horse of that epoch is encountered in three trackways; at
one place the crossing pathways of an adult and a younger animal suggest
a mare and her foal. The sequence of the old prints, hoof and side toe
marked, fits the pattern of the single-foot gait, "like a fast walk instead of
a slow run," during which one foot is always on the ground. It is favored
for surefootedness by equids "for instance when it suddenly starts snow-
ing." These prints have been compared with those of the Iceland pony,
specially bred for single-foot travel. By scaling from the modern pony, the
size and speed of the Laetoli horses can be estimated: the mare stood three
feet high at the withers, a good foot less than today's pony; she crossed
the slippery ash-covered terrain—a slip is marked in her hoofprints—at
some four miles per hour.

The beds at Laetoli are well dated; large flakes of mica with a good potassium content can be sorted from the ash at many levels and their radiogenic argon production measured. The Footprint Tuff itself is consistently found to be about 3.5 million years old. The geologist's interpretation of the fabric of that tuff is striking. The lower fraction of the tuff consists of 14 layers of ashfall. Those layers conceal local irregularities such as footprints without change in thickness; the material must have been undisturbed ever since it was deposited. Clear raindrop imprints are seen widely at several interfaces; the showers were enough to dampen the ash but not to erode it. Above those layers lie a few thicker ones, which show that heavier rainfall redeposited and mixed the layers of new-fallen ash. Footprints are found in many of the layers.

At the base of the tuff grass roots are visible, but no grass blades are seen in the tuff itself; the grass was kept short, probably by grazing. There were few trees nearby on this open land: the pollen found is grassy, and the birds are ground feeders, not forest dwellers. This ash was laid down at the close of the dry season, just as the first new rains came, each layer probably deposited by a new eruption. The annual wet season arrived as the upper layers fell. The prints in the lower part are those of dryland savanna creatures, hares, guinea fowl, rhinos; in the upper layers are the tracks of those animals that migrate, as they still do, when the rains come, chiefly the hoofed and horned herds and the baboons.

How can coarse ash, particles the texture of sand, record footprints so well? Just the right amount of moisture is needed; it is hard to see how that could have been managed for each of a dozen printed layers. the answer is that this was no commonplace volcano. Its clouds consisted of a carbonatite ash, rich both in sodium and in calcium carbonate. The first rainfall enabled the soluble soda ash to cement the surface layer. The very volcano is still visible, 15 or 20 miles to the southeast, its much eroded cone protruding from the flank of the grand caldera of the younger Ngorongoro. Its long-cold lava is of matching age, and its ash has the unusual carbonate-rich composition, a hint of reworked sea-floor material.

This archaeologically favored region, known as the East African Rift Valley, is a place where our own kind have long been at home. The layers preserve our ancestral bones and prints. Three trails of hominid tracks are there at one locality, where fortune exposed a single indentation of a heel. A few inches of darker material were then removed for a distance of some 100 feet to disclose those trails, shown here in a dramatic color photograph. (Someday a museum at the spot will house the wonders; for the time being they have been carefully covered up again with layers of sand and plastic sheet.) Two specialists agree: these are the prints of virtually human feet, whose age alone serves to part them from our own species. The prints show no features intermediate between apewalk and fully upright bipedal human stride; that transition must be older. While various beds have yielded portions of jaws and teeth from two dozen individual hominids, no worked stone at all is found. Everything fits the pattern of the gracile australopithecines. They are identical with individuals whose crushed bones in limestone caverns not far from Johannesburg show them somewhat later to have been regular prey to the big cats.

Indeed, that must have been so at Laetoli. Finds of outsize teeth and jaws point to truly lionlike felines (along with sabertooths), then at the pinnacle of the faunal pyramid. Apparently the savanna ecology was already fully formed in Laetoli days when across the slippery new ashfall a slight four-foot eight-inch tall hominid led a smaller one (by the hand?); their two trails are parallel at a nearly fixed distance, and the smaller prints show a quickstep maneuver to catch up. The leader had in fact walked in footprints left behind by a third individual, larger still, who had gone first across the ash. All were at daily risk from the hunting carnivores; these were nimble walkers, clever game animals, not yet Promethean. They had neither fire nor weapons. Or did those small brains already hold some idea of pit traps or of sharpened sticks?

The burden of this technical monograph with its 33 expert contributors from three continents is not new. The work was mainly completed by the early 1980's, much of it even published. More than half of the bulky text is not devoted to traces of behavior in all those footprints (and in intricate buried castings of termite nests, and of the brood cells of solitary bees). Instead it is the familiar technical paleontology of careful description and identification of skeletal fragments of all kinds, bone by bone and tooth cusp after tooth cusp. Recall that this site first came under the scrutiny of Louis and Mary Leakey 50 years ago for its fossil bones. They were digging in Olduvai Gorge when a Masai told them of many old bones on the surface 20 or 30 miles south at Laetoli, "the place of red lilies," and offered samples in evidence.

This report is worth the general reader's attention because the richness of specialists' detail makes it overwhelmingly persuasive. It is a nearly full account from the human past unrivaled in poignance. These finds are as startling as when 50 years ago a few big molars of our distant forebears showed up in the dusty wood drawers where old-fashioned Chinese pharmacies kept their best-quality dragon's bone.

(April 1988)

Quaternary Extinctions: A Prehistoric Revolution
Edited by Paul S. Martin and Richard G. Klein

Who killed the Great Auk? We know the names of the two fishermen who killed the last pair known, and destroyed their single egg, at Eldey Rock off Iceland in 1844. Who killed the giant moa? Moa bones by the wagonload and moa eggshells by the acre have been found in the middens and earth ovens of the Maori voyagers who entered the South Island of New Zealand. A hundred sites are dated by radiocarbon from about A.D. 1000 to about A.D. 1500. There is no sign of major climatic change during the protracted vanishing of the diurnal forest-fringe birds. The number measurably slaughtered over time is an order of magnitude greater than the best estimate of the available population. A New Zealand popular song sums it up: "No moa, no moa, / In old Ao-tearoa. / Can't get 'em. / They've et 'em; / They've gone and there aint no moa!" The scholars agree, and they add a word or two about deforestation by set fires and a footnote acknowledging the work of the dogs and rats that came as passengers and stowaways in the big canoes.

This volume of lively and expert papers by 50 field and laboratory scientists from around the world is more or less a debate about a bold generalization: that the wave of extinctions of many large land animals and birds so conspicuous in the geologically recent past is the bloody work of man the hunter. The concept of Pleistocene overkill is not new, but it was put forward afresh by the senior editor, who had made it the basis of a similar volume of argument in 1967. The indictment is strong, although the true bill has its defects; the case is subtly shifting. There is no clear verdict yet; the jury remains hung.

The prosecution's case is put impressively in one typical graph that shows the sharp decline in the North American mammoth population. The relative number of elephants — all known sites are mapped and dated to form the estimate — suddenly declines from a long-occupied plateau to a tenth of that number between 13,000 and 11,000 years before the present. The North American population of *Homo sapiens* shows its first sharp rise at just that time.

The indictment is worldwide. In Africa the Plains of Serengeti are current demonstration of what a world of large browsers and grazers and their big predators must have been like, when not so long ago bison, elephant and lion alike roamed France and the Dakotas. But African game have had a long time to adapt to the primate hunters, to their fire, to their developing tricks and tools. Ten times as many genera of large mammals have vanished from the Americas within the past 15,000 years as have vanished from Africa in 100,000 years. The islands tell their own special tales: join to the moas the big lemurs and the elephant birds — the rocs — of Madagascar and the cow-size marsupial browsers of Australia, all gone once humans arrived, and the courtroom grows still. The first sudden coming of the hunters spelled extinction to the biggest of their game.

The defense is eloquent too. Are those dramatic census changes real? Is the dating right? Is the time coincidence truly causal? If it is, how can a few mammoth hunters' butchering sites match the moa hunters' ubiquitous boneyards? The prosecution reminds us that if the hunt were suddenly begun and soon over, a blitzkrieg, then the total take would be small and hard to find. It will not escape a thoughtful juror that here the prosecutor has neatly found a way around the absence of the surest evidence, the corpse itself.

The ecologists weigh in with their diverse evidence, counting pollen and beetle species, tracing drainage regions and floral associations, looking at how plants change (herbivores feed on them at the grass roots) as the lands drifted toward aridity while the glaciers dwindled. The genetics of populations is drawn on: extinction seems associated with dwarfism. What forces selected for smaller individuals and shorter gestation periods? Could it have been hunting pressure?

A set of exemplary sites are given very interesting, knowledgeable and lengthy treatment by authors who know them well. An overview of the famous mammoth remains of Siberia is the kernel of an authoritative Soviet contribution. Here are structures made of mammoth bones, all right, but there are even larger graveyards that were certainly accumulated by long natural alluvial processes. The La Brea tar pits on Wilshire Boulevard are reviewed, with the valuable reminder that the scene at that live-baited natural trap was not quite as dramatic as some people imagine. Enmirement of a single creature every few years was plenty in due time to fill the museum cases. Caves in the lower Grand Canyon were long home to the big browsing Shasta ground sloth. Its well-preserved dung has been studied for a reading of the menu, and now that glimpse of the climate by way of the desert flora has been elaborated by study of the fossil middens of pack rats in the same locality. The ground sloth disappeared at "a time . . . which should have been nearly ideal for its continued existence." Hunters? No sites show them.

A couple of up-to-date bestiaries add concreteness. There were noble beasts in those days: consider a European rhino with a single six-foot horn, or a massive African antlered giraffe, neck unelongated. The Australian zoo of the past is vividly illustrated. The biggest marsupial was a strange browser with a clumsy-looking development of the upper lip, perhaps an incipient trunk? It is not hard to extrapolate and envision the coming of a fine marsupial mammoth.

The experts from down under are not impressed by the case against the hunters. All we know of the economic system of the aboriginals does not provide for hunting large game. Nowhere in Australia does the archaeology yet support overkill, and it is not hard to spell out how a climate turning dry increases the space between water holes beyond tolerable distances. In a desert world, megafauna depend on free water; effectively adapted small mammals do not.

There are three distinct summations, all full of interest, and an opening excursion into the history of the idea. What makes a verdict particularly hard to reach is the plain fact that the hunters too form part of the same climate-sensitive fauna. They could emigrate to the Americas in the first place, by way of the transient land bridge of Beringia, only as the result of "a unique set of climatic events." "Do I detect a conspiracy?" asks one judge. The thick volume is uncommonly readable and varied for watchers of paleontology and the rise of humankind.

(February 1985)

Stones, Bones and Skin: Ritual and Shamanic Art
Edited by Anne Trueblood Brodzky, Rose Danesewich and Nick Johnson

A shaman, a woman of the Mapuche Indians of Chile, looks gravely out of the page at you, bearing a shallow drum. The drum she beats as she stands on the notched pole (at once the world tree and her own celestial ladder) is not new to us. It is the very form of the drum, celebrated in Enlightenment Europe, that the dashing and ambitious Carl von Linné — Linnaeus himself — held as he stood for his portrait in the full shaman's dress he brought back from a journey among the Lapps. In this real medicine bundle of a book, with crowded pages bearing many images and diverse text, and with gatefolds and color plates as well, the editors assemble for us almost 20 picture essays on the theme of the title.

Our cultural sensitivity to the shaman of the hunting peoples has reached unprecedented heights. We easily accede now to the proposition that the "shamanic system . . . can be said to be mankind's oldest religion," for the evidence is strong. Depicted in the painted cave of Les Trois Frères, a half-animal, half-human figure appears to charm the deer and the bison — themselves not far from human — who dance around him. His music comes from what appears to be a small bow held in the mouth. Just such a musical bow is shown here in the hands of the Huichol shaman Ramón Medina, and another mouth bow of bent white birch is shown from the instrument collection of the National Museum of Man in Ottawa. A shaman healer in Nepal is seen ritually sucking the evil out of a patient's body, exactly as his counterpart operates in the delta of the Orinoco. Mankind spread past the edge of the ice to all the Americas, and clearly the marginal Old World peoples who are closest to the hunting life still practice the ancient periglacial arts, which lie, below the surface and much enriched, more or less everywhere. That ancient art is a la mode today. Consider the abstract, evocative intensity of "stones, bones and skin," the numinous union of animal and human, the living flesh revealing the bone within, the hallucinogens, the vocation sickness, the use of ecstatic trance to heal, the spirit language, the priestly guardianship of the public weal and even the selfish exploitation of those dark powers.

In these pages we watch a long-evolved Kwakiutl dance with great creative masks, cannibal birds, wasps and the raven, in a fine multiple-flash photographic record. In one colorful gatefold we see a shaman's costume in loving detail. It is a Siberian costume (now in New York) collected by the sinologist Berthold Laufer from the Goldi along the Amur River in 1900. (Why we see no drum is not explained.) A special feature of the volume is a set of accounts and displays of contemporary art inspired by shamanism. Bill Reid, an artist whose mother was a Haida, has brilliantly transformed the motifs and vision of that culture into intricately worked gold, silver and wood, the forerunner of a renascence of Pacific Northwest art. The six little heads peering out between the clamshell valves at a sheltering Creator Raven illustrate the Haida Genesis: "'Whah! Come out!' whispered the Creator. . . . Then human faces appeared one by one, in a row." It is all carved into one vibrant clam-sized piece of boxwood.

The fictionalized account of the Yaqui shaman Don Juan became a popular prototype of mysteries in the past decade. Much more wonderful is the honest account, together with photographs, of the Huichol shaman given us here by the anthropologist Peter T. Furst of the State University of New York at Albany. We see Don Ramón in "spectacular, and very dangerous, rapid-fire leaps — flights might be more appropriate" — from one slippery boulder to another at the lip of a high waterfall. He said, "I took you there to show you what it means 'to have balance.' So you could see and understand about the shaman." We see and in part do understand; he is a real shaman, acting as a human being is given to act at the farthest reaches. Here is no demeaning hyperbolic fiction.

At Baker Lake the story is told: "When the moon rocket went to the moon and some of the young kids were trying to tell the old people about this, they were getting really frustrated because the old people were saying, 'Oh, that's nothing, my uncle went to the moon lots of times.'" Uncle belongs to the *Apollo* story, all right; in a way, he first urged us to go, but we should not expect that he brought back samples.

(November 1977)

Man the Hunter

*Edited by Richard B. Lee and Irven DeVore
with the assistance of Jill Nash*

Nomads of the Long Bow: The Siriono of Eastern Bolivia
By Allan R. Holmberg

Is man in a state of nature a noble, free and happy being, chained to no onerous social contract? Or is he doomed to a life that is solitary, poor, nasty, brutish and short? It is the measure of the power of science that what was a grand philosophical cleavage is now the subject of empirical test.

But is it? In actuality the issue joined in both of these books remains unresolved. Yet the importance of the question, and the subtlety of the answer, come out in two very different but fascinating ways.

The population of heaven and hell, the total count of all the men and women who have ever lived out their lives on the earth, numbers somewhat less than 100 billion. A large fraction of all the members of our genus have lived by hunting and gathering. Lee and DeVore say nine-tenths, although they appear to overestimate it. If we are ever to understand ourselves, we need to understand that way of life. We know well that our entire biological makeup is adapted to it; all men were hunters up to 10,000 years ago, when they ate of the fruit of agricultural knowledge. What we learn of ancient man from the archaeologist, from all those deftly chipped tools and vigorous paintings, we must seek to test among that .001 percent of our fellow-men who still live as hunters, although they are no longer hunters in a world of hunters.

The main instrument of the inquiry among living hunters (we can extend this notion to our older anthropological colleagues, since the time of Captain James Cook, not to say Aristotle) is ethnography. This is a serious record of the culture of a group of humans. At its best, it is made by a man who lived among them, who spoke their tongue, who held them as friends, who thought deeply of their life while it was his own and who described it clearly in a context of sensible comparisons and explanations. Ethnography does not always reach that level. Too often it is secondhand, won by talking to intermediaries, frequently men who know hunters more as an enemy than as a friend. Even in the best case we expect to learn a way of life through one man's experience, through one observer who cannot, after all, be astronomer and zoologist, economist and sociologist as he trudges naked through the forest.

It is clear that the personal ethnography — all we shall ever have for most hunting groups — is too frail to carry the heavy load of our knowledge of mankind and its way into the world. There is only a little time left for doing better. That is one of the main burdens of the Lee-DeVore book, which reports a symposium of 67 participants (mainly American, but with other countries well represented) who read papers concerned with all continents, presented along with such a vivid, germane and meaty discussion as to set a model for symposium reports.

The paperback *Nomads of the Long Bow* is in contrast a classical one-man ethnography, one of the best. It is particular, genuine and moving. Holmberg's premature death in 1966 gives a poignant quality to the warmth and openness of this little book. It is his own reworking of his doctoral thesis, first published in 1950, eight years after his seasons in the field. He characteristically thanks his skilled companion of the bush, Don Luis Silva Sánchez, in appropriately courtly phrase, and his hosts the Siriono, who "tolerated a naïve but inquisitive anthropologist."

The life of the Siriono is Hobbesian. Wandering through the dense, wet forests, they are often hungry. In the rainy season the land turns into one vast swamp; they choose a stretch of high ground and stay on it. They clear garden plots with fire and digging stick and raise some crops; only maize, which they said had been known to them for 50 years or so, ever produces enough for serious storage. They have no canoes to travel their stream-filled world, little art, one story about the great hero Moon, poor huts, no clothing, numbers up to three. "Fire-making is a lost art"; once they could make it with a twirled stick. In that moist forest the skill was lost, and instead fire is carried from camp to camp in a burning brand made of the spongy spadix of a palm. At least one woman in every traveling band carries the fire.

The Siriono make eight-foot bows—each man makes his own—out of a special palm wood planed with a shell. A man who is busy is either hunting or working on arrows. There is great freedom in the matter of sex, for both men and women, married and unmarried. The dreams of the Siriono, like most of their constant quarrels and wrangles, are about food and drink rather than sex. The children are loved (a photograph of a father watching his young son draw the great bow is the happiest in the book) but the old are held as the burden they are. The people abandon the ill or the infirm without a word of farewell. Old age comes soon.

Holmberg and Silva themselves lived from the forest, but their lives depended on their shotgun and rifle, insect netting and knife. The Indians at once coveted the tools, the machetes in particular. Holmberg later introduced a few implements, a shotgun and the domestic hen. They enriched the individuals who received them, and began to spread to their kinsmen. Some of these very people have by now shifted from the nomadic to a settled way of life based on agriculture. "I am frequently disturbed," writes Holmberg, "by the fact that I had a hand in initiating some of the changes . . . over which neither I nor they had control. . . . Maybe they should have been left as they were."

Holmberg spent his remaining years as a conscious innovator. He bent his anthropology to the service of the people whose ways he studied, notably in the decade among his friends in the village of Vicos in the

Peruvian altiplano. They had been unable to free themselves from the peonage of centuries; today they live as hopeful men and women on their own lands. Their opportunity is also Holmberg's legacy.

The Lee-DeVore symposium, which is of course far wider in scope than any single ethnography, turns on the economics, demography and cultural patterns of hunters. The "devolved" Siriono are not even pure hunters and gatherers, of course. The wandering desert Bushmen, who have no gardens at all, make out contrastingly well. Their calorie intake is by actual count sufficient; they do not press their children to hunt food, nor do they dispose of unproductive oldsters. In one intimate ethnography they are called "the harmless people." They work an average 15-hour week gaining a living (plainly the envy of their hardworking Harvard observers!). This figure held true even during the third year of a severe regional drought.

The main economic basis for this inventory-free affluence appears to be the mongongo nut—abundant, reliable, drought-resistant, nutritious and good to eat even after lying a year on the ground. A Bushman, asked why he did not farm, reasonably answered: "Why should we plant when there are so many mongongo nuts in the world?" By and large hunters do not care for the morrow; they prodigally eat all there is on hand; they sleep a lot. Is that the "confidence born of affluence" or is it the lack of responsibility to their fellows of men who live by an intense individualism? Must we hold with Hobbes or with Rousseau? The answer is mumbled and incomplete, but it seems most unlikely to be unified.

Man is a plastic creature, as he is a powerful one. Only man can swim a mile, walk 20 miles and then climb a tree. There are Indians who can run down horse and deer, the runner making full use both of his physical superiority and of his mental one, in his knowledge of the prey and his planning for a coming day of rest. Professor William S. Laughlin has put it well: man the hunter domesticated only one species, but that was the vital one—himself. Natural selection made the hunter. The inventory he then made for himself was mainly informational; it was stocked in his speech, his pedagogy, his organizing, his skills. We cannot easily recover those things, at least not as easily as we dig up pots or expose the walls of Troy. Yet they lie everywhere, enciphered in the materials of the past, or in our old tales of the earth and the moon, or in the structures of speech and thought that still hold sway among men, a treasure trove too subtle for the spade.

(October 1969)

First Contact

By Bob Connolly and Robin Anderson

The mountains of New Guinea stretch nearly east and west for about 1,000 miles, the roof ridge of that great equatorial island. Their highest peaks outtop the Alps or the Sierras. Monsoon-drenched and malarial, all dense forests and tall grass, wide coastal lowlands border the entire central ridge. Even empire came late and thin to New Guinea: it is reported that 100 years ago not a single European lived north of the ridge on mainland Papua, the island's eastern half, an area twice the size of Florida. Colonial rule extended a few tens of miles in from the sea, since the people lived near the coasts, perhaps a million of them after World War I in all Papua, village farmers and fishermen. To planters, labor recruiters, missionaries, traders and officials they were hands, souls and customers. A few hundred such colonial outsiders were resident when for vaguely strategic reasons Australia took over the old British and German rule over Papua and the Territory of New Guinea. (The western half of the island is now part of Indonesia and is not treated here.)

Two large river valleys drain the interior. The Fly River flows a couple of hundred miles south to the sea and the Sepik flows north. Each rises far inland on wild, fog-shrouded mountain slopes. Along the wide valleys there is a diverse set of cultures, the population thinning out toward the steep foothills. There was an easy interpolation: out there on the high, narrow ridge between the slopes could be found only sparse nomadic mountain bands. They would be the highland people who traditionally had taken, through indirect trade from hand to hand, the cowries and the showy gilt-edged pearl shell gathered on the coasts, paying with plumage and bird skins. The best maps left a blank space as big as Scotland across the Papuan highlands, which were thought surely to be wild, rugged and empty. But then, in 1926, stream-borne gold was found near the northern coast of the island.

In May of 1930 two bold young Australian prospectors, Michael Leahy and Michael Dwyer, with 15 coastal men hired as carriers, six of them armed and licensed *gunbois*, climbed into the Bismarck Range, bound for the first of a set of short trips upriver seeking new placers. They started at a tiny foothills settlement the Lutheran missionaries had set up at the northern edge of the blank space. In one day's hard climb they had reached the lip of the mountain; before them spread a startling vista, a grassy plain, one of the few long plateau valleys that part the twin mountain ridges of the interior. By nightfall their wonder had turned to alarm: as far as they could see the stream-laced valley was filled with the pinpoint light of fires.

At sunrise the villagers came to meet them — men armed with bows and arrows and women offering sugarcane. Followed by crowds, touching and hugging, sharing the sweet cane, the travelers walked past endless hedged gardens with their long rows of beans, cane and sweet potatoes, while fat pigs wandered freely everywhere.

From time to time the smiling, excited people would drop away with tense warning gestures. Soon there would assemble a new emotional crowd: the strangers had entered a distinct but similar neighboring territory. After a week they reached a high vista and looked out to the horizon. An early photograph shows the wider scene: a grove of trees surrounds a ceremonial clearing amidst a dozen or two log huts adjoining large, neat gardens; within a mile in any direction there is another grove, another cluster . . . Thousands of enclaves, splintered into bands of friends and enemies, politically divided by language and by ancient ritual wars, spread over the fertile lands. There were no metals (a few steel knives and axes from trade), no malaria, no woven textiles, no beasts of burden, no chiefdoms; instead the competitive feasting displays of the hardworking and charismatic "big men." The populous highlands had at last been united with the rest of our species.

Mike Leahy was robust, inspired, brilliant, even though he never finished secondary school. His extraordinary story is not a new one; he published his account after six years of contact with the highlanders. That contact was as intimate as the begetting of his three sons by Mount Hagen women, as ruthless as his Mauser rifle (which, along with the shorter-range muskets of his *gunbois*, killed perhaps 40 of the people in swift encounters that met tragic misunderstanding with an old colonial ruthlessness), as fascinating as the 5,000 candid shots he took with his Leica, as novel as the light aircraft he talked the mining company into dispatching to link forever the million highlanders with the outside world they had never known.

It is a new story that is the core of this absorbing book by two Sydney filmmakers turned ethnographers. They present the testimony from the other side. In the early 1980's the authors followed Leahy's carefully recorded itineraries to seek out men and women who recalled the times of first contact, when tens of thousands of people first saw the outsiders. Some 60 interviews in eight highland languages are the ore they worked. They also present images made by Leahy and others, including a picture of Mike's influential and wealthy son Clem, shown with his mother in 1983, and two Leica shots of that same woman when, five decades earlier, she had both smiled and frowned at Mike Leahy in all her youthful beauty.

Concede that recollections told 50 years late are suspect; that cannot be helped. Moreover, these informants recall the most astonishing perception of their lives with utter clarity. Remembering just what they were doing at the time, these old people look around carefully to spot and point out "the boy or girl whose age they were when news first arrived."

The ancestors of the million people of the highlands have lived there for a time so long that it passes for always; archaeological dating puts some of the gardens at 9,000 years old. Thoughtful people knew there were other places, for they prized greatly the shells they gained by trade, exotic objects of enigmatic beauty. (The ocean itself was unguessed at; salt was a costly stuff.) Some, in places where the view was bounded by ridges, knew only that on the next ridge there were enemies: "We couldn't go past them." Others with a wider view of eye and mind "used to see smoke in the distance . . . I wonder who that is. I'd like to meet those people one day."

When the new men came, they were neither allies nor enemies. The cosmology had room for nothing besides, except spirits. The white men were just the color expected of those from the place of the dead, "our dead people, come back!" Even an Australian could be seen as a dead father by a bereaved young person and be taken before the uncles to be looked at straight in the eye for confirmation. The coastal men who were serving as carriers looked familiar enough, even if they could speak only gibberish: those men were often tearfully made out to be the familiar dead. "I saw half his finger missing, and I recognized him as my dead cousin . . . the very same man. His facial expression, the way he talked, laughed — exactly the same."

Perhaps they all turned into skeletons in sleep, befitting their spirit nature. In one place two heroic warriors are recalled by name as those who dared to enter the sleeping camp to peep into the tents. Elsewhere that story faded away slowly. Did all that wrapping mean they did not need to rid themselves of wastes? It did not: one man hid to watch them at the latrine pit. The smell was unifying. Was that loosely folded skin or a costume? Did those clothes-covered bodies mean they had something to hide, perhaps the giant penises of spirit myth? That was not true either, as watching the bathers soon proved. Were their women hidden, packed in the baggage? The prospectors spent much time panning stream gravel; the people long before had themselves regularly burned the bones of the dead and disposed of the ashes in the rivers. Were the strangers perhaps seeking their own old bones?

Above all, the newcomers had with them a partly decipherable but rich inventory. At first their goods were mainly magic: the lid of a tin can might become a precious talisman, or a discarded matchstick might be found and eaten for its unknown powers. Soon the loaded airplanes arrived (the first airstrip was prepared by late 1932), coming down among throngs swept by sudden terror as the daunting noise approached. Yet the thundering craft seemed always to be friendly; they "came with things — trade goods, axes, shells, to name just a few. Heaps of them! Then we said, 'These men must be men-of-all-things.'"

Fifty years have gone by. Many highlanders have themselves gone to view the salt sea. Papua New Guinea is a nation; the highlands grow coffee at profit, and now they know colleges and police barracks, movies and beer gardens, hospitals that admit both for arrow wounds and for heart attacks. The roar of heavy diesels rolling down dirt roads has also become familiar. The big men still aspire, but their lovely pearl shells, steadily inflated by air cargo from dazzling rarity into cloying excess, have lost their prestigious appeal; the profligate displays the big men now organize center around tusked pigs, motorcars and cold cash.

(October 1987)

Catal Hüyük: A Neolithic Town in Anatolia
By James Mellaart

There is something golden about our best archaeologists today. They inherit so strong a method and tradition, they find such remarkable objects, they write so brilliantly of such fascinating problems, they bring out so many books so well illustrated with photographs and reconstruction drawings, so personal and yet so clear in argument and so sound in substance, that other scientists cannot rival them. Here is such a book.

Three or four years of digging into the high 30-acre mound on the open wheatlands of the dry Anatolian plateau, carried out by an expedition from the University of London under the author's leadership, are the source of this work. The mound is an ancient town site, already 3,000 or 4,000 years old, by secure radiocarbon dating, when Ur of the Chaldees was founded. The people lived not only by the cultivation of wheat and barley but also by the taking of big game, the red deer and the aurochs with its great spreading horns. They knew pottery and weaving, even in the oldest levels yet reached; they smelted beads and trinkets of lead and perhaps of copper; they worked and polished stone and bone with high art; they maintained a complex terraced pattern of mud brick and frame construction, which remained stable sometimes over a millennium. They had no writing or accounts.

Only a small part of the town has been uncovered. Of the 139 rooms found, perhaps 40 were decorated with wall paintings, plaster reliefs, human skulls and horns of the great wild ox set in rows along walls or benches. Mellaart feels he has opened the religious quarter of the town and that most of these large and splendid rooms were devoted to a cult. What a cult! There are painted on the wall great black vultures attacking tiny headless humans. There are plaster heads of bulls, surmounted with real horn cores, in rows and sets, defining courtyards surmounted by the modeled figure of a goddess, flanked by still more bulls, who is giving

birth to a ram. The surfaces are painted, whitened, repainted and replas-
tered, with scores of layers of painting. The ritual function had to be
stopped and restarted many times. There are a few human skulls, and in
one pit the bones of a premature infant, offered to the goddess. The dead
were exposed to vultures, their bones stripped of the flesh and the skeletons buried in the platforms of houses and shrines.

We are offered a brilliant conjecture on the nature of this awesome
and barbaric ancient religion; the argument is based on the absence of any
overt reference to sexuality in the symbolism. Sexual organs are never
shown; breasts and pregnancy, horns and horned heads take their place.
Mellaart believes this shows that the religion was the creation of the
women, who became associated with the fertility of fields and of flocks,
with the idea of increase itself, "as the only source of life." Man appears
"as boy and as paramour," but the heads of the cult, its great deities and
their devotees, were women.

There is a decade of work ahead at this site. It shows man changing
from gatherer to farmer in that time of the greatest change men have yet
survived. One can only wait with fascinated expectation for what will be
found in the rest of that strange old town in sight of the snow-capped
volcanoes of eastern Anatolia.

(February 1968)

Aleuts: Survivors of the Bering Land Bridge
By William S. Laughlin

Professor Laughlin is plainly and
justly proud of the fact that the native village of Nikolski awarded him a
small "piece of land on which to build a home." It was as a graduate
student with the noted physical anthropologist Aleš Hrdlička that Laughlin first made his way to the windswept, treeless Aleutians. There he has
worked on and off ever since, living among their people, the Aleuts. In
1974 he shared the work and the excitement of excavation by a joint
Russian-American field party. This primer of Aleut life and its well-established lengthy history is one of a long series of brief case studies for
students of anthropology. Laughlin's study is "more than an interdisciplinary *tour de force.*" It reports, although very concisely, on the Aleuts as
a whole, from the high incidence of three-rooted first molars to the Aleut
semaphore signals invented by a few men before World War I (based on
the Cyrillic-derived alphabet the Aleuts have used for a century and a half)

and on to the Honda and walkie-talkie of today's Nikolski boatmen and hunters.

If that small house of Professor Laughlin's is ever finished, one will look from it out to the snowy flanks of the high volcanic cones across the bay, past a mile-long high island, transformed in August by a dense stand of deep-blue monkshood, loud with the bumblebee. On that island the excavators found acres of a stone-blade-working site, with a total inventory of some three million worked tools and cores, largely of obsidian. Dozens of fire hearths in the layered dig provided charcoal for the carbon-14 laboratories. The sequence is well dated and remarkable. People worked blades there 9,000 years ago. For 2,000 years the blade style remained unchanged: the tools were prismatic, blades and burins struck from a core of obsidian. The edges were very sharp but were flaked on one surface only. After that time both surfaces were worked, and bifaced tools show up along with stone lamps, dishes and grinding stones.

A couple of dozen house pits adjoin the blade site on higher ground They represent a transitional culture, which can be followed for 2,000 years more. The same objects reappear on the Nikolski shore, in an oval green mound just south of the present village. That mound is the midden of Chaluka. Within this century it still had some residents; now they have all moved down to the flatter ground adjoining to the north. The midden is an ancient village; 4,000 years more can be traced in the debris, including the buttons and rings and skeletal remains of an identifiable Russian party, massacred in thriving old Chaluka in the spring of 1764. The continuous occupation of the shores of Nikolski Bay by the Aleuts is thus witnessed by their own bones, their particular artifacts slowly changing in style, the circumstantial stories of their tradition. Theirs is a freehold without a break over nine millenniums, the settlements moving as the sea level changed.

Why should Nikolski, apparently only one island a couple of hundred miles out along the chain from the long mainland finger of the Alaska Peninsula, be such a key site? The casual map reader overlooks the work of time. When the old Aleuts came to Nikolski, it was at the point of the mainland. Perhaps a narrow seawater channel or two, or a couple of glacier tongues, made the outward trip something less than dryshod. But Samalga Pass, the arm of the ocean that flows past the headland a few miles south of Nikolski, is the first permanent deep-ocean pass out along the line of islands. It was there that the Aleuts ended their passage along the shores of the Bering Sea, when the sea level was 100 meters lower than it is today, the great ice sheet holding the waters.

These people turned seaward along the peninsula as they came south down the coast; the Eskimo peoples instead diverged northward to follow the Arctic coast, in the end all the way to Greenland. The Samalga Pass channeled the marine life of the entire Bering Sea past the Aleut hunters, and the exposed reefs provided a sea-plenty; indeed, the permanent up-welling in the pass enriches the local fauna. The Aleuts have long used octopuses, sea urchins, shellfish and seaweed, and the lakes and freshwater streams of the islands have yielded up salmon for a long time. Aleut culture adapted to the marine wealth; less than 5 percent of their diet came from plants, although shorebirds and their eggs were an important contribution of dry land. Here the Aleut culture centered; it slowly spread both ways, out to the lonelier islands westward, and eastward back toward Alaska.

The Aleuts are superb kayak hunters of the open sea, able to take the wary sea otter regularly even during foul weather, taking the abundant whales with a somewhat greater dependence on good fortune. They knew they were "better than anyone else" at kayak hunting. Their kayaks are distinct; the designs show a specialized variety, a three-hatch model becoming the standard transport of the clerics and the watchful administrators during Russian colonial rule. The Aleuts had a monopoly on sea-otter hunting; outsiders have never learned well enough. The historical experience of the Aleuts can be evoked by noting that over the years Aleuts have been sent to display their kayak skills both on the River Neva in St. Petersburg and in a pond at the St. Louis World's Fair.

These people are admirable, and Professor Laughlin admires them. They have a traditional school for boys, to teach kayak hunting. Its curriculum includes specific exercises, such as controlled finger hanging, arm twisting and other carefully constructed schemes to prepare the muscles for the demands of the kayak and the spear-throwing board. There were recognized Strong Men, with a lifelong regime of special training, thought to lead to premature death at the price of their great power, which was both physical and spiritual. One such man broke a hand-grip dynamometer in 1910 by too hard a squeeze. Another led the uprising against the Russian party at Nikolski. They know human anatomy well, and they conduct human autopsy along with comparative anatomy in dissecting sea mammals. Their language holds a specific anatomical vocabulary, well beyond common practice in English. The Aleuts used such skills in the frequent preparation of mummies of some of their dead, stored in caves with the tools of the hunt, the relics magically consulted and employed. The Aleut midwives could skillfully cope with breech delivery; they knew how to secure the afterbirth if it did not come naturally. The Aleut healers used acupuncture, bloodletting, massage, even sutures in surgery. The Aleut primary counting words went easily to five powers of 10. The Aleuts enjoy and elaborate word games and wordplay; storytelling was the great art.

They knew warfare and even slave raids for women and children, but these episodes were never on a large scale. There is an old suit of rod armor from a mummy cave, vertical wood rods held by sinew. The

Russian fur traders encountered the Aleuts in war, guns against stone weapons, until they crushed Aleut resistance after a major uprising in the 1760's. The Aleut population was sharply reduced from its peak of some 16,000 by a third or more within a decade or two. The Aleuts have not yet recovered; their well-attested longevity, known from the data yielded by their graves, is only now reappearing, more than a century after Seward's purchase. Before the Honda they had taken up Russian steam baths, the Russian Orthodox Church and literacy, all with enthusiasm. The enthusiasms remain strong, but now the people are learning to look to Washington and its processes as carefully as they watch the sea. "With their demonstrated skill in human adaptability, they may survive another 9,000 years," to see their lands once again extend as the ice cap grows.

(August 1981)

On Ancient Central-Asian Tracks
By Sir Aurel Stein

The Great Chinese Travelers
An anthology edited and introduced by Jeannette Mirsky

The Exhibition of Archaeological Finds of the People's Republic of China
An illustrated handlist

The Exhibition of Archaeological Finds of the People's Republic of China
Text by the Organization Committee of the Exhibition of Archaeological Finds of the People's Republic of China

In 1906 the little column started out for the lonely ruins in the waterless desert. Every available camel was loaded with 400 or 500 handy pounds of the chief necessity: ice (to provide water). Surprises such as ice-cold deserts abound in this charming, modest, somehow serene account of three remarkable expeditions to "innermost Asia" by a scholar-traveler, Sir Aurel Stein of the Indian Educational Service, during the Edwardian years. His book, first published in 1933, complements with a personal narrative his dozen heavy folio reports. He was a tireless "little gnome of a man," a superb Orientalist who knew Sanskrit, colloquial Turki, Early Iranian and much more. He walked and rode 25,000 insistent miles with a few Indian companions (a surveyor, a cook and a handyman), a couple of Turki camel-caravan specialists, a Chinese scholar-secretary ("for a serious study of Chinese . . . I regret I never had had needful leisure") and shifting bands of diggers he recruited locally when he needed them.

The main theater of these travels was the Tarim basin tucked north of the mountains fringing the high Tibetan plateau, south of the Tien Shan mountains and west of the snowy Pamirs, where the passes lie at 15,000 feet. Eastward is the outermost section of the Great Wall of China, a flanking portion built in Han times and first excavated on Stein's third trip. The central desert of this basin, the size and shape of California, is still uninhabited; it is perhaps the most barren region of such size in the world, with only one narrow transverse band holding a scant oasis population. Flanking the desert north and south, however, living wherever the snow-fed rivers come down from the mountain frontiers to sink into the rainless plain, a few million oasis dwellers grow grain and fruit under irrigation, and even cotton and grapevines in the lower altitudes, which fall to 500 feet below sea level in hot, arid, fertile Turfan.

Along this chain of oases Chinese travelers to the West have passed for two millenniums. The diplomat Chang Ch'ien, who visited the Huns in the second century B.C. and brought back news of their fine horses (and perhaps the first wine grapes), and the monk Hsüan-tsang, who in the seventh century of our era traveled to India to secure Sanskrit texts then known only in part to Chinese Buddhists, are two of the most famous. Stein studied the accounts of Hsüan-tsang and proclaimed his devotion to that "prince of pilgrims," whose footsteps he followed from India across mountain and desert. Marco Polo came too, and his account is also verifiable: the split track of the Old Silk Road, passing by the desert in the north and the south alike, is rich with the evidence of use.

Stein reclaimed from the dry, preserving sands (the glacier-fed streams have gradually dwindled over the centuries, so that not far beyond the present limits of irrigation there lie many abandoned and drifted-over settlements) many fascinating documents and a rich pictorial treasure of scroll painting and fresco. Here he found the oldest samples of paper known, made from hemp textiles reduced to pulp exactly as the old Chinese texts described paper on its invention in A.D. 105. Eight folded letters in a watch post along the oldest segment of the Great Wall were what he recovered. They were written in a novel script in Early Sogdian, an Iranian language, by Central Asian traders. All around lay Chinese military documents, wood tablets and thin slips of wood "stationery" to which "Chinese conservatism clung."

This region is a high crossroads of the Old World. A single shrine has painted panels with the clear "impress of Hellenistic style" depicting the

Chinese princess who first took contraband silkworm eggs out of China. A single document bears two seals side by side, one in Chinese lapidary characters and the other a "portrait head unmistakably cut after Western models."

The old seabed around Lop Nor at the eastern end of the basin, a terrain terrible with hard salt crust in big slanted cakes and pressure ridges, showed Stein a "straight wide track" worn by centuries of the passage of pack animals and probably even carts. Square-holed Han coins and government-issue bronze infantry arrowheads still lay on the salt surface. The find records the sizable traffic maintained for centuries by the Chinese across 120 miles of utterly barren ground for logistical and civil purposes, "an achievement fraught with momentous results for the exchange of civilizations."

When Sir Aurel traveled, the Chinese homeland was disunited and weak. His most famous disclosure to the world, 500 cubic feet of scrolls packed in the treasure recess of a chapel at the cave shrine of the Thousand Buddhas, was a scholar's library find more than it was an archaeologist's: the place was a living cult center, staffed by monks and thronged by pilgrims even though it was far from—and forgotten by—the officials and scholars of distant, preoccupied Peking. No longer, for China is now united and notably conscious of such things. "Let the past serve the present" is the watchword of Chinese archaeologists, who are busy now in the Sinkiang-Uigur Autonomous Region as they are over all China.

The catalogue of the Chinese Exhibition displays, among the yield of a hundred far-flung sites, a few recent finds from along the Old Silk Road. Here are damasks and twills of silk and wool excavated in Turfan and in Min-Feng, a site (Niya) first dug by Stein. There are even two dumplings, or *chiaotzu*; they are still available at your nearest northern-style Chinese restaurant, but these were prepared in the eighth or ninth century. (Stein reported similar grave goods, elaborate pastries preserved by the dryness of the climate.) The wonderfully lively little bronze horse on the front cover of the catalogue of this fine exhibition—the Flying Horse of Kansu —celebrates the "celestial horse," the tall Western strain introduced along the Silk Road about 100 B.C. to supplant the stocky, woolly horses traditional in China. It was unearthed at Wuwei, an interior town on the Silk Road.

These are three complementary books. The Stein work is an accessible paperbound presentation to a new generation of a masterwork, a fascinating volume whether read as travel, as archaeology or as autobiography. The companion anthology supplies an indispensable background to Stein and to Sinkiang (not to overlook the revealing pieces on 15th-century sea voyages to Africa or by the 19th-century Chinese travelers to our Western lands), but it is harder to read by a good deal. The variety of styles, and the antique quality of some of the reports and the stiltedness of others, do not ease the reader's path. The maps in both of these books are adequate but the recent atlas of the People's Republic of China (reviewed here in January, 1973) gives welcome aid. The exhibition catalogue provides a good pictorial introduction to the abundant legacy of ancient China, although it is only a start. It is more heartening, because these objects represent finds of the 25 years of the People's Republic, only a little of all to come: the "rich store" of the hard work of "the forefathers of the Chinese people."

(March 1975)

Great Zimbabwe
By P. S. Garlake

A couple of hundred miles inland in southern Africa lies the watershed plateau between the Limpopo and the Zambesi rivers, "cool, well-watered, gently rolling," free from the tsetse fly, its fertile open woodlands dotted with spreading acacias. The bones of the land are granite hills, pocketed here and there with the metamorphic rocks that yield gold ores to the miner today as they did millenniums ago. Near one edge of the plateau, where streams gather to flow seaward across the low, fly-ridden grassy plains, lies Great Zimbabwe.

The ruin occupies a dual site. The Hill Ruin displays one set of high walls. On the edge of a cliff half a mile away across the valley is the Great Enclosure, a masonry wall surrounding an ellipse some 800 by 300 feet, "by far the largest single prehistoric structure in sub-Saharan Africa." More than half of all the stonework at Great Zimbabwe is in this wall, which attains a height of 32 feet and a thickness of 17 feet. Within the Outer Wall and around the site are scattered a complex of lesser walls and platforms and one striking, completely solid conical tower. All the stonework is dry-wall masonry, well-laid or roughly laid courses of local granite blocks. The rock exfoliates everywhere on the smooth-domed granite hills that dominate the site, and thin slabs peel off and slide down slopes to collect as scree. There they can be cracked and taken away. Natural fracture planes give all the broken pieces a quite regular shape: cuboids, with even a standard thickness, that lend themselves to construction "based on more or less regular horizontal layers of stone." So was Great Zimbabwe built (the word probably means "venerated houses" in Shona), and so also were built 150 or 200 smaller and cruder ruins dotted over the high granite country. No sockets, beams or posts are found; apparently the stone walls never bore roofing. The walls are all curved, and they meander smoothly over the plan. The entire courtyard was once paved with the common indigenous building material called *daga*: a puddled, clayey soil binding gravel. Pits outside the walls show where the clay came from. *Daga* plastered the walls up to seven feet, and all the dwellings within were round huts of *daga* joined by abutting walls of stone. The walls are freestanding now and often one end of a wall is a finished doorway and the other end a jumble of collapsed stone, senseless once its abutting hut was washed away. The walls do resemble brickwork, but the resemblance is wholly superficial. There is no evidence of familiarity with brick bonding; these walls are never bonded, whether to break vertical joints, to link the two faces of rubble-filled sections or to join walls at a corner. Indeed, there are no angular corners.

The spade has not found very much more. Huge middens are present on every slope. Spindle whorls, shards, iron hoes and similar domestic artifacts of the Iron Age are abundant. Metalworking in copper, bronze, gold and iron was practiced. Radiocarbon dates are few; rock is not to be dated. The oldest timbers found are durable poles that have been dated to the seventh century. Garlake holds that these samples, cut from trees that live for 500 years, provide only the upper limit to the age of the structures: they might well have been taken from earlier structures on the sites and reused many times. Like all sites, Great Zimbabwe evolved; the few radiocarbon dates relevant to the footings of the great stone walls date from the 11th to the 15th centuries. A unique trade-goods cache, found buried in soil in an enclosure a few hundred feet from the Great Wall, can be dated more securely than anything else at Great Zimbabwe because it held Chinese celadon stoneware and an inscribed Persian bowl. The bowl was made in the 13th or 14th century. This hoard makes it plain that Great Zimbabwe then had far-flung trading contacts, the intermediaries being the Swahili coastal cities that flourished in those times. There is not much else, save for the remarkable and famous figurative carvings of soapstone (mostly removed), to add to the ordinary domestic goods. Those walls never enclosed a busy trading emporium; the very richness of the single hoard is evidence that a true center of trade would yield more. The celadon shards from China never give way to porcelain at this site in spite of the fact that in every trading post of the Portuguese, and in a number of other later ruins, the blue-and-white porcelain of the Ming is prominent. Great Zimbabwe was somehow preeminent when celadon came to the African coast but was in decline by the time the factories of the Ming sent porcelain, which was certainly by the late 15th century.

The enclosures were not mainly military, although they are protective. They have no slits or embrasures, even though the weapons of war in this land were arrow and spear. Walls do not defend other walls; nothing of the planned fortress is present. These structures were built and inhabited as a palace between A.D. 1000 and 1500 by a native people. They were built for "size and imposing grandeur, the product of two or three centuries of development of an indigenous stonebuilding technique, itself rooted in long traditions of using stone for field walls, building platforms and terraces." A small oligarchy—a royal and ecclesiastical court with sway over many vassals, if you will—grew out of an Iron Age subsistence economy, its growth based on political control of a vast region of gold and copper mining. The leaders dwelled there with a couple of thousand craftsmen, farmers and laborers to support the court. (Building the Outer Wall is estimated to have required 400 laborers working 50 days a year for four years.) The oligarchy's rule spread north and west over the plateau until, after some local decline in resources, the very strength of the wider society led the court to depart from Great Zimbabwe; the rulers moved north a couple of hundred miles into Matabeleland. Their new lands had no granite, so that all building in granite ceased. Tradition says that the old capital had "a severe shortage of salt"; we can read this as literally or as figuratively as we wish. Great Zimbabwe still stood, stripped of wealth and power; it remained for a while a provincial residence perhaps, and finally it became a religious monument of the old times.

When Carl Mauch, a young geologist, reached Great Zimbabwe in 1871, it was deserted and overgrown; the newly arrived people living there were led by an unimportant Karanga chief whose predecessor had taken the area away from the local people and turned the buildings into corrals. So was finally broken a tradition of sanctity that can probably be traced back 800 or 900 years. Mauch met a man of the ejected people whose father, a priest of Great Zimbabwe, had come every few years to sacrifice at the ruins. The last known sacrifice was in 1904. The structure remains, "a proud part of the Karanga and Shona past."

All of this describes only in part an enriching book by a Rhodesian trained in architecture and archaeology. Much of the careful, clear and handsome volume (there are many splendid photographs in color and in black and white), with a brief introduction by Sir Mortimer Wheeler, deals perforce with archaeology as a political battlefield. The early Portuguese never visited the site, but they spoke with Swahili traders who apparently had seen it. It was then within the Karanga kingdom of the Mwene Mutapa, ruling from the north, who held fief over the gold and the trading routes that had brought the Portuguese, as they had the Swahili before them. Since the Karange had no buildings of stone, the Portuguese ascribed the storied places to Prester John, to Solomon or to the Queen of Sheba. These are all folk figures in Islam. The "aged Moors" cited in 1609 by one Portuguese missionary suggested such an origin: "the factory of Solomon." When Cecil Rhodes and his colonizing British South Africa Company came, they seized with delight on such theories; to admit the local origin of Great Zimbabwe would fault their claims to a land they insisted had been settled no earlier by the Bantu than by the Europeans. In 1891, within a year of occupation by the company, it engaged the antiquarian J. Theodore Bent, a man who had studied the origin of the Phoenicians but who was without formal archaeological training or experience, to study the site. It was his vivid and uncontrolled imagination that first related Great Zimbabwe to a Sabaean temple in Marib in Yemen. This structure dates from the seventh century B.C.; it has an elliptical dry-wall enclosure of about the same size and shape as that of Great Zimbabwe. "However, all comparisons end there." Its blocks are limestone, carefully cut and pecked, the faces linked with cross walls, the entire structure joined to a rectangular building that was pillared and roofed, inscribed and linear in decoration: "products of a tradition and technology quite unlike those of Great Zimbabwe." Bent and his successors stripped the ruins "in an obsessive search for the exotic." In 1895 the company granted a firm the right to dig for gold in all ruins, Great Zimbabwe excepted ("at Mr. Rhodes' express desire"). After a few years public reaction to this greedy and foolish enterprise brought it to a half and a journalist, Richard N. Hall, wrote a book from the gold seekers' data that sought to build a coherent framework. Hall was made curator of Great Zimbabwe but himself stripped the ruins there lamentably, removing, as he said, "the filth and decadence of the Kaffir occupation." Outsiders complained again: "field work . . . worse than anything I have ever seen," wrote David Randall-MacIver after Hall was dismissed and MacIver was invited to investigate. He was a student and colleague of Flinders Petrie's and his skilled and honest, although hasty, work established that Great Zimbabwe was without alien influence. The opinion of the settlers has ever since been polarized against overseas experts. Gertrude Caton-Thompson followed MacIver around 1930, a generation later. She sought incontrovertible dating and carried out a model study. (Her team, by the way, was composed of women archaeologists; it is possible to see there the first excavation, made in her student years, by Kathleen Kenyon, who was later the famous excavator of ancient Jericho.) She too found almost no exotic objects, no easy dates. The Rhodesians Keith R. Robinson and R. F. H. Summers worked at the site in the late 1950's and early 1960's, and it was they who secured the radiocarbon dates (still rather vague) that are the foundations of the modern interpretation.

Garlake became Senior Inspector of Monuments in Rhodesia in 1964; he studied the digs, particularly the lesser sites, until 1970. Now he is at the University of Ife in Nigeria, and in secessionist Salisbury today "the Rhodesian museums no longer employ an archaeologist." Instead the official censor is at work. In the new guidebook "all theories relating to Zimbabwe will be presented absolutely impartially" and there will be no more search for unsettling evidence. It is distressing that in October, 1973, a national weekly in the U.S. published a piece lending strong endorsement to the most recent ascription of Sabean origins to the walls at Great Zimbabwe. But truth is more enduring than granite; it seems to beckon the reader from even a single aerial photograph of the ruins, where, as Garlake writes, stone wall and natural boulder are so interdependent on the ground that "each seems almost a natural outgrowth and extension of the other." That organic way of building with cracked granite scree surely evolved among a people long accustomed to and wholly familiar with the gray granite of their own hills, not among alien brickmakers from a far continent. One may hope that before too long archaeologists and freedom alike will return to the land of Zimbabwe.

(January 1974)

Monuments of the Incas
Text by John Hemming
Photographs by Edward Ranney
A New York Graphic Society Book

The joint effort of an American photographer and an English author, this extremely attractive volume transcends the merely showy to offer an honestly comprehensive if elegant photographic documentation of Tawantinsuyu, the empire built by the Incas within less than a century. What is left of its monuments lies beautiful and enigmatic before the lens, against the snowy peaks of the Andes along a sweeping arc from broad Lake Titicaca north to equatorial Quito. There are plenty of books about that empire conquered near its zenith, and images of its remains are commonplace, but Ranney had done more than any other photographer to show the works of the Incas as they are set into the numinous mountain landscapes that somehow called forth those superb forms in stone.

The first chapter of 15 sketches Inca history and presents an overview of Inca architecture, drawing explicitly on the admirable recent monograph of Graziano Gasparini and Luise Margolies, reviewed here (in translation) in March, 1981. Then the chapters treat, one after another, the famous localities more or less as they might be visited by a lucky traveler heading north from the Island of the Sun all the way to Ingapirca, the only surviving Inca ruin in Ecuador. About two-thirds of the book is devoted to the central region around Cuzco, that mountain capital planned in the form of a puma, here studied from Raqchi north to Vilcabamba. The illustrations are evocative and knowing, no less for a key carved detail than for a vista of meadow and peak. The text is sensitive and well documented; telling citations from the old chroniclers jostle the archaeological reports and the travelers' traditions. Hemming makes good use of the indispensable work of contemporary Peruvian scholarship; the footnotes are full and the bibliography is a find for serious beginners.

An armchair reader, envious of the fortunate who will visit the sites with this book behind them as a kind of hyperguide, found on page after page remarks and particularly scenes that escape notice in many a worthwhile book on the Inca world. The snow-covered peaks grandly tower over the rolling meadows of Soccllacasa pass, "near the rock shrines of Saihuite." There two rocks lie along in the high open rangeland, about 100 miles toward the sea from Cuzco. The principal stone of the pair "looks from a distance like a broken flint." It lies where it has lain for a very long time, a boulder of 200 or 300 tons, never much moved by human hands. But that broken surface 15 feet across has been fashioned into "an intricate mass of carving." Small figures, pumas and hunters, lizards, frogs, snakes, vicuñas and more, have been released there, all set into a labyrinth of tiny stairs, altars and platforms, through which a network of grooves once led liquid down from the highest point in some unknown "ceremony of divination." Iconoclasts have defaced the figures, save for one brooding puma. The two photographs of this monument are extraordinary; it is a statement as timeless as it is contemporary. A microcosm was somehow carved out by the Inca's craftsmen; the 19th-century travelers who saw an Andean topographic map in that carving were not far wrong.

The vista of the real city of Machu Picchu from the southern rise of its saddle in the mountains, a familiar and beautiful shot, given us by Ranney also, seems now at a glance only one more Saihuite rock. Notches in the stone rim offer evidence that the face of the Saihuite boulder once had a copper or gilded-copper cladding probably worked at a level of detail the relief carving in stone can never transmit to us. Perhaps the golden cities of the tall tales were real after all, even if they were only models. The strange gnomonlike platforms called inti-huatanas are called "hitching posts of the sun." Several are shown as they stand now in the Cuzco region. They are not, however, working gnomons or zenith markers as far as anyone can now make out; it seems a reasonable conjecture that here too what we now see is only a carefully carved stone base, its surfaces rounded and bland, never itself an astronomical instrument but only a kind of armature for a more intricate and controlled metal cladding. Together were they not working solar instruments?

The photographs and their excellent reproduction in duotone are so beautiful that they satisfy entirely; the work is a black-and-white prize and an archaeological introduction of real merit.

(July 1983)

The White Men: The First Response of Aboriginal Peoples to The White Man
By Julia Blackburn

"When I was a boy, the Sioux owned the world; the sun rose and set on their land; they sent ten thousand men to battle. Where are the warriors today? Who slew them? Where are our lands? Who owns them?" From the days of Captain Cook through the 19th century of European colonial expansion and the irresistible westering of the U.S. up to the post-World War II opening of New Guinea and Melanesia hundreds of smaller societies have known apocalyptic times. Troubled minds sought meaning. The undreamed-of white men suddenly arrive; their rule is based on strange secrets of artifact and action, on writings of power, on new weapons and new beasts. The strangers must be fitted somehow into a cosmology that had held no such beings; their coming "brought . . . countless and hitherto unknown ways of dying," from new disease to hopeless battle. Finally, the changed life can be managed to allow spiritual survival notwithstanding the mysterious presence.

This book is a poignant and beautiful anthology, remarkably fresh in its materials, collecting around each of five meaningful themes a chapter of some 10 texts as told by those to whom intruders once came. The cultures cited do not include those great states of the Andes or the Indus or the Yangtze where long ago men from Europe confronted societies of commensurate weight, even though they lacked the cannon or the rapacity of the venturers. That is a longer and richer tale. Here we read texts by people within the small polities, none larger than some kingdoms of South Africa, some as small and isolated at the foraging hunters of the Australian desert. The texts are all in translation, of course. They are somehow accidental; they are on record here only because someone who had the power of writing and detached observation could yet engage prophets and seers and chroniclers on other than hostile terms. In our times, when apocalypse does not seem remote from the most favored cities, these accounts are dazzling mirrors of our common humanity in the glare of inevitable change.

In 1786 the ships of La Pérouse came to the narrow Alaskan inlet of Lituya Bay; they stayed for four weeks to observe and to trade. In 1949 a Tlingit from Yakutat recounted the traditional story of that alien arrival, earlier recorded in 1886. "One spring a large party of men from the big village of Kaxnuwu went to get copper from the people at Yakutat. Four canoes were lost . . . and the first chief of the party was drowned. While the survivors were still mourning, two ships rounded the bay. The Indians thought they were two great birds with white wings, perhaps Raven himself. They fled to the woods. After a time they came back to the shore and looked through tubes of rolled-up skunk cabbage leaves, like telescopes, for if they looked directly at Raven they might turn to stone. . . . They were so frightened when thunder and smoke came from the ship that their canoe overturned. . . .

"Then a nearly blind old man said his life was behind him, and he would see if Raven really turned men to stone. He . . . induced two of his slaves to paddle him to the ship. When he got on board, his eyesight was so poor that he mistook the sailors for crows. . . . He traded his fur coat for a tin pan. . . . The people were surprised to see the old man alive. They smelled him to make sure that he had not been turned into a land-otter man, and they refused to eat the food he had brought. The old man finally decided that it must be ships and people he had seen, so the Indians visited the ships and traded their furs." Some of these details are confirmed in the French records; oral tradition can hold high events for centuries.

The most tragic account is that of the powerful Xhosa. A group of 10 strange young men appeared to a young girl, Nongquase (the text is her court testimony), at the river's edge where she was fetching water. She was fearful, but her uncle Mhala could see that they were the dead ancestors of the Xhosa. They promised victory over the English, if the corn was burned and the cattle were killed to feed the dead. The ancestors will soon return, and "they will rise at different kraals with cattle, corn, guns and assegais, and they will drive the English out of the country and make them run into the sea."

Both grain and cattle were indeed sacrificed over the whole of the Xhosa region. Three-fourths of the people died on this self-inflicted starvation between the spring of 1856 and the spring of 1857. "They waited for two red suns to rise over the hills in the east. Then the heavens would fall on the English and crush them. But the sun rose and set as usual and the ancestors did not come. My uncle . . . went down towards the sea where he could try to live on roots and shellfish. And when we were starving, I often heard him say that he regretted killing the cattle and destroying his corn."

The volume includes a striking collection of photographs, some of them portraits of the very prophets whose texts are quoted, such as Short Bull, a leader of the Ghost Dance. He looks steadily across 90 years at the reader in grave and charismatic nobility. Most of the photographs are less closely related to the texts; they present fascinating sculpture and graphics from many peoples showing the white man and his works as they appeared to the artist. The layout and presentation are particularly attractive, and the author, an English student of oral tradition, has sought her material in a wide variety of unusual sources, carefully cited. The famous report on the Ghost Dance by James Mooney and the material on the Tlingit are well known, but not many general readers will have encountered the Xhosa story, related in a book published in Kingwilliamstown, not far from the port of East London in the Republic of South Africa. An air of timelessness surrounds this work; in these words ring echoes of the tragedies of Hellas.

(July 1980)

Interstellar Migration and the Human Experience
Edited by Ben R. Finney and Eric M. Jones

In Advance of the Landing: Folk Concepts of Outer Space
By Douglas Curran

Enrico Fermi was a frequent visitor to early postwar Los Alamos. Once in the summer of 1950 he walked to lunch with three or four friends talking about the flying saucers at that moment ubiquitous in news stories and cartoons. After some speculation on interstellar travel the conversation shifted. A bit later, "apropos of nothing," one witness recalls, "Fermi said, 'Don't you ever wonder where everybody is?' Somehow . . . we all knew he meant extraterrestrials."

Fermi's point is now a pivot in the speculation about human uniqueness. If you see space rather as Antarctica, a fine place to visit although no agreeable residence, you are inclined to seek electromagnetic messages from distant starlit planets, arguing from some crude symmetry. If instead you see the dark interstellar volumes as so many Atlantics and Americas, you wonder at the absence of perceived fleets of voyagers, and not without a certain hubris you tend to view our own species as first in our galaxy to dream about spacefaring, and historically close to takeoff en masse.

This volume looks outward, in advance not of everyone landing but of many of us taking off. Clearly placed on the serious side of science's border with science fiction, it reports a conference at Los Alamos in the summer of 1983 that imaginatively extends some of Fermi's 1950 implications. The attention of about 20 authors, mostly astronomers, space engineers, anthropologists and historians, focuses on such topics as the means and modes of projected galactic travel, the demographic, evolutionary, genetic, social and moral issues raised by long-term interstellar migration of humans, and the lessons drawn from cross-cultural studies of human migrations of the past. Two final papers are more skeptical of mass space travel. They include a theoretical model of migration rate that points up the uncertainties of such extrapolation, and a summary of the status of the empirical search for microwave signals, much swifter and cheaper than travel.

A fascinating polarity is found in the extrapolations collected here, a duality of view: should we imagine bold, heroic voyagers or quiet, patient ones? We read of fastships and space nomads. Fastships might carry hundreds of expert colonists from the rich, sunlit oasis of home into the dark, the well-fitted ship powered by a fierce microwave beam. (Is anyone listening?) The nomad bands build their slower, lighter ships of cometary matter and power their extended-family lives by the concentration of pale starlight in huge farms of gossamer mirrors, a continental area devoted to each inhabitant.

We read of the real past, of !Kung hunters and gatherers, egalitarians and sharers, who spread by a random hiving-off into the desert emptiness, and of the Vikings, fleeing the populous but narrow arable fields crowded among the fjords, to found predator states whose most ambitious colonies did not survive. If a linear scale factor of tens of billions can be conceded, the Polynesians present the neatest analogue; their voyaging canoes, which over 10,000 years peopled the isolated atolls flung across the ocean wastes, are indeed evocative of wanderers among the stars.

A Malthusian engineering of boundless hope is also represented, its semilog plots rising linearly to the stars. One essay even suggests that the invisible mass that binds the orbiting stars of the spiral galaxies might turn out to be husbanded and converted stars. Gently unwrapped and reassembled into many long-lived little dwarfs, their dim light would be hidden under bushels of radiation-frugal macromachines, the "habitats . . . of advanced civilizations," albeit preternaturally inconspicuous ones, even shy.

The First Law is employed here scrupulously, so that uses of cosmic sources of matter and energy are optimized in detail. Yet a reader feels that the Second Law, with its insistence on noise, error and waste, its up-front costs for every structure and every choice, has been rather slighted.

The magical key to the future is the self-reproducing and exponentially growing construction system that can unwrap a sun, say by drawing off surface plasma into new-made magnetic channels. Diverted, the gas flies far into space, there to slow and condense onto prepared dust. Eventually the material would be gathered into self-gravitating, tiny sub-stars, cold warehouses for dwarf starry fusion furnaces to light the future. This audacious author, David R. Criswell, remarks that he will leave alternative schemes "to others with more imagination than myself."

There are other heroic forecasts, an evolutionist seeing a diversity of our descendants scattered across the galaxy "within 2 million years," novel hominid taxa that would astound us by their forms and adaptation. Another expert looks confirmingly to a far future Milky Way peopled by our prosperous progeny, by then hundreds of billions of intelligent species, dominated by those few more aggressive races of intrepid voyagers. This future includes rare conflicts. Within such a dilute regime even nations of heroes can support no more than a few million interstellar wars at a time. The editors (Finney an anthropologist at the University of Hawaii, Jones an astronomer at Los Alamos) comment elsewhere that the conquerors who roved in longship and caravel almost never made landfall on any coast to which the meek had not already spread in their slow and silent way.

This volume reasons out the hopes of an enthusiastic moiety of the technologically adept. Hard to test, its arguments by analogy and extrapolation are fine reading, if less than uniformly persuasive. Fermi's question may have a simpler answer. Everyone is trying hard to make a living not far from some long-lived star. They may be "noble in reason . . . in action how like an angel!" Yet they are finite beings just as we are; therefore they too are confined by logistic curves that having soared past the lively immaturities of exponential growth flatten to diminishing returns along every physical dimension. Such beings may even be freed of the old dream of immortality.

The second book is the work of a Canadian journalist-photographer who spent a few years on the road, seeking from Quebec to the Mojave the outward and visible signs of a new kind of inward grace: the sacrament of saucers from heaven. His remarkable photographs and clear first-hand accounts, always gentle and yet precise, disclose a widespread if small popular subculture that has about it the air of an inauspicious beginning. Once almost 2,000 years ago a traveler might have found something like this among small, serious groups gathered in Rome, Corinth or Ephesus; only 150 years ago noteworthy examples might have been visited in upstate New York. St. Peter's and Salt Lake City were hard to foresee.

The images of this particular salvation take a curious form. About a fourth of some 60 photographs display the structure of a rocket, represented in the round in a mater-of-fact way, at a scale practicable for local carpenters working plywood and sheet metal, an icon that is carefully modeled on the tangible results of the engineer. A somewhat larger number of these images represent no sight ever seen, no real contrivance. Instead they display at some scale in some material (a few are only painted) the prototypical flying saucer, a form familiar only from published artwork in the media, large and small. These are found on gas stations and in gardens, nestling in the woods or next to power pylons. Rather fewer than a third of the photographs document more complex social groupings among which the same roots have fully flowered into costume and ceremony, and a few show assemblages of real technology. Some here are recognizable cargo cults, not on an out-of-the-way Melanesian island but wistful social isolates within the ocean of American life.

There is strong continuity with past phenomena. The history of the late George Adamski, a prolific author and guru who dwelt at Mount Palomar, Calif. (below the observatory site), is revealing. By his own lengthy accounts a familiar of the flying saucers, he repeatedly enjoyed passage on interplanetary voyages, often to the dark side of the moon. Before the 1950's Adamski had been privy to quite distinct mysteries: he had founded a monastery in the 1930's to gather seekers after Cosmic Law (and to legitimate the sale of wine). He once frugally "resurrected a metaphysical tract he had written in the 1930's by substituting 'the Space Brothers' for 'the Royal Order of Tibet' throughout." Adamski is still revered by many, some of whom hold he has returned to earth. His feats went along easily with his status as minor celebrity in image and print, a man received during the unabashed heights of his appeal by members of Congress and by the Queen of the Netherlands. Adamski's photographs did much to establish the canonical form in which we conceive the flying saucer; there is evidence that one of the most celebrated of them presents a close-up of a small aluminum egg incubator.

We see a Hollywood service in which a Spiritual Battery is recharged; it is a little ceremony wherein by turns the gowned communicants gravely place their hands against the device, cradled on its tripod. Such a battery is rated at a capacity of 700 prayer-hours; several are kept at full charge ready to forestall world crises. Their efficacy has often been demonstrated. Some other views of taking part in the celebration of extraterrestrials of power and good will are here; often high planetary dignitaries and their servitors appear costumed in the satins and sequins of remembered theater.

Only two technical scenes occur. One shows a private roomful of relay racks, with which the complex spectral communications claimed are probably only simulated. (That judgment derives from the awry description and from the simple Lissajous figure seen on the big CRT screen central to the display.) Another site, on rolling land near Austin, Tex., was far more ambitious. There, a decade back, an array of lights flashed some coded function of pi; other saucer attractants, including a ruby laser under computer control, were deployed. The expense was borne by a few well-heeled followers.

The latest manifestation reported is not at all a folk phenomenon but a frank example of commercial theater, by Bob Gurr. The closing ceremonies of the 1984 Summer Olympics were ended by a lavishly staged night saucer visit to that packed and darkened stadium, complete with a probing searchlight from the hovering, flashing, responsive craft. "A seven-foot-eight-inch white-suited alien" visitor appeared, to voice a benign message as the fireworks rolled, the entire production carried worldwide on television. A single video image is shown.

In this volume the yearning is clear, the complexity of modern fears and hopes evident, the influence of newly predominant culture images pervasive. Both pathos and pleasure are to be seen in the poignant faces. Yet neither elegance nor wit is often tapped by these visually banal icons; only two beautiful images are found. One is a striking accident of a real effort; the big ring of lights that aspired to lure a passing saucer is magically inviting in the soft Texas night. The other serves as jacket photograph; it is not folk art but an abstracted small saucer form possibly of rock. Painted (it appears) by a genuine artist, Jene Highstein of Park Forest, Ill., it rests in a wide field of sere autumn grass against a twilight sky glowing green.

Both the well-argued forecasts of starship takeoff and the folk celebration of saucer landing may derive from a belief long ago defined by an American writer of insight; the two seem caught alike in the gleam of the green light at the end of Daisy's dock, where Jay Gatsby believed he might grasp "the orgastic future that year by year recedes before us. It eluded us then, but that's no matter—to-morrow we will run faster, stretch out our arms farther. . . . And one fine morning—"

(June 1986)

Album of Science: Antiquity and the Middle Ages
By John E. Murdoch

This excellent series seeks to convey the science of each period through its graphic representations. Professor Murdoch has marshaled his images mainly from the rich European holdings of the medieval manuscripts of the Latin West, thin booklike codices presented for the most part on parchment. He has by no means neglected the important Arabic and Persian material or the rarer papyrus scrolls of Egypt and the Levant. It is the Latinity, however, that is best preserved.

The science here is in large part the self-conscious preservation of and scholarly commentary on a few great classical authors, in particular the Greek mathematicians as well as Aristotle, Ptolemy and Galen. That pattern holds for Arabic and Latin scholarship alike, and sums up the lion's share of what we have. Discoveries, instrumentation, collections of material hardly figure. Science was *livresque*: it was "not just set down in books; it was largely carried out in books." The text was sovereign; even where it rested on empirical observation, once the theory inferred was written down, fresh appeal to the material itself rarely animated the continuators and commentators.

Copyists were trained for the task of writing, the tedious repetition of manifold permutations of few letters. It was hard enough, and costly enough, to perform that task well. The secondary task of getting pictures right lay outside that system. Talented specialists would have to be called on; a copyist could hardly be expected to be draftsman or painter. The bandwidth of illustration is too high; the very values it offers put it almost out of reach. It is no surprise to see model books, codices for the use of the trade, in which anatomical figures, foliage, diagrams from the theorems of Euclid and animals of various kinds are all provided for copying by illustrators. It is natural enough, but more of a surprise, to see a model drawing of the 13th century, here one of a stork, outlined in pinholes probably to allow quick copying by dusting with some powder. (No such use of the figure has been found.) Another page bears a specially drawn field, four bordered rectangles in a connected pattern, the frames left blank. The figure provided a logical format, useful for graphical explication of any number of textual arguments.

There are college textbooks, handbooks of simplification and synopsis, compact encyclopedic works meant for training and reference by clerics who would rarely need the full professional matter of the ancient masters. There are plenty of tables, mnemonic devices and systematic logical diagrams. The hand of the Venerable Bede was often drawn and elaborately annotated; his much-used eighth-century work on the reckoning of time gave explicit conventions for figuring with the fingers to derive the dates of a wide variety of religious feasts; it also offers a scheme for arithmetical finger reckoning up to 10,000.

Field guides serve physician and herbalist, surveyor and star clerk. Here one might expect more need to consult the objects of the world. A series of paintings of the wonderful herb mandrake is shown from medieval manuscripts. The version that went with an Arabic translation of the classical Greek text presents an unlikely stylized plant but not a magical one. Two more show the plant with roots that assume a magically human form: one still rootlike in texture and detail, the other about as good a drawing of the human body as its artist could make, topped by a wide foliage crown. The last version depicts a very believable but striking plant, its forked root real enough, although it still evokes the human form. Even this example was not drawn from a specimen plant; its prototype was realistically painted for a Paduan prince. One 15th-century artist illustrated his plants from the source by printing nature impressions made from real paint-coated leaves. Alas for his readers, he often misidentified the species.

All of this has a remarkably familiar look today, one that might have been missed even 10 years ago. These manuscript images are drawn from the same dwindled universe as today's computer graphics. Blank fields stand ready to accommodate some large class of data into a single neat format. Logical diagrams abound, often elaborated into trees and intricate flows. Realia, like flowers or animals or the human body, are stylized into conventional but recognizable outlines and shapes, easy to repeat (see Pac-man or any little red Apple). Simple transformations are much employed: the old manuscripts figured constellations twice, once as seen by looking out through the sphere of the sky and once by looking in.

The underlying reason is the same: copies are required fast. High resolution, any detailed attention to direct imaging from the variable and refractory outside world, takes too long. Today magnetic patterns are scarce goods, as paper was then, and copying too is simple, mainly symbolic. Presenting simplified images bit by bit is as much as either the old scribe or the modern microprocessor can generally do. Richly printed surfaces still offer more, perhaps through some powerful new form such as the video disk.

It is fascinating to see some fresh images. There is the painting of the Arabic library at Basra in the 12th century, the books neatly shelved; there are the varied exemplary bandages on arms and legs, teaching a medical art that appears to trace back long before the manuscript example, perhaps to the Hellenic original. Altogether the scholarly Harvard author-compiler has built us an exciting new vantage for looking at science's medieval past. Perhaps it is even a cautionary one. The sense that our quick digital descriptions are information-sparse compared with the dense thicket of real photons and atoms, that all theory is gray against the green world, is concededly a Romantic one. But is it outdated?

(January 1985)

Afterword

The literature of science grows almost by definition. A set of snapshots like these reviews can catch the past, but must leave unjoined threads towards the future. Have we read any more of the astronomical coding in the myths? Is the disease pattern of the Balkan villages better understood? Do some craters mark the scars left by comets that fell to bring an end to the Age of Reptiles? How does the count of the kingdoms of life now stand? Is QED as complete as it looks? What is the source of the distant x-ray background?

Let me know what you find out. As long as I can, I'll keep on reading.

The Books Themselves

The bookshelves of your favorite bookstore, of a friend, or of a local library are the first hunting grounds for those who would see a particular book. If you want to own that book, seeing it for yourself first is satisfying and provides firm identity.

Most of the books here reviewed are "in print." That term of art means that somewhere in a dry corner under the publisher's control there lies a pile of fresh copies of the book. The publisher is happy to supply a copy from that stock; you can order directly or through the good offices of a knowing bookstore. The full postal address of any publisher can be found through reference books held by most bookshops and libraries; our list does not include full addresses of the well-known publishers, though we offer more help for less-used addresses.

A decade or two is a considerable time in the life of a book, as of a reader. About twenty of these books bent to the passage of time, in that they changed publishers, or went out of print. Our list includes the original publishers for every book, whose enterprise earned them mention, and where a change has taken place the present publisher as well, whose copies now keep the book in print. A few titles are out of print; no publisher at all has a

*pile of those books. They must be sought out in
odd corners, often in bookstores that specialize in
old or used books. There is even a restless profes-
sion of booksleuths, who know where out-of-print
books might be found; given time they can usually
ferret out one to your order at a reasonable price.
We believe our information on books in print is
accurate for the last days of 1989.*

Adventures of a Mathematician. S. M. Ulam. Out of print. Originally published by Charles Scribner's Sons.

Akenfield: Portrait of an English Village. Ronald Blythe. Pantheon Books.

Album of Science: Antiquity and the Middle Ages. John E. Murdoch. Charles
Scribner's Sons.

Album of Science: From Leonardo to Lavoisier. I. Bernard Cohen. Charles
Scribner's Sons.

Aleuts: Survivors of the Bering Land Bridge. William S. Laughlin. Holt, Rinehart and Winston.

Ambidextrous Universe, The: Mirror Asymmetry and Time-reversed Worlds,
2d ed. Martin Gardner. Revised edition: W. H. Freeman and Company.
Second edition, originally published by Charles Scribner's Sons.

*Annotated Alice, The: Alice's Adventures in Wonderland and Through the
Looking Glass.* Lewis Carroll, with introduction and notes by Martin
Gardner. New American Library.

Art of Electronics, The. Paul Horowitz and Winfield Hill. Cambridge University Press.

Balkan Nephropathy, The. G. E. W. Wolstenholme and Julie Knight (ed.).
Little, Brown and Company.

Berenice Abbott/Photographs. Foreword by Muriel Rukeyser. Horizon Press.

Black Apollo of Science: The Life of Ernest Everett Just. Kenneth R. Manning.
Oxford University Press.

Book of Phänomena, The. Zürcher Forum, Gemeindestrasse 48, CH 8032
Zurich.

Breasts, Bottles and Babies: A History of Infant Feeding. Valerie A. Fildes.
Columbia University Press. Originally published by Edinburgh University
Press.

Bumblebee Economics. Bernd Heinrich. Harvard University Press.

Burgess Shale, The. Harry B. Whittington. Yale University Press.

Camel and the Wheel, The. Richard W. Bulliet. Harvard University Press.

Capitalism and Arithmetic: The New Math of the 15th Century. Frank J. Swetz. David Eugene Smith (tr.). Open Court Publishing Co.

Çatal Hüyük: A Neolithic Town in Anatolia. James Mellaart. McGraw-Hill.

Causes of Cancer, The: Quantitative Estimates of Avoidable Risks of Cancer in the United States Today. Richard Doll and Richard Peto. Oxford University Press.

Cecilia Payne-Gaposchkin: An Autobiography and Other Recollections. Katherine Haramundanis (ed.). Cambridge University Press.

Children's Games in Street and Playground: Chasing, Catching, Seeking, Hunting, Racing, Duelling, Exerting, Daring, Guessing, Acting, Pretending. Iona and Peter Opie. Oxford University Press.

Christo: Running Fence, Sonoma and Marin Counties, California 1972–76. David Bourdon and Calvin Tomkins. Harry N. Abrams, Inc.

Clever Hans (The Horse of Mr. Van Osten). Oscar Pfungst. Robert Rosenthal (ed.). Holt, Rinehart and Winston.

Collected Papers of Albert Einstein, The: Vol. 1: The Early Years; 1879–1902. John Stachel (ed.). Anna Beck and Peter Havas (tr.). Princeton University Press.

Confessions of a Psychic. Uriah Fuller. Karl Fulves, PO Box 433, Teaneck, NJ 07666.

Coral Seas, The: Wonders and Mysteries of Underwater Life. Hans W. Fricke. G. P. Putnam's Sons.

Deep Black: Space Espionage and National Security. William E. Burrows. Random House.

Desert Locust, The. Stanley Baron. Charles Scribner's Sons.

Dictionary of Scientific Biography. Charles Coulston Gillespie (ed.) Charles Scribner's Sons.

Dividing, Ruling and Mask-making. D. F. Horne. Crane, Russak & Company.

Earth at Night (poster map). Woodruff T. Sullivan, III. Hansen Planetarium.

East African Mammals: An Atlas of Evolution in Africa, Vol. 1. Jonathan Kingdon. University of Chicago Press. Originally published by Academic Press.

Edward S. Curtis: The Life and Times of a Shadow Catcher. Barbara A. Davis. Out of print. Originally published by Chronicle Books.

Energy in China's Modernization: Advances and Limitations. Vaclav Smil. M. E. Sharpe, Inc., 80 Business Park Drive, Armonk, NY 10504.

Epidemic and Peace: 1918. Alfred W. Crosby, Jr. Greenwood Press, Westport, CT.

Eradication of Smallpox from India, The. R. N. Basu, Z. Jezek and N. A. Ward. Southeast Asia Regional Office, World Health Organization, WHO Publications Centre USA, 49 Sheridan Avenue, Albany, NY 12210.

Everyone Here Spoke Sign Language: Hereditary Deafness on Martha's Vineyard. Nora Ellen Groce. Harvard University Press.

Exhibition of Archaelogical Finds of the People's Republic of China, The. Organization Committee. National Gallery of Art.

Explorations of Captain James Cook in the Pacific, as Told by Selections of His Own Journals 1768–1779, The. A. Grenfell Price (ed.). Dover Publications.

Exploring the Southern Sky: A Pictorial Atlas from the European Southern Observatory. Svend Laustsen, Claus Madsen and Richard M. West. Springer-Verlag.

Fads and Fallacies in the Name of Science. Martin Gardner. Dover Publications.

Famine and Human Development: The Dutch Hunger Winter of 1944/45. Zena Stein, Mervyn Susser, Gerhard Saenger and Francis Marolla. Oxford University Press.

Fertilizer in America: From Waste Recycling to Resource Exploitation. Richard A. Wines. Temple University Press.

Fertilizer Technology and Use, 3d ed. O. P. Engelstad. Soil Science Society of America.

First Contact. Bob Connolly and Robin Anderson. Viking Penguin.

Five Kingdoms: An Illustrated Guide to the Phyla of Life on Earth. Lynn Margulis and Karlene V. Schwartz. W. H. Freeman and Company.

Flight of Peter Fromm, The. Martin Gardner. William Kaufmann, Inc.

Food in Chinese Culture: Anthropological and Historical Perspectives. K. C. Chang. Yale University Press.

From Art to Science: Seventy-Two Objects Illustrating the Nature of Discovery Cyril Stanley Smith. MIT Press.

From One to Zero: A Universal History of Numbers. George Ifrah. Lowell Bair (tr.). Viking Penguin.

Further Confessions of a Psychic. Uriah Fuller. Karl Fulves, PO Box 433, Teaneck, NJ 07666.

Giant Meteorites. E. L. Krinov. J. S. Romankiewicz (tr.). M. M. Beynon (ed.). Pergamon Press.

Giving Up the Gun: Japan's Reversion to the Sword, 1543–1879. Noel Perrin. · Godine. Originally published by Shambhala Publications.

Gravity's Rainbow. Thomas Pynchon. Penguin. Originally published by Viking Press.

Great Barrier Reef, The. Isobel Bennett. Charles Scribner's Sons.

Great Chinese Travelers, The. Jeannette Mirsky (ed.). University of Chicago Press.

Great Zimbabwe. P. S. Garlake. Thames and Hudson. Originally published by Stein and Day.

Gypsies: The Hidden Americans. Anne Sutherland. The Free Press.

Gypsy on 18 Wheels: A Trucker's Tale. Robert Krueger. Sam Yanes (ed.). Praeger Publishers.

Gyroscopic Theory, Design, and Instrumentation. Walter Wrigley, Walter M. Hollister, and William C. Denhard. MIT Press.

Hamlet's Mill: An Essay on Myth and the Frame of Time. Giorgio de Santillana and Hertha von Dechend. Harvard Common Press, Boston. Originally published by Gambit Inc.

Handling the Big Jets. D. P. Davies. Civil Aviation Authority, 129 Kingsway, London.

Harvest of the Palm: Ecological Change in Eastern Indonesia. James J. Fox. Harvard University Press.

Healing Hand, The: Man and Wound in the Ancient World. Guido Majno. Harvard University Press.

How to Wrap Five Eggs: Japanese Design in Traditional Packaging. Hideyuki Oka. Harper & Row.

Hunters or the Hunted?, The: An Introduction to African Cave Taphonomy. C. K. Brain. University of Chicago Press.

Illuminations: A Bestiary. Rosamond Wolff Purcell and Stephen J. Gould. W. W. Norton.

In Advance of the Landing: Folk Concepts of Outer Space. Douglas Curran. Abbeville Press.

Inanna, Queen of Heaven and Earth: Her Stories and Hymns from Sumer. Diane Wolkstein and Samuel Noah Kramer. Harper & Row.

Incredible Dr. Matrix, The. Martin Gardner. Charles Scribner's Sons.

Insect Societies, The. Edward O. Wilson. Harvard University Press.

Intelligent Eye, The. Richard L. Gregory. Out of print. Originally published by McGraw-Hill.

Interstellar Migration and the Human Experience. Ben R. Finney and Eric M. Jones (ed.). University of California Press.

Invention of the Telescope, The: Transactions of the American Philosophical Society. Albert Van Helden. The American Philosophical Society.

Islands. H. W. Menard. W. H. Freeman and Company.

Journey to the West, The, Vols. 1-4. Anthony C. Yu (ed., tr.). University of Chicago Press.

Krakatau 1883: The Volcanic Eruption and Its Effects. Tom Simkin and Richard S. Fiske. Smithsonian Institution Press.

Laetoli: A Pliocene Site in Northern Tanzania. M. D. Leakey and J. M. Harris (ed.). Oxford University Press.

Late Great Subsistence Crisis in the Western World, The. John D. Post. The Johns Hopkins University Press.

Legends of the Earth: Their Geologic Origins. Dorothy B. Vitaliano. Out of print. Originally published by Indiana University Press.

Life of Captain James Cook, The. J. C. Beaglehole. Stanford University Press.

Magic Mirror of M. C. Escher, The. Bruno Ernst. Parkwest Publications. Originally published by Random House.

Magic of Uri Geller, The. The Amazing Randi. Ballantine Books.

Man the Hunter. Richard B. Lee, Irven DeVore and Jill Nash. Aldine Publishing Co.

Mathematical Circus. Martin Gardner. Penguin. Originally published by Vintage Books.

Mechanics and Energetics of Animal Locomotion. R. McN. Alexander and G. Goldspink (ed.). Halsted Press, John Wiley & Sons.

Mediterranean Was a Desert, The: A Voyage of the Glomar Challenger. Kenneth J. Hsü. Princeton University Press.

Melloni's Illustrated Medical Dictionary, 2d ed. Ida Dox, Biagio John Melloni and Gilbert Eisner. Williams & Wilkins.

Metric Change in India. Lal C. Verman and Jainath Kaul. Indian Standards Institution, New Delhi.

Metric System, The: A Critical Study of Its Principles and Practice. Maurice Danloux-Dumesnils. Anne Garrett and J. S. Rowlinson (tr.). Athlone Press. Originally published by Oxford University Press.

Military and Civilian Pyrotechnics. Herbert Ellern. Chemical Publishing Company.

Modern Rise of Population, The. Thomas McKeown. Academic Press.

Monuments of the Incas. John Hemming. New York Graphic Society. Originally published by Little, Brown and Company.

My Story. Uri Geller. Praeger.

Nature and Art of Worksmanship, The. David Pye. Cambridge University Press. Originally published by Van Nostrand Reinhold.

Nearby Galaxies Atlas. R. Brent Tully and J. Richard Fisher. Cambridge University Press.

Never at Rest: A Biography of Sir Isaac Newton. Richard S. Westfall. Cambridge University Press.

Niels Bohr: A Centenary Volume. A. P. French and P. J. Kennedy (ed.). Harvard University Press.

Night as Frontier: Colonizing the World after Dark. Murray Melbin. The Free Press.

Nomads of the Long Bow: The Siriono of Eastern Bolivia. Allan R. Holmberg. Waveland Press. Originally published by The Natural History Press.

Objets Fractals, Les: Forme, Hasard et Dimension. Benoît Mandelbrot. Flammarion Editeur, Paris.

Occult Sciences in the Renaissance, The: A Study in Intellectual Patterns. Wayne Shumaker. University of California Press.

Octopus: Physiology and Behavior of an Advanced Invertebrate. M. J. Wells. Chapman and Hall. Originally published by John Wiley & Sons.

On Ancient Central-Asian Tracks. Sir Aurel Stein. Oriental Book Store. Originally published by University of Chicago Press.

Path to the Double Helix, The. Robert Olby. University of Washington Press.

Patrick Maynard Stuart Blackett, Baron Blackett of Chelsea: A Biographical Memoir. Sir Bernard Lovell. The Royal Society, Carlton House Terrace, London SW 1.

Pedal Power: In Work, Leisure, and Transportation. James C. McCullagh. Rodale Press, Emmaus, PA.

Periodic Table, The. Primo Levi. Raymond Rosenthal (tr.). Schocken Books.

Perpetual Motion: The History of an Obsession. Arthur W. J. G. Ord-Hume St. Martin's Press.

Phänomena. Georg Müller (ed.). Zürcher Forum, Gemeindestrasse 48, CH 8032 Zurich.

Prepare Now for a Metric Future. Frank Donovan. Weybright and Talley.

QED: The Strange Theory of Light and Matter. Richard P. Feynman. Princeton University Press.

Quaternary Extinctions: A Prehistoric Revolution. Paul S. Martin and Richard G. Klein (ed.). University of Arizona Press.

Renaissance Rediscovery of Linear Perspective, The. Samuel Y. Edgerton, Jr. Harper & Row. Originally published by Basic Books.

Robert Oppenheimer: Letters and Recollections. Alice Kimball Smith and Charles Weiner (ed.). Harvard University Press.

Science and Civilisation in China, Vol. 5, Chemistry and Chemistry Technology, Part 1, Paper and Printing. Joseph Needham and Tsien Tsuen-Hsuin. Cambridge University Press.

Science and Civilisation in China, Vol. 5, Chemistry and Chemistry Technology, Part 7, Military Technology: The Gunpowder Epic. Joseph Needham, Ho Ping-Yü, Lu Gwei-Djen and Wang Ling. Cambridge University Press.

Science: Good, Bad and Bogus. Martin Gardner. Prometheus Books.

Science in France in the Revolutionary Era, Described by Thomas Bugge. Maurice P. Crosland (ed.). MIT Press.

Scientists under Hitler: Politics and the Physics Community in the Third Reich. Alan D. Beyerchen. Yale University Press.

Search for Structure, A: Selected Essays on Science, Art and History. Cyril Stanley Smith. MIT Press.

Shell Book of Country Crafts, The. James Arnold. Hastings House.

Single Lens: The Story of the Simple Microscope. Brian J. Ford. Harper & Row.

Sky at Many Wavelengths, The (11 color slides). Christine Jones and William Forman. Astronomical Society of the Pacific.

Smugglers, The: An Investigation into the World of the Contemporary Smuggler. Timothy Green. Walker and Company.

Snack Food Technology. Samuel A. Matz. Out of print. Originally published by the Avi Publishing Company.

Sport Science: Physical Laws and Optimum Performance. Peter J. Brancazio. Simon and Schuster.

Stones, Bones and Skin: Ritual and Shamanic Art. Anne Trueblood Brodzky, Rose Danesewich and Nick Johnson. The Society for Art Publications, Toronto.

Structures, or Why Things Don't Fall Down. J. E. Gordon. Plenum Press.

Sudden Infant Death: Patterns, Puzzles and Problems. Jean Golding, Sylvia Limerick and Aldan Macfarlane. University of Washington Press.

Sunsets, Twilights, and Evening Skies. Aden and Marjorie Meinel. Cambridge University Press.

Superminds. John Taylor. Viking Press, Inc.

Sweetness and Power: The Place of Sugar in Modern History. Sidney W. Mintz. Viking Penguin, Inc.

Thinkers and Tinkers: Early American Men of Science. Silvio A. Bedini. Landmark Enterprises. Originally published by Charles Scribner's Sons.

Think Tanks. Paul Dickson. Atheneum.

Tropical Nature. Adrian Forsyth and Kenneth Miyata. Charles Scribner's Sons.

Ultrapurity: Methods and Techniques. Morris Zief and Robert Speights (ed.). University Microfilm International, Ann Arbor, MI. Originally published by Marcel Dekker.

Uri: A Journal of the Mystery of Uri Geller. Andrija Puharich. Bantam Books, Inc.

Various Contrivances by which Orchids are Fertilised by Insects, The. Charles Darwin. AMS Press, New York. Originally published by University of Chicago Press.

Wheat: Botany, Cultivation, and Utilization. R. F. Peterson. Interscience Publishers.

Wheelwright's Shop, The. George Sturt. Cambridge University Press.

Whistled Languages. R. G. Busnel and A. Classe. Springer-Verlag.

White Men, The: The First Response of Aboriginal Peoples to the White Man. Julie Blackburn. The New York Times Book Co.

Whole Earth Catalog: Access to Tools. Portola Institute, Sausalito, CA.

Why Buildings Stand Up: The Strength of Architecture. Mario Salvadori. McGraw-Hill. Originally published by W. W. Norton.

Wild Boy of Aveyron, The. Harlan Lane. Harvard University Press.

Working Knowledge: Skill and Community in a Small Shop. Douglas Harper. University of Chicago Press.

World Armaments and Disarmament: SIPRI Yearbook 1975. Stockholm International Peace Research Institute. MIT Press.

Index